Female Well-Being

JANET MANCINI BILLSON AND
CAROLYN FLUEHR-LOBBAN | editors

Female Well-Being

Toward a global theory of social change

Zed Books
LONDON | NEW YORK

Female well-being: toward a global theory of social change was first
published by Zed Books Ltd, 7 Cynthia Street, London N1 9JF, UK
and Room 400, 175 Fifth Avenue, New York, NY 10010, USA in 2005

www.zedbooks.co.uk

Cover designed by Andrew Corbett
Set in FF Arnhem and Futura Bold by Ewan Smith, London
Printed and bound in Malta by Gutenberg Press Ltd

Distributed in the USA exclusively by Palgrave Macmillan, a division of
St Martin's Press, LLC, 175 Fifth Avenue, New York, NY 10010.

A catalogue record for this book is available from the British Library.
US CIP data are available from the Library of Congress.

ISBN 1 84277 008 x hb
ISBN 1 84277 009 8 pb

Contents

Acknowledgements

First and foremost, we want to express our sincerest thanks to the country teams, without whom this book could never have been written. Each team member shared our vision and commitment to documenting female well-being during a period of enormous transition. They doggedly tackled the formidable task of gathering statistical data for an entire century on several key indicators. Women and men, educators and activists, researchers and government statisticians, practitioners and administrators approached the task with the attention to detail that quantitative work requires – and with the historical knowledge and social insight essential to interpretive analysis. To each of them, we are deeply indebted.

We also want to thank Group Dimensions International research associates Kyra Mancini Reis and Susan J. Little for their invaluable assistance with headings, tables and references. They helped make the book easier for comparative reading. When we first started this project, Elena de Garcés Eder graciously set up two drawers' worth of file folders, all neatly labelled and filled with dozens of reports and articles relevant to *Female Well-being*. This jump-started our work in an organized fashion, for which we are extremely grateful.

Billson: During August 2003 and February 2004, I served as Visiting Scholar at the British Economic and Social Research Council's Research Group on Well-Being in Developing Countries – 'WeD'. The group focuses on the study of poverty, inequality and quality of life in Bangladesh, Ethiopia, Peru and Thailand, having set itself the daunting task of developing a 'coherent conceptual and methodological framework for understanding the social and cultural construction of well-being in specific developing societies'. WeD became my intellectual (as well as literal) home away from home as I struggled with defining 'well-being' and the question of how female well-being might differ from the well-being of males. Discussions with Laura Camfield (WeD) and Suzy Skevington (Department of Psychology at the University of Bath) about their work on quality of life and subjective well-being were especially helpful in this regard.

WeD Director Allister McGregor of the Department of Economics and International Development recognized at our first meeting that our scholarly agendas intersected in important ways. He encouraged me to apply for WeD's first Visiting Scholar Award in 2003–04, and facilitated the entire experience, which was pivotal for the book's development. I want to thank Allister for many hours of conversation about the complexities of conducting research across national boundaries. He and Ian Gough of the Department of Social and Policy Sciences, WeD's Deputy Director, were instrumental in identifying WeD researchers and collaborators to start the chapters on Thailand (Farung Mee-Udon and Ranee Itarat) and Bangladesh (Nasrin Sultana and Dan Feng Qin). Other WeD members David Clark, James Copestake, Joe Devine, Susan Johnson, Bereket Kebede and Faleke Tadele participated in the ongoing dialogues over morning coffee and afternoon tea that made this experience so rewarding. Many thanks are also due to those who handled logistics and provided technical support during my stays – Becky Lockley, Diana Duckling, Liz Graveling and Mark Ellison – without them, I would have been lost somewhere between Heathrow and Bath, or in cyberspace.

Closer to home, historian Marie Schwartz and other members of the Women's Research Group at the University of Rhode Island have provided an important place for sharing drafts and ideas about writing in various modes. Psychologist and author Mara Berkley has inspired me with her own love of writing, and my co-editor/author, Carolyn Fluehr-Lobban, has kept the project moving when it seemed too overwhelming. Her friendship since 1973 has been one of life's joys.

Always I must acknowledge the support of my parents, Kathleen and the late Clifford Ramey of London, Ontario, and my children, Kyra Mancini Reis and Mark F. Mancini. This book could not have been completed without the incredible nurturance shown by my husband, Norm London, who makes the best coffee in the world and seems to know exactly when the midnight oil is burning low. His love and daily kindnesses have sustained me. Obviously, he understands the meaning of patience as well as of female well-being.

JMB, Barrington, Rhode Island, USA
jmbillson@earthlink.net

Fluehr-Lobban: My first appreciation is to Janet Billson. In 1995, Janet and I met occasionally in Washington, DC, while I was working on a new code of ethics for the American Anthropological Association. We always enjoyed lively exchanges, but one morning, as we were driving from her home in West Virginia, we began to speak about the coming millennium and how to measure the impact of the twentieth century on women. We were both frustrated by the lack of adequate theory to explain the gendered face of this social change. Janet conceived the idea of a book that would examine women in various countries and would take the important step of attempting to build a new gendered theory of social change. Our conversation became more and more animated, and has remained so during the past nine years as we pursued the project. With critical assistance from colleagues around the world, I can honestly say that electricity is in the air when we are discussing 'Women 2000' or what evolved into *Female Well-being*. This has been a great journey, with many peaks and valleys along the way, but we have been sustained by the vision and by the old feminist and abolitionist slogan – 'failure is impossible'.

I thank all the contributors who have shared this vision, but I must single out Fusako Seki, whom I met on the 1996 voyage of *Semester at Sea*, when she joined the ship to sail with us from Hong Kong to Kobe, Japan. Fusako visited my class on women and anthropology, and displayed a keen analytical understanding of the condition of women in Japan. We spoke about the 'Women 2000' project; she grasped the vision immediately and organized a group at the University of Hokkaido, which began researching and writing drafts of the Japan chapter. She and her colleagues organized a conference, 'Women 2000', funded by the Japanese Education Ministry and held in 2000 in Nagoya and Sapporo, to which Janet and I were invited and honoured guests. This support and international solidarity sustained us more than Fusako and the Japan group can ever know. The South African authors were next to come on board, so I also thank Ria van Niekerk and Jopie van Rooyen for their early commitment to the project.

Many scholars and activists have been inspired by the mission and breadth of our project. I extend special thanks to Dr Krishna Ahooja Patel, Fatima Ahmed Ibrahim, Sayeda Khatnn, Amel Gorani and Laura Khoury. Students in several years of my class 'Women in World Perspective' have likewise embraced the power of this mission; papers by Mary Callahan and Meaggan Ward are quoted in this book.

Some of the boxed inserts (e.g. 'Nushu, women's secret language'), and all citations from the *Philadelphia Inquirer*, were derived from clippings sent to me by my mother, Anne Wolsonovich Fluehr. At eighty-six, she is still a tireless reader despite advancing glaucoma. She stays current with world events and has always been a key source of support for my travels and my work. My husband, Richard A. Lobban, has been an active supporter throughout our thirty-six years of married and intellectual life. Conversation has never been dull, especially when we turn to matters of gender and society. I have dedicated this book to our two daughters; with this dedication, I bear in mind all the mothers in the 'invisible nation of women' throughout the world who have wanted more

Acknowledgements

equality, more freedom, more agency and ultimately less patriarchy for their daughters than what they experienced in their lifetimes. They are, of course, the future, and that was uppermost in our minds as we reflected upon the past century and what it wrought for the world's women.

CFL, Cranston, Rhode Island, USA
cfluehr@ric.edu

Dedication

To my grand-daughters, Genevieve Lee London and Anne Patricia Mancini, who say they will find well-being by 'standing up and fighting for what we believe' ... And to my grandsons, Connor Ross London, Evan William London, Giorgio John Mancini, Eamon Patrick Reis and Stefan James Reis, who say they will foster well-being by 'treating women with dignity and respect, helping them as much as we can, and trusting in them to get the job done' ...

JMB

To my father, Clifford Ramey, who passed away just as this book was born and for my daughters, Josina and Nichola, and for all the daughters ...

CFL

Preface

> The last century saw a great leap forward in the struggle for women's
> rights, but women are still treated as second-class citizens all over the
> world. (Amnesty International 2000)

From many corners of the world we heard a common theme during the twentieth century: male dominance threatens women, building layer upon layer of disenfranchisement, abuse and subjugation. At the same time, we heard women's voices insisting that *not* all women are subordinate to men, as Billson found in her study of women in Canada, *Keepers of the Culture* (1996), and that the world of Islam is highly differentiated regarding the condition of Muslim women (Fluehr-Lobban 1994, 2004). We also learned that some countries do better than others in promoting and protecting female well-being. If we imagine a continuum of subordination, restricted opportunities and oppression, some women in each society lie closer to the extreme pole of total ill-being and others to total well-being. Similarly, if we place the countries of the world along the same continuum, some lie closer to the extremes of fostering or blocking female ill-being.

These contrasts raise several questions that will further our understanding of gender regimes in the twenty-first century: How can we account for changes in female well-being during the twentieth century? What were the driving forces behind positive social change for women and girls? What were the major catalytic events or factors that raised or lowered female well-being?

We have taken a collaborative approach to answer these questions and to ensure accurate documentation of female well-being. Therefore, at the heart of this book lie eleven case studies that throw into relief the significant markers and obstacles on the path towards gender equality for our sisters around the world. Because we cannot be authorities on all the countries, we assembled teams of scholars, educators and policy analysts who prepared a case study on the fate of women and girls in their own society. Because it was critical for comparative analysis and theory development, all teams followed the same set of guidelines for amassing statistical data in seven key areas: demographics; economics; education; family status and structure; politics; social conditions, health and deviance; and religion and culture. These data form the skeleton of each chapter, but country teams varied in their emphases within the structure.

Our collaborators chose to author or co-author their chapter. In some cases (as with Hokkaido University in Japan, the University of Bath in England or the University of Western Ontario in Canada), they formed working groups to discuss relevant issues and prepare their chapter. In other cases, authors formed collaborations across boundaries (as with Iceland's team, which was comprised of women from the University of Iceland's Women's Studies Centre and Statistics Iceland). The Bangladesh chapter was written by two Bangladeshi women – one in Dhaka and one at Rhode Island College in the USA, who communicated via e-mail.

As co-editors and co-authors, we contributed six chapters. Chapter 1 introduces the book's format and explores the cases in relation to other countries on several key indicators. In Chapter 2, we tentatively define well-being and relate it to the Millennium Development Goals. Chapter 3 directly addresses the failure of existing social change theory to account for the sources and impacts of social change on women (and vice versa).

The case studies follow, Chapters 4 to 14, to prepare the way for a significant statement in the last three chapters about the sources and implications of social change. The case study approach naturally tends to emphasize differences, but in Chapter 15 we carefully identify the patterns of change, oppression, liberation, strength and power that characterize females across cultures. The case studies provide a foundation for a new, gendered theoretical understanding of social change, which we attempt in Chapter 16. Because of the intensive involvement of country experts, *Female Well-being* has the potential to shape future policy and programme decision-making. To that end, we hope that Chapter 17 will help educators, policy-makers and practitioners rethink the choices that individuals and bureaucracies make regarding female futures. Our intention is that careful analysis of data on female well-being should support the work of scholars around the globe, but we also hope that women and men in all walks of life – and especially in the international development community – will find this book a valuable resource and an inspiration for research, practice and policy-making.

References

Amnesty International (2000) *Women's Rights are Human Rights: The Struggle Persists*, <www.amnesty.org>

Fluehr-Lobban, C. (1994) 'Toward a theory of Arab-Muslim women as activists in secular and religious movements', *Arab Studies Quarterly*, 15(2): 87–106

— (2004) 'Nubian queens in Nile Valley and Afro-Asiatic culture history', Proceedings of the 9th Conference of Nubian Studies, T. Kendall (ed.), Boston, MA: Northeastern University Press

ONE | Introduction

1 | The twentieth century as a transformative time for women

JANET MANCINI BILLSON AND
CAROLYN FLUEHR-LOBBAN

Until lions have their historians, tales of the hunt shall always glorify the
hunters.   African proverb

The fate of female well-being

The twentieth century was a transformative one for females and for gender
relations. Virtually everywhere in the world, women struggled towards new
freedoms and new identities. The century witnessed a surge of consciousness,
a proliferation of women's organizations and global conferences, the flourishing of sophisticated feminist scholarship, and the movement of literally
millions of women into the public sphere. The momentous positive transformations in women's lives – and the ways in which female well-being declined
or remained static – deserve to be fully documented and interpreted. *Female
Well-being* analyses this natural social experiment through the retrospective
lens and wisdom of elapsed time.

As we embarked upon the daunting task of looking back over the 1900s,
we also fortuitously found ourselves in the early 2000s with the technological
capacity to take a virtual 'data photograph' of women and girls across the
globe. Never before in history have humans been able to examine the fate of
females in countries in every region of the world and for an entire era. We
tackled the complexities of social change by examining statistical and historical data from several extremely diverse countries: Canada, Colombia and
the United States (the Americas); Croatia, Iceland and the United Kingdom
(Europe); Bangladesh, Japan and Thailand (Asia); and South Africa and Sudan
(Africa). With the help of modern technology – computers, the Internet, telephone, fax and flight – we assembled teams of experts who could write about
female well-being in these countries. The cases help illustrate the most critical
challenges that women faced during the last century and which are likely to
shape this century as well.

In this volume, we address the fate of female well-being in terms of four
basic indicators – life expectancy, maternal mortality, infant mortality and
literacy – but we also examine female political and labour force participation,

marital status, fertility, income, contraception, abortion and many other factors. Our exploration of female well-being goes beyond amassing statistics
on a single issue to a more holistic approach. Our teams discuss the effects
of chronic war on women and children; domestic violence and abuse; religious beliefs; and any other issues they felt were important for women in their
country.

Globalization shapes our standpoint in *Female Well-being*. Globalization
can be thought of as multi-dimensional interactions in all spheres that move
towards a 'crystallization of the entire world as a single place' (Croucher 2004:
10) and involves international movement of people (including labour), capital
and goods. Usually defined in terms of economics and trade, globalization
also implies technological, cultural and political interconnectedness which
may or may not support female well-being. In keeping with the spirit of global
sisterhood, we take a strong international, comparative and feminist perspective designed to uncover the fundamental processes that promote, sustain
or degrade the female condition. This helps us address the paucity of theory
regarding the impacts of social change on women (and vice versa). Ultimately,
we seek to move beyond feminism to a global humanism informed by feminist
thought, and to contribute to the growing awareness that solving the problems
that arise from female oppression will go a long way towards improving the lot
of the whole of humankind.

The uneven patterns of social change

Although the century witnessed an extraordinary convergence of feminism
and achievement, the process of change was neither uniform nor universal.
The ideology of female emancipation spawned during the nineteenth century
was put into practice in the twentieth century with differential and complex
results. From the medical establishment to organized religion, women have
made some inroads in challenging the male-dominated status quo and re-
integrating female perspectives into daily life (Aburdene and Naisbitt 1992;
Chant and McIlwaine 1998), but dramatic progress was matched by equally
dramatic reversion to past oppressions. Women made tremendous strides in
education but lost hard-won advances or failed to gain ground in important
economic and political arenas.

By looking back across the century, we can begin to answer the question
as to how progressive (or not) those changes were. Virtually every country can
point to significant improvements that occurred during the 1900s in the status
of women, shifting the balance towards liberation and equity. Generational differences that emerge during a period of rapid change can wipe out centuries

of tradition. Just as easily, though, the balance can revert towards subordination. A flurry of forces that keep women 'in their place' can very quickly rebuff a step forward.

The 1900s saw remarkable shifts in gender regimes (power relations between males and females) in some countries and virtually no change in others. Gender regimes are 'in transition under globalization and democratization, but the direction of change is neither unilinear nor inherently progressive' (Bayes et al. 2001: 2). Because gender emanates from a process of social construction, it is in constant flux and is never unitary, even within a specific time and place. The social inequality and well-being indices referenced in this book reveal this unevenness. Nevertheless, we believe that gender regimes vary enough across times and places to capture major patterns of both positive and negative change.

Assessment of female well-being as of 2000

Despite the fact that during the last two decades of the twentieth century national and international institutions intensified their focus on eradicating women's poverty and marginalization (Sweetman 2000), the work of redressing gender inequality has just begun. Women are still the poorest of the poor. In politics, women's voices are muted or silent. A woman in sub-Saharan Africa, where high fertility and high maternal mortality risks prevail, faces a one-in-thirteen chance of dying in childbirth over her lifetime; the rate is one in 160 in Latin America and the Caribbean; one in 280 in East Asia; and one in 4,100 in industrialized countries (Vandemoortele 2002: 8). The World Health Organization (WHO) estimates that one in five women globally is physically or sexually abused at some time in her life. Women's numbers as a percentage of the world's doctors, engineers and heads of state increased markedly in the twentieth century. Women – slightly more than half of the world's population – still perform two-thirds of the world's work hours, however, earn less than one-tenth of its income, and own less than 1 per cent of the property. Full participation in the labour force characterized some societies – discrimination and narrowly defined roles characterized others.

The invisibility of women Much research and policy analysis fails to acknowledge the informal and unpaid contributions of women to their country's economic base, so we asked our authors to examine this factor as well. In the twentieth century, women created multiple niches in the informal economies (where lack of security, pensions or benefits renders women fiscally vulnerable) at a greater rate than they advanced in the formal sectors (where greater

5

security, benefits and predictability prevail). Women in less developed countries produce 60 per cent of all food and run 70 per cent of small businesses, in addition to caring for families. Official data often ignore these contributions.

Not surprisingly, poverty wears a feminine and often invisible face: of the estimated 1.3 billion people living in poverty, over 70 per cent are female. When nations produce poverty figures for the entire population, without separating the figures by gender, female poverty is masked. As Jan Vandemoortele says, 'The failure to disaggregate for gender ... easily leads to the fallacy of "misplaced concreteness". Average household income is very much an abstraction for women who have little or no control over how it is spent; it may exist in the minds of economists but it does not necessarily correspond with the reality faced by millions of poor women' (2002: 1). In Cuba, for example, poverty has officially been 'eliminated', but women still bear the burden of unequal resources disproportionately.

Women own less than one hundredth of the world's property, but even as they win the right to vote, work outside the home or own property, they usually remain ensnared in the domestic sphere, too. Women who participate in the formal labour force (even in more developed countries) tend to carry the 'double day' burden – serving as wage earners by day and housekeepers/caregivers by night. Strong expectations that women should play their traditional role inside the home persist, buttressed by culture, patriarchy and custom. Moreover, when women gain access to public-sphere activities, they often find themselves victims of a male backlash in the form of stereotyping, ridicule, sexual harassment, pay inequities, glass ceilings, blocked opportunities, role conflict and battering (Faludi 1992).

Global issues Amnesty International (2000) offered an end-of-century reflection on the status and condition of females worldwide, which throws into relief some of the century's contradictions:

- Migrant workers: Because of crushing poverty, hundreds of thousands of women and girls seek work outside their country (or far from home in their own country) as field workers or domestic helpers, usually without government protection against abusive employers or basic human rights violations.
- Domestic violence: Violence against women continues unabated and remains under-reported across the globe. Government agencies, including the police and courts, often fail to protect victims or adequately penalize or restrict the movement of perpetrators.
- Refugees and internally displaced women: Women and girls make up 80

per cent of all displaced people and refugees (Mohanty 2003: 234–5). During armed conflicts, women and girls suffer from rape, sexual abuse and the burden of caring for children, the sick and the elderly in hostile circumstances. Malnutrition, illness and sometimes starvation follow refugees from camp to camp. Domestic violence rates escalate during war and chronic conflict.

- Torture: Even at the end of the century, women were being raped and subjected to multiple forms of abuse and sexual violence by the authorities that are supposed to protect them, both inside and outside prisons.
- Human rights defenders: Women who struggle for the rights of others often find themselves at risk for human rights abuses and violations.
- Discriminatory laws, practices and traditions: 'Profoundly discriminatory laws and practices – often in the name of religion, tradition or culture' continue to underscore the notion of male superiority and rights (Charlesworth 1997: 385). Controversial issues such as abortion rights and mandatory veiling persist, and millions of women and girls are subjected to female genital mutilation (FGM).
- Political voice: Freedom of expression and the right to live in safety are by no means universal: worldwide, the average level of women's representation in parliaments is only about 10 per cent.

The persistence of patriarchy At the dawn of the twenty-first century, it is still in many respects 'a man's world'. The tenacity of patriarchy is evident, although great strides in recognizing women's rights have been made in many countries. Despite the dramatic growth of female-headed households and some international gains for women in decision-making and positions of power, the twentieth century did not significantly undermine normative patriarchy. The slow advance of female well-being can be attributed in some instances to the existence of more rhetoric than material assistance or political will. The issues facing women and girls have been ignored for so long that solutions will take decades to make a real difference in female lives.

Furthermore, even when men reject the exercise of power over women, they benefit from the existence of male-biased structures and institutionalized sexism that favours males (Sweetman 2000: 9). Those who make public commitments to achieving gender equality are sometimes reluctant to renounce male privilege and the 'patriarchal dividend' they enjoy (Connell 1995). Just as whites in historically racist societies must give up some of their privilege in order to foster racial equality, so men will need to examine self-critically the consequences of centuries of male privilege.

7

A comparative case study approach

From the very inception of *Female Well-being*, we have worked from a comparative, cross-cultural and feminist framework. We approach the question of female well-being systematically and comparatively from the perspective of eleven countries. Because it is hard to construct a cross-national model for such a complex phenomenon as female well-being, there is a tendency to reify statistical analyses. Several scholars have attempted to construct a 'status of women index', but indicators vary in their power of cross-cultural comparability. This both reflects and results in biases. In *Female Well-being*, we try to minimize such biases through a solid, data-driven picture of the fate of women and girls that is broadly comparative in its reach but carefully focused through detailed and interpretive case studies. By using data from both wealthy and poor countries, we can pinpoint common sources and implications of female inequality. Issues relating to growth and development were written large across the twentieth century and will dominate this century. Therefore, we compare country profiles with global data on women. On the other hand, treating the status of women 'in general' as a unitary analytic category is misleading and unproductive, so we prefer to focus on female well-being within the context of national realities as females have shifted from traditional to contemporary lifestyles, rural to urban lifestyles, and domestic to public-sphere involvement. We hope to raise the level of feminist scholarship beyond single-country case studies, two-country comparative studies or international handbooks that present data without significant theoretical analysis. Data from across the decades of this turbulent period form the foundation for a comprehensive theory of social change that encompasses the core institutions of society. Grounding our theory-building in empirical data helps avoid the pitfalls of armchair philosophizing about how things work in the real world.

The country case studies In selecting the countries, we considered criteria such as political existence throughout the century, quality of historical data, and availability of scholars who could participate. India, China, Nigeria or Indonesia would have been informative cases, but finding a competent team willing and able to tackle their large size, heterogeneity and historical/political complexities proved to be an elusive task. Turmoil in the Middle East rendered data-gathering and locating teams problematic. Data in former Soviet bloc countries is notoriously inaccurate after decades of suppression and 'misinformation'. Communist countries, overt dictatorships and closed monarchies tended not to collect or make public data on many crucial indicators, therefore eliminating some countries from consideration.

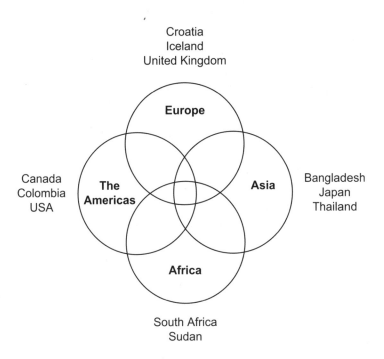

Croatia
Iceland
United Kingdom

Europe

Canada
Colombia
USA

The Americas

Asia

Bangladesh
Japan
Thailand

Africa

South Africa
Sudan

Figure 1.1 The case study countries

In the end, we chose countries from which we could learn something uniquely important about gender and social change. The cases come from every region of the world except Australia and the Middle East, and reflect many religious, racial, educational, income and occupational groups, varying degrees of urbanization, and different types of government. We include poor countries and rich countries, homogeneous and heterogeneous countries. All existed in 1900 (in some identifiable form), even if they were colonies and their boundaries later changed, and all existed until 2000 (Figure 1.1).

Since our task is to explore enhancements as well as declines in the status and condition of women, the case studies in *Female Well-being* underscore degrees of liberation as well as degrees of subordination. They make significant statements about the sources and implications of social change and the true nature of female contributions to their societies.

Country teams and a common structure Obviously, we cannot be experts on every country, so we extended our intellectual reach by assembling country teams of scholars, educators and policy analysts who prepared chapters on the societies they know best. These scholars identified catalytic events that tended to raise or lower women's status.

The teams assembled relevant data and identified key trends regarding infant mortality, maternal mortality, life expectancy, literacy, family structure, violence against women, labour force participation, school completion rates and political participation. To establish the sources of social change, we asked the teams to provide data for as many decades as possible from 1900 to 2000. Some countries did not have records for each data point throughout the century, so the teams assembled data as thoroughly as they could and turned to historical narratives for estimates. The key indicators of female well-being are relatively intact, as least since the Second World War. We provided the teams with Excel templates into which they could place their data to facilitate comparative analysis and theory development. No doubt the results are uneven across countries, but our attempt will surely lay the groundwork for future research that takes this broad view.

The teams answered specific questions: How has the condition of women and girls changed from 1900 to 2000? When the condition of women and girls improved or declined during the twentieth century, what forces helped create that change? Overall, in which respects did females leave the twentieth century better off than they entered it? What is the prognosis for the first decades of this century? The teams explored the conceptual links between political and economic realities, and the permeability of boundaries between public and private spheres. They also tackled analysis of the impacts on female well-being of educational and social policy, equal rights legislation and political direction.

Comparative analysis of the case study countries

This section offers a series of figures that show how our case study countries compare to each other on several important variables, including religion, involvement of females in agriculture, degree of urbanization, type of government, economics, demographics and education.

Religion Of the countries in our study, two (the UK and the USA) are predominantly Protestant (Anglican, Methodist, Presbyterian, Baptist, etc.) and two are predominantly 'other Christian' (Iceland, which is heavily Lutheran, and South Africa) (Table 1.1).

Three countries are predominantly Catholic (Canada, Colombia and Croatia) and two are predominantly Muslim/Sunni Muslim (Bangladesh and Sudan). Thailand and Japan are primarily Buddhist societies. Although the Japanese census does not ask about religion, surveys indicate that most Japanese relate to both Buddhism and Shintoism – or to no religion at all. In South Africa and Sudan, over a quarter of the population hold animist beliefs or follow an indigenous religion. No primarily Hindu or Jewish societies appear in

TABLE 1.1 Primary religious affiliations (%)

Country	Animist/indigenous	Buddhist/Shinto	Catholic	Hindu/Sikh	Jewish	Muslim/Sunni Muslim	Protestant	Other Christian	Other
Bangladesh		16.0				83.0			1.0
Sudan	25.0					70.0		5.0	
Japan		84.0						0.7	15.3
Thailand		95.0		0.1		3.8		0.5	0.6
Canada			46.0				36.0		18.0
Colombia			90.0						
Croatia			87.8			4.4	0.3	4.4	6.2
UK		0.3		1.6	0.5	2.7	71.6		0.3
USA			28.0		2.2	0.6	56.0	2.0	5.0
South Africa	28.5			1.5		2.0		68.0	
Iceland			1.7				4.0	87.1	7.1

Sources: For the UK, 23 per cent 'none' or 'not stated' (UKNS 2004); <www.wordiq.com>; <www.nationmaster.com>. For the USA, 8 per cent 'none' (USCB 2003).

our study, and up to 23 per cent of the population in some countries (e.g. the UK) report no religious affiliation.

Urbanization The case countries tend to be more urbanized than average, but vary from each other along this continuum (Figure 1.2). Iceland, which was virtually 100 per cent rural until the late nineteenth century, is now only slightly less urbanized than the most urban countries in the world (Guadeloupe or Singapore at 100 per cent). Thailand, our least urbanized case, is still relatively urbanized compared to the most rural country in the world (Rwanda at 6 per cent urbanization).

HIGHER URBANIZATION

Iceland	UK	Japan	Canada	USA	Colombia
93	90	79	79	77	75

MODERATE

Croatia	S. Africa
58	58

LOWER URBANIZATION

Sudan	Bangladesh	Thailand
37	26	20

World average = 47.6

Source: UNPD (2002). The Secretariat adjusts for some definitional inconsistencies in the term 'urban'. The world average is based on 2001 data from 204 countries.

Figure 1.2 Degree of urbanization (%)

Level of agricultural involvement Degree of urbanization does not correlate systematically with degree of participation in agricultural work, race or gender. For example, in Bangladesh females are more likely to live in rural areas and to be engaged in agriculture than are males (Table 1.2), but in Thailand and Iceland slightly more males are engaged in agriculture. Even urban dwellers can still be engaged at least part time in agriculture or in raising domesticated animals (as in the case of the 85,000 ponies who live in suburban Reykjavik, Iceland, or the countless vegetable gardens around Bangkok). Although South Africa is categorized as over 50 per cent urban, significant racial differences exist in that country's urbanization patterns. Colombia, which had been very agricultural and rural, has seen dramatic shifts towards urban lifestyles and occupations since the drug wars drove rural populations off the land during the 1980s and 1990s.

TABLE 1.2 Population engaged in agriculture by gender (%)

	Female	Male
Sudan	[90+]	[90+]
Bangladesh	78	54
Thailand	47	50
Croatia	17	16
Japan	6	5
Iceland	5	12
Canada	2	5
USA	1	4
UK	1	2
Colombia	[30]	[30]

Sources: ILO (2002); <www.nationmaster.com> (most recent year available between 1995 and 2001).

TABLE 1.3 Type of government by country

	Democracy	Federal democracy	Pseudo-democracy/ dictatorship
Bangladesh	Parliamentary democracy		
Colombia	Republic (dominated by executive branch)		
Croatia	Parliamentary democracy		
Iceland	Constitutional republic		
Japan	Constitutional monarchy/parliament		
Thailand	Constitutional monarchy		
United Kingdom	Constitutional monarchy		
Canada		Parliamentary confederation	
South Africa		Republic	
United States		Constitutional federal republic	
Sudan			Authoritarian regime (military/Islamist party)

Sources: <www.electionworld.org>; <www.nationmaster.com>.

The volatile political situation may account for the lower ratio of females to males in the Colombian countryside, where gender breakdown cannot be determined reliably, but about 30 per cent are engaged in agriculture; records are not available for Sudan, but the vast majority of the population is engaged in agriculture.

Type of government All the countries have adopted some form of democratic government in their primary political institutions, except Sudan (Table 1.3), which has had intermittent periods of democracy. Some democracies have experienced military regimes, as in Colombia and Japan. The countries' governments embrace the bi-level political system of the UK, which combines monarchy and parliament, the confederations that bond multiple provinces or states into a national body (e.g. Canada) and constitutional democracies (e.g. Iceland). In Colombia, democracy has been threatened twice in the nineteenth century and once in the twentieth century (1953–57) when the military seized power; chronic drug wars also pose threats to democracy there (see Chapter 6).

Economic position: GDP and poverty levels The countries span the economic spectrum, with five above the world average of $17,110 gross domestic product (GDP) per capita in US dollars (USD) and six below the average (Figure 1.3). Sudan and Bangladesh are the poorest countries in our set, both leaning towards the lowest-rated country of all (East Timor at $435 per capita). The USA rates highest among the eleven cases, although it is still considerably lower than the world's richest country (Luxembourg at $44,586).

LOWER INCOME

Sudan	Bangladesh
1,329	1,724

LOWER MIDDLE | | UPPER MIDDLE

Colombia	Thailand	S. Africa	Croatia
6,218	6,575	9,439	9,751

HIGHER INCOME

UK	Iceland	Japan	Canada	USA
25,427	27,560	27,958	28,932	35,935

World average = $16,441

Sources: World Bank (2002; purchasing power parity in USD, 2000). Low, lower middle and high income designations are from the World Bank and OECD; Croatian data for 2001 (UNDP 2003).

Figure 1.3 Economic position (GDP in USD per capita) (2000–2001)

Another way to look at economic position is through the percentage of a country's population living below the 'international poverty line', defined by the World Bank (2004b) as $2 per day. Figure 1.4 shows how our case countries compare on this measure. The relative rankings remain the same across groupings, although within each group the order changes somewhat using this measure. For example, although the USA is the wealthiest country in our sample on GDP, it has the highest percentage of children living in poverty among the 'high income' countries (22.4 per cent). A world mean is not available, but Nigeria is the poorest at 90.8 per cent.

HIGHER POVERTY		MID-LEVEL	
Sudan	Bangladesh	Colombia	S. Africa
[90]	29	20	12

		LOWER POVERTY			
Croatia	Thailand	Canada	Japan	UK	USA
2	<2	0	0	0	0

Sources: World Bank (2002); UNICEF (2000a); UNICEF (2000b); UNFPA (2001); no world average is available. Thailand data estimated as of 1998 (USCIA 2001); Croatia data from 1990–2001, using the $1 per day measure (UNDP 2003).

Figure 1.4 Economic position (% below the international poverty line)

By the $2 per day definition, the percentage of the adult population living below the poverty line in such 'developed' countries as the USA, Canada, Iceland, Japan and the UK is negligible. Figures for 'child poverty', however, would be higher. Over 90 per cent of Sudanese people live below the poverty line, using an older measure of $1 per day. The number of impoverished people has increased dramatically in the last thirty years from 52 per cent in 1968 to 91 per cent in 1993. Sudan ranks 143rd out of 174 countries for income. The high prevalence of poverty contributes to high maternal and infant death, widespread malnutrition and poor-quality healthcare.

Until recently, analyses of economic development largely overlooked women's productivity. Figure 1.5 shows our case study countries in terms of this dimension, and includes street traders and vendors, seasonal or itinerant workers, and others who earn a living outside of formal workplace settings. Although these figures are not gendered, most informal economy workers are female. Over half the population in Thailand works in the informal economy, compared to only 3 per cent in Canada.

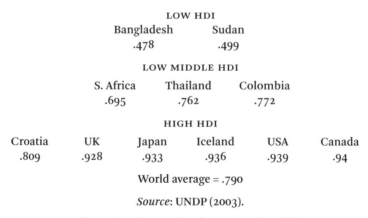

LOW INCOME

Sudan	Thailand
[high]	53

LOW MIDDLE INCOME

Colombia	Bangladesh	Croatia	S. Africa
39	36	33	29

HIGH INCOME

UK	Japan	USA	Canada	Iceland
13	11	9	3	–

World average = 26.47

Source: <www.nationmaster.com>.

Figure 1.5 Participation in the informal economy (%)

Human Development Index The Human Development Index or HDI (Figure 1.6) is also a useful indicator of well-being. The UNDP defines HDI as a composite of longevity, health, knowledge and standard of living. Again, Sudan and Bangladesh are among the lowest in the world (the lowest is Sierra Leone at 0.275). South Africa, Colombia and Thailand are in the low middle range and the other cases come in above the world average. Canada's score of 0.94 is virtually as high as the highest, Norway's 0.942. The HDI indirectly reflects other factors that contribute to health and standard of living – birth rate, death rate and population growth rate (Figures 1.7, 1.8 and 1.9).

LOW HDI

Bangladesh	Sudan
.478	.499

LOW MIDDLE HDI

S. Africa	Thailand	Colombia
.695	.762	.772

HIGH HDI

Croatia	UK	Japan	Iceland	USA	Canada
.809	.928	.933	.936	.939	.94

World average = .790

Source: UNDP (2003).

Figure 1.6 Human Development Index (HDI)

Birth rate The crude birth rate at mid-year per thousand persons is shown in Figure 1.7. Naturally, the birth rate is affected by trends in contraception use and abortion, as well as by age at first marriage. Birth rate tends to decline with increased female education (which reduces the fertility rate).

HIGHER BIRTH RATE

Sudan	Bangladesh
37.21	26.41

MIDDLE

Colombia	S. Africa	Thailand
21.99	20.63	16.39

LOWER BIRTH RATE

Iceland	US	Croatia	UK	Canada	Japan
14.37	14.1	12.76	11.34	11.09	10.03

World average = 17.85

Source: USCIA (2003).

Figure 1.7 Birth rate (per 1,000 persons)

Death rate The crude death rate is the average number of deaths per thousand persons at mid-year (Figure 1.8). The death rate is very sensitive to the age structure of the population, so most countries eventually show a rise in the death rate even though deaths may be declining in each age category because of healthcare improvements; declining fertility rates result in a 'greying' of the population.

HIGHER DEATH RATE

S. Africa	Croatia	UK	Sudan
18.86	11.25	10.30	9.81

MIDDLE

USA	Japan	Bangladesh
8.70	8.53	8.47

LOWER DEATH RATE

Thailand	Canada	Iceland	Colombia
7.55	7.54	6.93	5.66

Average = 9.42

Source: USCIA (2003).

Figure 1.8 Death rate (per 1,000 persons)

Population growth rate Population growth rate, a third HDI indicator, can be positive or negative (Figure 1.9). This rate refers to the average annual percentage change in the population when births, deaths, in-migrants and out-migrants are tallied. Immigration heavily influences the population growth rate (as in the UK, the USA and Canada), as does a high birth rate after war (as in the 'baby boom' effect after the Second World War).

The twentieth century

HIGHER GROWTH RATE

Sudan	Bangladesh	Colombia
2.71	2.06	1.56

MIDDLE

Thailand	Canada	USA	Iceland
.95	.94	.92	.49

LOWER GROWTH RATE

Croatia	UK	Japan	S. Africa
.31	.3	.11	.01

World average = 1.01

Source: USCIA (2003).

Figure 1.9 Population growth rate in % (2003)

Educational levels Iceland and the UK are close to being the highest in the world for average number of years of education completed (Norway at 17.6 years for females and Australia at 16.4 for males are highest); Figure 1.10 shows data for the cases.

LOWER NO. OF YEARS

	Sudan	Bangladesh
Female:	n/a	4.2
Male:	n/a	5.9

LOW MIDDLE

	Thailand	Colombia	Croatia	S. Africa	Japan
Female:	10.8	11	11.5	14.1	14.1
Male:	10.7	10	11.3	14.1	14.4

HIGHER NO. OF YEARS

	Canada	USA	Iceland	UK
Female:	15.3	15.7	16.5	16.8
Male:	14.4	14.8	15.1	–

World average: males = 10.6, females = 13.2

Sources: <www.nationmaster.com>; for Colombia, UNESCO (2004). Croatian data are for 1994; the female literacy rate in Croatia is 97.4 per cent, compared to the overall literacy rate of 98 per cent, as of 2001.

Figure 1.10 School life expectancy (female vs male)

As of 2003, females were either at a par with males in terms of average number of school years completed or ahead of males, except for Japan, where boys have slightly higher school life expectancy. There is greater gender disparity in the wealthier countries than in the poorer countries in our set.

Women in development statistics Table 1.4 summarizes some of the key gender statistics that portray female well-being in our case study countries. The most prominent female advantage can be seen in life expectancy. In all our cases, females outlive males – sometimes by a considerable margin, as in Croatia, which experienced so much war in the twentieth century. In the poorest countries in our sample (Bangladesh and Sudan), the sex ratio favours males, even though life expectancy is higher for women.

The percentage of females who receive pre-natal care varies widely from country to country. Again, Bangladesh and Sudan show very low rates on this dimension, which directly affects not only female but also child well-being. This percentage does not appear to vary according to degree of development: Colombia and South Africa have pre-natal care rates almost as high as those of Canada and the USA; a few percentage points on this variable can make a large difference in maternal and infant mortality rates. The Literacy Gender Parity Index (which reflects access to basic education rather than school life expectancy) is another area in which females aged fifteen to twenty-four seem to be reaching male levels; the exception is Bangladesh, where for every ten literate males there are only seven literate females, and Sudan (nine females to ten males). In the countries with square brackets around their figures, the female literacy rate is virtually 100 per cent and has perhaps even surpassed that of males.

The Labor Force Gender Parity Index, which measures the ratio of females to males actively involved in the labour force, has remained relatively constant during the last ten years of the century; not surprisingly, Sudan has the poorest showing on this index, followed by Colombia and South Africa. The labour force gender gap rose slightly for Canada, Croatia, the UK and the USA. As of 2000–2002, no country in our sample had more than 50 per cent of females working in the non-agricultural workforce. The lowest percentage was in Bangladesh at only 22.9 per cent. Except for Canada, Colombia and the USA, the percentage of unpaid family workers was at least two females for every male, and in some cases, such as Bangladesh, Thailand and Japan, the proportion was even higher.

Finally, in our sample South Africa, Canada and Croatia have the highest percentage of female parliamentarians; Bangladesh, Japan and Thailand all rate lower than the world average of 10 per cent.

According to the World Bank (2004b), life expectancy at birth is the 'number of years a newborn infant would live if prevailing patterns of mortality at the time of its birth were to stay the same throughout its life'. Teenage mothers are defined in terms of the percentage of women aged fifteen to nineteen 'who

19

TABLE 1.4 Women in development gender statistics

	Female population (% of total) 2002	Life expectancy at birth (in years) 2002 Male/female	Pregnant women receiving pre-natal care 1995–2002	Literacy Gender Parity Index 15–24 2002 (%)	Labor Force Gender Parity Index 1990/2002	Women in non-agricultural sector (% of total) 2000–2002	Unpaid family workers (% of employment) 2000–2002 Male/female	Women in parliaments (% of total seats) 2003
Bangladesh	49.7	62/63	40	0.7	0.7/0.7	22.9	10.1/73.2	2
Canada	50.5	76/82	–	–	0.8/0.9	48.8	0.1/0.3	21
Colombia	50.5	69/75	91	1.0	0.6/0.6	49.1	5.1/7.1	12
Croatia	51.7	70/78	–	1.0	0.7/0.8	45.9	2.4/7.8	21
Iceland	50.0	78/82	[99]	1.0	–	98	–	30
Japan	51.1	78/85	–	–	0.7/0.7	40.4	1.6/10.1	7
South Africa	51.7	46/48	94	1.0	0.6/0.6	–	0.7/1.4	30
Sudan	49.7	57/60	60	0.9	0.4/0.4	–	–/–	10
Thailand	50.8	67/72	92	1.0	0.9/0.9	46.8	16.4/39.8	9
UK	50.8	75/80	–	–	0.7/0.8	49.7	0.2/0.5	18
USA	51.1	75/80	99	–	0.8/0.9	48.4	0.1/0.1	14

Source: World Bank (2004a). Data are for the most recent year available.

already have children or are currently pregnant'. Pregnant women receiving pre-natal care are defined as the 'percentage of women attended at least once during pregnancy by skilled health personnel for reasons related to pregnancy'. Women in parliaments are defined as the 'percentage of parliamentary seats in a single or lower chamber occupied by women'.

A road map for this book

Although a retrospective analysis of statistical data supplies a springboard from which we can understand gender issues in the twentieth century, it is not enough. From the moment we conceived the idea of *Female Well-being*, we thought of it as a project with serious implications for social policy, legislation, programme development and action. In the last chapter, we suggest some strategies to help ensure that any laudable goal that supports gender development and female well-being will come to fruition.

Before we begin our journey through the eleven countries, in the next two chapters we explore definitions of well-being and critique existing theories of social change. Chapters 4 to 14 present the case studies in alphabetical order. Our final chapters outline comparative highlights and present a new social change theory based on the country data.

References

Aburdene, P. and J. Naisbitt (1992) *Megatrends for Women*, New York: Villard Books

Bayes, J. H., M. E. Hawkesworth and R. M. Kelly (2001) 'Globalization, democratization, and gender regimes', in R. M. Kelly et al. (eds), *Gender, Globalization, and Democratization*, Lanham, MD, and Oxford: Rowman & Littlefield

Billson, J. M. (2005) *Keepers of the Culture: Women and Power in the Canadian Mosaic*, Boulder, CO: Rowman & Littlefield

Chant, S. H. and C. McIlwaine (eds) (1998) *Three Generations, Two Genders, One World: Women and Men in a Changing Century*, London: Zed Books

Charlesworth, H. (1997) 'Human rights as men's rights', in C. C. Gould (ed.), *Key Concepts in Critical Theory: Gender*, Amherst, NY: Humanity Books

Connell, R. W. (1995) *Masculinities*, London: Blackwell

Croucher, S. L. (2004) *Globalization and Belonging: The Politics of Identity in a Changing World*, Lanham, MD, and Oxford: Rowman & Littlefield

Faludi, S. (1992) *Backlash: The Undeclared War Against American Women*, New York: Anchor

ILO (International Labour Organization) (2002) *Key Indicators of the Labour Market, 2001–2002*, Geneva: ILO

Mohanty, C. T. (2003) *Feminism without Borders: Decolonizing Theory, Practicing Solidarity*, Durham, NC: Duke University Press

Sweetman, C. (ed.) (2000) *Gender in the 21st Century*, Oxford: Oxfam (Focus on Gender)

UNDP (United Nations Development Programme) (2003) *Human Development Reports 2003*, New York: United Nations

UNPD (United Nations Population Division) (2002) *World Urbanization Prospects: The 2001 Revision: Data Tables and Highlights*, New York: United Nations

UNICEF (United Nations Children's Fund) (2000a) *Innocenti Report Card No. 1, a League Table of Child Poverty in Rich Nations*, Florence: Innocenti Research Centre

Vandemoortele, J. (2002) *Are the MDGs Feasible?*, New York: United Nations Development Programme, Bureau for Development Policy

World Bank (2002) *World Development Indicators 2002*, Washington, DC: World Bank Group

— (2004a) *Women in Development*, Washington, DC: World Bank Group

— (2004b) *World Development Indicators 2002*, Washington, DC: World Bank Group

Websites

Amnesty International (2000) *Women's Rights are Human Rights: The Struggle Persists*, <www.amnesty.org>

UKNS (United Kingdom National Statistics) (2004) *Census Report 2001*, <www.statistics.gov.uk/census2001,8June>

UNESCO (UNESCO Institute for Statistics) (2004) <www.uis.unesco.org>

UNFPA (United Nations Population Fund) (2001) <www.unfpa.org/arabstates/sudan/2sud0206.pdf> (Report #DP/FPA/SDN/4)

UNICEF (United Nations Children's Fund) (2000b) <www.unicef-icdc.org/publications/pdf/repcard1e.pdf>

USCB (United States Census Bureau) (2003) *Statistical Abstract of the United States*, <www.census.gov/prod/2004pubs/03statab/pop.pdf>

USCIA (US Central Intelligence Agency) (2001, 2003) *World Fact Book*, <www.worldfactsandfigurescom/countries>

<www.electionworld.org>

<www.nationmaster.com>

<www.wordiq.com>

2 | The complexities of defining female well-being

JANET MANCINI BILLSON

A better life for me is to be healthy, peaceful and to live in love without hunger. Love is more than anything. Money has no value in the absence of love. (Ethiopia) (Narayan et al. 2000: 22)

The complexities of well-being

As midnight of 2000 approached, individuals, communities and organizations all over the world reflected upon the legacy of the twentieth century and the promise of the twenty-first century. These reflections undoubtedly culminated in many dreams and disappointments, predictions and anxieties. Many crafted or solidified ambitious plans for the new century, but these plans rested on attempts to define well-being and the proper goals for development efforts (Qizilbash 2004). Our task in this chapter is to explore the meaning of well-being in general and for females, as the definition of well-being most assuredly will shape action strategies on behalf of girls and women in the next decades.

Beyond wealth Well-being has been systematically studied for many years in fields such as psychology, epidemiology and healthcare, and in philosophy since Aristotle's forays into defining 'happiness' (Barnes 1984). No culture defines well-being simply in terms of wealth (Dasgupta 2001: 139–61). Women and men around the world give definitions that are complex and multi-dimensional – yet common threads run from one society to the next.

The term 'well-being' is often used to refer to an optimal condition that entails some measure of satisfaction, confidence, physical fitness and health. For our purpose, well-being extends to a state of social, economic, political and individual well-being that implies the opposite of isolation, poverty, disenfranchisement, poor health, alienation or powerlessness. New perspectives on well-being must come from a broad social scientific perspective based on analysis of data from disparate regions of the globe. The perspective must reflect differences in religious beliefs, socio-economic conditions, histories, values and institutional frameworks; it must also reach across time to capture trends and patterns of change. Although this is a monumental task, the complexities of well-being deserve careful analysis.

TABLE 2.1 Dimensions of well-being and ill-being

	Well-being	Ill-being
Material	Enough to eat, shelter, clothing, land tenure (rural), capital (urban), dependable work, money *Not being out of work*	Lack of food, water; starvation, poor shelter and clothing, uncertain livelihood, little or no money; subsistence living
Bodily	Good health, a strong body, good appearance, looking well *Good health* **Life (expectancy)** **Bodily health** **Bodily integrity**	Sickness, feeling weak from hunger or illness, exhaustion, looking pale, skinny or old
Social	Good relations within the family and the community; being able to care for, raise, marry and settle children; peace and calm *Marriage* **Affiliation**	Not being able to sustain traditions, give gifts; loneliness, isolation and estrangement; feeling disconnected; worrying about problematic relations with others
Self-respect and good community relations	Social respect and being part of a community; being listened to, being popular, and being able to fulfil social obligations and help others *Membership of non-church community organizations* *A belief that others can be trusted and that it is never justifiable to cheat on one's taxes* **Emotions** **Affiliation**	Stigma of poverty; shame of having to ask for and accept help; being rejected or treated badly because of being poor; low self-confidence; feelings of vulnerability and fear

Security	Peace of mind, confidence in survival, absence of constant fear and worry **Emotions**	Insecurity, feeling vulnerable, lack of predictability and stability, being subjected to widespread crime, domestic violence, corruption
Freedom of choice and action	Power to control one's life, to plan and take action; power to avoid exploitation, rudeness, humiliating treatment; ability to acquire skills, education, loans, information, services and resources; to live in 'good places'; to not slip farther into poverty; helping others in need *Education* **Practical reason** **Control over one's environment (political and material)** **Play**	Constrained choices; inability to control what happens; being forced to accept trade-offs; having one's voice silenced; inability to challenge authorities; living in 'bad places'; being forced to take risks to survive
Spiritual	Regular church attendance Belief in god(s)	

Source: Adapted from Narayan et al. (2000: 22−43).

Well-being and ill-being Analysis of female well-being is intricately tied to the assumption that certain basic human needs must be met in order to achieve a good quality of life; these needs are, of course, debatable, multi-levelled and diverse (Doyal and Gough 1991; Gasper 2004). *Voices of the Poor: Crying out for Change* is based on a massive set of interviews with over twenty thousand poor people in twenty-three countries (Narayan et al. 2000). The research team asked, 'How do you define well-being or a good quality of life, and ill-being or a bad quality of life?' The team concluded that the core dimensions of well-being and ill-being include several interconnected internal and external dimensions: material well-being, physical well-being, security, freedom of choice and action (Dasgupta 1993), and good social relations.

Well-being and ill-being are firmly rooted in social structures. Ill-being, which is not simply the opposite of well-being, is closely associated with certain aspects of poverty, which McGregor (2004: 4) sees as both an outcome and a process – both a cause and an effect of structure.

Another study that has embraced different countries on a large scale is the World Values Survey (WVS) (Inglehart et al. 2000). The WVS focuses on basic values and beliefs in sixty-five countries that were studied in waves between 1981 and 2001. These data show that subjective well-being is positively correlated with certain age groups (higher in the early forties and higher in the over-sixty-five age group than among eighteen-to-twenty-four-year olds). *Relative* income also has an impact on well-being: as income rises, self-estimations of well-being rise until the person reaches the middle of the national income distribution, then the relationship between well-being and income decays. The WVS data suggest that higher subjective well-being appears to come from higher than average participation in community organizations. When individual and societal levels of social capital are higher, subjective well-being is higher. Well-being has to do with a discrete set of dimensions that have been observed across cultures. Table 2.1 displays key findings from Narayan; the WVS (in italics); and Martha Nussbaum's theory of central human capabilities (1995, 2000) (in bold). Obviously, there is much overlap in these conceptualizations of well-being. Narayan and her team also found that:

- 'Well-being' has to do with 'happiness, harmony, peace, freedom from anxiety, and peace of mind', which ultimately stem from having 'enough' to survive physically, but also from good relations with others.
- Poverty is deepening for many people and is associated with failure of governments and public institutions to perform adequately and honestly.
- Poverty, gender and violence mix inextricably with a sense of powerlessness, frustration, anxiety, depression and anger.

As with well-being, the nature of ill-being is multi-dimensional and inter-woven. Ill-being and well-being are not just opposite experiences; describing one does not automatically describe the other in reverse, as Narayan found:

- Corruption, violence, powerlessness, incapacity and bare subsistence living serve as interlocking forces that keep people poor and in a state of ill-being.
- Steps backward reflect a failure to sustain improvements, blocking of new opportunities, or denial of inclusion.

Subjective versus objective measures of well-being Some researchers have taken a distinctly psychological or 'subjective' view of well-being, using such measures as life satisfaction scales. Others emphasize 'objective' factors such as income. Quality of life within the context of national norms and networks cannot be measured in terms of productivity and income alone. That is, well-being *is not simply a question of materialism*. In fact, according to Helliwell (2002), economic equations that attempt to measure well-being show that gains in social capital have more direct and more sustained effects on well-being than do the effects of income gains.

Values also play an important role in these definitions. In one culture, the good life may revolve around money, material possessions and occupational status; in another, well-being may centre on harmony, peace and positive family relations, regardless of material status (Brock 1999). As Narayan et al. point out, seemingly objective measures of poverty (low income or sub-standard housing) may not adequately define well-being or ill-being – rather, they have a distinct psychological and spiritual side. Wealth and well-being are not necessarily coterminous. Thus, a woman living in Bangladesh with little income but good health, enough food for her family, and close friends may say that her life is full of well-being. Her neighbour, who suffers from depression or lack of self-confidence, might describe her life in terms of ill-being. Ill-being often results from poverty, but it often stems from other factors as well (as expressed in the saying 'Money can't buy happiness'). Gough (2003) adds that autonomy and competence needs, which are often suppressed in women, are enhanced by subjective life satisfaction; at the same time, they contribute to subjective well-being.

Both individuals and cultures define in different ways the details of 'the basics' necessary for a decent life. Narayan found that 'across cultures and contexts, being able to dress well and appear well is repeatedly stated as part of a good quality of life' for women (2000: 26). For example, in Bangladesh younger women point to such items as clothes, oil for the hair and soap as important to their sense of well-being. In countries that are ravaged by war or chronic conflict, respondents identify the cessation of violence and chaos as the most important component of well-being: 'Be hungry but live in peace' (ibid.: 27).

Well-being and relative deprivation Although well-being is not singularly related to income, research at the country level shows an improvement in subjective well-being when individuals move out of poverty (Helliwell 2002: 50). Gains in income are relative, regardless of one's socio-economic position, although the positive impact on well-being is greatest as one moves upward from the lowest level to the middle level in any society. The move from the middle into the higher brackets shows smaller relative impacts on subjective well-being (ibid.: 49). This finding shifts the argument and analysis of well-being away from income and GDP towards social capital. When average national income increases but a person's own income does not, however, she may report a decrease in life satisfaction and well-being (ibid.: 50; Frey and Stutzer 2000). This is true even in relatively affluent countries. Sociologists refer to this phenomenon as 'relative deprivation' (Merton 1957: 185–214), and it cannot be ignored in analysing either subjective or objective well-being data.

Furthermore, subjective well-being is generally higher in richer countries than in poorer countries, especially during the rise from poverty to moderate affluence (as mentioned above). Indeed, the recognition that one group enjoys superior well-being compared to another has been the driving force behind countless social movements, including the global women's movement, aboriginal rights movements and racial equality movements. Underprivileged groups in one society may seem privileged in another, but if they perceive their situation as less privileged, they will feel deprived relative to others. This is true for social capital as well as for income. For example, the language of the Declaration on Women's Rights at the Seneca Falls (New York) convention that was called by two abolitionists, Lucretia Mott and Elizabeth Cady Stanton, in July 1848 reflects women's clear statement of deprivation relative to the rights accorded males in the United States (Stanton et al. 1881: 70–73):

> The history of mankind is a history of repeated injuries and usurpations on
> the part of man toward woman, having in direct object the establishment of an
> absolute tyranny over her. He has never permitted her to exercise her inalien-
> able right to the elective franchise. He has compelled her to submit to laws
> in the formation of which she had no voice. He has withheld from her rights
> which are given to the most ignorant and degraded men, both natives and
> foreigners. Having deprived her of this first right of a citizen, the elective fran-

28

chise, thereby leaving her without representation in the halls of legislation, he has oppressed her on all sides. He has made her, if married, in the eye of the law, civilly dead. He has taken from her all right in property, even to the wages she earns.

The language in this statement points to the crisis in both subjective and objective well-being for women at the time. Research and history suggest that there is a bar below which poverty is all-consuming and so keenly felt that the capacity to meet basic material and bodily needs is threatened (Doyal and Gough 1991). In any country, falling below a certain (undefined) level of income means that other factors that might ordinarily affect well-being recede. As with the Declaration of Women's Rights, so for social capital measures of well-being.

The male–female differential: unmasking inequality Well-being is complicated by many factors, but the most significant (and under-studied) may be gender. Amartya Sen's observations (1993) have particular relevance for female well-being. Sen defines quality of life in terms of one's 'capability' to lead a 'valuable' life. Capability has to do with what people can do or be – 'positive freedoms' that lead to a flourishing life (Nussbaum and Glover 1995; Nussbaum 2000). Clark and Gough, in their attempt to interrelate well-being with the human capabilities notion, conclude that 'well-being is multidimensional, but basically composed of physical and mental states' (2003: 17). Because capability for females has been severely restricted by prejudice, discrimination and barriers to full and equal participation, quality of life for girls and women has been jeopardized. By extension, female mental states are in jeopardy (as documented by many studies that show a higher depression incidence among North American women, especially those who were trapped in the suburbs of the 1950s and 1960s in narrowly defined homemaker roles).

Development can be thought of as programmes, policies and activities that expand capabilities and positive freedoms (Sen 1999). Poverty, in turn, can be seen as a failure to create the expansion of opportunities that lead to well-being. Positive development that fosters enhanced capabilities should lead ultimately to greater female well-being; failed development leaves women and girls with restricted life chances. The factors that detract from well-being apply to males as well as females in any country, but females also suffer from the institutionalized sexism that pervades so many societies. For women, 'development as freedom', in Sen's terminology, cannot coexist with gender discrimination and stratification.

When we look at development indicators for countries as a whole, the danger of a 'masking effect' emerges. For example, as mentioned earlier, using average income can hide basic gender inequalities. Always, we must ask the question, 'Where is the country's wealth and income located – with an elite or equally distributed among citizens and across genders?' Country comparisons that look only at average income may be inherently misleading for two reasons. First, the mean is always the least reliable measure of central tendency, because it is sensitive to the extremes (Vandemoortele 2002); an essentially impoverished country whose power elite controls an enormous percentage of the wealth may show a higher mean income than actually reflects the 'average' person's life – or that of women. Second, the percentage living below the poverty level must be examined before undertaking national analysis; in other words, we must know the proportion of those who cannot adequately meet basic needs such as housing, food, water and clothing. The masking effect occurs with other basic indicators as well, including school completion rates, literacy rates and GDP.

Female well-being is extremely prone to deterioration or blockage. When a society defines any segment of the population as 'less than' and denies access to education, healthcare, employment, upward mobility, secondary associations, government and other sources of self-respect, well-being is by definition jeopardized. What happens to societies in which access to education, meaningful work, personal income, participation in organized religion, membership of community organizations and a voice in decision-making – the key sources of well-being – are systematically denied to females simply because they are females? Females are likely to experience lower subjective *and objective* well-being levels, but their lower levels of well-being will negatively affect societal levels as well. (The effect would be similar for any group that is systematically excluded.)

Furthermore, denial of access and opportunity creates a structural portrait of gender stratification, characterized by the barriers and abuses that women describe in our case studies and which serve to threaten female well-being: sexual abuse and harassment, domestic violence, unequal inheritance, arranged or forced marriage, female infanticide, low-paying or unpaid work, pay inequities, and silencing of one's political voice. When gender stratification is complicated by other types of stratification based on race, ethnicity, language, religion or sexual preference – which may also be experienced by males – then female well-being is seriously compromised. In other words, gender stratification creates an 'overlay effect' that amplifies other types of societal layering.

The Cycle of
Well-Being

Access to Education ← → Quality of Institutions

Individual Well-Being ← → National Well-Being

Figure 2.1 The cycle of well-being

The cycle of well-being It seems logical to use a combination of subjective and objective measures in defining or determining well-being: beyond income, it is critical to acknowledge the role of subjective measures such as quality of family relations, trust in community and government, physical and psychological health, strength of institutions, and access to participation in all aspects of life. These factors influence each other in a cycle that moves from individual through community and institutions up to the national level and back to the individual. Various types of stratification and discrimination can block that movement, especially the multiple disadvantages related to gender stratification.

Helliwell's extensive meta-analysis of well-being research concluded that the direct links between social capital and subjective well-being must be drawn via the links 'flowing indirectly through physical health to subjective well-being' (2002: 47). Education, as the purveyor of societal values and the crucible of skills and knowledge essential for participation in other institutions and for improvement of physical health (for self and for children), acts as a conduit between individual and society, which is why unblocking girls' access to education during the twentieth century had such a salutary effect on female well-being (Figure 2.1).

The cycle of well-being suggests that testimonials regarding subjective well-being (as found in *Voices of the Poor*) – as enriching as they may be – must be heard in tandem with the quantitative data on standard indicators such as maternal mortality, infant mortality, literacy and life expectancy (as the case studies in this volume elucidate). Our case studies look at these issues over a long enough period to avoid single-point or recent-point observations that might be dramatic or even revolutionary. Rather, they trace the long-term view of what contributes to or detracts from female well-being.

We examine country differences (rather than local or regional differences, because census and other statistical data are less reliable at those levels, especially over time) and intentionally explore the gap between female and male well-being. Variations in culture – each social system's blueprint for language, religion, values, beliefs, lifestyles and norms – link to both equality and oppression. We were mindful of these subtleties as we wrote *Female Well-being*.

International efforts to improve female well-being

During the twentieth century, many countries passed laws guaranteeing women equal rights; important progress has been made. Many governments have enacted legislation to promote equality and have established national machineries to enforce the law and to bring women's voices into major centres of decision-making. Importantly, international agencies have made concerted efforts to highlight gender stratification and oppression and ways to improve female well-being all over the world. These efforts have met with uneven success in the face of centuries of female disadvantage.

The differences in male and female power and well-being dominated conversations among women during international conferences in the late twentieth century. Through intense discussion, women recognized that resource disparities among nations, particularly between nations of the 'North' and 'South' (often referred to as 'developed' and 'developing' nations), are complicated by social and gender differences. Even within developed countries, gender disparities and gender oppression keep women from fully accessing the wealth and opportunities available to men. Everywhere, religious, cultural and racial differences exacerbate economic oppression.

Some important twentieth-century landmarks Because these awakenings and conversations affected women in each of our case study countries, it will be useful to review some of the pivotal points of the century's time line:

- By 1930: Women's suffrage obtained in all nations except Saudi Arabia and Kuwait.
- 1931, 1946: Women's International League for Peace and Freedom awarded Nobel Prize for Peace.

- 1948: Universal Declaration of Human Rights.
- 1975: The UN General Assembly's International Women's Year spawned a series of worldwide meetings and legislative efforts to enhance female well-being.
- 1976–85: The UN Decade for Women flowed from the International Women's Year and galvanized efforts around the globe on behalf of women; goals included a massive review by participating countries 'to examine the status and rights of women and to bring women into decision-making at all levels' through country-based legislation.
- 1975: The UN First World Conference on Women was held in Mexico City and subsequent world conferences were held in Copenhagen, 1980; Nairobi, 1985; Beijing, 1995 (attended by 40,000 women).
- 1979: The Convention on the Elimination of All Forms of Discrimination Against Women (CEDAW) was adopted by the UN General Assembly – the first human rights document devoted exclusively to women.
- 1985: The World Conference to Review and Appraise the Achievements of the UN Decade for Women: Equality, Development and Peace adopted the Nairobi Forward-looking Strategies for the Advancement of Women, which were to be implemented by the year 2000.
- 1990: The UN Commission on the Status of Women recommended a minimum of 30 per cent women in decision-making positions in national governments.
- 1990: Discussions began on the Millennium Development Goals (MDGs), following the 1990 World Summit for Children.
- 1993: The UN Second World Conference on Human Rights was held in Vienna; the Vienna Declaration and Programme of Action defined women's rights as an inalienable, integral and indivisible part of universal human rights; implementation has yet to be realized.
- 1994: The UN International Conference on Population and Development met in Cairo; feminist groups urged integration of human rights issues into development planning and population policies.
- 1994: The UN appointed the first Special Rapporteur on Violence Against Women, Radhika Coomaraswamy.
- 1995: The Fourth World Conference on Women (Beijing) called on all governments to develop implementation strategies or plans in support of the Platform for Action; the Division for the Advancement of Women (DAW) asked all UN member states to supply copies of these strategies in order to bring the goals of the International Women's Year into reality.
- 1996: The International Women's Leadership Forum was held in

Stockholm, Sweden, chaired by Vigdís Finnbogadóttir (president of Iceland, 1980–96); many women prime ministers and presidents in attendance; the Council of Women World Leaders was created.

- 1997: Mary Robinson (former president of Ireland) was appointed UN High Commissioner for Human Rights.
- 1998: The Council of World Women Leader's first Summit of Women World Leaders was held; the second Meeting of High-Level Women in Finance and Economics was held in collaboration with the World Bank; the inaugural Meeting of High-Level Women in Justice, Law and Equality was held in collaboration with the UN.
- 2000: The Millennium Development Goals were officially adopted by 191 member states of the UN General Assembly, the International Monetary Fund (IMF), the Organization for Economic Cooperation and Development (OECD) and the World Bank.
- 2000: The UN Millennium Women's Summit was held with sitting women heads of state and government, and women heads of specialized UN agencies; they met with UN High Commissioner for Human Rights President Mary Robinson to discuss the grave situations affecting women and girls around the world.
- 2002: The UN Commission on the Status of Women met; no plans were initiated for the fifth UN International Women's Conference in 2005, following the every-tenth-year tradition.
- 2004: The Millionth Circle Initiative worked towards an international women's conference in 2010.

Of all these late-twentieth-century events, perhaps CEDAW and the MDGs will have the most far-reaching impacts. Therefore, they deserve further explanation.

Eliminating discrimination against women: CEDAW

CEDAW, the Convention on the Elimination of All Forms of Discrimination Against Women, set a definitive international standard for gender equality to which national governments can comply by signing the convention. CEDAW defines discrimination as '... any distinction, exclusion or restriction made on the basis of sex which has the effect or purpose of impairing or nullifying the recognition, enjoyment or exercise by women, irrespective of their marital status, on a basis of equality of men and women, of human rights and fundamental freedoms in the political, economic, social, cultural, civil or any other field' (UN 2003).

CEDAW REQUIREMENTS By accepting the convention, countries commit themselves to undertake measures to end discrimination against women in all forms, including: incorporating the principle of equality of men and women in their legal system by abolishing all discriminatory laws and adopting laws that prohibit discrimination against women; establishing public institutions that ensure the effective protection of women against discrimination; and ensuring elimination of all acts of discrimination against women by persons, organizations or enterprises. The convention provides a legal instrument to ensure women's equal access to, and equal opportunities in, political and public life – including the right to vote and to stand for election – as well as education, health and employment. State parties to the convention agree to take all appropriate measures, including legislation and special measures, to protect essential freedoms and rights for women and to guard against all forms of traffic in women or exploitation of women.

The convention is the only human rights treaty that affirms the reproductive rights of women and specifies culture and tradition as influential forces shaping gender roles and family relations. It recognizes women's rights to acquire, change or retain their nationality and the nationality of their children. Countries that have ratified or acceded to the convention are legally bound to put its provisions into practice. They are also committed to submitting national reports, at least every four years, on measures they have taken to comply with their treaty obligations.

SIGNATORIES TO CEDAW By 1999, 163 countries had ratified this 'international bill of rights for women'. As of 6 October 2004, 179 countries – over 90 per cent of the members of the United Nations – were party to the convention. Within our study, the following countries have signed the CEDAW convention: Bangladesh, 1984; Canada, 1980; Colombia, 1980; Iceland, 1980; Japan, 1980; the USA, 1980; Thailand, 1985; the UK, 1986; and South Africa, 1993. Croatia became a party to the convention in 1991 and succeeded to it in 1992 ('succession' allowed Croatia to continue the former Yugoslavia's ratification in the early 1980s). Sudan was not at the time of writing a state party to the convention. The Bush administration in the USA has tried to block CEDAW, although the US State Department initially backed it; the administration also cut its contribution to the United Nations Fund for Population Activities (UNFPA) because of concerns that funds were being used for contraception or selective abortion, especially in China (Kristof 2002).

CEDAW RESERVATIONS In spite of CEDAW's potential influence, the UN's

Division for the Advancement of Women (DAW) points out that the number of 'reservations' officially logged for this convention is substantial; most reservations are against Articles 2 and 16, which DAW considers to strike at the very heart of the convention. For example, among our case studies Bangladesh does not consider as binding the provisions of Article 2 as they 'conflict with Shari'a law based on Holy Quran and Sunna' (UN 2000). Bangladesh expressed its reservations about Articles 2 and 16 because of perceived contradictions between these articles and certain provisions of the civil and personal laws in Bangladesh. Since the provisions of the CEDAW charter are not yet incorporated into the laws of Bangladesh, the government is not legally bound to follow them (UN 2003).

Thailand 'expressed its understanding that the purposes of the Convention are to eliminate discrimination against women and to accord to every person, men and women alike', equality before the law, and in accordance with the principles prescribed by the constitution of the Kingdom of Thailand. Some Islamic states and the Vatican opposed the 1995 platform, arguing that CEDAW could jeopardize marriage, motherhood and the family, the 'backbone' of society.

The millennium development goals relating to female well-being Another important global change instrument of the twentieth century was a set of far-reaching aspirations, the Millennium Development Goals (MDGs). The Millennium Declaration was designed to throw into relief the values of various organizations concerned with international development, and to stimulate concerted action (UN 2000). The International Conference on Financing for Development examined in 2002 how to mobilize development resources in support of the MDGs. Emerging out of several international meetings and summits, 'the adoption of the Millennium Declaration in 2000 was a defining moment for global cooperation in the 21st century' (UN 2002).

The declaration recognizes the critical importance of improving female well-being worldwide for achievement of all MDGs, resolving 'to promote gender equality and the empowerment of women as effective ways to combat poverty, hunger, and disease, and to stimulate development that is truly sustainable'. Three of the eight MDGs relate directly to gender, indicating main areas that international development agencies, governments and non-governmental organizations (NGOs) consider most critical for the advancement of female well-being. Goal 2 has the intent of ensuring education for all children, but includes a component of gender equity, and so is included in this discussion.

Although the gender development goals relate to the next two decades, they also help place the achievements of the last century into perspective. That is, they highlight the fact that women and girls still lag behind males in many of the most important aspects of a life well lived. Achievement of the other MDGs, which involve alleviation of poverty and improvement of health worldwide, presumably will also contribute to female well-being. Those goals include eradicating extreme poverty; achieving universal primary education; combating HIV/AIDS, malaria and other diseases; ensuring environmental sustainability; and developing a global partnership for development.

The following organizations are the UN bodies responsible for working towards these goals: the United Nations Educational, Scientific and Cultural Organization (UNESCO); the International Labour Organization (ILO); the Inter-Parliamentary Union (IPU); the United Nations Children's Fund (UNICEF); and the World Health Organization (WHO) (as indicated in parentheses below).

ENSURE PRIMARY EDUCATION FOR BOTH SEXES (UNESCO) Goal 2 calls for every child, male or female, to be able to complete primary schooling. The target date is 2015. This key goal expects both literacy and gender equity in basic primary education and is closely tied to Goal 3.

> Indicators: The net enrolment ratio in primary education; the proportion of pupils who start Grade 1 and ultimately reach Grade 5; and the literacy rate of fifteen-to-twenty-four-year-olds.

PROMOTE GENDER EQUALITY AND EMPOWER WOMEN (UNESCO, ILO, IPU) The target of Goal 3 is to eliminate gender disparity in primary and secondary education, preferably by 2005, and in all levels of education no later than 2015. This goal is actually a cluster of goals pertaining to the need for females to gain equality of opportunity and access to social, economic and political power. The goal calls specifically for open access to education, more work in non-agricultural sectors, and greater participation in decision-making bodies. Goal 3 assumes that bringing more of the world's women into literacy will open doors that have been closed to females. Two objectives underpin this goal: protection against discrimination and full access for females at every age to pursue their aspirations.

> Indicators: The ratio of girls to boys in primary, secondary and tertiary education (UNESCO); the ratio of literate women to men, fifteen to twenty-four years old (UNESCO); the share of women in wage employment in the non-agricultural sector (ILO); the proportion of seats held by women in parliaments (IPU).

EARNING POWER AND INCOME Although not specified in Goal 3, another way to measure its progress is the Gender Income Ratio, which compares female income as a proportion of every male dollar earned. Belize, at .24 cents to the male dollar, is the lowest in the world; Latvia, at .72 cents to the male dollar, was the highest as of 2000. Figure 2.2 shows how our case countries compare on this dimension (literacy, school completion rates and parliamentary seats appear in Chapter 1).

LOWER RATIO

Sudan	Japan	Colombia	S. Africa
0.33	0.44	0.47	.51 (white)

LOWER MIDDLE RATIO

Croatia	Bangladesh	Iceland	UK	Canada	Thailand	USA
.56	.57	.61	.61	.62	.62	.62

World average = .57

Source: <www.nationmaster.com>. For women of colour worldwide, the GIR is much less than the .54 average for the countries in this study. In South Africa, the GIR for black women is a low .12.

Figure 2.2 Gender Income Ratio (GIR) (female income as a proportion of male income)

REDUCE CHILD MORTALITY (UNICEF, WHO) By 2015, the target of Goal 4 is to reduce by about 66 per cent the mortality rate of children who are under five years of age. Goal 4 recognizes that female well-being depends on dramatic reductions in the devastating phenomenon of infant mortality. The highest rate in the world occurs in Angola, where almost 200 out of every 1,000 live births end in death before the baby's first birthday. In contrast, countries such as Iceland and Sweden have essentially eliminated infant mortality, with rates of three or four deaths per 1,000 live births. Addressing infant mortality requires improved pre-natal care for pregnant mothers, better birthing care, and eradication of preventable diseases of young children (such as tuberculosis and measles). This goal also has implications for ending selective abortion of female fetuses, killing newborn female babies and differential malnourishment of female infants and toddlers.

Indicators: The under-five mortality rate; the infant mortality rate; and the proportion of one-year-old children immunized against measles. Figure 2.3 compares our case countries on this dimension.

IMPROVE MATERNAL HEALTH (UNICEF, WHO) By 2015, the target of Goal 5 is to reduce by about 75 per cent the maternal mortality rate worldwide. This

HIGH MORTALITY

Bangladesh	Sudan	S. Africa
68.05	67.14	61.78

MIDDLE LOW

Thailand	Colombia
29.5	23.21

LOW MORTALITY

Croatia	USA	UK	Canada	Japan	Iceland
7.06	6.69	5.45	4.95	3.84	3.53

World average = 25.56

Source: USCIA (2003). The infant mortality rate is the annual number of deaths of children under one year old per 1,000 live births that occurred in the same year. It is a strong indicator of overall health, especially maternal health and pre-natal care.

Figure 2.3 Infant mortality per 1,000 births

goal reflects the assumption that female well-being depends on extinguishing unacceptable rates of maternal mortality. The maternal mortality data are those reported by national authorities. UNICEF and WHO periodically evaluate these data and make adjustments that account for well-documented problems of under-reporting and misclassification of maternal deaths; they also develop estimates for countries with no data. The maternal mortality rate is defined as the number of deaths that result from pregnancy, delivery and related complications. Dying in childbirth (or shortly thereafter) must become a relic of the past throughout the world, not just in the countries that can presently afford good pre-natal and birthing care. That it can be drastically reduced through provision of appropriate medical care and other supports is proved by the contrast between Mozambique, which has the highest rate of maternal deaths in the world – 1,100 per 100,000 births – and Greece, which has the lowest rate of only one death per 100,000 births. Croatia, at an estimated six per 100,000, is the lowest-rated country in our data set.

Indicators: The maternal mortality ratio (UNICEF/WHO) and the proportion of births attended by skilled health personnel (UNICEF/WHO). Figure 2.4 shows this dimension for our cases; attended births percentages appear in Table 1.4.

Globalization versus local networks

When we approached this project, we struggled with the question of whether to examine data for whole countries or for themes (such as poverty or mortality rates across the globe). Although much homogenization of culture

Defining female well-being

39

HIGHER MORTALITY

Sudan	Bangladesh	S. Africa
550	350	239

MIDDLE LOW

Colombia	Thailand
80	44

LOWER MORTALITY

Iceland	Japan	USA	Canada	UK	Croatia
10	8	8	7.8	7	6

World average = 132

Sources: <www.nationmaster.com>; UNFPA (2003); <www.globalis.gvu.unu. edu>. The maternal mortality rate for Croatia, 1985–2001, is based on the observed value adjusted by a nationally reported adjustment factor, if available, or by 1.5 if not; estimate developed by WHO, UNICEF and UNFPA. Prior estimates for 1995 levels may not be comparable. Data are reported per 100,000 births for the latest year between 1985 and 1999.

Figure 2.4 Maternal mortality per 100,000 births

has taken place, local networks and norms are still powerful according to Helliwell and Putnam (1995). In fact, 'networks are much tighter close to home and in the same country' than they are across societies (Helliwell 2002: 39), which suggests that culture is a critical determinant in outcomes. Borders, though often imposed and arbitrary, frequently reflect choices of people whose cultures differ on fundamental dimensions. Even in the case of the longest undefended border in the world, which separates Canada and the United States, the differences between cultures are subtle but real. Societies construct policies that reflect deeply held values, but we must be vigilant in recognizing that those values might not be gender neutral (Billson 1996). Societies that exclude women and girls from education and health do grave damage at the higher levels of social well-being, because these two variables have such far-reaching direct and indirect impacts on both individual and social health. This relates directly to how societies define the value and nature of being female. Therefore, choosing countries as the unit of analysis made sense.

At the same time, the negative and positive impacts of globalization on female well-being cannot be denied. As Bayes et al. (2001: 2–3) argue, globalization during the twentieth century spawned changes in foreign investment; extensive feminization of labour (often involving low wages and poor conditions); damage to subsistence economies as more women worked outside the home or engaged in large-scale migrations to urban areas; degradation of female labour (prostitution, sex slavery and sex trafficking); altered consumption patterns and creation of false needs; and impoverishment. On the positive side, some women prospered during the century because of globalization; for some, gender roles and gender regimes became more flexible and positive; some women were able to create more individualistic lives; and many became politically conscious activists. All these outcomes triggered the emergence of human rights groups that demanded rights for women. In some cases, a backlash against these demands set female well-being back and led to hardening of gender biases.

That 'economies are not just more national but more local than assumed' (Helliwell 2002: 11) has significant implications for the impacts of globalization. We suggest that economies are less local only because social, cultural and religious values are equally as powerful determinants of cross-national contact as are trade and economic market processes. Differences between nations persist, are transported with immigrants, and are often embedded in (or reflective of) government policies. This appears to justify the selection of countries over regional or local data and has implications for the impacts of global trade.

Globalization tends to distract societies from focusing on the welfare of citizens as leaders begin to look outward for economic competition, political alliances and technological innovations. Whether the balance has been more positive or more negative for female well-being, it is certain that the tentacles of globalization caused various degrees of social disruption in the twentieth century. We chose the key indicators of infant and maternal mortality, literacy and life expectancy to help measure that disruption and to suggest where improvements may have occurred.

The 'gender differential'

When we asked our key research questions – what supports female well-being and what detracts from it? – we turned to existing theories of social change. We found them inadequate in their explanatory power when it comes to unravelling the connections between gender and social change. Although many theorists have stressed the complexity of change, most have been silent on women. That is, they have not included what we call the 'gender differential' – the fact that the entire experience of social change is often fundamentally different in its source, nature and consequences for females compared to males. Therefore, we assigned ourselves a double task: first, to assess retrospectively the dynamics of social change in the well-being of women between 1900 and 2000; second, to generate a new, 'gendered' theory of social change that will shed light on advances and reversals in female well-being. Such a theory must hold up across cultures.

Helliwell wondered 'whether it might be possible to obtain comparative measures of subjective well-being from enough countries, and covering enough years, to provide a comprehensive assessment of how individual-level and societal-level influences combine to shape well-being' (2002: 45). We asked each team to gather objective data from the entire century and to supplement it with analytical, interpretive research as found in reports, articles, books, working papers and statements from NGOs, women's organizations, international development agencies and from their own perspectives. Altogether, these data will paint a portrait of well-being, ill-being, change and stasis in societies and for females across a clearly defined time span.

It is understandable that theory has lagged behind both research and ideology, for the need to include women as part of history and culture, of production as well as reproduction, has been a vigorous and enduring struggle. In the next chapter, we critique existing theories of social change with respect to their limitations in addressing the gender differential. In Chapter 16, we seek to move towards a more systematic, gendered theory that directly does justice to the intricacies of the gender differential and the cycle of female well-being. In doing so, we are not just theorizing about gender, social change and female well-being, but are providing a foundation upon which women around the world can use theory to inform action.

References

Barnes, J. (1984) *The Complete Works of Aristotle: Volume One*, Princeton, NJ: Princeton University Press

Bayes, J. H., M. E. Hawkesworth and R. M. Kelly (2001) 'Globalization, democratization, and gender regimes', in R. M. Kelly et al. (eds), *Gender, Globalization, and Democratization*, Lanham, MD, and Oxford: Rowman & Littlefield

Billson, J. M. (1996) *Keepers of the Culture: The Power of Tradition in Women's Lives*, New York: Lexington Books

Clark, D. and I. Gough (2003) 'Needs, capabilities and well-being: relating the universal and the local', paper presented at the Inaugural Workshop of the ESRC Research Group on Wellbeing in Developing Countries, 13–17 January, Bath

Croucher, S. L. (2004) *Globalization and Belonging: The Politics of Identity in a Changing World*, Lanham, MD, and Oxford: Rowman & Littlefield

Dasgupta, P. (1993) *An Inquiry into Well-being and Destitution*, Oxford: Clarendon

— (2001) *Human Well-being and the Natural Environment*, Oxford: Oxford University Press

Doyal, L. and I. Gough (1991) *A Theory of Human Need*, New York: Guilford Press

Frey, B. S. and A. Stutzer (2000) 'Happiness, economy and institutions', *Economic Journal*, 110(466): 918–38

Gasper, D. (2004) 'Conceptualizing human needs and well-being', paper presented to the International Workshop on Researching Well-being in Developing Countries, Hanse Institute for Advanced Study, Delmenhorst, Germany, 1–4 July

Gough, I. (2003) 'Quality of life and human wellbeing: bridging objective and subjective approaches to well-being', paper presented at meeting of the Development Studies Association, Strathclyde, September

Helliwell, J. F. (2002) *Globalization and Well-being*, Vancouver: University of British Columbia Press

Helliwell, J. F. and R. D. Putnam (1995) 'Economic growth and social capital in Italy', *Eastern Economic Journal*, 21(3): 295–307

Inglehart, R. et al. (2000) 'World Values Surveys and European Values Surveys, 1981–1984, 1990–1993, and 1995–1997', computer file, ICPSR Version, Ann Arbor, MI: Institute for Social Research, University of Michigan

Kristof, N. D. (2002) 'Bush vs. women', *New York Times*, 16 August

McGregor, J. A. (2004) 'Researching well-being: communication between the needs of policy makers and the needs of people', paper presented to the International Workshop on Researching Well-being in Developing Countries, Hanse Institute for Advanced Study, Delmenhorst, Germany, 1–4 July

Merton, R. K. (1957) 'Social structure and anomie', in R. K. Merton, *Social Theory and Social Structure*, New York: Free Press

Narayan, D. et al. (2000) *Voices of the Poor: Crying out for Change*, New York: Oxford University Press (for the World Bank)

Nussbaum, M. C. (2000) *Women and Human Development: The Capabilities Approach*, Cambridge: Cambridge University Press

Nussbaum, M. C. and J. Glover (eds) (1995) *Women, Culture and Development: A Study of Human Capabilities*, Oxford: Clarendon Press

Sen, A. K. (1993) 'Capability and well-being', in M. C. Nussbaum and A. K. Sen (eds), *The Quality of Life*, Oxford: Clarendon Press

— (1999) *Development as Freedom*, Oxford: Oxford University Press

Stanton, E. C. et al. (eds) (1881) *History of Woman Suffrage*, vol. I, New York: Fowler and Wells

UN (United Nations) (2000) *Road Map towards the Implementation of the United Nations Millennium Declaration*, New York: United Nations

USCIA (United States Central Intelligence Agency) (2003) *The CIA World Fact Book*, Washington, DC: USCIA

Vandemoortele, J. (2002) *Are the MDGs Feasible?*, New York: UNDP, Bureau for Development Policy

Websites

Brock, K. (1999) 'It's not only wealth that matters – it's peace of mind too: a review of participatory work on poverty and illbeing', <www.worldbank.org/poverty/voices/reports>

Qizilbash, M. (2004) 'On ethics and the economics of development', newsletter of the International Development Ethics Association, 29 November, <www. development -ethics.org>

UN (United Nations) (2002) *The United Nations and the MDGs: A Core Strategy*, www. unitednations.org.

— (2003) *Convention on the Elimination of All Forms of Discrimination Against Women (CEDAW)*, <www.un.org/womenwatch/daw/cedaw/cedaw.htm>

UNFPA (United Nations Fund for Population Activities) (2003) *State of the World Population*, <www.unfpa.org>

<www.globalis.gvu.unu.edu>

<www.nationmaster.com>

3 | A critique of social change theories

CAROLYN FLUEHR-LOBBAN AND
JANET MANCINI BILLSON

A person doesn't have the strength or power to change anything, but
if the overall system changed, things would be better. (Bosnia) (Narayan
et al. 2000: 34)

The weakness of existing theories of social change

From around 5000 B.C.E., the world's population tripled in size after
the birth of agricultural societies. As the traditional gatherers in pre-state
societies, women were in all likelihood the domesticators of grains. Between
1900 and 2000, the world's population tripled again (Chirot 1994: 7). The
staggering multiplication of human beings on the face of the earth during the
twentieth century has also meant staggering social change. Change affected
women differently from country to country (and even within countries), but
the changes of the twentieth century were monumental relative to those of
earlier centuries. The average standard of living worldwide rose from 1900 to
2000, though serious inequities still exist within and between all societies.
Not only astonishing technological inventions but also rapidly changing values and social norms marked these hundred years. Thus, the lives of females
born in 1900 were significantly different from those of females born at the
end of the century.

Although many theorists talk about change being progressive, linear or
cyclical, change in the twentieth century did not follow an ever progressive,
linear pathway to improved female well-being worldwide, nor was it cyclical,
as many Western theories of social change would postulate (Rihani 2002).

We recognize the possibility that change may stem from random, coinciden-
tal or geographic factors. Undoubtedly, significant society-wide changes have
emanated from natural disasters or war, but we want to offer students and
researchers throughout the world a richer and more comprehensive perspective on how change occurs. To begin this task, we assess selected theories for
their value in developing a global, gendered theory of social change.

In addition to facile explanations of change, theories reflected an endemic
male bias. Most theorists do not attempt to account for social change that
occurs for one part of the population (e.g. males) but not for another part

(e.g. females). For example, some argue that the spread of democratic ideas has produced more autonomy for individuals than was possible in the past. Since in so many societies men but not women have had education, suffrage and associated freedoms, at least in the early years of democracy, the effects on female autonomy are questionable.

The conceptualizations of change and culture were constructed by early sociologists and anthropologists, most of whom were Western males. The same is true for historians and philosophers. The androcentric bias is best illustrated in what have been called 'Great Man' theories, whereby social change is understood as the result of the acts and influence of powerful males, such as Alexander the Great, Thomas Jefferson or Adolf Hitler. History is often narrated as a history of male leaders. Similarly, Western political theory ontologically is male, focusing on the 'reasonable man' from Plato to Locke, Rousseau, Hume, Hegel, Marx and Nietzsche. That social institutions are fundamentally masculine remained virtually unchallenged until fairly late in the century (and usually by feminists). For example, the female 'underside' of history was explored by Elise Boulding (1992), using a counter-narrative to respond to male bias. Boulding's feminist analysis is hardly mainstream and her preoccupation was with correcting history, not with generating theoretical hypotheses. Similarly, the pioneering efforts of Margaret Mead to correct Western male bias had limited success, in part because her theory was ideologically driven in an attempt to undermine Freudian theories about the nature of female and male by using cases from 'primitive' societies in the Pacific. It remains the task of twenty-first-century scholars to review and replace this fundamental paradigm with alternative constructions (Clark and Lange 1979).

Male bias in research and theory-building was evident, too, in the classical Marxist and materialist analyses focused on class as the major independent variable in human history, generally leaving out the social markers of gender, race and ethnicity. A singular exception was Frederick Engels' *Origin of the Family, Private Property, and the State* (1972 [1884]), which acknowledged female status as inferior within the rise of class society. Building upon theories of the matriarchate developed by J. J. Bachofen on the 'The Mother-Right' (1861), in which an original matriliny (descent through the female line) and matriarchy was argued, and the later ethnographic research among the Iroquois of North America by L. H. Morgan which appeared to confirm Bachofen's argument, Engels and the subsequent Marxist tradition asserted that women's power and status were higher in pre-state society. Fluehr-Lobban (1979) argued that the matriarchate was in need of reappraisal in light of twentieth-century ethnographic knowledge and that widespread matrilineal descent does not necessarily translate into female dominance or matriarchy, although it often signifies some status and influence.

Despite this theoretical advance, women's status in Marxist theory was not treated with the significance that half of humanity deserves, primarily because the Marxists subsumed gender as a category of analysis under class (Guettell 1974). Likewise, classical Marxism did not organically incorporate the colonized nations, and post-colonial Marxian theories focused little upon the 'double colonization' that women suffer, subordinate both to foreign rule and to males in their own countries. Nevertheless, classical Marxist theory did place 'the woman question' on the social and historical agenda; we are still attempting to fulfil this mission.

In a parallel mode to economic reductionism, biological reductionism theories flourished over the twentieth century and are enjoying a revival now. Such theories simplify cultural and gender differences, as well as race and class differences, by positing that the sexual division of labour is essentially natural: men are natural hunters and women are natural gatherers; men are natural wagers of war and women are natural pacifists; men are the 'breadwinners' and women the dependent child bearers and caretakers.

In early twentieth-century attempts to explain social change, sociological theorists such as Talcott Parsons (1937/1966) elaborated upon nineteenth-century structural-functional systems theory, which assumes interconnections and adaptations among economic and political systems, social institutions and culture. Parsons occasionally mentioned gender in his analysis of change, but simply appended women to the status they derived from their kinship networks (i.e. their husband's status).

Modernization theory

Modernization theory has said little specifically of theoretical significance about gender and social change. If theorists have considered gender as an important variable at all, they have generally seen modernization as emancipatory for women, because they have assumed (erroneously) that industrialization would undermine patriarchy. Typically, social change theory that attempts to explain modernization has been dominated by attention to urbanization and the economic processes related to globalization. These theories have contributed little to explain women's enduring inequality.

All modernization theorists have tended to stress economics, trade and finances in their explanations of social change. They have pointed to technology, invention and knowledge explosions as key sources of growth (e.g. Abramovitz 1989, 1990). Financial and legal systems that allow mobilization of savings and investment under stable government conditions contribute to restructuring and change throughout society (for example, the creation of stock markets or, later, the international monetary instruments such as structural adjustment policies and development lending).

Trade routes have historically led to urbanization, usually at the junction of two or more modes of transportation (for instance, a river and a footpath or a river and a railway line). Urbanization is both an outcome of change and a source of change (Shackman et al. 2002). Although urbanization began with the creation of surpluses in agricultural societies millennia ago, in the twentieth century it was marked by the growth of mega-cities that threaten the environment. These urban cauldrons of unmanaged poverty and inequality have resulted in 'consequent weakening of the state, civil unrest, urban-based revolutions, and radical religious fundamentalism' (Brockerhoff 2000). This pattern integrally and unequally affects women's lives as they struggle to eke out a living in overcrowded urban areas with stretched or failing infrastructures. The harshness of life for millions of families who are living under elevated highways in Manila, in the *favelas* of Latin America or in the urban ghettos on every continent bears witness to this struggle.

A major effort was made by Daniel Chirot to trace social change from the agricultural through the industrial, urbanized periods (in some cultures). Like others, he explains social change in terms of climate shifts, advancing or receding glaciers and over-hunting, which eventually led to ecological pressures in early societies. In later societies, he lists the process of settlement into villages, cultivation and storage of grains (which created surpluses) and consequent overcrowding as sources of change (one could argue that these were the changes, which still need explanation – or that each one represented a change and a source of change).

Fully developed agriculture, increasing population density (and pressure) and social conflict within and between groups produced the formal state, which Chirot considers the 'single most critical innovation in human organization ever undertaken' (1994: 1). Strong leaders (all male) floated to the top in this period, which was characterized by increasing specialization and role differentiation. Chirot then postulates that 'economic pressures and changing ideas are really the main causes of change' (ibid.: 119). Surely, this begs the question – change is the cause of change. Not only is there no mention of women, females or gender, but Chirot also assumes that economic pressures signal that a society is failing in its performance in comparison to others.

As with so many others who have tackled social change theory, Chirot falls into the 'change is cyclical' trap (that is, assuming that simply recognizing the cyclic nature of change explains its causes). He also swings between two typical explanatory poles: change is rooted in either cataclysmic or evolutionary sources, born of failures in competition with other societies, or else it is the result of human strivings for survival of the fittest. While economic and political pressures undoubtedly produce both social change and impinge on female well-being, this type of instrumentalism and economic reductionism places culture and values in the back seat as sources of change in their own right. Culture and values carry patriarchal modes of oppression.

Murdock's earlier work (1961) explored how cultural (rather than general) change occurs. He defined culture as a system of collective habits that are learned collectively and either shared throughout society or limited to certain classes or groups within society. His notion that each generation is prone to adopting the habits that were adaptive for previous generations helps explain the persistence of patriarchy. Social pressure ensures that new members of society conform to the habits that are viewed as 'right' (meaning those that the elite and privileged groups view as appropriate). Change occurs in the face of 'some significant alteration in the life condition of a society' (ibid.: 249) such as an infusion of immigrants with differing habits, natural disasters, wars, discoveries, specific leaders, cross-cultural contact and so forth. We can add an unspoken implication of Murdock's work for women: when the 'habits' are male defined, women as the primary socializers of children project those habits to the next generation until they are no longer seen as right and appropriate.

For Murdock, the process of cultural change depends upon innovation (stemming from inventions, experimenting with new habits, crises, such as famines or epidemics, or cultural borrowing and diffusion). Murdock did not directly address gender but acknowledged that intermarriage might enable borrowing. With innovation, the next change process is social acceptance (or backlash), followed by selective elimination of old habits that are less rewarding than their alternatives. Finally, integration means that new habits are adapted into other habits to form an integrated whole. Of course, we now realize that competing cultural forms exist side by side in tension or conflict and that social acceptance is rarely uniform across whole populations. Ruth Benedict (1961) saw this in her depiction of cultural change as complex and not capable of logical explanation. She mentioned that habits of culture are deeply ingrained and hard to change. As we had learned by the end of the century, that was particularly true of the rigidity of patriarchal cultural forms.

Anthony Giddens (1999) has offered several elaborate explanations of social change, mostly related to globalization and trade economics, but also with

A critique of social change theories

social, political and cultural implications. He said that globalization affects local cultures and identities, which means that people must lead a more re-flexive life but also have more options in creating identities. Certainly that has been true for females as well as males in the twentieth century (though not addressed directly by Giddens). Giddens also cites the electronic world com-munication revolution as a feature of globalization that requires new political, economic and social systems. The danger is that during change processes the state can become an instrument of exploitation, as with women in some world regions, extracting surplus value from workers (Tilley 1997).

Giddens defines democracy as a system of competition between political parties that is marked by fair elections and civil liberties. By this definition, Western 'democracies' such as the United States, Canada and the United King-dom (and others) were not true democracies until suffrage was granted in the early to mid-twentieth century. Female inclusion and consultation in the power brokering of their societies are requisite to both the emergence of democracy and the shaping of future change. Failure to grant suffrage and a wider political voice stimulated the feminist social movements of the nineteenth and twentieth centuries, which, in turn, led to shifts in old habits (even such a small habit as opening one's own door rather than expecting a man to do so, or using the term 'chairperson' instead of 'chairman', began to change the gender paradigm).

Several theorists have pointed to social movements in response to inequity or crisis as a spur for social change, but few have acknowledged the role of the feminist movement (outside of feminist literature). For example, Guillén (2001) mentions that global movements have been necessary to address global prob-lems such as the AIDS epidemic and global warming, but does not identify gen-der differentiation as a global problem that spawned the feminist movement. Similarly, Held et al. (1999) view globalization in terms of trade, diplomacy, multilateralism and environmental issues, and the global treaties necessary for regulating common issues such as war and toxic wastes. No mention is made of CEDAW or other international women's conferences, movements or understandings that have been essential to address gender discrimination.

Other social change theorists have emphasized demographic changes as the most significant stimuli for change, specifically rapid population growth (Gel-bard et al. 1999). A high rate of growth affects not only population size but life ex-pectancy, declines in childbirth and population shifts. These explanations lead into discussions of cultural traditions that govern age at first marriage, fertility rates and the role of women in child or elder care. Kinsella and Velkoff (2001) talk about the increasing number of elderly women relative to elderly men as a source of change in pension schemes, disability care and female roles.

Many theorists have social institutions as the mechanism through which individuals pursue goals, but ignore the ways in which institutions shut out women in a systematic fashion. For example, they have not fully realized the extent to which institutions (such as the Catholic Church) have obstructed individual agency of women and girls. This affects both change processes and change outcomes. Virtually all recent theorists insist that for societies to change (and, implicitly, to grow), institutions need to invest in education and training to sustain their competitive capacity. Theoretically, this could advantage females because their labour is essential to survival, but investment in female education and training was minimal until mid-century in most countries and later in many. Thus, theories that focus on the pivotal role of institutions in growth have accounted for only part of the story; what happened to the others while this was taking place for the privileged members of societies? Theories must encompass both sides of the power equation.

The most recent modernization theories have done a better job of taking gender into account. For example, Eisenstadt (1983) couches the dynamics of modernization in terms of social mobilization, structural differentiation, development of free resources, role specialization, diversity of social organization, and the development of regulative and allocative mechanisms in all institutions. Change occurs when economic markets and political parties differentiate and expand. Interestingly, Eisenstadt says that for societies to modernize they need to absorb change, including demands from emergent constituencies which arise during the process of increasing specialization and differentiation. Although gender analysis was not central to Eisenstadt's work, he recognizes the role of civil and human rights movements during the change process: if a society cannot respond to demands for suffrage or national independence, continuity will be jeopardized.

Similarly, in the human development approach to social change, democracy, modernization and economic growth all depend on development of individual capabilities and 'opportunities to base their lives on free choice' (Welzel et al. 2000: 7). Human development in the economic sense reduces constraints on individual well-being and enlarges physical and cognitive resources. This should enhance *female* well-being, assuming that a woman is not restricted from participation in developing capabilities because of her gender. Human development feeds into value changes (rendering the patriarchal dividend less acceptable), reduces constraints on aspirations (for girls as well as for boys), and intensifies human striving for self-expression (in all fields, regardless of gender).

Clement and Myles (1994) argue that the post-industrial world will draw its vitality from the knowledge explosion and creative productivity of both sexes, but post-industrial society has also been associated with super-exploitation of female labour, the global sex trade and persistent gender differentiation in power and resources. Postmodern theories have not yet explained fully how female well-being is elevated or diminished or how social change occurs within a gendered context.

Contributions of 'second wave' feminist scholars

Feminist theory has challenged traditional Western philosophical ideas of 'mankind' which leave out half of humanity. Feminist researchers have established that the androcentric (male) bias in social and physical sciences is pervasive and must be balanced by female perspectives. Unfortunately, however, even much feminist theory is based on narrow class, cultural or racial perspectives or fails to include women who are living outside developed Western democracies. Although there is a growing body of research on native, minority and immigrant women in various countries, most studies fail to take into account regional or cross-global differences in social change processes. Positivist theories that emphasized data-gathering and theory-building from an empirical base were more popular among late-nineteenth and early-twentieth-century social scientists, but this comparative approach has not been employed as fruitfully as it might have been by feminist scholars, even when numerous studies of women in the last decades of the twentieth century produced a significant new database. It is an impossible task to summarize or review the feminist scholarship of the second wave for this volume, but many works are cited in the various country chapters and a few influential thinkers are explored here.

In the early efforts at theory-building in the second wave of feminism, e.g. in the work of Shulamit Firestone (1970) and Michelle Rosaldo and Louise Lamphere (1974), biology-as-destiny arguments were challenged by using cultural examples to show that women are much more than the bearers of children and the reproducers of culture and the labour force. Limitations of the biology-as-destiny argument abound, especially when a cross-cultural framework is established. Transformations in industrial societies have witnessed women breaking so-called natural barriers in sports previously dominated by men, in the military, where they have performed as equals with men, in the sciences, and in the professions. Research on women and war challenges the hereditarian view of natural differences between men and women which render women the logical victims and refugees, and all the male soldiers willing killers or rapists.

Rosaldo and Lamphere shaped the conceptualization of female–male relations in their 1974 delineation of the public versus private spheres of life: males dominate the public spheres of power and influence and females are relegated to the private sphere of domesticity. This dichotomy moved feminist thinking about patriarchy and liberation to a new level and stimulated a great deal of research. The public–private-sphere model applies more to some cultures and times than to others, but the essential distinction between male and female worlds was heuristic for later theory development.

In her influential book *The Creation of Patriarchy*, Gerda Lerner (1986) stressed the significance of the archaic state that was centred in the patriarchal family at least four thousand years ago and depended on the commodification of women's sexual and reproductive capacities. Through inter-group exchange of women in marriage and the use of the labour of women and children to increase production, surpluses were accumulated in emergent agricultural societies. Females and land were treated in much the same way – as property capable of generating wealth and security. Men as a group had rights regarding women (including ownership and enslavement) that women as a group did not have regarding men.

This early framework based on gender and racial stratification pre-dated stratification based primarily on socio-economic status. In fact, Lerner argues that class and class oppression were from the outset expressed in terms of patriarchal relations: class is not a separate construct from gender; rather, class is expressed in 'genderic' terms. The gender differential is an old phenomenon that continues to shape power relations today. Lerner warned that the patriarchal family (throughout the world) reinforces and reproduces itself through a 'cooperative omen' and that moving from female 'unfreedom' to freedom will require a complete overturn of patriarchy. When it appears that women's position has improved, it is only an improvement in economic status and minor political leverage *within* the system of patriarchy. Reforms and legal changes are an essential part of improving female well-being but do not change the essential patriarchal nature of societal arrangements. That will require a 'vast cultural revolution' to transform and abolish patriarchy throughout all institutions. Lerner mentioned women's networks as essential to accomplishing this type of change.

Canadian sociologist Dorothy Smith extended Marx's concepts of false consciousness and alienation into a gendered notion of the 'feminist standpoint', which refers to women's bifurcated consciousness in trying to negotiate two worlds: the male-created and -dominated world and the lived female experience (1987, 1990, 1999). That males in this perspective govern female thought and action forms a disconnect that results in a loss of 'authority to speak'. By treating this disconnect as 'problematic', women can begin to unpeel the layers of power that affect their lives. Other feminists whose work has addressed social change include Paula England (1993), Janet Chafetz (1990), and Randall Collins et al. (1993). These theorists have laid a solid foundation for further theory construction in the social sciences which aims to uncover gender differentiation, gender hierarchies and the constraints on equity and empowerment for both females and males in all societies.

Globalization and feminist theories

Globalization began centuries ago but dominated the twentieth century after the Second World War, when international economic and political reconstruction shaped post-colonial, post-conflict and post-Soviet bloc realities. This overriding economic and political context, which involved heightened contact between the world's peoples through travel and communications, has produced an unprecedented connectivity of the globe.

Globalization theory is rooted in macroeconomics, but women's pivotal role in social change might better be explained by microeconomic theory; this distinction has been appreciated anecdotally but not theoretically. The assumption is that economic development, measured by such fictions as GDP, reflects the status of whole populations. As we now realize, 2 billion people in the world live on less than a dollar a day and the majority of them are women and children. Yet women, for the most part, have been left out of globalization theory, much as they were left out of mainstream historical paradigms.

The great reserve of female labour has been tapped but women were employed more in temporary jobs in the industrial nations and in the informal economic sector in the predominantly agrarian nations. While a majority of the world's women are employed in the workforce, the sexual division of labour has changed very little. In the developing countries, women are working double days that amount to longer and harder work days than for men. Where patriarchy actually threatens women's lives – e.g., in those cases where men outnumber women, such as in India and China, this is due to practices that severely limit economic resources for women.

First World–Third World conflicts in feminist frameworks Feminists have disagreed on whether 'women' or 'gender' is the relevant theoretical construct. Western feminists have treated 'women' as a unitary category, often failing to address issues of race, class, colonization or culture that are likely to draw the attention of minority, Third World and aboriginal women. Gender theory signifies analysis of power relations between females and males, or females and social institutions and systems, while the study of women has tended to be more descriptive.

INDIGENOUS FEMINISMS Certain regional or religious feminisms such as African or Islamic feminism have attempted to theorize the new world order (Arndt 2002). Obioma Nnaemeka (2002) suggests that African women attempt to redefine feminisms for their own purposes. She is an African woman who is 'African' when she speaks in Africa and is referred to as 'black' when she speaks in North America. She notes that African women speak of geography, while others speak of colour. Anti-feminist positions are widespread in Africa because of feminism's twentieth-century Western character and essence, although radical and Marxist feminists are sometimes seen as an exception. It is alleged that white women focus only on gender, while Africans see gender in the context of the society's institutions and social formations.

An 'anti-movement' of African women tries to bring balance into the discourse through contextualizing gender issues; in this respect, African women are dissociating themselves from African-American feminism because of its focus on race. Within the United States, African-American women criticize second wave feminists for ignoring race in their theoretical analyses. Again, these chasms are not only ideological but theoretical, in that building theories of social change must be able to address the gender differential and at the same time understand women within the contexts of their daily lives.

Islamic feminists have challenged the Western essentialist view that Muslim women constitute an exceptional case of patriarchy, indeed the worst case. They have pointed to the common threads of patriarchy in the Judeo-Christian and Islamic faiths, all emanating from a core Middle Eastern social base. Muslim feminist writers, such as Fatima Mernissi (1975) and Leila Ahmed (1982, 1992), have asked Westerners to examine multiple realities of life for women in the Islamic world 'beyond the veil', which represents for some an icon of inferiority. They have documented the participation of Arab and Muslim women in independence movements, and have viewed sexual segregation as engendering female solidarity and therefore as more empowering than disempowering.

Ackerly (2000) argues for the continued use of the designation 'Third World' for theories of women because it evokes the once colonized nations and peoples. Feminist theory that is embedded in the experience of colonialism is also embedded in struggles against colonialism, which means a heightened consciousness of the dynamics of race and class, national liberation

movements, and the necessity of autonomous women's movements to successfully advance feminist agendas. Ackerly believes that Third World women
activists today seek what Third World leaders in the 1950s sought, but in
another way.

Third World feminists have also focused on the standard-of-living gap between North and South; the different experiences of former colonizer and
colonized; and the separate feminist agendas of industrial and post-industrial
societies versus predominantly agrarian nations. Many have rejected the
essentialist paradigms of Western scholars and have analysed differences in
the experiences of Latin American, Asian or African women. Open differences
along this theoretical fault line broke out in the International Women's Congresses in Copenhagen, Mexico City and Nairobi.

The question of the class position and relative power of women's voices is
an important one: richer women may gain the attention of state forces more
easily than poorer women. Although women's position and condition in the
world's 'South' differs from women in the 'North', adjustment to the new
economic realities in both regions depends on the assumption of gender differences. The super-exploitation of the world's women as labourers in the
international workforce is frequently overlooked as the newly rich Asian 'tiger'
nations have been extolled as a model for the road to prosperous economic
development. In fact, the treatment of female labour as cheap, temporary,
passive, reliable and more readily manipulated is central to any appraisal of
these economic 'miracles'.

Collectively, feminists have pioneered a model of patriarchal oppression
that critiques existing values, practices and norms that perpetuate inequalities, although they have not always built a systematic model of social change
or taken a global approach. Exceptions include Bernard (1987), Morgan
(1984/1996) and Seager (1997). Like other feminist scholars, Jessie Bernard
critiques Western male bias by citing international development reports that
rarely mentioned women. She challenges the fundamental assumption that
basic institutions are under male control, including reproduction as well as production. Bernard identifies the 'separate worlds' that women and men occupy,
making the task of incorporating women into analysis even more difficult.

After exploring the challenge of 'equitable integration' between the have
and have-not nations, and how local women's development programmes have
sought to achieve this integration of rural women into national economies,
Bernard discusses the relations between these disparate worlds in the post-
colonial era, using case studies. She notes that the status of rural women can
easily be overlooked. Bernard also broaches the issue of Western parochialism

in feminism, and discusses opening 'new channels' of international contact and discussion as tactics for raising consciousness in a 'shared female world'. She highlighted the significance of the UN Decade for Women 1975–85 and the multiple conferences that resulted in new international networks. Guilt is increasing in the 'have' nations, but this too has a gender face. Bernard argues that with equal opportunity comes equal responsibility. Throughout her work, however, Bernard fails to develop a systematic, gendered theory.

Robin Morgan has been a pioneer in internationalizing the women's movement and in drawing together data from countries around the world which permit comparative study. Her various editions of *Sisterhood is Global* have documented basic social, political, demographic, legal, family and reproductive trends for dozens of countries. Her method of inclusion of the world's women is similar to our own in *Female Well-being*, and her observations and analysis are consistently feminist. The global activist reach of *Sisterhood is Global* and the valuable networks that the project stimulated are a signal achievement of the elevated consciousness of the Western-based women's movement. Other initiatives, such as Women in Development (WID) and the United Nations special research and activist task force, UNIFEM, are in part a response to the feminist internationalism framed by Morgan.

Morgan's analytical constructs delineated a universal female subordination well before the 1993 Vienna Conference that declared women's rights as human rights. Morgan saw the universality of denial of human rights to females in both the relatively richer industrial and the relatively poorer agrarian nations. This was a significant contribution to the conceptualization of female well-being, but compilations of data such as Morgan's summaries have not generated much theory-building. Given the activist orientation of Morgan's work, her strategies for the future are couched in terms of a coordinated global activism. This leads to a greater awareness of the ways in which women around the world are truly interconnected and share common fates in a multitude of ways. That the world is shrinking makes these interconnections even more obvious.

The rise of female-headed households and matrifocal families The rise of female-headed households represents one of the most significant trends of the twentieth century, but little theoretical attention has been paid to this phenomenon, either. Female-headed or matrifocal families are increasing everywhere as a direct outcome of globalization, the absence of urban-bound male heads, and economic stresses on the family. Matrifocal families are increasing rapidly in the industrialized nations (about one quarter of all families in Australia, New Zealand, Canada and the USA). They make up between 16 and 22 per cent of households in various parts of Europe and are also rising in the Caribbean (17.7 per cent); Latin America (14.5 per cent); East Asia (14 per cent); sub-Saharan Africa (13.6 per cent); and South Asia (5.7 per cent) (Chant 1997: 70).

Generally, women in matrifocal families of the South are older, in contrast to the lone-female households that are more common among affluent, professional women of the North (e.g. the UK, the USA and Finland). The usual definition of female-headed household places the female as breadwinner and decision-maker, but matrifocal families are differentiated by stage of life, class, race, marital status and child support. The term covers a broad spectrum of social forms that have emerged in social and economic crises and for different reasons. Single-sex/female-only households have grown in East Asia, where female factory workers set up single-sex dormitories, and in certain West African societies, such as among the matrilineal Ashanti and Ga people. Grandmother-headed households are common in areas where matrilineal societies are strong, such as West Africa, Indonesia and the Caribbean; and in African-American families in the USA and in Caribbean families that have emigrated to the UK and Canada (Billson 2005).

Female-headed households can be viewed as emancipating for women, as in the case of women escaping from patriarchal and abusive social relations (Chant 1997). They can also be viewed as impoverished families that are struggling to survive. The overarching contrast between the North and South is that female-headed households in the North are comprised of divorced, separated or never-married women, while in the South the majority are married women with husbands who are away working, or women who are alone through widowhood, desertion or migration.

Some see female-headed households as the dysfunctional, 'problem family' that signals breakdown of the traditional (patriarchal, male-headed) family (ibid.: 31–2). Marxist feminist scholarship did not engage in head-on confrontation with these theories, although it diverted attention from the deviance model by focusing upon the contradictions between patriarchy and capitalism. By adding the variables of age, class and race, a different picture emerged.

Studies of female-headed households reveal several important findings that are relevant to theorizing about female well-being. These include: 1) the value of comparative research and analysis as a basis for theorizing; 2) a methodology to strengthen the empirical basis for theory; 3) the value of the grassroots perspective and the importance of accuracy of representation; 4) the continued male bias in female-headed household research; 5) the importance of female agency; and 6) the value of synthetic theories that bring multiple variables into analysis. The study of female-headed families illustrates the importance of reconstructing masculine and feminine identities.

Chant raises the question as to whether women-headed family units are 'victims' or 'survivors'. Studies show that the matrifocal family is an emerging social form that is becoming increasingly normative because of female preference. What if the female-headed family is an escape from patriarchy, a form of feminine survival where the absent male is neither problematical nor a disadvantage?

At the same time, powerful countervailing forces of female unity have begun to bridge these divides in the feminist dialogues. The common ground of being female in patriarchal societies, regardless of world region and however disparate, has become better understood. The world congresses patterned themselves on global meetings and agreements initiated by the United Nations, as well as by world heritage and environmental conventions. An increasingly self-conscious scholarship among Western women has begun to embrace the view that they are First World scholars whose privileged position influences their work (Momsen and Kinnaird 1993). As Lerner (1986) points out, however, it is the elite women in any society who are likely to be the fundamental change agents because they are most likely to be admitted to the halls of education or the realms of power.

Gender and development Although the North–South discourse was critical to feminist theory, it did not solve other issues. Many argue that alternative conceptual approaches to gender must be sought (Waylen 1996). For example, feminist discourses sparred with development discourses towards the end of the century. A dominant theoretical strand focused on 'women in development' (WID). Caroline Moser created one of the most influential frameworks by elevating gender roles and gender needs, as NGOs, planners, international development agencies and governments tried to understand and create the practical mechanisms of change. Moser identified five basic approaches to WID that ultimately relate to female well-being, each one revealing a fundamental assumption about gender, class and social change (adapted from the Royal Tropical Institute 1996). Each approach reflected the gender paradigm of the moment:

- *Welfare*: This was the approach in the early days of development (1950–70), when the goal was to help women become better mothers. Females were viewed as passive beneficiaries of development in their reproductive role, as recipients of food aid and programmes to reduce malnutrition or improve family planning.

A critique of social change theories

59

- *Equity*: This approach, triggered by the UN Women's Decade, redefined women as active participants in development. The first WID movement (criticized as Western feminism) stressed gender equality and equal participation in society and development processes.

- *Anti-poverty*: The less threatening second WID approach from 1970 focused more on women's productivity and less on gender equity. Women's poverty stems in this framework from poverty in general, not from gender subordination or oppression. NGOs like this approach, which emphasizes supporting women in micro-enterprise income generation.

- *Efficiency*: The third WID approach (from the 1980s) has turned the paradigm upside down: instead of women benefiting from development, women are seen as directly engineering change through their economic contributions and productivity: participation means equity and equity means productivity. This model assumed elasticity of women's time – that women would continue to function as full-time homemakers and mothers without compensatory wages, benefits or support from publicly supported services (e.g. day care).

- *Empowerment*: In the most recent approach, articulated by Third World women, development should empower women through greater self-reliance in the context of gender subordination and colonial and neo-colonial subordination. This, too, is self-limiting since it tends to define Western feminists as part of the problem, thereby fragmenting women's interests worldwide.

The strength of Moser's framework is that it looks behind technical planning and development strategies to uncover the entrenched assumptions and fundamental conflicts of interest that divide the world's women. The weakness stems from using gender roles and gender needs as pivotal concepts in development, thereby running the risk of masking gender power relations and issues of equity. Obscuring the notion of gender regimes could be interpreted as avoiding head-on analysis of fundamental power relations between men and women or the impact of differential male–female socialization, regardless of society.

Ester Boserup pioneered analysis of women and economic systems in *Women's Role in Economic Development* (1986), in which she stressed the primary importance of the sexual division of labour; the roles of women in the marketplace as producers, sellers, and consumers; and the transformation in women's economic roles that occurred in the transition (still ongoing) from agricultural to industrial production and the shift from rural to urban life. She discovered that, overwhelmingly, development projects ignored women and their economic contributions. Subsequent critical analysis has revealed women's pivotal role not only in the management of household finances but in microeconomic development projects. The majority of women are working while the division of labour in the house has changed little. On average in developing countries, women are working longer and harder than men. Although women's position and condition in the South differ from those of women in the North, adjustment to the new economic realities in both regions depends on the assumption that gender differences figure both in theory and in practice.

Even though these theoretical forays have been imperfect, they have helped to compensate for previous explanations of social change which lacked a gender narrative. Perhaps the greatest contribution of the second wave feminist scholars is that it is no longer possible to write historical or social scientific works without including women, at least as a part of the story.

The case studies as a basis for new theory Before we can fully comprehend the potential impacts of CEDAW or the MDGs, we must have a clearer picture of what has transpired in the past century. We also need to have a better grasp of how positive social change occurs, which the case studies will provide. The cases in this book provide concrete data on our key questions as we try to determine the sources of female well-being in various regions of the world. Insights from each country form the springboard for a new theory of social change that encompasses the core institutions of society (educational, family, work, political, economic, health, cultural and religious systems), but also accounts for the gender differential *within* different racial, class and cultural contexts.

In *Female Well-being*, we reach beyond the narrow limits of Western feminism to a global humanism informed by global feminism. With our country teams from around the globe, we look to empirical data to try to understand the nature of inequities that are rooted in gender. These cases will help us build new theory. In the final chapter, we develop a strategy for negotiating change-policy in a world that is still marked by a troubling gender differential.

References

Abramovitz, M. (1989) *Thinking About Growth and Other Essays on Economic Growth and Welfare*, Cambridge: Cambridge University Press

— (1990) 'The catch-up factor in postwar economic growth', *Economic Enquiry*, 28: 1–18

Ackerly, B. A. (2000) *From Political Theory and Feminist Social Criticism*, Cambridge: Cambridge University Press

Ahmed, L. (1982) 'Western ethnocentrism and perceptions of the harem', *Feminist Studies*, 8(3): 521–34

— (1992) *Women and Gender in Islam*, New Haven, CT: Yale University Press

Arndt, S. (2002) *The Dynamics of African Feminism*, trans. from the German by I. Cole, Trenton, NJ: Africa World Press

Bachofen, J. J. (1861) *Das Mutterecht*, Stuttgart

Benedict, R. (1961) 'The growth of culture', in H. L. Shapiro (ed.), *Man, Culture and Society*, Oxford: Oxford University Press

Bernard, J. (1987) *The Female from a Global Perspective*, Bloomington: Indiana University Press

Billson, J. M. (2005) *Keepers of the Culture: Women and Power in the Canadian Mosaic*, Boulder, CO: Rowman & Littlefield

Boserup, E. (1986) *Women's Role in Economic Development*, New York: Gower

Boulding, E. (1992) *The Underside of History, a View of Women Through Time*, vol. 1, Newbury Park, CA: Sage Publications

Brockerhoff, M. (2000) 'An urbanizing world', *Population Bulletin*, 55(3)

Chafetz, J. S. (1990) *Gender Equity: A Theory of Stability and Change*, Newbury Park, CA: Sage

Chant, S. (1997) *Women-headed Households, Diversity and Dynamics in the Developing World*, London: Macmillan Press

Chirot, D. (1994) *How Societies Change*, Thousand Oaks, CA: Pine Forge Press

Clark, L. M. G. and L. Lange (eds) (1979) *The Sexism of Social and Political Theory, Women and Reproduction from Plato to Nietzsche*, Toronto: University of Toronto Press

Clement, W. and J. Myles (1994) *Relations of Ruling: Class and Gender in Postindustrial Societies*, Montreal: McGill-Queen's University Press

Collins, R., J. S. Chafetz, R. L. Blumberg, S. Coltrane and J. Turner (1993), 'Toward an integrated theory of gender stratification', *Sociological Perspectives*, 36: 185–216

Eisenstadt, S. N. (1983) *Tradition, Change, and Modernity*, New York: Wiley

Engels, F. (1972 [1884]) *Origin of the Family, Private Property, and the State*, ed. E. B. Leacock, New York: International Publishers

England, P. (ed.) (1993) *Theory on Gender/Feminism on Theory*, New York: Aldine de Gruyter

Fluehr-Lobban, C. (1979) 'A Marxist re-appraisal of the matriarchate', *Current Anthropology*, 20(2): 341–60

Firestone, S. (1970) *The Dialectic of Sex: The Case for Feminist Revolution*, New York: Morrow

Gelbard, A., C. Haub and M. M. Kent (1999) 'World population beyond six billion', *Population Bulletin* 2, 26 March

Guettell, C. (1974) *Marxism and Feminism*, Toronto: Hunter Rose

Guillén, M. F. (2001) 'Is globalization civilizing, destructive or feeble? A critique of five key debates in the social science literature', *Annual Review of Sociology*, 27

Held, D. et al. (1999) *Global Transformations: Politics, Economics and Culture*, Cambridge: Polity Press

Kinsella, K. and V. Velkoff (2001) *An Aging World: International Population Report*, Washington, DC: US Census Bureau and National Institute of Aging

Lerner, G. (1986) *The Creation of Patriarchy*, New York: Oxford University Press

Mernissi, F. (1975) *Beyond the Veil*, Cambridge: Cambridge University Press

Momsen, J. H. and V. Kinnaird (eds) (1993) *Different Places, Different Voices, Gender and Development in Africa, Asia, and Latin America*, London and New York: Routledge

Morgan, L. H. (1851) *The League of Ho-De-No-Sau-Nee, or Iroquois*, Rochester: Sage and Browa

Morgan, R. (ed.) (1984/1996) *Sisterhood is Global*, New York: Anchor Books

Murdock, G. P. (1961) 'How culture changes', in H. L. Shapiro (ed.), *Man, Culture and Society*, Oxford: Oxford University Press

Narayan, D. et al. (2000) *Voices of the Poor: Crying out for Change*, New York: Oxford University Press (for the World Bank)

Nnaemeka, O. (2002) 'Contribution on African feminism', in S. Arndt (ed.), *The Dynamics of African Feminism*, trans. from the German by Isabel Cole, Trenton, NJ: Africa World Press

Parsons, T. (1937/1966) *The Structure of Social Action. A Study in Social Theory with Special Reference to a Group of Recent European Writers*, New York: McGraw-Hill.

Rihani, S. (2002) *Complex Systems Theory and Development Practice: Understanding Non-linear Realities*, London: Zed Books

Rosaldo, M. Z. and L. Lamphere (eds) (1974) *Women, Culture and Society*, Stanford, CA: Stanford University Press

Royal Tropical Institute (1996) *Training Workshop for Trainers in Women, Gender and Development, June 9–21, Programme Handbook*, Amsterdam: Royal Tropical Institute

Seager, J. (1997) *The State of Women in the World Atlas*, New York: Penguin

Smith, D. (1987) *The Everyday World as Problematic: A Feminist Sociology*, Boston, MA: Northeastern University Press

— (1990) *The Conceptual Practices of Power: A Feminist Sociology of Knowledge*, Boston, MA: Northeastern University Press

— (1999) *Writing the Social: Critique, Theory, and Investigations*, Toronto: University of Toronto Press

Tilley, C. (1997) 'Democracy, social change, and economies in transition', in J. M. Nelson, C. Tilley and L. Walker (eds), *Transforming the Role of the State*, Washington, DC: Task Force on Economies in Transition, Commission on Behavioral and Social Sciences and Education, National Research Council, National Academy Press

Waylen, G. (1996) *Gender in Third World Politics*, Boulder, CO: Lynne Rienner

Welzel, C., R. Inglehart and H. Klingermann (2000) 'Human development as a universal theory of social change: cross-level and cross-cultural evidence from 63 societies', paper presented at ECPR Joint Sessions, Copenhagen, 14–19 April

Wichterich, C. (2000) *The Globalized Woman*, London: Zed Books

Websites

Erlich, S. D., R. J. Franzese and R. F. Inglehart (1999) 'Democracy, economy, and values: estimating a recursive system', <www-personal.umich.edu/˜franzese/publications.html>

Giddens, A. (1999) *The Director's Lectures: Runaway World (The Reith Lectures Revisited – Globalization)*, <www.lse.ac.uk/Giddens/lectures.htm>

Shackman, G., Y. Liu and X. Wang (2002) 'Brief review of world socio-demographic trends', <www.gsociology.icaap.org/report/socsum.html>

TWO | **Case studies**

4 | Women in Bangladesh: a journey in stages

NASRIN SULTANA AND ALEMA KARIM

This chapter explores how the last century has shaped the lives of women in Bangladesh. The dynamics of change have made this a complex journey of many stages. The state has enacted laws prohibiting unjust behaviour towards women but, because of the sociocultural construction of gender attitudes, immoral practices and arrangements of old persist. Bangladesh has experienced considerable socioeconomic development and changing values relating to women's family status. Despite these positive social changes, it will be a long journey to eradicate the rigid patrilineal system that obstructs female well-being and legal rights.

Status of women in the constitution of Bangladesh

The constitution guarantees women fundamental rights and forbids any form of discrimination based on sex, pledging that the state will aim to realize, through the democratic process, a society free from exploitation and subject to the rule of law. This means securing fundamental freedom, equality and political, economic and social justice through guarantees of human rights and equal protection for all citizens. Articles 10 and 28 forbid discrimination among citizens and especially ensure women's participation in all spheres of life. Article 19 ensures equality of opportunity to all citizens and places emphasis on removing inequality between men and women. Article 29 forbids discrimination among citizens in employment. Article 26 confirms that any law inconsistent with the constitution should be void (MLJ 1972; Sultana 2003).

A demographic portrait of Bangladeshi women

Urbanization After independence, Bangladesh experienced phenomenal urban growth. Now, 25 per cent of the population live in urban areas compared to only 5 per cent thirty-five years ago (BBS 2000). In 1997, agriculture contributed more than 31 per cent towards the GDP of Bangladesh. Although the country is slowly becoming more urban and industrial, 82 per cent of the labour force was still in agriculture and 81 per cent lived in rural areas as of 1991. Figure 4.1 reflects the country's shift towards urban residence and work.

Life expectancy Life expectancy at birth has reached sixty-one years for males

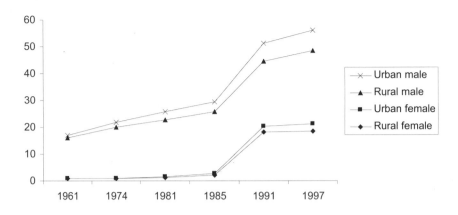

Figure 4.1 Civilian labour force by gender and residence (millions)
Source: **BBS (1996)**

and sixty-two years for females. The crude death rate has decreased from 19.4 in 1974 to 11.9 in 1987 and 8.1 in 1996 (BBS 1997). Thus, Bangladesh has begun to enter the first stage of the demographic transition towards lower death rates and lower birth rates.

Population growth, fertility rate and male–female ratio Many circumstances evolved over time to determine the economic well-being of women. Widespread illiteracy, severe malnutrition and extreme poverty characterize women in Bangladesh, who constitute roughly 49 per cent of the population. After marriage, women's reproductive role is to ensure the existence of succeeding generations through child bearing. Giving birth to a male child is critical to strengthen a woman's position in her new family. The patrilineal descent system leads to strong son preferences. A daughter's birth is an event of sorrow, so trying for a son increases the number of children. In consequence, as a result of negligence, female infant mortality rates are high.

Despite these factors, the fertility rate has fallen dramatically from 6.34 per woman in 1975 to 3.8 in 1996. From 1975 to 1996, there was a reduction of about 3.16 children per woman. Effective family planning measures, increased age of marriage and reduction of child mortality through immunization have contributed to declining fertility. Even though family planning programmes started in the 1960s, the transition towards reduced fertility did not begin until the 1980s. Fertility is higher in rural areas (2.76) than in urban areas (2.48), especially among women between twenty and thirty-five years old. The increased participation of urban women in the labour force, starting at adolescence, contributes to lower fertility (ADB 2001).

Maternal mortality rate Over the last three decades, the health situation has improved for all, but both primary and specialized healthcare services are still inadequate, especially for women. Infant mortality and maternal mortality rates, though improved substantially, are still relatively high compared to other South Asian countries (FYP 1997–2002). Owing to an inadequate focus on maternal care, women in Bangladesh have a lower health status compared to men; the mortality rate and life expectancy at birth for women were lower until the 1990s. Even though women are the primary care-givers in the household, and their well-being is crucial for the family's well-being, their health has been neglected for generations. From childhood on, females experience neglect in every sphere of life. In a poor household, women are the ones who suffer the most. Women customarily eat last, after everyone else in the household has had their share of the food. Boys receive preference in food consumption and healthcare.

RURAL WOMEN Bangladesh has very high rates of maternal mortality and morbidity because of frequent pregnancy and childbirth-related complications. Religious beliefs, cultural norms and family traditions shape women's antenatal care practices. Most rural women do not seek antenatal care, some visit untrained village practitioners. A study by Ahmed et al. (1998) found that one third of women did not consult anyone for pre-natal or antenatal care. Rahman et al. (1997) found that only 24 per cent of women consulted trained providers and 13 per cent utilized the free government health facilities. Lack of education, social and cultural biases, and superstitions prevent women from seeking medical attention. They prefer to go to the untrained village practitioners because they are cheap and readily available. Decision-making is a complicated process that the husband and older family members influence. Younger women with five years or more of schooling are more likely to seek medical care from qualified practitioners during pregnancy and after childbirth (ibid.), because they are more informed about the availability and benefits of facilities.

URBAN WOMEN The healthcare situation in urban areas is equally poor. Even though the number of healthcare facilities has grown, the increase has unfortunately not kept pace with unprecedented urban growth. Women must depend on an infrastructure that can no longer cope with their increasing needs (Thwin and Jahan 1996). Pregnant women need good nutrition and pre-natal care, but age-old biases and sex discrimination give men priority in access to food and healthcare.

Case studies | 4

Infant mortality rate Low calorie and nutrient intake contribute to widespread malnutrition, especially among women and children. The nutritional inadequacy of lactating mothers has serious implications for the well-being of children in rural Bangladesh (Chowdhury 1994). Malnutrition results in low-birth-weight babies, who are likely to be unhealthy and susceptible to infection and disease.

The infant mortality rate plays a crucial role in determining the number of children a woman decides to have. The rate decreased from 116 per 1,000 in 1988 to sixty-seven in 1996; this reduces the need to have more children. In poor countries, households see children as an investment for the future. Parents prefer to have more children, especially boys, to guarantee the survival of a few who can provide security for them in old age. Boys are preferred because they can work in the family farms as well as outside the home in paid employment to supplement the family income. Since child survival has a positive impact on contraception, it is important to provide mothers with children's healthcare services. A study by Latif (1994) found that it was most effective for programmes to supply children's healthcare services to women receiving contraception.

Contraception and abortion Women are the major contributors to fertility reduction because they are the major users of family planning measures. In 1975, when the women's decade started a flow of women's development worldwide, Bangladesh took many measures, primarily in fertility reduction. The state has been dominated by patriarchal attitudes, so women had been victims without control over their own bodies. As the government took initiatives to reduce fertility, though, it encouraged people through media advertisements to have fewer children and focused on equal treatment for both boys and girls. Various non-government organizations work for gender-neutral behaviour and on positive programmes that favour females.

Since then, contraceptive use has shown a huge increase from 8 per cent of eligible couples in 1975 to 40 per cent in 1991 and 54 per cent in 2000. Modern methods appeared, but female methods predominate, indicating the strong gender bias in family planning (Figure 4.2). Women rather than men are obligated to control births, just as they are obligated to produce offspring and care for them (BBS 1994). The government persisted in its efforts to introduce modern methods of family planning by using a very labour-intensive, door-to-door delivery strategy sponsored by bilateral and multilateral donors. The relentless use of the media in educating the public about the benefits of having a small family was successful.

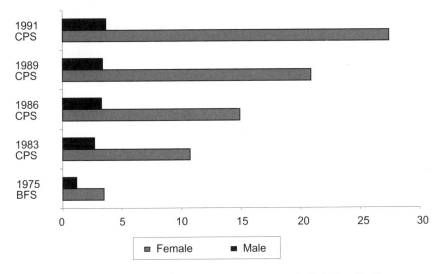

CPS = Contraceptive Prevalance Survey; BFS = Bangladesh Fertility Survey

Figure 4.2 Contraceptive use by gender (per cent)
Source: **BBS (1994)**

As with declining infant mortality rates, women's education has a positive impact on the decline in fertility. A minimum level is necessary to follow the birth control instructions. As women's education level increased, the contraception rate increased as well, allowing women to feel more confident in communicating with their husbands about trying contraception.

NGOs played a vital role in Bangladesh through poverty alleviation programmes that provided small credit to rural women, as well as family planning information. Income-earning opportunities and self-employment bring financial independence and give women an upper hand when negotiating family size with their husbands. Latif (1994) found, however, that women's employment *without* health and motivational services did not have a great impact on contraception practices and fertility regulation. The more successful programmes dovetail with health programmes, especially those for children and mothers, linking family planning and early intervention to sustain children's health (Lynn 2003).

Family status and structure

Marriage age In 1931, the average age at marriage was twelve for females and nineteen for males; the mean increased through the century but an age gap still exists between males and females (Figure 4.3). This demographic shift has lowered the number of reproductive years, but more rural women still tend to

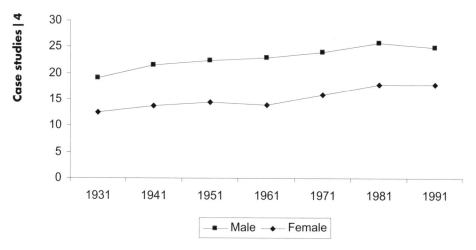

Figure 4.3 Mean age of marriage by gender
Source: BBS (1999)

marry young than do urban women. Although the national average is following the legal age of marriage, in rural Bangladesh early marriage is prevalent.

Livelihoods of the Extreme Poor (LEP), a long-term study conducted by the NGO PROSHIKA and the Department for International Development (DFID) in sixteen rural villages, showed that early marriages occur mostly with poorer families; parents are criticized if they fail to arrange their daughter's marriage at an early age. Younger girls are considered more attractive than older ones – and their youth guarantees their purity. Many of the poorest are not concerned about the legal age of marriage; social custom is stronger than law.

Marriage and divorce Women have multiple identities in the life cycle, which strongly influence their authority and autonomy, preferences and household status (Gibson et al. 2004). In general, women are not treated as people with their own rights (Nussbaum 2000); rather, they are treated as fulfillers of the needs of others as reproducers, care-givers, sexual outlets and agents of a family's general prosperity. The female's position in the family is not as positive as the male's. Social, cultural and religious traditions structure the status of women in Bangladesh, and men's decisions in a patriarchal social system shape women's lives. Discrimination starts from childhood and dominates the life of a woman, which threatens her well-being.

The nuclear family – a married couple with unmarried children – characterizes over half of all households in Bangladesh (52.7 per cent in rural areas and 48.1 per cent in urban areas; BBS 1992). The second-most common form, the non-nuclear family, consists of more than one married couple (around 40

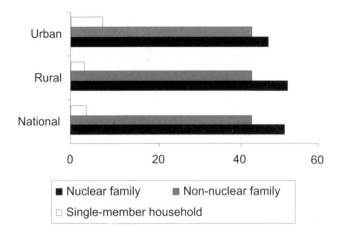

Figure 4.4 Households by family type and residence, 1982 (per cent)
Source: BBS (1992).

per cent of all households, both urban and rural). The third form, the single-member household, is comparatively more common in urban areas (7.8 per cent) than in rural areas (3.4 per cent) (Figure 4.4).

For poor rural families, poverty creates regular intra-household conflict between a daughter-in-law and her mother-in-law or other in-law; this influences the move towards nuclear households. Those who favour non-nuclear families focus on help from other members of the household, especially for childcare. Older parents play a pivotal role by caring for children while parents work outside the home.

Many educated women now prefer to live in a non-nuclear family, ignoring the everyday conflict, to ensure their children's security. People who migrate for work make up the single-headed households. Women living alone in cities for employment have most likely secured government or other public sector jobs.

Muslim family laws Marriage is a fundamental institution in a patrilocal and patrilineal setting, fulfilling a social obligation rather than individual choice. In the rigid patrilineal kinship system of Bangladesh, the status of men and women is not equal. Women generally find themselves in a disadvantaged position during their entire marital life. Girls usually have little or no voice in marital choices, so the institution of marriage is a significant factor in women's well-being (or ill-being).

Religious precepts have a profound effect on female well-being in Bangladesh, since the legal system incorporates the religious values and injunctions of different communities (ADB 2002; Huda 1999; Monsoor 1999; Chowdhury 1997). Because these precepts strongly influence women's status in the family and society, Muslim family laws require explanation. Some provisions protect women; others restrict their freedoms and rights.

EARLY MARRIAGE The Child Marriage Restraint Act (1929) stipulates punishment for violating the legal age of marriage. A male adult above twenty-one or a female adult above eighteen can be punished for marrying a child; penalties occur for the parents or guardians concerned (Chowdhury 1997).

DOWRY The Muslim Family Law Ordinance (MFLO, Section 10, 1961) outlines options for the bride's dower money, which is security for the wife in case of divorce or widowhood. It also operates as a check on the man's arbitrary exercise of the right of divorce. According to the Dowry Prohibition Act (1980), 'dowry' means any property or valuable security given either directly or indirectly by one party to a marriage to the other party (or by the parents) (ibid.: 176–7). In practice, in Bangladesh the bride party always gives dower to the groom party. To protect women from violence, the Dowry Prohibition Act (1980) stipulates a penalty for giving or taking dowry and a penalty for demanding dowry. The Cruelty to Women Ordinance (1983) outlines a penalty for 'causing death for dowry'. Lately, the Oppression of Women and Children Act (XVIII, 1995) has regulated punishment for causing death or grievous harm for dowry (ibid.; Mansoor 2000). The Women and Children Repression Prevention Act (2000) raised punishment to the level of the death penalty for crimes against women and children (Mansoor 2000).

The emergence and spread of dowry in rural Bangladesh derives from the cultural construction of gendered positions in the family. Women's capability is not recognized (Sultana 2004). The dowry system is closely linked with women's role in productive activities: where women are regarded as an unproductive burden, a dowry is given to the bridegroom's side as compensation (Monsoor 1999). It is not clear when the dowry culture began but, according to villagers, the amount has been changing over time. Volart (2003) says that since the 1970s dowry has substantially increased in rural Bangladesh. Unequal inheritance underlies the dowry system (ibid.; Botticini and Siow 2003).

Ironically, despite the push for girls' education by government and non-governmental organizations, some parents resist having well-educated daughters because the dowry amount generally increases with girls' age and educational attainment. Currently, dowry is a prerequisite for marriage. Some meet the obligation by selling land; others offer payment in kind; and some borrow the amount. Sometimes extra dowry is demanded; if the bride's family does not agree to pay more, the bride has to face severe physical and psychological torture, including the threat of divorce and/or her husband taking another wife. Murder attempts and death due to failure to pay the full amount of dowry also occur. Parents commonly fear having daughters – a son is a helping hand, a daughter is a burden and security risk – because it entails giving multiple dowries and weddings (Sultana 2004).

POLYGAMY Polygamy is common in rural Bangladesh, compared to urban areas, encouraged by the strong desire for a son and the opportunity for multiple dowries. Especially among the poor, men view wives as income-generating assets (Sultana 2003). Men engage in multiple relationships openly, although this is not as socially accepted now as it was in the past. Many husbands who have migrated to urban areas become involved with another woman, leaving their wife behind in the village. A few women (an insignificant number) may quietly become involved with another man during their husband's long-term absence. Household conflicts and other problems occur because of polygamy.

According to the MFLO, specific conditions govern a second marriage: permission in writing from the Arbitration Council; following an application stating reasons for the proposed marriage and whether the consent of the existing wife or wives has been obtained; and payment of the prescribed fee. The penalty for contracting another marriage is immediate forfeit of the entire dower to the first wife; if the dower is not paid, it is recoverable as arrears of land revenue, and punishable by imprisonment, and/or fine (Chowdhury 1997).

DIVORCE Muslim jurisprudence confers on the husband almost absolute right of divorce but denies similar freedom to the wife, who can divorce only under certain conditions. The MFLO introduced some restrictions to the husband's right to divorce: he must give ninety days' notice to the chair and a copy of this notice to the wife, omission punishable by imprisonment and/or fine. Section 8 addresses the pregnancy period and the right to divorce option (ibid.; Huda 1999). In Hindu law, there is no provision for divorce, other than the fact that men can divorce their wives on the grounds of adultery. A Christian woman has to prove adultery and other matrimonial offences.

MAINTENANCE According to the MFLO, maintenance signifies provision of food, clothes and lodging to the wife during marriage and during the *iddat* period after divorce (Chowdhury 1997). A wife may file a civil suit for maintenance under the Family Courts Ordinance or under the MFLO (Huda 1999).

CUSTODY OF CHILDREN Islamic law does not regard a mother as the legal guardian of her children. Upon divorce, she is entitled to custody of her son until he reaches seven years old and of her daughter until puberty. Hindu law also sees the father as the natural legal guardian of the minor child. The court decides on custody, maintenance and guardianship of the Christian minor after the father's death; he is considered the natural guardian. Under any religion, however, the court may appoint any person as guardian if the father is proved unfit (ADB 2001).

INHERITANCE Women's rights to property and inheritance are not equal to those of men, which affects their economic status. Under Muslim law, a daughter inherits one half the share of her brother. A wife receives one eighth of the deceased husband's property, whereas the husband receives a quarter of his deceased wife's property, when there is a child. Hindu women's right to inheritance is limited. Christians provide for equal inheritance between sons and daughters (ADB 2001).

Women's economic participation

The division of labour The social status of a woman depends largely on her economic status, which depends on education, training, skills, background and opportunities (Chowdhury and Ahmed 1980). Traditional sociocultural practices limit women's opportunities in education and skill development, which limits participation in income generation. Even in rural agricultural labour, rigid gender role differences mean that women work in and around the house and men work in the fields.

Women's participation in the labour force The increase in women's participation in the labour force has several explanations. First, as the overall economy of the country stagnated, especially in the rural areas, many households faced the hard choice between starvation and the need to look for paid work for all members of the family, including women. Second, a number of government-sponsored programmes (e.g. Food for Works programmes and other institutional supports for employment in the rural areas) attracted poor women to work outside the home. Third, as men migrated to urban areas in search of employment, women found themselves managing their families with little financial support. The civilian labour force has increased dramatically from 30.9 million in 1985–86 to 56 million in 1995–96 (BBS 1997). This leap stems from migration to urban areas but also from 'definitional changes in the economic activities, which include activities like caring for domestic animals and poultry, threshing, boiling, dying and husking crops, processing and preserving food ... usually carried out by the females in the rural agricultural households' (ibid.: 57). For both genders, the shift has been towards urban labour.

In 1982, according to the Third Five Year Plan, 1985–90, women headed 16.5 per cent of all households. Because of large age differences between husbands and wives, more women are widowed (and with few assets). The severity of economic suffering broke down traditionally rigid gender differences some-what and allowed rural women in Bangladesh to participate in agricultural as well as non-agricultural wage-earning activities. Simultaneously, increased institutional support provided by government and non-government institu-tions widened opportunities for rural women. Social norms and local customs do not necessarily determine women's time-use pattern. Economic constraints play a significant role in women's participation in wage-earning activities, even under patriarchy. This suggests that women in rural Bangladesh respond to market opportunities when available (Khandker 1988).

Cultural and structural changes may be weakening patriarchy in Bangla-desh, thereby opening the way for women to take part in market-based agricul-tural and non-agricultural activities. This evidence provides support to theories of liberal feminism which claim that patriarchal Asian societies have allowed women to gain more status through education and more income-earning op-portunities through agricultural employment (Lantican and Gladwin 1996). With increased women's participation in agricultural activities, in 1990/91 average wages for women were just 14 per cent lower than those of men, reducing the wage gap between men and women (Mahmud 1997).

Types of occupation As Figure 4.5 shows, Bangladeshi women have been

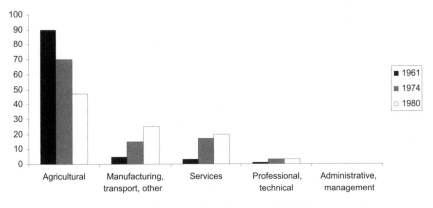

Figure 4.5 Female occupational types, 1961–80 (per cent)
Source: **Adapted from Khan (1993)**

active primarily in the agricultural sector, at a rate of 88.1 per cent compared to 55.8 per cent for males (Kabir 1997). Women's participation in professional and technical occupations increased from 0.3 per cent in 1961 to 2.5 per cent in 1980. In administrative and management areas, it was nil before 1974 and rose to 0.2 per cent in 1980 (Khan 1993). Highly educated and emancipated women belong to professional women's organizations that play a significant role as pressure groups for women's socio-economic rights, but their presence is small in high-level positions.

URBAN WOMEN AND THE INDUSTRIAL SECTOR Women's labour force participation in the industrial sector is a new and growing phenomenon which started only in the early 1980s, when Bangladesh began to pursue an export-led development policy (FYP 1997–2002). Young women especially came from rural areas in large numbers to work in the rapidly growing ready-made garment industries in the cities. Globalization has been responsible for this new phenomenon in other countries of South Asia as well, but Bangladesh and Sri Lanka are the two countries where women's participation has shown record progress. An ILO report (cited in Khundker 2002) concluded that there are wide differences in the proportion of women employed in the garment industry (15 per cent in Nepal, 10 per cent in Pakistan, 89 per cent in Sri Lanka, and 90 per cent in Bangladesh). Export-based industrialization has significantly altered women's lives, making them more visible in public spaces, especially in cities, thus altering gender relations.

RURAL WOMEN AS ENTREPRENEURS Increasingly, women in Bangladesh are breaking taboos and stepping outside the social norms to explore the market economy. As Khan and Noman point out, 'Most of the women entrepreneurs in Bangladesh work in rural areas and are engaged in micro-enterprises ... characterized as having minimal capital and relying on indigenous materials and use antiquated technology' (2002: 57–74). Because of gender segregation in Bangladesh, women feel much more comfortable working from home and for themselves, so setting up a small home-based business can offer independence and raise self-esteem. Because women usually do not own land or other assets, and financial institutions refuse to lend money to those without collateral, women find it almost impossible to borrow money to set up a business. Under these precarious conditions, targeted credit programmes that lend without collateral have provided a critical service to poor rural women (Box 4.1).

As Khundker (2002) points out, the 'Bangladesh experience is unique from

Grameen Bank and other NGOs have provided a much-needed support system for rural women in Bangladesh. When private financial institutions failed to provide credit to the most needy, Grameen Bank offered small loans to those without assets – mostly women. The bank started on an experimental basis in 1976 and received governmental approval in 1983 as a regular bank. Landless, poor women welcomed this rare opportunity and started tiny home-based businesses in an effort to better their lives and raise the family out of perpetual economic misery. Of the 2,294,637 borrowers up to 1998, 94.61 per cent were poor rural women (Grameen Trust 1998). Following in the footsteps of Grameen Bank, many other NGOs are now providing micro-credit and other institutional support to rural women, many of whom have been able improve their lives.

As encouraging as these micro-credit programmes are, problems exist. Credit was intended for the poorest women, but in many villages it was also extended to the affluent. In some cases, husbands or other males took the money from the women, defeating the purpose of empowering women. The imbalance in loan allocation worked to the advantage of richer households and landowners (Kabir 1997).

Despite their high rate of repayment, women in Bangladesh are facing various constraints in access to credit. Kabir (1996) shows that, despite the endeavours of development organizations in upgrading the socio-economic condition of women, credit has not yet reached the poorest families.

other south Asian and developing countries in terms of access to micro-credit generating self-employment for poor women, particularly in rural areas'.

Urban women and entrepreneurship Since the 1980s, a small group of women have emerged as entrepreneurs in the urban areas. Women needed significant courage to venture into the male-dominated world of business. They faced many obstacles but some succeeded in such specialized areas as boutiques, beauty parlours, tailoring shops, handicrafts and food catering services. Some women became heads of businesses, not by virtue of their business expertise or entrepreneurial skills, but because the male members of their families wanted the female members to be directors in order to avoid taxes. Nevertheless, a handful of women, with the help and encouragement of non-government organizations and financial institutions, took risks and made their mark as

Women in Bangladesh

entrepreneurs. A separate Ministry of Women was established to house governmental organizations that were created to address women's issues. Unfortunately, the high level of corruption means that government help does not always reach the deserving; instead, financial and other support goes to those with financial means and contacts in the government.

Income and poverty In 2002, per capita income was $360 ($1,720 as per the Purchasing Power Parity method), still very low compared to the other South Asian nations, where it was on average $460 ($2,390) (<www.worldbank.org>). The traditional System of National Accounting (SNA) estimate of GDP excludes home-based, non-market activities performed mostly by women, such as food processing, vegetable gardening, cleaning, cooking and childcare. Official statistics indicate that men contribute 75 per cent and women 25 per cent to the country's total production. If non-market production were added to conventional GDP estimates, then women's contribution to total production would escalate from 25 to 41 per cent, while that of men would decrease from 75 to 59 per cent (Hamid 1994).

Employment in the garment industry has changed women's lives by providing income, raising their standard of living, and stimulating ambition. Women lag behind men in terms of wages, however. They work in less than satisfactory environments and lack job security, which makes them vulnerable to their employers (Paul-Majumdar and Zahir 1994). Globalization has been a mixed blessing for women in Bangladesh, creating low-skilled, low-paying and unsecured jobs. In the industrial sector, women have come a long way, but a much longer and tougher road lies ahead.

Literacy and education

Historically, women in Bangladesh have faced disparities in education because of unequal treatment in every sphere of life in the strong patriarchal social structure of this sub-continent. The approach taken to different communities by the British colonial government left Muslims farther behind than Hindus. Women's movements began to flourish among Hindus, supported to some extent by the modernization of educated middle-class men. Traditional Muslim society did not allow similar space for women. Changes for Bengali Muslims started nearly a hundred years later than for the Hindus, so education and economic participation levels of Muslim women remained much lower.

Literacy rates The movement to educate Bengali Muslim girls started when Rokeya Sakhwat Hussain founded a girls' school in 1911. The 1931 census

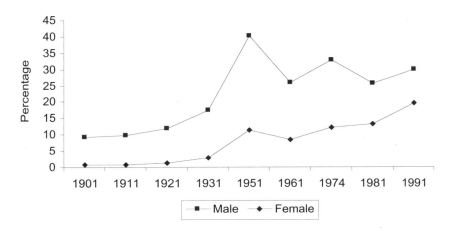

Figure 4.6 Changes in literacy rate by gender (per cent) *Source*: **BBS (1999: 554 and various years, data not available for 1941)**

gives the literacy rate for men as 11.7 per cent and for women as 1.9 per cent; only about twelve Muslim women in a thousand were literate (Khan 1993). By 2000, the literacy rate was 30 per cent for women of fifteen and older and 52 per cent for males (USCIA 2004) (Figure 4.6). While this rate may seem low, there was remarkable improvement in the female literacy rate during the twentieth century, from a base of less than 1 per cent in 1901 (when it was 9.3 per cent for males). The gender gap has narrowed – in 1974 the gender gap in adult literacy was 35 per cent; it declined to 26 per cent in 1999 (BIDS 2001).

School completion rates

PRIMARY LEVEL Primary schooling is free in Bangladesh and lasts until Class 5. Enrolment in primary schools has increased dramatically over the last two decades because of a strong emphasis on primary education. In 1974, girls' enrolment was 34 per cent among enrolled students overall; it rose from 45 per cent in 1990 to 49 per cent in 2000 (ADB 2001). Although primary school enrolment had increased to 96 per cent by 1999, the drop-out rate continues to be high and is similar for both boys and girls. Nearly a quarter of students leave after one year. The rate remains 15–20 per cent up to Class 4, and then declines to 10 per cent by Class 5. Simply increasing access to educational facilities does not address the problem of sustaining school attendance (BBS 1994).

SECONDARY LEVEL The improvement in secondary education is relatively slow. Enrolment increased from 21 to 32 per cent between 1982 and 1992, rising further to 41 per cent in 1999 (BBS 2000). The gender gap narrowed, however, from 1951 (when only 3.4 per cent of females were enrolled in secondary

Women in Bangladesh

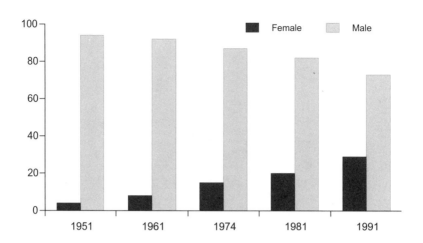

Figure 4.7 Secondary school enrolment by gender, 1996–97 (per cent)
Source: **Estimated from BBS (1999)**

schools, compared to 96.6 per cent of males) to 1991 (when 24.5 per cent of females were enrolled, compared to 75.4 per cent of males) (<www.sanisoft. tripod.com>; JICA 1999). This is a positive gain for girls, which improved further in 1997, but the gap is considerable (Figure 4.7).

The grant for girls in secondary schools has a great impact in this respect. Government support covers tuition fees and stipend, both of which vary by class. One DFID study (Gibson et al. 2004) revealed that the stipend ensured that all girls, but especially those from poorer families, could participate in school. It has also influenced traditional attitudes towards girls, allowing them to be more visible outside the home, using public transport, and even studying the same subjects as boys. Some have questioned the stipend programme because of cost and quality. The most common concern is that the size of the stipend is not sufficient to meet the costs associated with education. One main reason for dropping out at Grade 9 is lack of money to manage additional private tuition (which is almost universally required if a child is to pass the public examinations). Other limitations are lack of awareness about the latest status of the stipend, changing rules on eligibility criteria (now requiring the attainment of certain grades rather than just attendance) and the extension of the programme from Grades 10 to 12 (ibid.). Poor families sometimes use the stipend money for meeting basic needs and not for girls' educational attainment.

SECONDARY LEVEL AND HIGHER EDUCATION From secondary level to higher education, women's representation is increasing (BBS 1994, 1999),

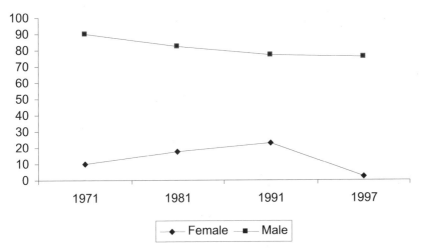

Figure 4.8 University students by gender (per cent)
Source: BBS (1999: 510)

although women are noticeably less likely than men are to complete four years of college or university (Figure 4.8). The difference has narrowed but the educational gender gap in Bangladesh is still striking. At university level, 13 per cent of the teachers are women, but the female proportion drops significantly in such male-dominated professional disciplines as agriculture and engineering (BBS 1994).

Constraints on girls' education

VALUE CONSTRAINTS From the secondary level on, the drop-out rate for girls is much higher than that for boys. Girls have had little access to education, especially in poor families. Parents invest scarce resources in sons as potential providers; they are reluctant to send daughters to school out of fear for their safety and chastity. The reputation of an unmarried girl determines her value in the eyes of her potential husband and in-laws. Girls are potential mothers and homemakers, so priority is given to training in domestic chores rather than academic disciplines (ADB 2001). Although poverty is the overriding reason for not sending children to school, the culture of poverty also creates illiteracy: the fact that many villagers believe that educated girls are rude, disobedient and less affectionate works against female education (Khan 1993).

PRACTICAL CONSTRAINTS Money is not the only concern for parents in sending adolescent girls to school. Physical considerations such as school location and distance, lack of basic facilities (e.g. separate latrines for girls and clean water) and culturally appropriate facilities for girls also hinder girls' education.

Women in Bangladesh

83

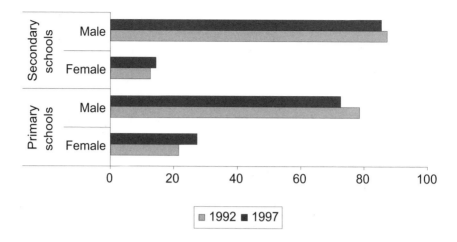

Figure 4.9 Teachers by gender in primary and secondary schools (per cent)
Source: BBS (1999: 533, 543)

The presence of female teachers creates positive parental attitudes in terms of sending their daughters to school (ibid.). In rural areas, parents generally do not send girls to schools with male teachers – but most teachers in Bangladesh are male (Figure 4.9), although their predominance slipped very slightly between 1992 and 1997. The social construction of attitudes still renders this a violation of the custom of keeping young girls secluded from outsider males. Other bottlenecks for women's education include poorly trained teachers, problems with curricula, calendar issues and poor enforcement of child labour laws (UNICEF 2001). Enrolment will not improve unless the social aspects of the problem are resolved.

POLICY CONSTRAINTS In Bangladesh's recent five-year plans, ambitious ideas have focused on accelerating female education; unfortunately, most of the plans have not been feasible because of traditional urban-based education systems, imbalances between male and female educational facilities, and for other reasons given above. Moreover, education policy formulation has overlooked the importance of non-formal education for women who have not had access to the formal education system. NGOs started non-formal primary education (NFPE) in the 1990s for primary age, adolescent and adult people in specific areas. Most teachers are female (above 90 per cent). These schools are close to homes and take account of student work hours in order to ensure attendance (Sharafuddin 1998). The Women's Affairs Sector of Alema suggests NFPE as a suitable strategy to be linked with income-generation activities (but not as a substitute for formal education).

84

Efforts by NGOs to target girls and women in non-formal education pro-grammes have been more successful than opening access to formal primary schools because of the minimal cost to parents of sending their daughters. The retention rate is nearly 100 per cent in the non-formal schools, which run for three years, compared to the government primary schools (where about 20 per cent of boys and girls drop out at Grade 3). The schools provide flexible hours and a practical curriculum. Successful linking of students to the mainstream education system has yet to be realized.

Political, educational and cultural leadership

Political empowerment for both genders is vital for national progress. The constitution gives equal rights to men and women, but for many women politi-cal participation remains out of reach.

Suffrage: participation in voting and elections Voting is the key element in women's political participation, an essential part of the democratic process, and a right protected by law in Bangladesh. Women's political participation is closely linked to their mobility, often for economic and educational pur-poses, which has been restricted in keeping with traditional beliefs about women's position held in the Indian sub-continent. Until the early part of the twentieth century, both the upper-class Hindu and Muslim women of Bengal had to live in *Zenana* (in the strict privacy of home), in total seclusion. Dur-ing the period of British rule, women awoke to their political rights. In 1917, Annie Besant insisted that the same tests be applied to women as to men with regard to the franchise. In 1921, the Madras Legislative Council passed a resolution calling for the registration of women on the electoral rolls. In the Indian sub-continent, women gained the right to vote in the Calcutta Muni-cipal Corporation in 1923, whereas the Pakistan government did not offer women the political right to cast their votes in local bodies until 1956, ten years after independence. The Bengal Legislative Assembly passed the wom-en's franchise resolution in 1925. It was not until 1926 that women gained the right to sit on legislative councils in the provinces of then British India. The constitutional right for women to vote was finally granted in 1935.

A remarkable change has occurred in the democratic power struggle: women are now mobilizing as voters and hold the balance of voting power. The highest turnout was when 73 per cent of the voting population cast their votes in the parliamentary election of 1996; over 56 million people voted, 28.7 million males and 27.9 million females (Rahman and Rahim 2001), revealing a narrowing gender gap. In the union-level elections held in 1997, there was

85

a massive turnout of female voters for the first time in Bangladeshi history. About 76 per cent of male voters and 83 per cent of female voters cast their votes during the last union *parishad* election (ibid.).

Political leadership In the 1930s and 1940s, a few educated women, inspired by revolutionary male leaders, played an active role in the anti-British movement. Women have been involved in the language movement, the liberation war and the civic movement against the autocratic Ershad government in 1992. Women participate now through electoral activities, trying to influence the votes of others, attending political meetings or rallies, and working for or contributing funds to a party or candidate. NGOs involve women in grassroots organizations and encourage them to participate in community activities. Many organizations are working for women's legal support (e.g. Ain o salish kendro, BLAST, BNWLA), awareness (e.g. Bangladesh Mahila Parishad, Nari pakhha, BNPS), and research or academic issues (e.g. Women for Women).

Political participation was most extensive in the liberation movement of 1971, in which women from all walks of life rendered support to the freedom fighters. The independence of Bangladesh in December 1971 created a growing awareness among women of their rights and responsibilities in the new society. The new government headed by Sheikh Mujibur Rahman drafted a fair constitution that guarantees fundamental rights for women (as mentioned earlier): the right to vote, the right to form a political party and the right to political participation (Khan 1993).

HEADS OF STATE AND GOVERNMENT Since independence, Bangladesh has had five heads of state through direct election. Tragic incidents propelled two women into leadership, although neither had a political career before inheriting the top position in their political party. In 1981, Sheikh Hasina was elected president of the Bangladesh Awami League, one of the largest political parties in Bangladesh. She is the daughter of Sheikh Mujibur Rahman, the country's main liberation leader and the first prime minister, who was killed in a military coup in 1975. She had some experience in student politics.

In 1981, Begum Khaleda Zia took a strong leadership role after the assassination of her husband, the late President Ziaur Rahman; she became chairperson of the Bangladesh Nationalist Party (BNP). She had no prior political involvement and was a homemaker before she became party leader. In the 1991 parliamentary election, Begum Khaleda Zia was elected as the first woman prime minister in Bangladesh. At the time, Sheikh Hasina was the leader of the opposition in parliament. In the 1996 parliamentary election,

Hasina was elected prime minister. Begam Khaleda Zia was re-elected as prime minister for a second term in 2001 and Sheikh Hasina once again holds the position of opposition leader.

MINISTERIAL (CABINET) Despite the unique situation of having women as both prime minister and leader of the opposition, women's participation in decision-making is minimal at the highest policy level. Only six women have been cabinet ministers since independence (Chowdhury 2003). The 1996 cabinet had three women ministers, and for the first time women were given responsibility over important sectors (agriculture; forest and environment). These two women had long political careers with the Awami League; others were state or deputy ministers responsible for less significant ministries (Table 4.1).

TABLE 4.1 Women ministers in different regimes

Administration	Number of ministers	Number of women ministers	Percentage
Sheikh Mujibur Rahman (1972–75)	50	2	4
Ziaur Rahman (1979–82)	101	6	6
Hussain Mohammed Ershad (1982–90)	133	4	3
Khaleda Zia (female) (1991–96)	39	3	5
Sheikh Hasina (female) (1996–2001)	46	4	8.69
Khaleda Zia (female) (2001–)	60	2	3.5
TOTAL	429	21	–

Sources: Chowdhury 1994; Rahman and Rahim 2001; Chowdhury 2003.

PARLIAMENTARY The national parliament, Jatiya Sangsad, consists of 300 general seats filled by direct election from single-member territories. The constitution reserves fifteen additional seats for women for fifteen years; the elected 300 legislators elect them indirectly. As women were in a 'backward' position at the time of independence, this rule was intended to ensure their future participation in government (Chowdhury 2003). This number was later increased to thirty and then to forty-five seats (fourteenth amendment, 2004). After independence, women members in parliament gradually increased, but as Table 4.2 shows, representation of women remains very low. Note that in 1988, when no seats were reserved for women, the percentage of females in parliament was zero.

TABLE 4.2 Women members of parliament (elected and reserved seats)

Year	Women candidates (%)	Elected women (%)	Reserved seats for women	Women as (%) of total seats
1973	0.3	0	15	4.8
1979	0.9	0.7	30	9.0
1986	1.3	1.7	30	10.6
1988	0.7	1.3	0	0
1991	1.5	1.7	30	10.6
1996	1.36	2.33	30	11.2
2001	2.0	2.33	*45	2.33

Sources: Chowdhury (1994, 2003); Rahman and Rahim (2001); Khatun et al. (1995). The option of reserved seats for women has expired; the present parliament has submitted a bill for forty-five reserved seats.

LOCAL GOVERNMENT Male members continue to dominate local government, which the British first introduced in 1970 under the Bengal Village Panchayat Act. The constitution encourages women's involvement. A four-tier system was recommended by the Local Government Commission of 1997. Union *parishad* (council) is the second tier, consisting of 4,472 *parishad*, each comprising ten to fifteen villages (Chowdhury 2003). The government made provision in 1997 for three reserved seats for women in the *parishad*, elected directly from each of the three wards. Women can also contest any general seat. Previously, selection of women representatives was based on nominations or indirect election. In the 1997 election, 45,000 women were in competition for 13,000 reserved seats. The number of candidates declined from 3.6 per cent in 1997 to 3.1 per cent in 2003. Greater interest, however, has been shown for the open position of chairman and for general seats (Chowdhury 2003).

The majority of women representatives regularly attend *parishad* meetings, but only a few of them participate in the deliberations and decisions. Female representatives usually involve themselves in mass education, family planning, immunization, handicrafts, relief activities and *shalish* (mediation in the village court). The women representatives have the potential to become agents of change for rural women and various NGOs.

PARTY LEADERSHIP Women's participation in political parties is insignificant in terms of both number and position (Khatun et al. 1995; Chowdhury 2003), and women are less likely than men to receive nomination during elections.

Towards gender equality

The future for female well-being is bright despite significantly unequal status at present. Because education has become a priority in Bangladesh, positive policy initiatives are reflecting changing attitudes. Awareness programmes encourage people to think positively about girls' education. In a remarkable shift in public attitudes towards girls' education, parents are considering their daughters' education positively and are focusing on maximizing their daughters' capabilities through education. Increased access to educational facilities is a major initiative, and the proportion of female primary school teachers has risen markedly from 5 per cent in 1974 to 20 per cent in 1991. These women are pioneers and role models for girls.

Research shows that parents of educated and employed girls may find relief from giving a dowry to the groom's family at marriage if the bride earns an income. One study found that mothers' expectations of their daughters' futures, and girls' own aspirations, have significantly changed in the last decade. Many girls now desire 'a good job' (Gibson et al. 2004). In middle-class families, factors such as building identity and self-esteem, having a voice at home and achieving dignity are becoming more important.

Despite initiatives and shifting attitudes, progress has not reached an optimal level because of policy inconsistencies. The Bangladesh Poverty Reduction Strategy Paper focused on reducing inconsistency and encouraging coordination among agencies (EXD 2002). Party ideology politicizes education in Bangladesh, so positions change when different parties come into power. Fostering an appropriate education policy requires accelerating a broader view and concentrating on policy stability.

A gap exists between legal provisions and social practice. In the political sphere, it is more complicated, as Bangladesh has had two women prime ministers in three sequential terms. This scenario contradicts the country's generally male-dominant structure. That these two women came to supreme command does not reflect the actual political empowerment of women. Statistical analysis shows that, despite having a female head of state and opposition leader, Bangladesh has remained inequitable in terms of gender composition in the political arena. Lower numbers of women in cabinet – and with responsibility for soft ministries – do not make women's participation in the decision-making process at the highest policy level secure (Rahman and Rahim 2001; Sultana 2001). Although Bangladesh is the only country where the prime minister and the leader of the opposition are both women, one cannot conclude that it is one of the most progressive countries in the world. Both women came to power because of family connections, and their governments proceed with little regard for protecting female well-being. Although the limitations of the situation are real, it is also true that these two women became leaders during crisis periods and have been successful as driving forces and unifying factors for their respective parties. Once placed in the position of leadership, they were able to generate their own dynamics and momentum to lead their parties through difficult times. In a male-centred political environment, they have been performing their leadership role in public life and helping to liberalize sociocultural values in a patriarchal society. More needs to be done, however.

Women's equal participation in parliament is important to change the conventional male-dominant environment of politics, but the negligible percentage of women parliament members has limited influence over government commitment to women's concerns. The party that has won the majority of general seats usually uses the reserved seats option as a vote bank. Despite experiencing continuous pressure from women's groups, no major political party agrees to change the existing indirect selection process; all ignore the requirement of direct election, in which eligible candidates compete for a seat in parliament. In this system, these reserved-seat members are bound to act as their party asks them to do; they have no true voice.

Rural women have been playing a crucial role in improving women's mobility and participation in the political process. In the *parishad*, it is very positive that women are coming to the fore, but social stigma limits their role. Women have not been given many responsibilities in the *parishad*; rather their roles and responsibilities have been curtailed (Chowdhury 2003).

Women in Bangladesh must play a dual role, facing the challenges of professional life and of the domestic sphere. This places restrictions on political ambition (Huq et al. 1995). Although women in Bangladesh are far from gaining an equal partnership in the political, economic and educational spheres, they have started their journey through a different sort of participation, working through different stages.

References

Ahmed, S. (1999) 'Role of women entrepreneurs in the national economy', in *Unnayan Podokkhep: A Quarterly Publication of Steps Towards Development*, Dhaka

Ahmed, S., P. A. Khanum and A. Islam (1998) 'Maternal morbidity in rural Bangladesh: where do women go for care', Working Paper no. 147, Dhaka: ICDDRB

Ashford, L. S. (2003) 'Empowering women', in R. J. Griffiths (ed.), *Annual Editions: Developing World*, Windsor Locks, CT: McGraw-Hill/Dushkin

Asian Development Bank (ADB) (2001) *Women in Bangladesh*, Country Briefing Paper, Manila: ADB

— (2002) *Sociolegal Status of Women in Indonesia, Malaysia, Philippines and Thailand*, Manila: ADB

BBS (Bangladesh Bureau of Statistics) (1990, 1992, 1996, 1997, 1999, 2000) *Statistical Yearbook of Bangladesh*, Statistics Division, Ministry of Planning, Government of the People's Republic of Bangladesh, Dhaka: BBS

— (1994) *Women and Men in Bangladesh: Facts and Figures 1970–90*, Statistics Division, Ministry of Planning, Government of the People's Republic of Bangladesh, Dhaka: BBS

BIDS (Bangladesh Institute of Development Studies) (2001) *Fighting Human Poverty: Bangladesh Human Development Report 2000*, Dhaka: BIDS

Botticini, M. and A. Siow (2003) 'Why dowries?', forthcoming, *American Economic Review*

Chaudhury, R. H. and N. R. Ahmed (1980) *Female Status in Bangladesh*, Dhaka: Bangladesh Institute of Development Studies

Chowdhury, D. (2003) 'Women in local government', in M. Haque (ed.), *Local Governance*, Legislative Support Service Project of MSS, funded by the European Commission

Chowdhury, N. (1994) 'Bangladesh gender issues and politics in patriarchy', in B. Nelson and N. Chowdhury (eds), *Women in Politics Worldwide*, New Haven, CT: Yale University Press

Chowdhury, O. H. (1997) *Handbook of Muslim Family Laws: The Dhaka Law Reports*, Dhaka: At al Afsar Press

CPD (Centre for Policy Dialogue) (2001) 'Policy brief on "education policy"', CPD Taskforce Report, Dhaka: CPD

— (2002) 'Impact of globalization on gender: the Bangladesh perspective', in *Bangladesh Facing the Challenges of Globalization: A Review of Bangladesh's Development 2001*, Dhaka: University Press Ltd

ERD (2002) *Bangladesh: A National Strategy for Economic Growth and Poverty Reduction*, no. 8217, Dhaka: Economic Relations Division, Ministry of Finance, Government of the People's Republic of Bangladesh

FYP (1997–2002), *The Fifth Five-Year Plan*, Dhaka: Ministry of Planning

Gibson, S. et al. (2004) *Breaking New Ground: Livelihood Choices, Opportunities and Tradeoffs for Women and Girls in Rural Bangladesh*, Dhaka: Department for International Development

Grameen Trust (1998) *Grameen Bank Dialogue*, Dhaka: Grameen Trust

Halim, M. A. (1995) *Women's Crisis within Family in Bangladesh*, Dhaka: Bangladesh Society for the Enforcement of Human Rights

Hamid, S. (1994) 'Non-market work and national income: the case of Bangladesh', in S. Amin (ed.), *The Bangladesh Development Studies: Special Issue on Women, Development and Change*, Dhaka

Haque, M. (ed.) (2003) *Mainstreaming Women in Politics*, Legislative Support Service Project of MSS, Dhaka

Huda, S. (1999) *Registration of Marriage and Divorce: A Study on Law and Practice*, Dhaka: Bangladesh Legal Aid and Services Trust

Huq, J. et al. (1995) *Women in Politics and Bureaucracy*, Dhaka: Women for Women

JICA (Japan International Cooperation Agency) (1999) *Country WID Profile (Bangladesh)*, Tokyo: JICA

Kabir, N. N. et al. (1996) *Non-formal Education and Gender Development: Hopes and Realities*, Camilla, Bangladesh: BARD

— (1997) 'Rural poverty and women: socio-cultural and economic dimensions', *Women and Poverty: A Journal of Women for Women*, 1: 18

Kamal, M. K. and I. A. Mia (2003) 'Women's empowerment through micro-credit: some important analytical observations', *Development Review*, 15

Khan, A. M. and S. Noman (2002) 'Women's participation in economic activities', *Empowerment: A Journal of Women for Women*, Dhaka

Khan, S. (1993) *The Fifty Percent: Women in Development and Policy in Bangladesh*, Dhaka: University Press

Khandker, S. R. (1988) 'Determinants of women's time allocation in rural Bangladesh', *Review of Economics and Statistics*, 37(3): 111–17, Chicago, IL: University of Chicago Press

Khatun, K. et al. (eds) (1995) *Nari O Unnayan: Prasangik parishagkhan*, Dhaka, Women for Women

Khundker, N. (2002) 'Bangladesh facing the challenges of globalization', in R. Sobhan (ed.), *A Review of Bangladesh's Development 2001*, Dhaka: Centre for Policy Dialogue, pp. 313–32

Koenig, M. A. et al. (2003) 'Women's status and domestic violence in rural Bangladesh: individual- and community-level effects', *Demography*, 40(2): 269–88

Lantican, C. P. and C. H. Gladwin (1996) 'Income and gender inequalities in Asia: Testing alternative theories of development', in *Economic Development and Cultural Change*, Chicago, IL: University of Chicago Press

Latif, M. A. (1994) 'Determinants of antenatal care-seeking behaviour programme impact on current contraception in Bangladesh', *Bangladesh Development Studies*, XXII: 27–61, Dhaka: Bangladesh Institute of Development Studies

Lynn, S. R. (2003) *Economic Development: Theory and Practice for a Divided World*, Englewood Cliffs, NJ: Prentice Hall

Mahmud, S. (1997) 'The structural adjustment programme in Bangladesh: implications for women in poverty', *Women and Poverty: A Journal of Women for Women*

MLJ (Ministry of Law and Justice) (1972) *Constitution of People's Republic of Bangladesh*, Dhaka: Government of the People's Republic of Bangladesh (rev. 1996)

Monsoor, T. (1999) *From Patriarchy to Gender Equity: Family Law and Its Impact*, Dhaka: University Press

Nussbaum, M. C. (2000) *Women and Human Development: The Capabilities Approach*, Cambridge: Cambridge University Press

Paul-Majumdar, P. and S. C. Zahir (1994) 'Dynamics of wage employment: a case of employment in the garment industry', in S. Amin (ed.), *Bangladesh Development Studies: Special Issue on Women, Development and Change*, Dhaka

Rahman, A. S. M. and M. A. Rahim (2001) 'The political empowerment of women in Bangladesh: an overview', in *Social Science Review: The Dhaka University Studies, Part D*, 18(2), December

Rahman, M. M. et al. (1997) 'Determinants of antenatal care-seeking behaviour in rural Bangladesh', Working Paper no. 126, Dhaka: ICDDRB

Shamim, I. (2002) 'Trafficking in women: the worst form of women's human rights violation', in K. Salahuddin, R. Jahan and L. Akanda (eds), *State of Human Rights in Bangladesh: Women's Perspectives*, Dhaka: Women for Women

Sharafuddin, A. M. (1998) *Innovations in Primary Education in Bangladesh*, New Delhi: Indira Gandhi National Centre for the Arts

Sultana, N. (2001) *Women's Political Participation and Partnership: Bangladesh Perspective*, unpublished MPhil thesis, Dhaka University

— (2003) *Is Marriage a Safe Haven for Women? A Critique of Existing Laws and Practices, Research Report 10: The Livelihoods of the Extreme Poor (LEP) Study*, Dhaka: IMEC, PROSHIKA

— (2005) 'The role of dowry and early marriage in shaping the livelihoods of poor rural women', in K. Iqbal and J. Seeley (eds), *Making a Living: The Livelihoods of the Rural Poor in Bangladesh*, Dhaka: University Press Ltd

Thwin, A. A. and S. A. Jahan (1996) 'Rapid appraisal of urban health needs and priorities', Working Paper no. 22, Dhaka: ICDDRB

USCIA (United States Central Intelligence Agency) (2004) *The CIA World Fact Book*, Washington, DC: USCIA

Volart, B. E. (2003), 'Dowry in rural Bangladesh: participation as insurance against divorce', draft paper, London School of Economics and Political Science

Websites

Mansor (2000) <www/thedailystar.net/law/2000307/04/>

UNICEF (2001) 'Barriers to girls' education, strategies and interventions', <www.unicef.org>

<www.sanisoft.tripod.com>

<www.worldbank.org>

5 | Women in Canada: a century of struggle

TESS HOOKS, PATRICE LECLERC AND
RODERIC BEAUJOT[1]

Social change seems inevitable, so it is no surprise that women in Canada have experienced an enormous amount of change in the last hundred years. At the beginning of the century, women were fighting for the right to vote. Now most Canadian women have been exercising their franchise for over eighty years and some hold elected office. As of 1900, women were excluded from most institutions of higher learning; now they gain more undergraduate degrees than do men.

Many assume that women today are much better off than in 1900, but the changes have not been unidirectional in nature, nor have they all necessarily been positive. For example, women gained the freedom to smoke; now lung cancer is more prevalent among women. Although it is unclear how the rates of violence against women in Canada have changed over the century, most would not consider the current level of violence against women in a positive light. The increased rates of crime and incarceration among women are also worrisome. Our exploration of seven dimensions of female well-being will help document the patterns of change.

A demographic portrait of Canadian women

Urbanization, immigration and the Canadian mosaic Changes stem from many factors, including urbanization and immigration, which have changed Canada's face literally as well as culturally. In 1901, 36.5 per cent of the population was classified as urban; by 2001, the country was almost 79 per cent urban (Figure 5.1). In 1991, 16 per cent of Canadians were not born in Canada, and the percentage was even higher in urban areas (Finkel et al. 1993). The 1997 change in immigration laws facilitated settlement in Canada (Mensah 2002), as decisions were now made on education and abilities rather than national origin. People came from Asia, the Caribbean and Africa at the rate of over 200,000 a year, contributing to the country's urbanization and increasing heterogeneity. The arrival of so many who were perceived as different from the 'traditional' Canadians of English and French ancestry produced problems and contradictions. While most celebrated the Canadian mosaic and a tradi-

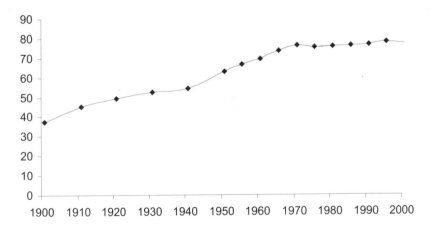

Figure 5.1 Urban population 1860–2000 (per cent)
Source: UNDP (2003)

tion of tolerance, racism and ethnic violence also emerged, especially in such urban areas as Toronto (40 per cent foreign-born).

In mid-century, the immigrant experience was very different for women than it was for men. Many women who arrived from the West Indies or the Philippines were recruited for domestic service, even though they may have been teachers or nurses in their home countries (Billson 2005a). Others who arrived with families were unemployed, as they did not speak English or French; they were ineligible for government support programmes, including language training (Prentice et al. 1996).

Life expectancy Women made more life expectancy gains compared to men from 1901 to 1976, and lower gains up to 2001 (Figure 5.2), but females still outlived males by five years as of 2001 (Beaujot and Kerr 2004: 45; SC 2003a: 1). In 1921, between the ages of twenty and twenty-four, the male probability of death was equal to that of women, while in 2001 it was three times that of women (SC 1994: 58–60). Especially at ages forty-five and over, men have made greater gains since 1976.

Beyond stress or lifestyle, biology plays a part in the gender difference: boys are more likely to die before birth and at very young ages. In the first year of life, the male mortality rate has consistently been 125 per cent of the female rate. Other factors can be identified (Beaujot and Kerr 2004: 54–5); for example, men are more likely to engage in unhealthy or dangerous activities, especially smoking, drinking and risk-taking. Among the population aged sixty-five and over, where death is more likely to occur, data from the mid-1980s indicate that a fifth of men but two-thirds of women had never smoked. The female risk in

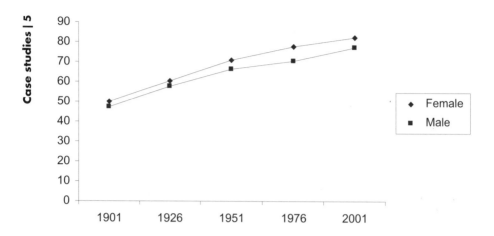

Figure 5.2 Life expectancy by gender (years) *Sources:* **Beaujot and Kerr (2004: 45); SC (2003a: 1)**

this regard was lower than the male risk, but increased over the century as their smoking rates grew. In 1998–99, the proportion who had ever smoked at age fifteen to nineteen was 32 per cent for girls compared to 23 per cent for boys. Women's deaths from lung cancer have increased over the 1990s, while men's rates have declined. Women retain the advantage of less dangerous working conditions. For instance, among fatalities that were subject to workers' compensation boards between 1988 and 1993, 4 per cent were women and 96 per cent were men (Marshall 1996: 30). Women are more likely to admit to illness and to solicit assistance. The 1998–99 Population Health Survey showed that 16 per cent of women compared to 32 per cent of men aged twenty-five to forty-four had not consulted a physician in the previous twelve months.

Population growth, fertility rate and male/female ratio From 1901 to 1971, there were fewer women than men in Canada, owing mostly to the lower proportion of women among the foreign born. The proportion of females was lowest in 1911 at 47 per cent of the population (McVey and Kalbach 1995: 57). With the increase in the proportion of women among immigrants, and their increased advantage in life expectancy, women outnumbered men after the 1971 census, with females reaching 51 per cent of the total population in 2001. With women's greater gains in life expectancy, the changes are more dramatic in the population aged sixty-five and over, where women comprised 49 per cent of the total in 1901 but 57 per cent in 2001 (SC 2002a: 28). Women's share of the total widowed population increased from 67 per cent in 1901 to 82 per cent in 2001 (Leacy 1983: A110–24; SC 2002a).

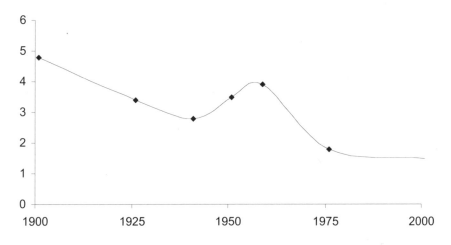

Figure 5.3 Fertility rate, 1901–2001 *Sources:* **Henripin (1968: 30);**
SC (1993: 45–6)

Women's mortality declined relative to men between 1901 and 1976, with the decline in deaths associated with childbirth, women's greater willingness to take advantage of the health system, and men's relative disadvantages in terms of lifestyle. Since 1976, however, men have made relative gains, especially in terms of heart disease and cancer.

Immigration has become more balanced between women and men. In the 1911 census, 38 per cent of the foreign-born population were females, compared to 51 per cent in 2001. Important differences remain, with men representing a higher share of the principal applicants of the economic class of immigrants; women are more likely to arrive as dependants. The overall trend in child bearing has been downward, from a total fertility rate of 4.8 births per woman in 1901 to 1.5 in 2001, except for the post-Second World War baby boom and affluent 1950s (Figure 5.3).

Age structure of the population The median age risen steadily since the baby boom ended in 1966, from 25.4 to 37.6 in 2001 (<www12.statcan.ca/english/census01>).

Maternal mortality rate Deaths associated with pregnancy and childbirth were once an important form of mortality for women, but essentially disappeared in Canada and are still among the lowest in the world. The rate dropped from 4.7 in 1921 to 0.1 in 1974. It climbed to 5.8 during the depression of the 1930s and peaked again at 7.8 in 2001 (SC 2004b).

Women in Canada

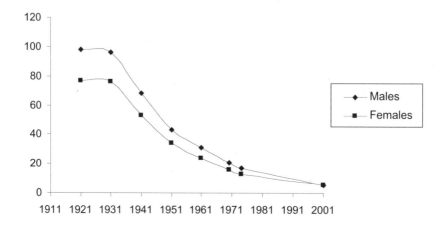

Figure 5.4 Infant mortality rates 1911–2001 (per 1,000 live births)
Source: **SC (2004b)**

Infant mortality rate Infant mortality rates, which are very low in Canada, occur primarily from low-birth-weight babies and pre-term births. The rate has been about twice as high for First Nations families (among whom birth weights are higher); these babies are more prone to post-natal causes of death such as sudden infant death syndrome, infection and poor living conditions, which suggests that poverty and lower education levels play a significant part in infant mortality (ibid.). The rate increased from 5.2 deaths per thousand in 2001 to 5.4 in 2002, caused by an increase in the female rate, especially among females one day old (Figure 5.4).

Contraception and abortion/average age at first child The median age for women at first birth declined to as low as 22.5 in 1961, then increased to 27.6 in 2001. Because they had higher marriage rates, women born in 1941–45 had the lowest childless rate at only 10 per cent by age forty-four (Beaujot and Muhammad 2003).

Family status and structure

Marriage age The timing of marriage provides other avenues through which to highlight the changing situation of women. The median age at first marriage declined over the century, to reach its lowest point at just over twenty-one for brides and twenty-three for grooms in the early 1970s, then increased to twenty-six and twenty-eight for women and men respectively in 2001 (Beaujot and Kerr 2004: 212; SC 1992: 47, 51–4). While the trends in age at marriage have reversed over the century, the gap between women's and men's average ages has been consistently downward, from a four-year difference in 1926 to 2.8 years in 1951. The gap underlies greater similarity in the roles of marriage and work for women and men. A larger age difference at marriage occurs typically when gender roles are more complementary in terms of family and work.

A first and second demographic transition, with an interlude between transitions, can explain these trends (Beaujot 2000). The first transition (1870 to 1945) involved a change in the economic costs and benefits of children, along with a cultural environment that made it more appropriate to control family size. The second transition (since the mid-1960s) involves various family changes, especially increased levels of cohabitation and divorce. We can understand the uniqueness of the 1950s as a period between the two transitions. Not only was this the peak of the baby boom, but it was also a period of 'marriage rush' (young ages and high proportions of persons married at least once in their lives). During this 'golden age of the family', many families corresponded to the new ideal of domesticity, especially in the suburbs, so there was less variability in the population (Skolnick 1987: 6–16).

In his model of marriage, Becker (1981, 1991) proposed that there are lower gains to marriage when there is less gender specialization in the division of labour in couples. This 'independence hypothesis' argues that women who have higher levels of achieved (rather than ascribed) characteristics would be less likely to marry. That is, men of higher status would 'buy marriage' as part of the package, while women use their higher achieved status to 'buy out of marriage', fearing ways in which marriage could limit their opportunities (Goldscheider and Waite 1986). In her alternate 'Theory of marriage timing', Oppenheimer (1988, 1997) attributes the delay to the difficulty that young men have in establishing their work lives, and to the importance attached to the work lives of both spouses.

The determinants of marriage timing show change over time, implying alternative dynamics associated with forming relationships. Using the 1995 General Social Survey, Turcotte and Goldscheider (1998) found that more highly educated women from the pre-1950 birth cohorts were less likely to marry, but the opposite applies in the post-1950 cohorts. For men across these cohorts, education relates positively to entry into unions, but that relationship has declined in importance. Mongeau et al. (2001) also found that the Becker model applies to older cohorts, where women were more likely than men to marry sooner and to have more work interruptions. In the more recent cohorts, however, significant work interruptions reduce men's likelihood of marriage, and uncertainties increase the likelihood that women will cohabit rather than marry. Over the century, union formation in Canada has increasingly required the earning power of both partners.

Marriage and divorce Not all was ideal in the golden age of post-war affluence. Isolated housewives experienced the 'problem with no name' (Friedan 1963: 15). Idealism created blinkers regarding such realities of family life as violence and abuse, which meant there was little recourse for the victims of violence. There was also a lack of autonomy, especially for women, to pursue routes other than the accepted path of wife, mother and homemaker (Veevers 1980). Many people considered childless couples as selfish, single persons as deviants, and working mothers as harming their children. Single women who became pregnant were required either to marry or to give up the child for adoption in order to preserve the honour of the family (Beaujot 2000: 85–96). The second transition started in the 1960s.

Especially through the demographic transition, it appeared that women's status increased more within the family than in non-family institutions (McDonald 2000). That is, women gained greater control over child bearing, which permitted access to other roles. In contrast, the 1950s saw an accentuation of the breadwinner model of families. For example, the following appeared in *MacLean's* magazine in June 1942: 'What will they [women workers] demand of [post-war] society? Perhaps – and we can only hope – they'll be tired of it all [working outside the home] and yearn in the old womanly way for a home and a baby and a big brave man' (cited in Boutilier 1977: 23). Folbre (2000) further reads gender change as women being allowed to make decisions based on their self-interests. As women gained greater control over their marital and reproductive status by virtue of the birth control pill in the early 1960s and the Divorce Act of 1968, other possibilities of self-actualization emerged.

Divorce was once rare, with most marriages ending with the death of a partner, but increased, especially mid-century. In 1921, there were only 558 divorces in all of Canada and fewer than 1,000 in 1965 – and then over 50,000 by 1975 (Wargon 1979: 87). The 1968 Divorce Act allowed divorces on fault-related grounds besides adultery and on marriage breakdown when a couple had lived apart for three or more years. In 1986, living apart for one year was sufficient to obtain a divorce. Data from later in the century indicate that a third of marriages end in divorce. Although most marriages remain intact until death, the substantial increase in separations means that marriage is no longer defined as 'till death do us part'. This has reduced the extent to which women can depend on marriage for economic security.

Trends in family patterns On many family dimensions, we cannot speak of a long-term trend over the century in Canada. For instance, today's two-income families share more similarities with the two-parent farm families of the beginning of the century than with the breadwinner families of the 1950s. The uniqueness of the 'baby boom period' (1946–66) can be seen in terms of fertility and timing of marriage. Other trends have been more consistent over the century, such as a decline in the age difference at marriage. The greater looseness in relationships, manifested by separations and later by cohabitation, is a unidirectional trend, but it is best to speak of a long period of stability, followed by marked changes in the period starting in the late 1960s. These trends in marital stability have differentially affected the lives of women and men, especially at ages thirty-five and over. Because of women's higher life expectancy, earlier age at marriage and lower remarriage rates, they are less likely to be living in a relationship, but are more likely than men are to live with children.

Both of these features undermine women's economic well-being, since they can depend less on the income of a partner, but have the additional costs associated with raising children. The negative side for men is that they are less likely to have enduring relationships with children and associated intergenerational support.

Cohabitation Another visible change in families is the greater prevalence of cohabitation, especially since 1976; in fact, cohabiting unions were considered too sensitive to be enumerated in the 1976 census. By 1986, most tabulations on families were treating cohabitations as marriages. By 2001, 63 per cent of first unions among women aged twenty to twenty-nine were common-law rather than marriages (SC 2002b).

The greater prevalence of both separation and cohabitation is part of a long-term change that has de-institutionalized the family, so that relationships are increasingly based on companionship (Burgess et al. 1963; Harris 1983; Thornton 2001; Dagenais 2000). Relationships are not maintained as institutions, but as a *'projet de couple'* (Roussel 1979) or as a 'pure relationship' (Giddens 1991).

Lone-parent families The percentage of children living in one-parent families was 11.9 in 1931, but as parental deaths declined, this proportion reached a low of 6.4 per cent of children in 1961 (Wargon 1979: 108). With increased separations, the proportion of children in lone-parent families reached 9.5 per cent in 1971 and doubled to 20.9 in 2001. In 1931, 75 per cent of lone parents were widowed, compared to two-thirds in 1951 and only one fifth in 2001 (Milan 2000).

With the decreased importance of death in the genesis of lone-parent families, and the tendency for children to live with their mother in cases of separation, the proportion of lone-parent families that involved women increased from 70 per cent in 1931 to 78 per cent in 1971 and 82 per cent in 2001 (Beaujot and Kerr 2004: 212; Wargon 1979: 87, 108). While joint custody has increased, the cases in which the father has sole custody have remained in the range of 12 to 15 per cent (SC 2000: 44).

Violence against women

In 1982, a report on wife battery introduced in the House of Commons was met with laughter and ridicule. In 1991, a subcommittee on the status of women of the Standing Committee on Health, Social Affairs, Seniors, and the Status of Women (SCHWSA) released a report with the provocative title *The War Against Women*. The catalyst for this report was the 'Montreal Massacre': on 6 December 1989, Marc Lepine entered an engineering class at the École Polytechnique of the University of Montreal, separated the women from the men, and murdered fourteen women students in twenty minutes while shouting, 'I hate feminists!' Lepine resented their presence in an institution that

TABLE 5.1 Key demographic data 1901–2001

	1901	1926	1951	1976	2001
(%) female in population	49	48	49	50	51
Median age at first marriage					
Brides	–	23.7	22	21.6	26
Grooms	–	28	24.8	23.7	28
Divorces per 100,000 married couples	–	34	180	990	1,110
Births to non-married women (%)	–	2.6	3.8	10.9	38.4
Median age at first childbirth	–	–	23.5	23.4	27.6
Lone-parent families as % of all families	–	–	9.8	14.0	24.7
% of children in lone-parent families					
Male-head	–	3.6	1.8	2.1	3.7
Female-head	–	8.3	6.2	7.4	17.2

Sources: Beaujot and Kerr (2004: 45, 212); McVey and Kalbach (1995: 57); Henripin (1968: 30); SC (1992: 47, 51–4); SC (1993: 36, 41, 45–6); Wargon (1979: 87, 108); Nagnur (1986: 195); Leacy (1983: B1–14). For 1926 and 1951, births to non-married women were designated as illegitimate births. The 1926 data on median age at first marriage were estimated by the authors based on mean age for all marriages; total fertility rate for 1901 estimated from 1891, 1911; 1931 data on children living with one parent used for 1926 and 1971 data used for 1976; 1961 data for median age at first birth used for 1951; 2000 data for median age at first marriage for 2001.

had until recently been an exclusively masculine domain. He left a list of other women he hoped to kill; all were successful women (Box 5.1).

Although feminists had been working on violence against women since the 1970s, the Montreal Massacre put the issue on the public agenda. As Mary Collins, the Minister Responsible for the Status of Women, stated in her appearance before the parliamentary committee, 'the events that took place in Montreal are reflective of the same kind of violence that destroys the lives of so many women in Canada every day, in their homes, on the street, and at work' (SCHWSA 1991: 1). Public outrage was immediate, and responses came from the government, women's groups and journalists to increase public awareness (Finkel et al. 1993; Prentice et al. 1996).

The standing committee subsequently refused to endorse *The War Against Women*. Unfortunately, as elsewhere in the world, changing expectations, female role expansion and the education of women are still perceived by some as threats. The debates surrounding this report were indicative of the contentious nature of violence against women as an issue and signalled the beginning of a reassessment of Canada's strategy for dealing with domestic violence. This reassessment included recognition that information on the extent of the problem was lacking (see Box 5.1 for further discussion of the Montreal Massacre).

In the early 1980s, parliament initiated a review of the Canadian Criminal Code provisions related to assault, resulting in three assault offences and three corresponding sexual assault offences. Assaults are categorized according to the degree of injury or harm done (Johnson 2002: 24). After this change, wife battery was subsumed under the categories of assault when police reported crime data. The offences of rape, attempted rape, sexual intercourse with the feeble minded, and indecent assault on males and females were abolished and replaced with three levels of a new sexual assault offence (ibid.: 25).

In 2001, of all women victims of a violent offence, 58.5 per cent were victims of assault and 10.2 per cent were victims of sexual assault (SC 2001b). Two crime victim surveys have documented the prevalence and severity of spousal assaults: the 1993 Violence Against Women Survey (VAWS) and the 1999 General Social Survey (GSS). According to the GSS, the rates of spousal violence experienced by men and women were only slightly different – 8 per cent for women, 7 per cent for men in relationships over the last five years, and 4 per cent for both men and women in their current relationships. Taking this data at face value is deceiving because women are more frequently subjected to severe forms of violence. Two and a half times as many women as men are beaten, five times as many are choked, and twice as many have a gun or knife

Box 5.1 After the Montreal Massacre: gender and the pervasiveness of violence

In spite of the fact that Canada has one quarter of the violent crime of the United States, stricter gun control and a tighter criminal justice system, and that Canadians have a deeply rooted societal ethos that supports 'peace, order, and good government', one of the most heinous crimes committed in modern North America took place when Marc Lepine shot and killed fourteen female engineering students at the University of Montreal, and then committed suicide.

Some view the events of 1989 as the isolated act of a madman, a random event. In retrospect, the 'Montreal Massacre' ranks as one of the century's clearest expressions of the intimate linkage between pervasive societal violence and the degradation of women. Although Lepine was a terribly disturbed individual, his behaviour goes far beyond that of mere mental instability or misogyny. While the planned, cold-blooded killing of several young women was not the act of a 'normal' person, it could be argued that society provided the language from which Lepine crafted a discourse of antipathy towards women. Violence, like sexism, is a state of mind, a bad intellectual habit, a mistake of logic, a failure of a warped spirit – but it is also the logical culmination of humanity's collective mistaken assumption that those who are more powerful have the right to keep 'the others' – whoever they are – in their place. It is in this sense that society is at fault. Society, by institutionalizing violence, even celebrating it, provided a sociocultural legitimization of this murderous choice. Society, in supporting violence against women for so long by ignoring it and failing to punish it adequately, sent a clear message to Lepine and others who have killed or injured literally millions of women in North America: it is acceptable to harm women; female lives are not as deserving as male lives. Even though crime rates are lower in Canada, Canada nevertheless has its share of violence, both individual and institutional. Patricia Monture-Okanee, a Mohawk lawyer, expresses the view of many Native women: violence against women is only one type of assault on human lives – racism, classism and violation of the rights of Native people to pursue their own destinies lie at the historical base of both Canadian and American cultures. The explanatory and real-life power of interlocking dynamics of oppression helps to put Lepine's actions into perspective.

In a very real sense, Lepine's gendered imperialism and cultural chauvinism was and is supported by the living arrangements and assumptions all around him. Though most males would not consciously condone his specific act of heartless violence, many still uphold by deed or word or indifference the mechanisms through which women are subordinated. Barriers remain and biases persist, in spite of significant gains tethered to the 1981 Canadian constitutional protection of women.

To Lepine, these bright young women engineering students symbolized an entire army of females that were receiving the education he coveted for himself – an education that would lead them to a life of privilege in a society that until very recently afforded that kind of education and privilege to men only. The University of Montreal women were pioneers who constituted a tangible threat in the war between the sexes. Lepine was not unique among males in believing that education was a uniquely male right.

That Quebec came late to women's rights may have an impact, according to Micheline Dumont. Canadian women won the right to vote in 1918 – Quebec women in 1940; Canadians began co-education in the late 1800s – Quebec did not dismantle its separate school systems for males and females until 1965; Canadian women gained access to universities in 1850 – Quebec women in 1907; in Canada, women won civil rights in marriage in 1872 – Quebec women in 1964. Dumont points out that the strong feminist movement in Quebec also appeared later than in the rest of Canada. Thus, the publicly held concept of women's equality was relatively new in the historical sweep of things. In Quebec, Canada and the USA, women are still under-represented in the highest managerial, executive positions and policy-making positions and salary categories. Slow but threatening change has begun.

Two other factors feature in the backdrop of Lepine's action: the proliferation of weapons and the secondary violence that is done to women who are victims of sexual harassment, rape and battery in how they are treated by the police, courts, psychiatrists and the media (being accused of asking to be victims, enjoying the assault, or lying about it in the first place). This informal system undergirds the individual male's choice to harm women throughout the world. (*Janet Mancini Billson*)

used against them. Women are also more likely to have experienced repeated incidents of violence: 65 per cent of all women who reported being assaulted by a partner were victimized more than once, with 26 per cent victimized more than ten times. The comparable figures for men are 54 per cent and 13 per cent, respectively. Female victims were more likely to report being afraid for their children, to have sleeping problems, to suffer from depression or anxiety attacks, and to report lower self-esteem. Of women living in violent relationships during the past five years, 38 per cent feared that their lives were in danger. This was the case for only 8 per cent of male victims (SC 2000: 166–7).

A comparison of the VAWS and GSS suggests that the severity of the assaults has diminished slightly. The proportion of victims who reported injury requiring medical attention or experiencing chronic assaults also declined. There may be a decline in five-year prevalence rates. Spousal assault of women within the previous year, however, does not appear to have decreased (FPTMRSW 2002). One important difference is the increase in the number of female victims who reported to the police: 37 per cent in 1999 compared to 29 per cent in 1993 (SC 2000).

Police-reported data do not parallel self-reported data from the surveys. Police data indicate that women represented 85 per cent of victims of spousal assault from 1995 to 2000. The number of assaults against women reported to the police dropped between 1995 and 1997, and then increased between 1998 and 2000. The number reported by male victims increased steadily over this six-year period (FPTMRSW 2002: 16). Reported sexual assaults show a steady increase from 1983 to 1993, but declined steadily from 1993 to 2000. Even though there was a 1 per cent increase from 2000 to 2001, the rate of sexual assaults is still 35 per cent lower than in 1993 (Savoie 2001: 6). The vast majority of sexual assault victims are women (over 85 per cent). Over 90 per cent of these sexual assault incidents are recorded as Level I assaults – that is, assaults involving minor or no physical injury. VAWS data indicate that 10 per cent or fewer women report their assaults to police (FPTMRSW 2002: 19).

For the third consecutive year, homicide rates in Canada remained stable (1.8 per 100,000) after a steady thirty-year decline (Savoie 2001: 6). Spousal homicide rates are also declining. Between 1974 and 2000, the homicide rate for women decreased by 62 per cent, from 16.5 to 6.3 women per million couples, and the homicide rate for men dropped by more than a half from 4.4 to 2.0 men per million couples (Bunge and Sauvé 2002: 9). Several possible explanations exist for this decline: an increase in community-based supports; mandatory charging policies when police suspect that an assault has occurred; and better training for police in dealing with family violence. It may also be that women have developed a lower tolerance for spousal violence and leave relationships before the violence reaches a critical, deadly stage (FPTMRSW 2002: 17–18).

Crime and deviant behaviour Women are much more likely to be victims of crime than perpetrators of crime. As criminal offenders, women account for a minority of all persons charged by police in Canada each year, and rarely pose the same kind of threat to public safety as men, who commit more numerous and more violent offences. In 2001, women were charged with committing 19 per cent of adult crimes of violence and property, but females represented 54.6 per cent of all victims of violent crime. Nevertheless, the level of female criminality has nearly doubled in the last twenty years. In 2001, adult women were charged with 16.7 per cent of all violent offences, compared to 8.1 per cent in 1981; they were charged with 26.6 per cent of all property offences in 2001 and only 14.8 per cent in 1981. Female criminal activity peaks at about age fifteen; girls have accounted for a greater proportion of youth crime than women have of adult crime. Except for young offenders, adult women account for a higher proportion of adults charged with property offences than they do for violent offences (SC 2000: 172–3).

Johnson and Rodgers (1993: 98) argue that there is a link between socio-economic status and female criminality: ' ... women who come into conflict with the criminal justice system tend to be young, poor, under-educated, and unskilled. A disproportionate number are Aboriginal. Many are addicted to alcohol, drugs, or both. A majority have been victims of physical and sexual abuse, and many are emotionally or financially dependent on an abusive male partner.' Some observers have blamed the feminist movement for the increase in female criminality, arguing that feminists encourage women to imitate the behaviour of men. The above characterization of female offenders lends little support to this notion. The women described hardly sound like 'liberated' women.

Women are also a much smaller proportion of the prison inmate population than men are, but the number of women prisoners nearly doubled towards century's end (from 2 per cent federal and 6 per cent provincial/territorial in 1981 to 5 and 9 per cent respectively in 2001). Women sentenced for two years or more are incarcerated in the federal prison system. The federal Prison for Women (P4W) housed all federally sentenced women between 1934 and 1995. Cooper asserts that Canada's treatment of female offenders reveals a 'mixture of neglect, outright barbarism, and well-meaning paternalism' (1993: 33). P4W's sixty-year history helps to illustrate Cooper's assertions. During the prison's lifetime, it was subject to fourteen inquiries and commissions, many of which recommended its closure, which occurred in 1994 (Correctional Services of Canada 1995). Federally sentenced women are less likely than men to have access to rehabilitation and treatment programmes, more likely to be in facilities further away from family and support networks, and more likely to be in multi-level facilities. Their relatively small numbers help to explain these differences.

Economic participation

The division of labour Families can usefully be described in terms of the division of labour, especially associated with earning a living and caring for each other (Beaujot 2000). Until the mid-1930s, when over half of the population was rural, the prevalent form was the two-parent farm family. With the differential economic opportunities by gender associated with early industrialization, and with the push of the first generation of feminism, the breadwinner model became the dominant division of labour and probably reached its peak in the 1950s. The two-worker model became dominant in response to greater economic opportunities for women and the second generation of feminism. 'Head of household' was last used in the 1971 Canadian census. Among couples with children under sixteen, one third were dual-income in 1961, but this had become almost a two-thirds majority by 1997 (Marshall 1998). By the mid-1990s, a quarter of couples with employment income showed higher income for the wife than for the husband, compared to 11 per cent in 1967 (Crompton and Geran 1995).

Women's participation in the labour force Women's labour force participation has increased substantially since the beginning of the last century. In 1901, only 14.4 per cent of women over the age of fourteen were in the labour force. By 2003, over 57 per cent of women over the age of fifteen undertook paid work and they accounted for nearly half (46.6 per cent) of the total labour force (SC 2004a: 11). This does not account for the significant amount of informal, unpaid work that women do, but which is not recorded as formal participation.

During the early twentieth century, Canada was an agrarian society. Many women worked on family farms. They took in boarders or did the laundry for others; a few engaged in prostitution. Even though many of these activities brought money into household economies and were often essential for survival, most did not appear in official labour force statistics.

While women have increased their rates of formal labour force participation, the pattern for men has been the opposite, from 84 per cent of men aged fifteen and over in 1951 to about 68 per cent in 2003. The availability of pensions helps explain this trend: men are now living longer and retiring earlier. By the end of the century, participation rates of women and men had become more similar than different (Figure 5.5) (Creese and Beagan 2004: 246).

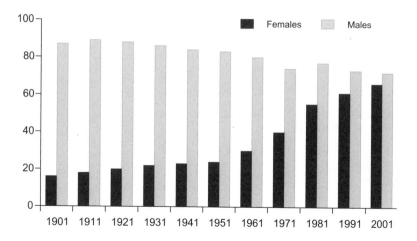

Figure 5.5 Labour force participation by gender (per cent) *Sources:* **Krahn and Lowe (1993: 62) for 1901–91; SC (2001)**

Notwithstanding women's increased participation in the labour force, women's share of unpaid work hours is still greater than men's share. According to analysis of 1992 data, the unpaid work of women represented between 32 and 54 per cent of Canada's GDP that year, depending on the valuation method used (SC 2000: 97). The 1986, 1992 and 1998 Canadian surveys have given similar results in terms of the overall distribution of time in total productive activities for men and women, both paid and unpaid. For paid work, men's time has been stable while women's has increased. In 1986, women's average time in paid work was 63 per cent of that of men, increasing to 70 per cent in 1998. For unpaid work, men's average time represented 45 per cent of women's time in 1986, compared to 60 per cent in 1998 (Beaujot and Liu 2005).

FULL/PART-TIME Women's participation in the labour force is still at variance with men's in that women are much more likely to work part-time. In 2003, 28 per cent of all women in the paid workforce worked less than thirty hours per week in their main job. Though the numbers of men working part-time have increased, women have made up about 70 per cent of the part-time labour force since the mid-1970s (SC 2004a: 8).

A century ago, women included in labour force statistics were most often young and single. Upon marriage, but most certainly after the birth of a child, most exited the labour force. Some re-entered after their children had grown up and left home. In 2003, nearly 72 per cent of women with children under sixteen undertook paid work, including 63 per cent of those with children under the age of three (ibid.: 14). Figure 5.6 shows the strong increase in participation of

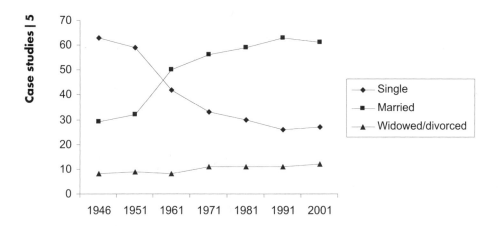

Figure 5.6 Marital status of women in the labour force, 1946–2001 (per cent)
Sources: **SC (2001); SC (1971–2001)**

married women in the labour force during the century, reflecting shifting definitions in the family division of labour and changing family patterns.

TYPES OF OCCUPATION In 1901, just five occupations accounted for nearly three-quarters (71 per cent) of women in the labour force (Krahn and Lowe 2002: 183). Most worked as domestic servants (36 per cent), seamstresses (13.5 per cent), or teachers (13 per cent). All three occupations could be classified as female job 'ghettos', with over 75 per cent women in each occupational grouping. Only 5.3 per cent of women worked as office clerks; men still dominated the clerical profession. By mid-century (1951), sales clerks, hotel, café and domestic workers, and teachers made up 44 per cent of the female workforce (ibid.: 183). As the century continued, and up until the 1980s, clerical work took on increasing importance for women. By 1987, around one in every three women workers (30 per cent) in Canada was employed in a clerical occupation (SC 2000: 128).

At the beginning of the new century, women work in a broader range of occupations, including professional occupations. Women now constitute 52.1 per cent of all doctors, dentists and other health professionals. In addition, they make up nearly half (48.4 per cent) of those in business and finance. Despite these gains, 70 per cent of women workers are still concentrated in four traditionally female occupational categories: clerical and administrative (24.1 per cent), sales and service (32.2 per cent), nursing (8.4 per cent) and teaching (5.2 per cent) (SC 2004a: 8–9, 20).

UNEMPLOYMENT There is a great deal of diversity among Canadian women;

some groups are clearly more disadvantaged than others. Immigrant and visible minority women experience lower rates of employment, higher rates of unemployment, and lower employment earnings. Aboriginal women are among the most disadvantaged. Their rates of unemployment are twice those of other Canadian women and their incomes are significantly lower. Women with disabilities are similarly disadvantaged (Creese and Beagan 2004: 246–7).

During the 1950s and early 1960s, male unemployment rates were about twice as high as female rates (Krahn and Lowe 2002: 76). From 1976 to 1989, however, women were more likely than men to be unemployed. During the 1990s and into the twenty-first century, women's unemployment levels have been slightly lower than men's. In 2003, 570,000 women, 7.2 per cent of all female labour force participants, were unemployed, compared with 8 per cent of male labour force participants (SC 2004a: 9).

Despite the fact that women are almost as likely to be unemployed as men, women are much less likely to be eligible for government unemployment insurance. During the 1990s, the Liberal government drastically overhauled the system, slashing benefits and entitlements (Phillips and Phillips 2000) and in 1999 only 32 per cent of unemployed women in Canada qualified for benefits – 10 per cent lower than the comparable figure for men (Income Security Advocacy Centre 2003).

Income and poverty Because of the gendered division of labour in the home and the workplace, women are significantly disadvantaged economically. According to Phillips and Phillips (2000: 56), in 1911 the average wage of employed women stood at 53 per cent of average male wages. In 1931, it was 60 per cent. This ratio between men and women's earnings remained relatively unchanged over a forty-five-year period. It was not until the late 1970s that women's earnings began to increase in relation to men's. If we compare full-time, full-year workers with full-time, full-year workers in 1981, women were earning about 64 per cent of male earnings. Even though more women were entering higher-paying managerial and professional jobs in the 1980s, the wage gap narrowed ten percentage points over the twenty years between 1980 and 2000 because increased employment in high-paying jobs was offset by an expansion in low-paying (mostly service sector) employment (Krahn and Lowe 2002: 190–91). The best year for women was 1996, when women earned 73.4 per cent of the earnings of male workers. When part-time workers are included for 1996, women's average earnings drop to 65 cents for every dollar men earned (SC 2000: 155). Wages have improved for both genders but by 2000 women still earned only about 71 per cent of men's wages (Figure 5.7).

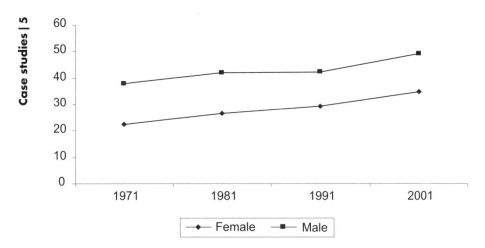

Figure 5.7 Average earnings by gender (Canadian dollars)
Source: SC (2000)

Given their lower earning potential, it is not surprising that at all stages of their lives women are more likely than men to live in poverty. Women on their own (single mothers and widows) are the most vulnerable. In 1971, 16.9 per cent of women lived in poverty and women made up 45.6 per cent of all those living in poverty (Gunderson et al. 1990: 7–8). By 1981, 18 per cent of women lived in poverty and women made up 56.4 per cent of all those living in poverty. Since 1981, the percentage of women living in poverty has hovered around 55 per cent of the total (SC 2000: 149). Poverty levels peaked in Canada in 1996. In that year, almost 20 per cent of women as compared to 16 per cent of men lived in poverty. Since then, the number of people living in poverty has declined (11.1 per cent of women and 9.6 per cent of men) (SC 2001a).

Literacy and education

As with all retrospective analyses that span many decades, data collection and recording must be recognized as uneven and not strictly comparable over time. This is particularly true for Canada in the area of education. According to the British North America Act of 1867, education falls under the jurisdiction of the provinces (excluding Aboriginal peoples, whose education is the responsibility of the federal government). The provinces varied considerably in their data classification and collection systems, and many school types existed (public, private and confessional), especially in Quebec and Ontario.

School completion rates Early in the twentieth century, schooling for women and men was variable. A range of schooling options existed, all of them gendered. For women, there were some public schools and many religious ones; higher education occurred primarily in normal schools, which prepared women and men for elementary and secondary teaching. Women were barred from professional educational opportunities.

PRIMARY AND SECONDARY By 1905, all provinces except Quebec had free and compulsory schooling for *all* children ages seven to twelve (Finkel et al. 1993). This development increased the need for teachers, most of whom were women. Girls and boys had different curricula, with the girls working mainly in the 'domestic sciences' (Prentice et al. 1996), which was considered vocational training. Gender segregation was also physical: there were different entrances in the schools for boys and girls, as well as separate playgrounds. By 1931, most children were spending about ten years in the classroom, particularly in urban areas, but the *percentage* of girls (and boys) enrolled in school had declined from 1901, though actual numbers increased (ibid.). The percentages had risen dramatically by 1961 (Figure 5.8).

Attendance rates were high by 1961, but varied by province and region. Rates were much higher in urban areas (Guppy and Davies 1998). Elementary schooling was now well entrenched in Canadian society, but less so in Quebec, with its great disparities in language and religion. Francophones from working-class backgrounds attended school at a far lower rate than did anglophones. The Catholic Church opposed compulsory education – in 1926 only one Catholic child in twenty attended schools beyond the primary grades (Finkel et al. 1993). In 1943, Quebec instituted compulsory school attendance,

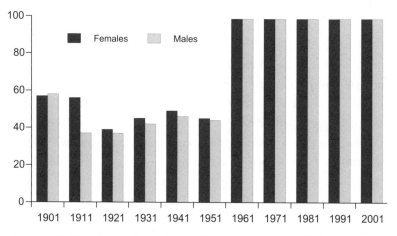

Figure 5.8 School attendance by gender, age eight and older (per cent)
Source: Prentice et al. (1996)

which increased the need for teacher training and furthered the debate about women's place in schools.

By 1960, Canadians were attending primary and secondary schools at the rate of 90 per cent (Guppy and Davies 1998). People of European descent were most likely to attend school, as were the native-born. Between the Second World War and the 1970s, enrolment in elementary and secondary schools doubled (SC 1992). There was some concern about increasing egalitarianism in the schools and differing expectations for boys and girls continued, particularly in Quebec, where girls were channelled into Instituts Familiaux and taught to be good housewives (Prentice et al. 1996). First Nations boys and girls experienced the abuses of residential schools well into the 1970s.

HIGHER EDUCATION Compared to public and secondary education, which had achieved enrolment of almost 100 per cent by the middle of the century, post-secondary enrolment was lower. Early in the century, women's role in society and the education needed to fulfil that role centred on domesticity. The classical education offered to boys was thought to harm women's reproductive capacity and even their physical appearance. Thus, considerable debate occurred about women attending university and professional schools; many females who requested admission were rejected. Despite this pattern, by 1900 women constituted 11 per cent of students in university and college. New careers were opening, if slowly, and women were demonstrating that they could equal men intellectually. The proportion of women students increased steadily throughout the century (Figure 5.9) (Prentice et al. 1996).

The women's suffrage movement of the late 1800s was still inspiring demands for women's social and legal rights. Women within their own class, geographic and ethnic groups had formed many organizations. The start of the First World War, with the need for more women to participate visibly in the paid workforce, stimulated women to press for more gains, and membership in voluntary associations increased. Schooling was also a technique to assimilate immigrants (Finkel et al. 1993). After the First World War, more occupations were opening for women, many of which required training and schooling. The post-war emphasis was on returning to traditional life and gender roles. Although more young women were attending school, educators re-emphasized training of women for 'marriage and motherhood, and for careers that complemented these roles' (Prentice et al. 1996: 280).

In 1940s Quebec, clergy still controlled the schooling. For young men of wealth, higher education took place in the 'classical' colleges, to prepare them for professions and business; few young women were educated beyond the

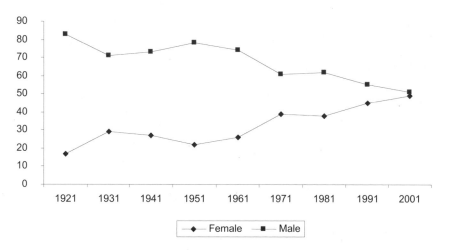

Figure 5.9 Females as a percentage of all college/university graduates
Sources: **Census Office (1906); Prentice et al. (1996); SC (later years)**

public schools (Clio Collective 1987). Females still dominated in *les écoles normales*, which existed until the 1950s (ibid.). Enrolment in domestic science courses decreased in the 1950s, as more women took commercial courses. The *instituts* continued until 1964 when Quebec, as part of the Quiet Revolution and reflecting awakening nationalist goals, restructured schooling to include the two-year, post-secondary *Colleges d'enseignement général et practique* (CEGEPS) (ibid.; Prentice et al. 1996).

Before the 1960s in Quebec, three times as many Protestants as Catholics completed Grade 11 (Finkel et al. 1993). Despite the new structures and opportunities created by the Parent Report on Education of Girls, and the increase in young women attending higher education, girls were still channelled into traditional female roles and occupations. By 1976, 54 per cent of girls were in vocational studies at the CEGEPS, meaning that far more young men than women went on to college. Females and males were still not taking the same courses. Females, because of the structural impediments present in society, continued to focus on teaching, nursing and dietetics (Clio Collective 1987). These structural changes disadvantaged some women, particularly teaching nuns, who lost their positions (Prentice et al. 1996).

A boom in post-secondary education swept Canada after the Second World War. Veterans were supported to attend university as part of the government's efforts to reintegrate returning soldiers into society. Of course, most veterans were men. Despite the fact that women and men now attended public school in generally equal numbers, sex-role stereotyping in materials and gendered expectations of roles meant that there were two education systems in the public schools and higher education. Both women and men were prepared by the schools for their assigned (traditional) roles in life. In the 1960s and 1970s, there was a huge increase in attendance at colleges and universities, as the 'baby boom' generation reached majority in a time of economic prosperity. Immigration was increasing and the women's/feminist movement in Canada and worldwide was re-emerging, which affected all aspects of Canadian life, including education.

Feminists worked to open up more programmes for women and to change gender stereotyping of professions and occupations. Although many more women were achieving higher education, they were still concentrated in primarily 'female' areas. One reason for this was lack of women role models both in occupations and in the academy; in the mid-1960s, only 10 per cent of university teachers were women and they were concentrated in education, nursing and the arts (Prentice et al. 1996). Early in the century, men dominated in completing one or more years of graduate school, but the rates converged to a virtual 50/50 situation by the end of the century.

By the 1990s, education through secondary school was definitively the norm in Canada, with high percentages of students going on to various forms of higher education. In all provinces, more women than men held university degrees but women outnumber men at a higher rate the lower the degree. Today, women earn over 19,000 more bachelor's and first professional degrees than men do each year. As in the beginning of the twentieth century, however, the gender distribution by field remains skewed, with women predominating in nursing, education, social work and fine arts, and men predominating in engineering, physics and computer science.

The development of women's studies programmes at many universities had a major impact on the academy. By the 1980s, these programmes were well established in many Canadian universities; three scholarly journals flourished in the emerging field; and the federal government had endowed five regional women's studies chairs (ibid.). Women and men now receive approximately the same number of master's degrees, but again women are concentrated in the traditional female specialities. Of all full-time women pursuing master's degrees, women represented only 27 per cent in mathematics and physical sciences, and 18 per cent in engineering and applied sciences, towards the end of the twentieth century (Normand 2000). Women receive approximately one third of all PhDs but the concentration is in education, the fine and applied arts and the social sciences. There is little substantial change across recent decades (Guppy and Davies 1998).

Variations by region, gender and rural versus urban populations persisted through the end of the twentieth century. The lower rates of higher education attendance among First Nations males and females continued. Geographic isolation makes education difficult for many; for example, there are no universities in the Yukon, Northwest Territories or Nunavut (some communities have two- or four-year colleges). In 1991, of Aboriginal women aged twenty-four to thirty-four, only 2.6 per cent had obtained a university degree, compared with 11 per cent of those with English ethnic origin and 15.7 per cent overall. For Aboriginal men, 1.9 per cent had a degree, with an overall population rate of 15.9 per cent (ibid.). These gaps are closing but major differences remain.

Political, educational and cultural leadership

Suffrage: participation in voting and elections The Royal Commission on the Status of Women (RCSW 1970) pointed out that women's participation in the political process takes several forms, ranging from slight involvement (voting and following the political news of the day) to high involvement (standing for election to public office). Intermediate levels of involvement might include contributing money, working for political parties or engaging in the activities of a social movement that seeks to influence the political process.

During the nineteenth century in Canada, women began organizing to gain access to the ballot box. The suffrage movement reached its peak in the early years of the twentieth century (ibid.: 334). Because of this campaign, women gradually won voting privileges in Canada. Manitoba was the first province in 1916; Quebec was the last in 1940; most others fell between 1916 and 1922. In 1918, parliament passed a Women's Franchise Act, which extended the right to vote in federal elections to women aged twenty-one and over who possessed the same age, income or property qualifications for provincial voting as those required for males in their province or territory. The Dominion Elections Act (1920) separated federal voting from provincial voting qualifications and affirmed the right of women to be elected to parliament. Canada did not achieve universal suffrage until much later in the century, though: Canadians of Chinese, Japanese and East Indian descent were not eligible to vote until 1948, and Status Indians were denied the franchise until 1960 (ibid.: 336–8).

HEADS OF STATE AND GOVERNMENT Conservative Kim Campbell held the position of prime minister for three short months in 1993.

MINISTERIAL (CABINET) Women hold just nine of thirty-nine cabinet positions (less than 25 per cent); five women hold minor portfolios while four hold key cabinet posts (Simpson 2004). In spite of their strong voting record, women have not been rewarded with commensurate cabinet representation. For example, despite the strong evidence that Prime Minister Paul Martin may owe his 2004 minority victory to female voters who would have supported the Liberal agenda more strongly than male voters, his July 2004 cabinet has two fewer women than the pre-election cabinet.

The Supreme Court is another forum to which the federal government makes appointments. The Supreme Court has achieved more authority since the Constitution Act of 1982 and the adoption of the Canadian Charter of Rights and Freedoms. Some argue that the court may be more important than parliament because it can declare laws and government decisions to be unconstitutional and in violation of the charter, as in 1988, when the court found the government's abortion law in violation of the charter (Historica Foundation of Canada 2004).

The first woman was appointed to the nine-member Supreme Court in 1982, and seven women have been appointed to the court since then. The first woman Chief Justice, Beverley McLachlin, was appointed in 2000. In October 2004, when Canada swore in two new women justices, it brought the number of acting women in the court to four. This brings a gender balance to the bench that is unprecedented, not only in Canada but also elsewhere in the world (Richer 2004: A1).

PARLIAMENTARY AND PROVINCIAL After winning the right to vote, women participated in the electoral process, but this did not translate into seats in government. In fact, the RCSW report in 1970 noted that women were almost completely absent from elected office. Between 1920 and 1970, only eighteen women were elected to the House of Commons. In the 1968 election, only one woman, Grace McInnis of the New Democratic Party, won a seat in the 264-member House. Between 1920 and 1970, only forty-nine women were elected to provincial legislatures. As of June 1970, only twelve women were members in the provincial houses. There were 134 federal and provincial elections between 1917 and June 1970; out of 6,845 people elected, only sixty-seven were women, just under 1 per cent of the total (RCSW 1970: 339).

Women's representation improved after the RCSW report. Between 1970 and 1985, the number of women elected grew slowly but steadily. Women's representation in all legislatures across the country exceeded 10 per cent by 1985. During the last fifteen years of the century, significant increases to almost 20 per cent occurred by 2000. Thus, the percentage of women elected to Canadian legislatures increased tenfold over a thirty-year period (Trimble and

Box 5.2 Is a woman a 'person'?

Under Section 24 of the British North America Act (1867), which created the 'Dominion' of Canada, any qualified person could be appointed to the Senate. After the enfranchisement of women in the early twentieth century, Canada still took the position that there was ambiguity about whether women qualified as 'persons' and chose not to appoint any women to the Senate.

In 1927, five women in the province of Alberta initiated the 'Persons Case'. They presented a petition to the federal government requesting that the Supreme Court be required to provide an interpretation of the word 'persons'. On 24 April 1928 the court ruled that 'persons' did *not* include women. Since ultimate constitutional authority at the time resided in Great Britain, the women appealed this decision to the Privy Council of the United Kingdom, where it was decided that 'persons' did, in fact, include members of the male and female sex (RCSW 1970: 338-9).

Arscott 2003: 30–31). Despite these significant gains, women's representation falls well short of equal, which makes it difficult to maintain the critical mass of elected women needed to have significant influence over public policy and political institutions. Indeed, many observers of the political process are concerned that women's level of representation has plateaued. In 1997, 20.6 per cent of elected federal parliamentarians were women. In 2000, this level of representation remained unchanged, and in the most recent Canadian elections (2004), women's representation increased by just 0.5 per cent.

The other significant political body in Canadian federal politics is the Senate, whose members are appointed. The first woman was appointed in 1930, but only after a court challenge (Box 5.2). By 1970, women comprised 4.5 per cent of the Senate. The RCSW recommended that women be appointed in greater numbers, which appears to have occurred. In 1988, women comprised 12 per cent of the Senate and in 2000 almost 37 per cent. In the second half of his term, Prime Minister Jean Chrétien (1993–2003) began appointing women in almost equal numbers to men, surpassing the numbers elected to the House of Commons: 'However, women have tended to be appointed later in life than men and to serve relatively short terms by longevity standards of that chamber' (ibid.: 32). Women's representation in the Senate and the House of Commons has increased, but Canada's diversity is still under-represented. More women

Women in Canada

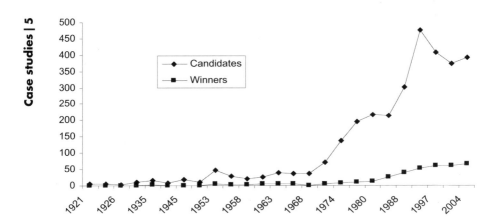

Figure 5.10 Female candidates vs female winners, House of Commons (numbers) *Source*: **Heard (2004)**

tend to be white, older (mid-forties), better educated and in professional oc-cupations than other Canadians (Trimble and Tremblay 2003).

What accounts for women's general lack of representation in Canadian politics? According to Brodie and Chandler (1991: 17), gender differences in voter turnout do not account for the limited representation of women in the House of Commons. Data taken from Canadian National Election Studies between 1965 and 2000 show that voter participation rates are virtually iden-tical by gender, but women candidates are more likely to lose than are men candidates (Figure 5.10).

The results of Canada's most recent elections have been discouraging enough for many women to now be calling for reform. A multi-partisan action group, Equal Voice: An Action Group for the Election of Women, wants the cur-rent winner-takes-all system to be replaced by a system of proportional repres-entation to give women a fairer chance at political success (<EqualVOICE. ca 2004>). A 1997 referendum that would have created gender parity in the new, predominantly Inuit, Nunavut Territory (created 1999) failed miserably, however. The plan would have allowed voters to select one candidate from a women's slate and one from a men's slate in each community. Women as much as men defeated the referendum and, in the first election, only one woman was elected to the new nineteen-person legislature – the woman who had led the fight against the gender parity referendum (Billson 2005b).

PARTY LEADERSHIP MacIvor (1996) identifies other factors that may account for lack of female representation, including the gendered division of labour at home and at work. Because of this, women are less likely to work in the high-status, high-paying jobs from which politicians are drawn. MacIvor also identifies sexism in the political parties and the masculine nature of conventional politics as other factors that tend to keep women on the sidelines. The low number of winning candidates may have to do more with party structures and parties not choosing to run women for winnable seats rather than the appeal of women candidates per se.

PARTICIPATION IN RELIGIOUS INSTITUTIONS The influence of religion in Canada has changed significantly over the century. A country that was predominantly Protestant and Catholic has been transformed into today's multicultural, multi-religious or non-religious community. In the last few decades, the number of persons identifying with the Catholic faith increased slightly; those identifying with the Protestant faiths decreased, and there has been an increase in those who report no religious preference or allegiance to non-Christian religions (Mori 1990). Attendance at services and other religious activities is dropping, especially among people under the age of forty-five (Bibby 2000). Those who do attend are older and widowed people, and more women than men are active in religious activities: 40 per cent of women and 32 per cent of men stated that they attended services at least once a month in 1990.

Non-Christian traditions are also increasing in Canada, which will shape how female identity is defined and female roles are delineated. For example, numbers of Buddhists increased by 84 per cent from 1991 to 2001; Hindus and Sikhs increased by 89 per cent; and Muslims doubled in this period. These groups report greater importance of religion and demonstrate a more active involvement in their faith activities than the Christian groups. A study by Janhevich and Ibrahim (2004) showed that the percentage of those who report participation in religious activities at least once a week varies by religion: Muslims 42 per cent, Sikhs 32 per cent, Protestants 28 per cent and Catholics 25 per cent.

Women more than men are active religious participants, but they did not hold religious leadership positions until 1951 (though for many decades Roman Catholic nuns were the primary teachers of children in Quebec). For many denominations, women were not permitted to act as clergy until recently: Anglicans ordained the first woman in 1976 (Prentice et al. 1996).

Artistic, creative and cultural contributions

'CANADIAN' CULTURE AND IDENTITY Defining 'culture' is extremely problematic for a century during which Canada became a multi-ethnic, post-industrial society. Many elements go into what Pierre Berton (1987: 9) calls the 'mucilage' that holds the country together. For Canadians, culture, both high and low, is an essential aspect of identity, especially given the tendency to define Canada in contrast to the USA. The government has used funding, legislation and organization to preserve and protect Canadian culture. The North American Free Trade Agreement specifically excludes Canadian culture, as the government insisted that federal funding of cultural industries should be non-negotiable, even in a trade treaty (Thompson 1995).

Today, Canadians point with pride to the long list of internationally known Canadian artists and performers (for example, Margaret Atwood, Carol Shields, Margaret Lawrence, Celine Dion, Shania Twain, Alanis Morissette, k. d. lang, several hockey teams, Cirque de Soleil, and even Peter Jennings). Yet, as in other countries, much of women's culture was not recorded in malestream history and much was discounted as unimportant – handiwork, for example. Direct barriers were placed on many cultural producers because of gender, going back to women who later became recognized for their enormous contribution to Canadian culture (Box 5.3).

As Scott See (2001) notes, several institutions crucial to Canada's cultural future had their roots in the Depression. First, with the spread of radio (including US programmes broadcast into Canada), a conscious decision was made to design a federally funded broadcaster to link the vast nation: the forerunner to the Canadian Broadcasting Corporation was founded in 1932 and the National Film Board was established in 1939. Further efforts to promote and protect Canada's culture included the establishment of the Canada Council in the 1950s, which funded artists, musicians and writers. Women artists, however, already marginalized, were further disadvantaged by regulations that made distinctions (and funding decisions) based on a division between traditional crafts (female) and art (male) (Prentice et al. 1996). On the other hand, the *Refus Global* in 1948, a manifesto calling on artists in Quebec to express themselves as part of the modern age, meant that Quebec became an active centre for abstract art, particularly that of women artists (ibid.).

THE PRESENCE OF WOMEN From the 1940s onwards, women played major roles in the arts as fund-raisers, writers, actors and feminists. They formed theatre companies, ballets and a women's symphony in Montreal. The first solo exhibition of work of a living Canadian woman at the National Gallery of Art, Joyce Waveland, took place in 1971, and focused explicitly on women's history and experiences (ibid.).

With the major increase in education in the 1960s and 1970s, the market for literature expanded. In English Canada, the themes focused on survival,

Box 5.3 Emily Carr: the struggle for artistic recognition

Emily Carr (1871–1945), artist and writer, was isolated from mainstream acceptance for most of her career. In spite of her brilliance and prolific output, she gave herself the nickname 'Small'. She was an independent woman and a Westerner (born in Victoria, British Columbia), at a time when independent women were anomalous. She was considered eccentric, perhaps because she lived in her 'House of All Sorts' with numerous cats, dogs, birds and her monkey, Woo.

Carr studied art in Paris, London and San Francisco, but as of 1913, after many years of path-breaking painting, she still had to supplement her income by growing vegetables, making pottery and taking in boarders. Even her sisters ignored or condemned her progressive images of Native Canadian scenes: 'Having so few pupils, I had much time for study. When I got out my Northern sketches and worked on them I found that I had grown. Many of these old Indian sketches I made into large canvases. Nobody bought my pictures; I had no pupils; therefore I could not afford to keep on the studio. I decided to give it up and to go back to Victoria. My sisters disliked my new work intensely. One was noisy in her condemnation, one sulkily silent, one indifferent to every kind of Art' (Carr 1946).

In 1927, Carr was finally invited to exhibit her work in Ottawa, where she met Lawren Harris, one of the prestigious 'Canadian Group of Seven' whose work had inspired her for years. Although her paintings by any measure fit into the Group of Seven style, which centred on evocative, stylistic renderings of Canadian scenery (especially of the north), admitting her into the illustrious all-male Group was not entertained. Meeting Harris rekindled her spirit and confidence, however, so Carr returned to her first love with renewed vigour: painting the images of ancient totem poles and haunting trees in northern British Columbia and the Queen Charlotte Islands. Harris encouraged Carr through letters until her death.

Although she was never officially admitted to the inner circle, in 1932 Emily Carr became a charter member of the Canadian Group of Painters, after the Group of Seven disbanded. Slowly, Emily Carr's work was recognized as a monumental contribution to Canadian culture. Her first solo exhibition (at the Vancouver Art Gallery) finally occurred in 1938. She was sixty-seven years old.

Carr did not begin to write until the age of seventy, after her second heart attack. Her first effort, *Klee Wych*, won the coveted Governor General's

Literary Award. Playing on her nickname, she wrote *The Book of Small*, which became the Canadian Book of the Year in 1942. Just before she died in 1945, Carr finished her autobiography, *Growing Pains*, a title that reflected the difficulties she had experienced as a woman breaking into the artistic community. Her struggle is emblematic of so many women born at the dawn of the twentieth century, such as her contemporary, poet E. Pauline Johnson, who also found acceptance late in life.

Three days before she died, Carr learned that the University of British Columbia had decided to grant her an honorary Doctor of Letters. Today, there is no question about the quality of Emily Carr's work. The Vancouver School of Art became the Emily Carr Institute in 1978; her paintings fill galleries across Canada. Ironically, her work is often shown in conjunction with the Group of Seven: 'She will always be remembered as one of Canada's most talented artists' (Collections Canada 2004). (*Janet Mancini Billson*)

resistance, and women as exemplars of the country, with particular sensitivity to region, ethnicity and gender (Finkel et al. 1993). In Quebec, the Quiet Revolution, the secularization and expansion of education and the increase in nationalism produced a new literature of modernity and new ways to express identity, many led by women's art. Although Quebec had been modernizing since the turn of the century, this was at a slower pace than in the rest of Canada. In the decade 1960–70, a new government transformed the social and political face of society, introducing a civil service and new government-sponsored social programmes. The power of the Church declined. The development of 'Can Lit' (Canadian Literature) courses in the 1970s was led by women who celebrated their womanhood and Canada's diversity.

Both federal and provincial governments fund a variety of cultural enterprises, which range from libraries to heritage resources to performing and visual arts. Recently this funding has slowed (SC 2004c). Employment growth in cultural industries seems to have peaked in 2001. Today, musicians are the largest group of cultural producers. In 1995, women musicians' income was $20,162 per year while men's incomes averaged $31, 917 (SC 2001).

Hockey, 'Canada's Religion' (See 2001), was introduced in schools in 1915. By the 1920s, women's teams were participating in provincial and dominion championships, but during the post-Second World War rise in domesticity, women's

TABLE 5.2 Cultural participation by gender (numbers)

		1901	1941	1951	1961	1971	1981	1991	2001
Religious leaders	F			272	301	700	1,610	2,290	5,420
	M			16,097	18,623	17,930	20,415	20,925	21,845
Teachers (elem./sec.)	F	21,164	55,970	74,319	118,807	120,160	197,160	116,885	294,755
	M	6,205	19,417	28,259	49,219	25,900	113,570	125,040	118,195
Educators (higher ed.)	F		n	812	2,366	3,915	8,125	9,750	16,665
	M			4,610	8,779	19,540	25,200	31,545	30,220
Musicians	F		8,023	4,598	6,802	2,430	3,245	13,440	13,310
	M		3,435	3,435	4,469	6,645	9,160	11,675	16,795
Artists	F		63	479	834	3,610	3,610	3,110	24,875
	M		87	631	1,454	4,275	4,275	45,665	21,345
Conductors	F						215	391	755
	M						730	1,175	1,620
TV Announcers	F			64	111	255	1,080	1,935	2,485
	M			948	1,552	2,268	4,755	7,210	6,120

Sources: Census Office (1901: 2); Government of Canada (1993).

team sports generally fell out of favour. After the RCSW report, concern for women's lack of equal participation in sport led to the first National Conference on Women and Sport in 1974. Considerable growth in women's team sports ensued, including a female hockey team. Females suffer inequities in participation, coaching, organizations and sports journalism, however (especially minority and francophone women) (Status of Women Canada 2002). Other opportunities expanded for women as a result of the RCSW. For example, the prestigious Studio D of the National Film Board was established in 1974 to make films by and about the condition of women (Status of Women Canada 2002).

Women participate in the culture of Canada in a number of ways, from formal production to their influence through voluntary and waged employment, but in Table 5.2 many cells are empty until 1941. Women either did not formally participate or were not counted in many of the cultural production fields until mid to late century.

A significant number of women faculty members did not appear until the 1980s; although there has been continued growth in the professoriate, women still lag significantly behind. Across all university faculties today, women represent 33.9 per cent and are paid at 85.3 per cent of the level of men's wages (Robbins et al. 2004). Men continue in positions of power and authority in the academy.

Towards the future

Social and cultural movements have been characterized as 'three steps forward and two steps back'. Canada in the twentieth century can be described in this way as well. Although women's participation in education has increased tremendously, many groups of women have remained disadvantaged as their sisters advance: immigrant women, First Nations women, rural women, some visible minority women, and women of the working classes. History shows us that in time of social or economic crises there is a reversion to traditional norms of behaviour for women; this was true during the post-war periods and the economic stress of the 1980s. Despite tremendous gains for women in higher education and the professions, men still dominate the advanced degrees and high-paying fields. A continued structural lack of acceptance of women in positions of power, in both the academy and the workforce, reveals itself in all fields. Sexism and gender violence characterize educational and economic institutions, and confining gender norms, while continually challenged by brave women (and some men), still persist. Trends towards equality of opportunity and social acceptance for broader female roles are counterbalanced by inequities that negatively affect all Canadians.

Given the current rhetoric of 'inclusion' and 'equal rights', it seems likely that individual women in Canadian society will be given the opportunity to make outstanding and notable contributions to Canadian life. Women achieving the position of CEO in large organizations, being appointed to serve on the Supreme Court, writing the great Canadian novel or being named to the presidency of a Canadian university may all come to be less remarkable because of the gender of the achiever. The picture for women as a whole may be much more mixed, but many areas look hopeful. Gender equity depends on practices and public policies that utilize new ways of defining goals and measuring success.

Women and men are gradually renegotiating the traditional division of labour in the home. Unfortunately, although considerably more gender balance exists in school attendance at all levels, there is less balance in programmes, opportunities and occupations pursued. Combined with global pressures on the Canadian economy, this may mean the continued over-representation of women in part-time work and a limited number of female-dominated occupations. If this pattern continues, we will not see a significant narrowing of the wage gap between men and women; most women living on their own will find their economic circumstances challenging. Consequently, areas of women's lives that are tied to economic well-being, such as health status, victimization and criminality, are not likely to improve significantly.

In sum, the future for Canadian women holds promise for those whose achievements are recognized at the highest levels. For the majority of Canadian women, daily life may show modest improvements but diligence will be needed in order to avoid social backsliding. The struggle for gender equality and female well-being that began in the nineteenth century and dominated the twentieth will surely continue well into this century as well.

Note

1 We would like to thank Suzanne Shiel, of the Populations Studies Centre (UWO), for her help in collecting data for this chapter, and the library staff at UWO and St Lawrence University for their support.

References

Beaujot, R. (2000) *Earning and Caring in Canadian Families*, Peterborough: Broadview Press

Beaujot, R. and D. Kerr (2004) *Population Change in Canada*, Toronto: Oxford University Press

Beaujot, R. and J. Liu (2005) 'Models of time use in paid and unpaid work', *Journal of Family Issues*, forthcoming

Beaujot, R. and A. Muhammad (2005) 'Transformed families and the basis for child-bearing', forthcoming in K. McQuillan and Z. Ravanera (eds), *Canada's Changing Families*, Toronto: University of Toronto Press

Becker, G. (1981) *A Treatise on the Family*, Cambridge: Harvard University Press

Berton, P. (1987) *Why We Act Like Canadians*, Markham: McClelland and Stewart

Bibby, R. W. (2000) 'The persistence of Christian religious identification in Canada', *Canadian Social Trends 3*, Toronto: Thompson Educational Publishing

Billson, J. M. (2005a) *Keepers of the Culture: Women and Power in the Canadian Mosaic*, Boulder, CO: Rowman & Littlefield

— (2005b) *Inuit Women: Their Powerful Spirit in a Century of Change*, Boulder, CO: Rowman & Littlefield

Boutilier, M. (1977) 'Transformation of ideology surrounding the sexual division of labour: Canadian women during World War II', paper presented at the Second Conference on Blue-Collar Workers, London, Ontario

Brodie, J. and C. Chandler (1991) 'Women and electoral process in Canada', in K. Megyery (ed.), *Women in Canadian Politics: Toward Equity in Representation*, Toronto: Dundurn Press

Bunge, V. P. and J. Sauvé (2002) 'Declines in spousal homicide', *Family Violence in Canada: A Statistical Profile*, Ottawa: SC Catalogue no. 85-224-XIE

Burgess, E. W., H. Locke and M. Thomas (1963) *The Family: From Institution to Companionship*, New York: American

Caldwell, J. (1999) 'The delayed Western fertility decline in English-speaking countries', *Population and Development Review*, 25(3): 479–514

Carr, E. (1946) *Growing Pains: The Autobiography of Emily Carr,* Toronto: Oxford University Press

Census Office (1901, 1906) *Fourth Census of Canada, 1901, 4, Vital Statistics; School Attendance; Educational Status; Dwellings and Families; Institutions, Churches and Schools; Electoral Districts and Representation*, Ottawa: The Census Office

Charles, E. (1948) *The Changing Size of the Family in Canada*, Ottawa: Dominion Bureau of Statistics, 8th Census, 1941

Citizenship and Immigration (2002) *Facts and Figures 2001: Immigration Overview*, Ottawa: Citizenship and Immigration

Clio Collective (1987) *Quebec Women: A History*, Toronto: Women's Press

Cooper, S. (1993) 'The evolution of the federal women's prison', in E. Adelberg and C. Currie (eds), *Conflict with the Law*, Vancouver: Press Gang Publishers

Creese, G. and B. Beagan (2004) 'Gender at work: strategies for equality in neo-liberal times', J. Curtis et al. (eds), *Social Inequality in Canada*, 4th edn, Toronto: Pearson Education Canada

Crompton, S. and L. Geran (1995) 'Women as main breadwinners', *Perspectives on Labour and Income*, 7(4): 26–9

Dagenais, D. (2000) *La fin de la famille moderne*, Quebec: Presses de l'Université Laval

Finkel, A., M. Conrad and V. Strong-Boag (1993) *History of the Canadian Peoples: 1867 to Present*, Toronto: Copp Clark Pitman

Folbre, N. (2000) 'Sleeping Beauty awakes: feminism and fertility decline in the 20th century', paper presented at meetings of the Population Association of America, Los Angeles, 23–25 March

Ford, D. and F. Nault (1996) 'Changing fertility patterns, 1974 to 1994', *Health Reports*, 8(3): 39–46

FPTMRSW (Federal-Provincial-Territorial Ministers Responsible for the Status of Women) (2002) *Assessing Violence Against Women: A Statistical Profile*, Ottawa: Catalogue no. SW21-101/2002E-IN

Friedan, B. (1963) *The Feminine Mystique*, New York: Norton

Giddens, A. (1991) *Modernity and Self-Identity: Self and Society in the Late Modern Age*, Cambridge, Polity Press

Goldscheider, F. and L. J. Waite (1986) 'Sex differences in the entry into marriage', *American Journal of Sociology*, 92(1): 91–109

Gunderson, M., L. Muszynski and J. Keck (1990) *Women and Labour Market Poverty*, Ottawa: Canadian Advisory Committee on the Status of Women

Guppy, N. and S. Davies (1998) *Education in Canada: Recent Trends and Future Challenges*, Ottawa: Statistics Canada

Harris, C. C. (1983) *The Family and Industrial Society*, London: George Allen and Unwin

Henripin, J. (1968) *Tendances et facteurs de la fécondité au Canada*, Ottawa: Federal Bureau of Statistics

Historica Foundation of Canada (2004) 'Supreme Court of Canada', *The Canadian Encyclopedia*, <www.thecanadianencyclopedia.com>

Janhevich, D. and H. Ibrahim (2004) 'Muslims in Canada: an illustrative and demographic profile', *Our Diverse Cities*, 1, spring

Johnson, H. (2002) 'Methods of Measurement', *Violence Against Women: New Canadian Perspectives*, K. M. J. McKenna and J. Larkin (eds), Toronto: Ianna Publications and Education

Johnson, H. and K. Rodgers (1993) 'A statistical overview of women and crime in Canada', in E. Adelberg and C. Currie (eds), *Conflict with the Law*, Vancouver: Press Gang Publishers

Krahn, H. J. and G. S. Lowe (1993) *Work, Industry and Canadian Society*, 2nd edn, Scarborough, Ontario: Nelson Canada

— (2002) *Work, Industry and Canadian Society*, 4th edn, Scarborough, Ontario: Nelson

Leacy, F. H. (1983) *Historical Statistics of Canada*, 2nd edn, Ottawa: Supply and Services Canada

McVey, W. and W. Kalbach (1995) *Canadian Population*, Toronto: Nelson

MacIvor, H. (1996) *Women and Politics in Canada*, Peterborough, Ontario: Broadview Press

Marshall, K. (1996) 'A job to die for', *Perspectives on Labour and Income*, 8: 26–31

— (1998) 'Stay-at-home dads', *Perspectives on Labour and Income*, 10(1): 9–15

McDonald, P. (2000) 'Gender equity in theories of fertility', *Population and Development Review*, 26(3): 427–39

Mensah, J. (2002) *Black Canadians: History, Experiences, Social Conditions*, Halifax: Fernwood

Milan, A. (2000) 'One hundred years of family', *Canadian Social Trends*, 56: 2–12

Mongeau, J., G. Neill and C. Le Bourdais (2001) 'Effet de la précarité économique sur la formation d'une première union au Canada', *Cahiers québécois de démographie*, 30(1): 3–28

Mori, G. A. (1990) 'Religious affiliation in Canada', *Canadian Social Trends* 1, Toronto: Thompson Educational Publishers

Nagnur, D. (1986) *Longevity and Historical Life Tables 1921–1981, Canada and the Provinces*, Ottawa: Statistics Canada, Catalogue no. 89-506

Normand, J. (2000) 'Education of women in Canada', *Canadian Social Trends*, 3, Toronto: Thompson Educational Publishing

Oppenheimer, V. (1988) 'A theory of marriage timing: assortative mating under varying degrees of uncertainty', *American Journal of Sociology*, 94: 563–91

— (1997) 'Women's employment and the gain to marriage: the specialization and trading model', *Annual Review of Sociology*, 23: 431–53

Pelletier, A. J., F. D. Thompson and A. Rochon (1938) *The Canadian Family, 1931 Census Monograph, No. 7*, Ottawa: King's Printer

Péron, Y. (1999) 'The evolution of census families from 1971 to 1991', in Y. Péron (ed.), *Canadian Families at the Approach of the Year 2000*, Ottawa: Statistics Canada, Catalogue no. 96-321-MPE no. 4

Phillips, P. and E. Phillips (2000) *Women and Work*, Toronto: James Lorimer

Prentice, A. et al. (1996) *Canadian Women: A History*, Toronto: Harcourt Brace

RCSW (Royal Commission on the Status of Women) (1970) *Report*, Ottawa: Queen's Printer

Richer, S. (2004) 'Supreme Court gender balance unprecedented', *Toronto Globe and Mail*, 25 August

Roussel, L. (1979) 'Générations nouvelles et mariage traditionnel', *Population*, 34(1): 141–62

Savoie, J. (2001) 'Crime statistics in Canada', *Juristat*, Ottawa: Statistics Canada, Catalogue no. 85-002-XIE

SC (Statistics Canada) (n.d.) *Culture*, Municipal Expenditures on Culture, Catalogue No. 87-206

— (1901, 1911, 1921, 1931, 1941, 1951, 1961, 1971, 1981, 1991, 2001), *Census of Canada*, Ottawa: Statistics Canada

— (1932, 1992, 2001, 2000) *Canada Year Book*, Ottawa: Statistics Canada

— (1990) *Women in Canada,* 2nd edn, Ottawa: Statistics Canada

— (1992) *Selected Marriage Statistics*, 1921–90, Ottawa: Statistics Canada, Catalogue no. 82-553

— (1993) *Selected Birth and Fertility Statistics*, Canada, 1921–90, Ottawa: Statistics Canada, Catalogue no. 82-553

— (1994) *Selected Mortality Statistics*, Canada, 1921–90, Ottawa: Statistics Canada, Catalogue no. 82-548

— (1995) *Women in Canada*, 3rd edn, Ottawa: Statistics Canada

— (2000) *Women in Canada 2000: A Gender-Based Statistical Report*, Ottawa: Statistics Canada Cat. no. 89-503

— (2001a) *Income in Canada*, Ottawa: Statistics Canada, Catalogue no. 75-202-XIE

— (2001b) *Canadian Crime Statistics*, Ottawa: Statistics Canada, Catalogue no. 85-205

— (2002a) *Marital Status of Canadians*, 2001 Census, Ottawa: Statistics Canada, Catalogue no. 97F0004XCB01040

— (2002b) *Changing Conjugal Life in Canada*, Ottawa: Statistics Canada, Catalogue no. 89-576-XIE

— (2003) 'University enrolment by age groups', *The Daily*, Ottawa: Statistics Canada

— (2003a) 'Deaths', *The Daily*, 25 September, Ottawa: Statistics Canada

— (2004a) *Women in Canada: Work Chapter Updates 2003*, Ottawa: Statistics Canada, Catalogue no. 89F0133XIE

— (2004c) 'Government expenditures on culture', *Focus on Culture*, 14(3), 7 January

SCHWSA (Standing Committee on Health, Welfare, and Social Affairs, House of Commons) (1991) *The War Against Women*, Ottawa: Ministry of Supply and Services

See, S. (2001) *The History of Canada*, Westwood: Greenwood Press

Simpson, J. (2004) 'Not exactly a brave new Cabinet', *Toronto Globe and Mail*, 21 July

Skolnick, A. (1987) *The Intimate Environment*, Boston: Little, Brown

Thompson, J. H. (1995) 'Canada's quest for cultural sovereignty: protection, promotion and popular culture', in S. J. Randall and H. W. Konrad (eds), *NAFTA in Transition*, Calgary: University of Calgary Press

Thornton, A. (2001) 'The developmental paradigm: reading history sideways, and family change', *Demography*, 38(4): 449-65

Trimble, L. and J. Arscott (2003) *Still Counting: Women in Politics Across Canada*, Peterborough: Broadview Press

Trimble, L. and M. Tremblay (2003) 'Women politicians in Canada's parliament and legislatures, 1917–2000: a socio-demographic profile', in M. Tremblay and L. Trimble (eds), *Women and Electoral Politics in Canada*, Don Mills: Oxford University Press

Turcotte, P. and F. Goldscheider (1998) 'The evolution of factors influencing first union formation in Canada', *Canadian Studies in Population*, 25(2): 145–74

UNDP (United Nations Development Programme) (2003) 'Human Development Indicators 2003', *Human Development Reports*, New York: UNDP

Urquhart, M. C. and K. A. H. Buckley (eds) (1965) *Historical Statistics of Canada*, Toronto: Macmillan

Veevers, J. E. (1980) *Childless by Choice*, Toronto: Butterworth

Wargon, S. (1979) *Canadian Households and Families*, Ottawa: Statistics Canada, Catalogue no. 99-753

Wisenthal, M. (1983) 'Education', *Historical Statistics of Canada*, Ottawa: Statistics Canada

Websites

Canadian Heritage (2004) 'Sport participation in Canada', <www.pch.gc.ca>

Collections Canada (2004) <www.collectionscanada.ca>

Correctional Services of Canada (1995) Regional Facilities for Women Offenders, <www.csc-scc.gc.ca>

Equal Voice: An Action Group for the Election of Women (2004) <EqualVoice.ca>

Heard, A. (2004) Canadian Elections, <www.sfu.ca>

Hockey Canada (2002) 'Female hockey statistics', <www.canadianhockey.ca>

Income Security Advocacy Centre (2003) 'The Attorney General of Canada v. Kelly Lesiuk', <www.incomesecurity.org>

McFarlane, B. (n.d.) 'Women's hockey: a proud past, a bright future', <www.collectionscanada.ca>

Robbins, W., M. Ollivier and R. Morgan (2004) 'Ivory towers: feminist audits', <www. fedcan.ca/engish/policyandadvocacy>

SC (Statistics Canada) (2004b) <www.statcan.ca>, Daily, 9 November

Status of Women Canada (2002) 'Women's History Month 2002, Adult Fact Sheet: Women and Sports in Canada', <www.swc-cfc.gc.ca/dates whm/2002>

6 | Women in Colombia: 'you forge your path as you walk'

ELENA GARCÉS DE EDER WITH
ADRIANA MARULANDA HERRÁN

Why do they shut me out of Heaven? Did I sing – too loud?
Emily Dickinson

Colombia lies on the north-western coast of South America. Totalling 439,737 square miles, it is bounded by Venezuela, Panama, Ecuador, Peru and Brazil. The country is part of one of the three Latin American regions that begin in Mexico and end with Tierra del Fuego at the tip of Argentina, near Antarctica. The inhabitants of Latin America, north, central and south, come from all races of the world including, first, the Aborigines or indigenous people, then the Caucasians or Europeans, Africans, Arabs, Asians and the children of these races who have intermarried throughout time. Latin America is a melting pot of races with a population in excess of 430 million inhabitants who share the Mediterranean culture, the Catholic religion at large and, with the exception of Portuguese-speaking Brazil, Spanish as their mother tongue.

The historical context

The Spanish colonizers named the upper region of South America 'New Granada'. After the wars of independence (1870) the name was changed to Colombia. Cultural upheaval brought about by the colonizers set the rules for later participation by women in Colombia. Asunción Lavrin sees the sixteenth century as the crucible for later social and cultural differences between Colombian men and women: '[Colombia was] a pre-capitalist new world in which the encounter of several cultures produced important cleavages in culture concepts of family and social orders. New forms of familial and personal relationships developed in the fissures created by the confrontation and eventual adaptation of conquered and conqueror to each other' (1987: 110).

The white male Spaniards (*conquistadores*) brought with them their own customs and civil and religious laws. When they encountered the indigenous people in the New Kingdom of Spain, they tried to influence them with their European customs and Catholic religion. The civil laws of Spain are solidly based on Christian doctrine. The Spaniards were convinced they were to conquer the world so that they could Christianize the heathen; it was a holy war

133

in the name of the Christian God. For the indigenous people of Colombia, the arrival of the Spanish *conquistadores* was marked by human calamities and spiritual distress. The men brought with them illness, death and destruction of innumerable Indian cultures.

The political context

Colombia has the oldest democracy in Latin America, but violence permeates the country's social, political and economic arenas. The situation is unstable because of warfare that has plagued Colombia for more than thirty years. Forty years ago, two Marxist guerrilla groups, the Fuerzas Armadas de Colombia (FARC) and the Ejército de Liberación Nacional, started fighting for a more just and equal society. Later, forgetting their ideological commitment, they became the most infamous drug dealers in the world, making them feared as drug terrorists. Auto Defensas Unidas de Colombia, a right-wing paramilitary group, has been fighting the guerrillas, competing with them in the drug trafficking business and spreading terror. The Colombian army fights these three groups, contributing to a never-ending fratricidal confrontation that makes Colombia one of the most violent countries on earth – fed by worldwide drug consumption.

From the 1960s until today, the drug wars between guerrillas, paramilitaries and the Colombian army have created a general atmosphere of danger, terror and death that magnifies, undoubtedly, the traditional oppression and subordination of females. Every year in Colombia, 30,000 people die because of the war with the insurgents. Decades of fraternal warring have resulted in greater suffering for women and children in a country submerged in a chaotic social atmosphere. Tied to the seemingly endless armed conflict is great economic poverty that degrades the well-being of any person's life. The United Nations High Commissioner for Human Rights in Bogotá describes this conflict as demoralizing for the population, since it continuously affects the economic and social rights of Colombians. Poverty and social injustice increase daily with the armed conflict. Displacement has a devastating effect, particularly as regards the rights of vulnerable groups such as women, peasants and rural citizens, among whom the war is most aggressively fought.

Thus, the situation for Colombian women was still far from favourable at the end of the twentieth century, in spite of apparent progress in legislation, education, employment and healthcare. It is in this context that we understand the fate of Colombian women in the twentieth century.

The social context

The situations that adversely affect Colombian women include relationships with men that are based on political, legal and religious laws; patriarchal cultural values; socio-economic conditions that challenge survival and decent living; and a cult of machismo, the cult of virility and male dominance. Even everyday language reflects machismo, and the degradation of women that it causes. For example, when a man likes a woman, he might say, '*Esta vieja, está tan buena que me la voy a comer!*' ('This chick is so good that I will eat her up' – meaning to have sex with her).

Women's lives in Latin American countries are still heavily influenced by gender role asymmetry. Hierarchy and gender stratification – the results of patriarchal ideology – are blended with machismo's male philosophy, which is based on honour, shame and protection of the virginity of young women (Schneider 1971: 1). Machismo permeates Colombian society. It shapes male and female identity, social imagination, gender relations, family structures, the education of girls, and opportunities for women. Lavrin argues that traditional relations between the sexes deeply affect female existence within the social, political and private spheres of the Latin nations (1987: 110–11). From an early age, the differences between boys and girls are accentuated through many forms of differential socialization influenced by machismo, a legacy left by 800 years of Moorish cultural influence in Spain and transported to the New World with the Spanish conquerors (Pitt-Rivers 1966: 45).

The counterpart of machismo is marianismo, which is equally prevalent. This 'cult of feminine spiritual superiority ... teaches that women are semi-divine, morally superior to and spiritually stronger than men' (Schneider 1971: 91). This dual ideology creates a division among women – those who are good and those who are bad, Mary and Eve – that has helped to objectify women as the 'other', making them less than human, which lays another foundation stone for sexism. By understanding how these two myths – that of the Virgin Mary as a pure, selfless being and Eve as a temptress and bad woman – have manipulated women's lives women in Colombia we will be able to shatter these images and change their destinies by consciously abandoning a fate that tends to obscure their existence.

A demographic portrait of Colombian women

Unfortunately, statistics are scarce on gender participation in the social, economic and political agendas of Colombian life. The national institute for statistics in Colombia, Departamento Administrativo Nacional de Estadisticas (DANE), is not very thorough on women's participation in the labour force,

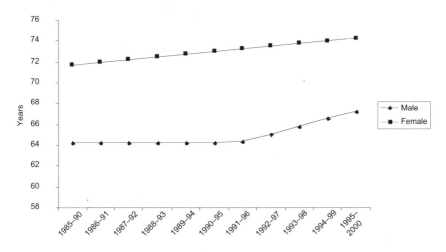

Figure 6.1 Life expectancy by gender 1985–2002
Source: **DANE (2004)**

literacy and education, reproductive health services, and political and public
posts, especially before 1950. Nevertheless, we present available statistical data
to outline the basic picture of female well-being in Colombia.

Urbanization It is significant that in 2000, 74 per cent of the population lived
in urban areas and 26 per cent lived in rural areas (DNP 2000). The war has
displaced millions of Colombians from the countryside. It is estimated that
between 1996 and July 2004, 3,100,000 people were displaced, of which 50 per
cent are women.

Life expectancy In 1999, life expectancy was 74.1 for women and 68.1 for men
(Figure 6.1). This is one area in which women have had a distinct advantage
(about eight years more of life); in recent years, men's life expectancy has improved at a higher rate than female life expectancy.

Population growth, fertility rate and male–female ratio The Colombian population multiplied tenfold between 1900 and 2000, with the largest jump occurring in the relative prosperity of the two decades after the Second World War.
The population is growing at an annual rate of 1.7 per cent (as of 2000). The
birth rate continues to decline (Figure 6.2). Only the census of 1940 shows a predominance of males (50.5 per cent), suggesting that the depression of the 1930s
affected females more than males. The population now stands at 42,321,000,
with 50.6 per cent females, although other reliable statistics say that females
comprise 52 per cent and males 49.5 per cent (a result of the armed conflict).

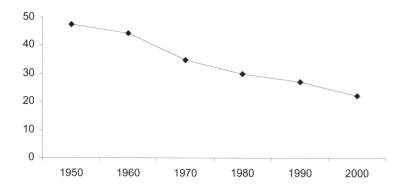

Figure 6.2 Birth rate (per 1,000 women)
Source: **CEPAL (2001)**

The fertility rate in 1950 was 6.7 per thousand, and then started to fall until 2000, when it reached 2.0 in younger women and 2.6 in older women (Figure 6.3). The average age of females at birth of first child was twenty-two in 2000.

Age structure of the population At the end of the twentieth century, 33 per cent of the population was below the age of fifteen; 60 per cent between fifteen and sixty-four; and 7 per cent over the age of sixty-four.

Maternal mortality rate In 1940, the maternal mortality rate stood at 2,198 per 100,000 women (Figure 6.4). Maternal deaths dropped each decade to a low of seventy-one in 2000, primarily through improvements in educational levels for females. Women in Colombia today have more knowledge about

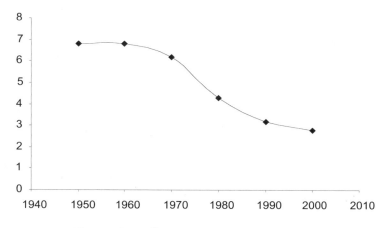

Figure 6.3 Fertility rate 1940–2000 (per 1,000)
Source: **CEPAL (2001)**

Women in Colombia

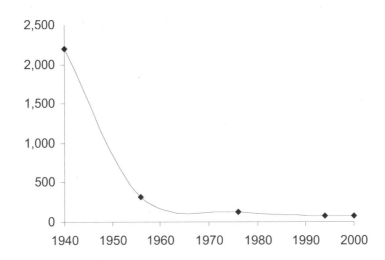

Figure 6.4 Maternal mortality rate (per 100,000) 1940–2000 *Source*: **Report from the Women's Net, presented to the Colombian Senate in 2001**

healthcare in general, more access to hospital delivery (for women in urban areas) and better-trained midwives (for women in rural areas). Nevertheless, compared to that of other developing countries, the rate is still high because of poor access to pre-natal and institutional obstetric care (UNICEF 2003). At 15 per cent, abortion is the second-highest cause of maternal deaths each year (Cabal et al. 2001: 492; Murdock 2003).

Infant mortality rate Statistics are available for infant mortality only since 1940, when it was 142 per 1,000 live births. The rate dropped steadily through-out the century to approximately 41 in 1985 and 30 per 1,000 as of 2000, because of better medical care, but it is still higher in rural areas (DANE 2004). Another threat to children is the persistent conflict that plagues the country-side, the villages and even the cities (Box 6.1).

Contraception and abortion Reproductive rights are not an issue unless the right to become a mother is at stake. The situation changes if the woman wishes not to have the child because 'the courts have emphatically affirmed the constitutionality of the prohibition of abortion' (Cabal et al. 2001: 19). That is, the Colombian Constitutional Court protects the rights of the fetus before the mother's rights, even if the woman was raped, underwent non-consensual artificial insemination, or becomes dangerously ill because of the pregnancy. This limits her reproductive autonomy.

Colombian statistics on contraception and abortion are vague. As of 1970,

Box 6.1 *Threats to the well-being of children in Colombia (UNICEF 2003)*

Child soldiers: It is estimated that 6,000 to 7,000 children have been recruited by illegal armed groups. The government deals with released children through the Colombian Institute for Family Welfare. UNICEF has been working for the release of children from all illegal groups through the Church and other grassroots organizations, and is supporting the social reintegration of released children. Over six hundred children have been released during the last three years. UNICEF is also promoting an integrated preventive approach focusing on two actions that should significantly reduce child recruitment: improving education and addressing the economic situation of families with children aged seven to sixteen.

Landmines: UNICEF is providing technical and financial support to a plan of action approved by the government. Municipalities affected by landmines have increased from 125 in 1999 to nearly 500 in 2002. Nearly 20 per cent of victims are under eighteen.

Kidnapped children: In 2002, nearly 300 children were kidnapped in Colombia.

27.5 per cent of Colombian women were using some form of contraception. Contraception use increased dramatically to 76 per cent in 2000, as more women gained access to higher education – even though the practice is contrary to the teaching of the Catholic Church. Indirectly, the Church promotes abortion by condemning birth control. The means of birth control available to large segments of the population are not reliable and are often difficult to obtain. The Instituto Colombiano de Bienestar Familiar (ICBF), responsible for the government's birth control programme, helps women only to space their pregnancies and does not reach a great number of Colombian women.

An estimated 365,000 women undergo abortions every year in Colombia. A quarter of all women between the ages of fifteen and fifty-five (29.9 per cent) and one third of all women in this age group who have been pregnant say that they have had at least one induced abortion. Public debate in the media took place in 2001 when the Catholic Church announced that if a woman in Colombia underwent an abortion, she and the person who performed the medical procedure would be excommunicated. The woman can also be imprisoned if found guilty. The law punishes the person who performs the abortion (and involvement can be difficult to prove) but not the father of the child (ibid.:

67). Both the Church and the law agree that the man should escape sanction; secular and religious laws are thus intertwined.

Family status and structure

Three family types lie at the foundation of Colombia's culture: the patriarchal family; the indigenous Amerindian family and the African-Colombian family.

The patriarchal family Simone de Beauvoir (1952) argued that in early times men and women participated equally in the construction of daily life. Later, with the beginning of agriculture, the domestication of animals and the genesis of private property, female status changed. Patriarchal rule determined the legal and religious laws that shaped women's destinies. Private property and inheritance gave absolute power to men, denying women the possibility of owning anything, even their own bodies. Like land, animals and slaves, women have been owned in societies with modes of production that benefit property and the rule of the father/patriarch, to whose authority they were subjected (Lerner 1986).

The Spanish women who later accompanied the males were subjected to a double and hypocritical sexual morality. A 'lady' had to adhere 'strictly to the model of the virginal, chaste woman, submissive to the male, dedicated to perform domestic work, as the only given status to her was that of spouse' (Restrepo 1995: 29). Husbands could freely enjoy their sexuality with lovers from any social class. In colonial times, the ideal woman was constructed by male fantasy. The feminine virtues were chastity, modesty, piety, discretion, obedience, prudence and an affable nature, and the model woman was expected to be a good administrator of her home (Luna 2001). Mary became the symbol of the ideal woman (white), while Eve portrayed evil (the Indian, black or woman of mixed race) (ibid.: 68). The 'honest woman's' best destiny was to be confined in her home or in a convent (Ranke-Heineman 1990; Warner 1976). Unfortunately, writes Ivonne Gebara, there is a belief in Christian theology that man by nature possesses an original goodness that has been given to him by God, but woman's self is irremediably linked with evil.

The bourgeois world and the patriarchal ideology of the Spanish universe influenced the New World dramatically. At the same time, Castilian law was different for men (to whom it gave privileges) than for women (to whom it restricted privileges). Females were considered feeble, unable to defend themselves, and the inheritors of Eve's sinful nature. The belief arose that, after human beings were thrown out of paradise, men were bound to protect women, who were not to be left alone without a father, brother or husband (Segura Graiño 1995: 75). The idea of the pure woman with a frail nature still pervades women's lives and destinies in Colombia, regardless of their social or economic class. This perception of how a woman should behave may not be discussed openly in the twenty-first century, but the idea permeates how women think about themselves and their life choices. Since the 1500s, regardless of socio-economic class, the purpose of Colombian men has been to redress women's evil nature (Eder 2002).

The Amerindian family In Colombia, there are at least eighty indigenous groups with their own cultures, languages and beliefs. Many have been affected by Western civilization and by four decades of warfare to the point of being on the verge of extinction. Before conquest, the Indian family's sole purpose was to benefit the community. The man was responsible for the woman and the children. Everywhere, Indian laws protected women against the physical or sexual violence of men; women were respected and appreciated. The leaders paid women benefits during pregnancy, widowhood and old age (Acosta-Belén and Bose 1995; Restrepo 1995). Marriage was extremely important, but could be dissolved by the wife or the husband if it did not work. Either party could remarry without fear of stigmatization. Children usually stayed with their mother.

To be a 'virgin' did not bring respect. Rather, virginity was a 'shortcoming' and a reason for shame, meaning that the woman was not good enough for a man to wish to be with her. The colonizers were surprised to see the freedom men and women had over their sexuality (Restrepo 1995). Men practised polygamy (chiefs had six or seven wives) but polygamy placed women at a disadvantage. When the Spaniards started killing the Indians, they took men as slaves and women as concubines. The survivors of the Spanish massacres adopted the culture of their enemies, including to some extent the patriarchal value system.

The African-Colombian family Africans came to Latin America as slaves to help the Spanish in the gold mines, serve as soldiers against the insurgents, and do work the white people would not perform. The Africans did not know the cultures or languages; they were poor and miserable, having been dispossessed and separated from their families and their countries. Today's Colombian black populations are the country's most vulnerable: they are the least educated, the poorest, the most disadvantaged, and have the least cohesive social structures, which leads to abandonment of women and children at a higher rate than in other groups, relatively more female-headed households, and less societal respect.

Marriage and divorce Over time, these three groups – African, Indian and white – have intermarried to some extent, creating racially and culturally mixed families. Immigrants from other countries have more recently contributed to a multiracial, multi-cultural society that has been heavily influenced by the Catholic Church.

In 1974, the husband's legal power over women's assets, children and decisions was eliminated by Congress. The *Patria Potestad*, which was the legal authority that fathers had over their children until they reached majority, was abolished. Thus, married women acquired legal civil rights and the husbands' control over their wives, their children and their family wealth was terminated by law. In 1991, legal divorce was approved and women could end their marriages without losing their legal rights. The Catholic Church condones religious divorce.

BIGAMY Although adultery is considered a sin by the Catholic Church, in Colombian culture it has always been socially accepted for men because of the social belief in a male's 'libidinous' nature. In June 2001, the Colombian government gave bigamy legal status simply because it was impossible to punish the bigamous man. The bigamous man is protected not only by society but often by the women who share him. Florence Thomas writes in *El Tiempo* (16 August 1998) that 'bigamy is an affective mistreatment of women that clearly reflects Colombian patriarchy, which is resistant to change'. The lawful acceptance of bigamy will promote further infidelity among spouses or couples with a long-term living commitment, and negatively affect the family unit, especially the children.

INHERITANCE In 1932, Colombian women obtained the right to inherit property and money, and were allowed to manage their wealth.

Violence against women

Discrimination against women in Colombia is a well-documented phenomenon. A woman in Colombia is far from being considered a valuable, autonomous subject, despite her social status: 'Sexism and *machismo* are continuously reproduced by formal education and the media' (Tokatlián 1998: 6A). The violence perpetrated against women within the family unit injures them throughout life. The alleged love and attention amid which girls are raised is actually infused with repression and violence mischaracterized as concern.

Wife-beating existed in pre-capitalist societies, when men were allowed to dominate their wives with 'the rule of the thumb' (Lerner 1986; Schechter 1982). Violence and domination were integral to the patriarchal family under the control of the father (Schechter 1982: 216).

Today, the nuclear family has replaced the self-sustaining family of earlier cultures, but patriarchal structures have not yet been eradicated. The Colombian National Association of Nurses has characterized Colombia as a 'scenario of patriarchy, misogyny, and *machista* par excellence' (OIM/ANEC 2002: 14). Importantly, they argue that the underlying reasons for sexual violence are exacerbated in times of armed conflict because the aggressors are protected and surrounded by cultural symbols of masculine strength and the ideology of war. Rape becomes a weapon of war, another way to degrade females and attack the honour of their male partners and families with impunity.

The Inter-American Convention of Belem do Pará (Inter-American Commission of Women 2004) for the prevention of violence against women defines violence as 'any act or conduct, based on gender, which causes death or physical, sexual, or psychological harm or suffering to women, whether in the public or the private sphere'; often, it includes battery of the couple's children. Battery is assaultive behaviour between adults who are in an intimate, sexual and (often) cohabiting relationship. The batterer uses violence to dominate, control and punish the victim. The perpetrator has no regard for the victim's wishes, and beatings and violence may occur without any previous reason or provocation (Eder 1988). Battery may also end with 'life-threatening and seriously injurious behaviour such as choking [or] breaking bones' (NCADV 1989) that may lead to the victim's death. The principal methods of aggression against women in Colombia are physical violence (36.7 per cent of cases reported), verbal abuse (26 per cent), economic abuse (18 per cent) and psychological abuse (12.6 per cent) (NCADV 1989).

Victims of sexual abuse or crimes usually do not report them to the police because they feel ashamed, guilty and afraid of the consequences. Their families may not believe them. These crimes have increased by 200 per cent a year in Colombia (UNIFEM 2004) from 12,736 reported cases in 1994 to 36,149 cases in 2002. For example, in September 2004 the media reported the pregnancy of an eight-year-old who was raped. The ratio of sexually assaulted females to males is six to one.

On sexual harassment, there is a complete lack of debate in the Constitutional Court, and the Supreme Court requires 'high evidentiary standards', which makes women's cases more difficult to prove. In Colombia, the 'spirit of the law is that of the dominant religion' (Cabal et al. 2001: 54–6).

Literacy and education

In Colombia today, men and women are educated equally; there is no discrimination in terms of access to educational opportunity.

Literacy rates The literacy rate was about 52 per cent in 1940 (not broken down by gender) and rose to 79 per cent in 1970 (Florez et al. 1987). By 1990, the rate was slightly higher for males (87.5 per cent) compared to females (85.9 per cent). By 2000, however, the literacy rate was 91 per cent for both males and females (UNICEF 2003) and in 2004 it was virtually 100 per cent for both sexes (DANE 2004). Females appear to be doing better than males in this regard. The rate of illiteracy was slightly higher for males than females in the fifteen-to-twenty-four age group in 1993, but similar among older adults; the rates were virtually identical by 2000 (UNESCO 2002). By 2000, for every 100 literate males there were 101 literate females, and for young females (aged fifteen to twenty-four), the literacy rate increased from 96.7 per cent in 1995 to 97.9 per cent in 2002 (UNIFEM 2003: 10).

School completion rates

PRIMARY According to Corpoeducación (2002), the average number of school years completed rose steadily between 1950 and 2000 from just over two years to about 7.5 years, with virtually no gender gap (Figure 6.5), but school life expectancy in Colombia is still low compared to other countries. In 1998, 18 per cent of children dropped out of first grade, but in rural areas the percentage was much higher at 30 per cent. Girls are less likely to withdraw from school

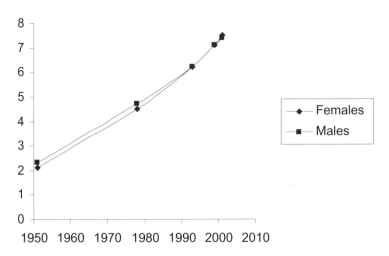

Figure 6.5 School life expectancy by gender (years completed)
***Source*: DNP (2000)**

or to repeat grades than are boys, because fewer girls work in the fields or help their families in hard labour in the cities. Pre-school attendance is low, although it increased from 31.6 per cent in 1993 to 46.8 per cent in 2000; rural children, especially those from indigenous and Afro-Colombian families, have far less access to education (UNICEF 2003). Since 1991, by law every child must have at least ten years of education, but Corpoeducación (2002) found that illiteracy in the rural population is comparatively high and that 18 per cent of children do not complete the required schooling in rural areas (perhaps another impact of the drug wars).

SECONDARY According to UNIFEM (2003: 4), for every 100 males enrolled in secondary education in Colombia there were 111 females. The main reason for children leaving school is lack of economic means (40 per cent). The second reason is having no desire to study. Around 11 per cent of children between the ages of twelve and seventeen desert their studies because they marry or the girls become pregnant. It is more frequent for boys to drop out than for girls, because boys are expected to work outside the home. Educational levels have improved with economic growth. In 1951, only 8 per cent attended secondary school. That figure increased to 30 per cent in 1985 and about 39 per cent in 2000. A lack of secondary schools in rural areas depresses attendance rates outside of cities (PAHO 1998).

HIGHER EDUCATION Women began their struggle for equal rights in the 1930s; in 1933, Law 132 was passed, requiring universities to open their doors to females. Today many more women go to university than men. Although there are more than 200 institutions of higher education in Colombia, including seventy-one universities, most are private and beyond the reach of poor families.

Economic participation

The division of labour Throughout history, women have been consigned to the private sphere of the family, the world of human reproduction and reproduction of ideologies and values. Men have been in charge of the world of production and exchange (Momsen 1991; Medrano and Escobar 1985). The sexual division of labour in Colombia still relegates women to the home, even after women's struggle for political, economic and social rights and respect. Female labour is least valued and is often entirely ignored (for example, in statistical reports and computations of the gross domestic product and other such measures of economic productivity). Capitalism and socialism view reproductive and/or use-value labour as unimportant for economic development, even though women reproduce and maintain the labour force.

Since the institution of patriarchy, the definition of economic activity has included only market production for the growth and accumulation of capital (Benería 1985). Work outside the formal labour force is regarded as natural, not economic, and invisible. 'Housewifization' refers to domestic labour that is not valued or defined as economic activity (Acosta-Belén and Bose 1995: 26).

Although some Colombian women appear to fare better than others because of social class differences, gender bias also plagues economically well-off women. There is a general belief that women of the upper classes do not suffer discrimination, intra-family violence or rape, and are free from reproductive problems. The assumption is that if they are well educated, they will receive pay equal to that of their male colleagues. Material comfort is thought to solve any problem an individual faces in her lifetime, so women in Colombia from the bourgeoisie are assumed to be free from hardships. These fallacies must be acknowledged, analysed and interpreted. The entrapment and discrimination a bourgeois woman suffers are real and must be corrected. Social class, ethnicity and religion drastically separate women from each other and diminish the chances of achieving positive action through solidarity.

Women's participation in the labour force As of 1936, Colombian women were allowed to work in the public sector. After the UN Decade for the Advancement of Women (1975–85), new opportunities opened up for women. The decade's forward-looking strategies emphasized that women must be active participants in their progress to help generate equality, constructive development and peace (Fraser 1987: 25).

UNIFEM (2004) reported that even though the economic participation of women in the labour force has risen tremendously in the last few years, women's participation in relation to men's is still very low (38 per cent for women in contrast to 66 per cent for men as of 2000). The unequal percentage is quite significant because there are more women than men in the age band eligible for employment. A study by Farnsworth-Alvear (2000) showed that women were gradually squeezed out of textile mills in the 1950s and 1960s because of male perceptions that females did not belong in an industrial setting. She disputes the idea that the shift in the workforce over several decades from mainly women to almost exclusively men was based on economic factors and concepts of 'improper' versus 'proper' female behaviour.

FULL-/PART-TIME Colombian women who work outside the home work two shifts, since males do not participate in household labour: ' ... the workday is

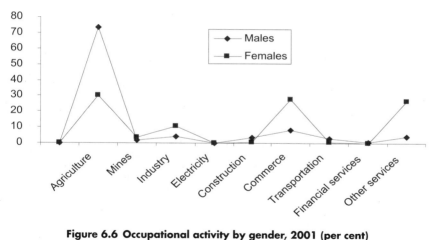

Figure 6.6 Occupational activity by gender, 2001 (per cent)
Source: DANE 2004

longer than eight hours, because [women] also perform household chores ...
and use week-ends as time to catch up on the housekeeping ... Women [can]
work a total of 60 hours per week' (IDB 1990: 127, 217–18). In rural areas, cooking is 100 per cent women's labour. For domestic activities overall, women's
participation is 95.6 per cent and men's 4.4 per cent (La Red de Mujeres 2001).
Cultural factors stemming from the traditional, gendered division of labour
contribute to this pattern.

TYPES OF OCCUPATION At the end of the twentieth century, males predominated in agricultural work (over 70 per cent), leaving female participation
proportionately higher in certain kinds of industry (textiles), commercial positions and the general service sector (Figure 6.6). Women have moved farther
into agriculture and commercial employment since 1964 but their industrial
sector and service sector participation has declined since that time.

UNEMPLOYMENT The unemployment rate rose from 11.2 per cent in 1992 to
20.4 per cent in 2000, the highest in Latin America (Figure 6.7). For females,
the rate has been substantially higher than for males (22 per cent as opposed
to 12 per cent for males in 1999). For all Colombians, the last decade of the
twentieth century brought severe economic conditions and unemployment,
but the unemployment rate for young females (eighteen to twenty-four) was
even more devastating, at 39.1 per cent in 2000 compared to 30.2 per cent for
young males.

Income and poverty In 1999, Colombia's gross domestic product (GDP) per

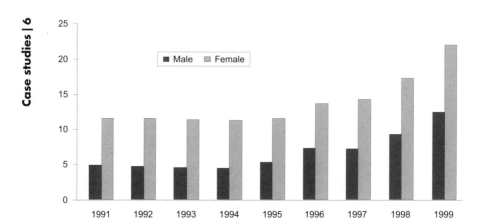

Figure 6.7 Unemployment rate by gender, 1991–99 (per cent)
Source: **DNP (2000)**

capita was $6,200 (National Geographic 1999: 1). In 1996, there were 20 million people living under the poverty line – over half of the population; in 2000, the figure rose to 24.7 million, and as of 2004 it had reached 26 million: 51 per cent were women and 49 per cent were men (UNIFEM 2004). Colombian rural and urban women are among the poorest of the poor as their pay is low and they have poor qualifications. In 1981, legislators determined that there was to be no salary discrimination between men and women.

Political, educational and cultural leadership

Thanks to the fourth International Feminist Congress, which took place in Bogotá in 1930, Colombian women started gaining social and legal status, which had been denied to them since the nineteenth century. They created a slogan to help in their political fight: 'Partner, but not serf!'.

Undoubtedly, in the last seventy years Colombian women have obtained innumerable advantages that have enhanced their social and legal status. Nevertheless, this does not mean that women's fight for their human rights has ended, nor that women's struggle for social and political rights has been achieved. Thus, the law may be on the books, but fair legislation often does not produce the desired results.

Suffrage: participation in voting and elections The wife and daughter of a military dictator were the catalysts for women's suffrage in Colombia. In 1954, Colombia's only twentieth-century dictator, General Gustavo Rojas Pinilla, granted the vote to Colombian women. He took this step because he had listened to the requests of his wife, Carola de Rojas (who was the first Colombian woman to receive a social ID), and of his daughter, Maria Eugenia Rojas, whom he loved dearly and educated to become a senator and presidential candidate (Zuñiga 2004). Rojas Pinilla's criterion for women to acquire political rights was based on their being mothers, which gave them a superior status as worthy citizens with suffrage rights (Luna 2001: 16–17). Congress agreed that Colombian women could have suffrage, but it was not until 1957 that women actually exercised their right to vote, during the government of President Alberto Lleras Camargo.

With women's suffrage, the slogan 'the private is political' started to modify women's lives and destinies. Today – on the surface – Colombian society appears to approve of women's social and political participation. Yet a recent CEDAW report emphasized that during the 1990s there had been little change for Colombian women in politics and public life. Women vote but few are elected.

Political leadership Women are mentioned infrequently in Colombian and Latin American history, even though some women have participated actively in the social, political and artistic developments of the region. Countless Latin American women have contributed to revolutionary movements and have undertaken acts of resistance. When La Gran Colombia – the geographic and political entity formed by Venezuela, Colombia and Ecuador – began its battle for independence from Spain, women participated actively alongside men. Before and during these wars of independence (1780–1822), the women of La Gran Colombia donated homes as well as jewellery and money to support the cause of freedom (Cherpak 1985).

Later, Colombian women not only participated in the fighting but helped wherever women were needed, usually in espionage, nursing and in traditional roles (ibid.: 83–116). When the wars of independence began, women from all strata of society participated in the fight against the colonizers. Two of the most renowned Colombian women, who died in the name of independence, were Policarpa Salavarrieta and Antonia Santos (Guhl 1997: 118–30). A few women historians speak about women's accomplishments since the times of the Spaniards (e.g. Magdala Velásquez Toro).

HEADS OF STATE AND GOVERNMENT The formal participation of women in Colombian politics is still very low (Craske 1999; Luna 2001). Women have very little chance to create laws that favour female rights. No matter how many years have gone by since the revolutionary legal transformation of women's civic and political conditions and status, 'cultural traditions still bind women

149

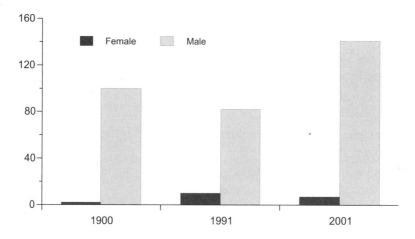

Figure 6.8 Women in the Colombian parliament (numbers)
Sources: **La Red de Mujeres 7 (2000); DANE (2004)**

to concepts that ... consider women infants and thus submit them to their father, brother, or husband' (de los Rios 1995: 422). Despite protests, Colombia disregards female existence by ignoring women's political capacity and human rights (Thomas 1999: 117).

MINISTERIAL (CABINET) In the last twenty years, Colombia has had three female ministers in the International Relations Office. At ministerial level, the percentage of women stood at only 1.1 per cent in 1994; at sub-ministerial level, it was 5.6 per cent (La Red de Mujeres 2000). In 2000, the Colombian legislature passed Law 581, which required that 30 per cent of governmental posts be filled by females, but this law has not been observed. As the Inter-American Development Bank (IDB) affirms, even with quotas, governmental posts are 'still monopolized by men'. Meanwhile, women's posts are often restricted to traditionally female issues such as home economics, education, the environment and the arts.

In spite of the legislation, in peace negotiations with the guerrilla group FARC there was not one single woman representing either the government of President Andrés Pastrana or FARC. Despite protestations, Colombian society continues to do very little for female existence, women's political capacity or human rights.

PARLIAMENTARY Women in Colombia have by and large marginalized themselves from political participation, although the presence of females in the political arena has been growing (Figure 6.8). For example, in 1990 only one woman was elected to the Senate compared to 114 males. Between 1990 and

2000, the percentage of female senators rose to 12.7, but the body is still heavily tilted towards males (Blum 2001).

LOCAL GOVERNMENT The proportion of female mayors in 1990–92 was 8.3 per cent, while in 1995–2000 it fell to 5 per cent. The disparity between women and men participating in the country's political life is still large.

PARTY LEADERSHIP Acosta-Belén and Bose argue that '[I]n many Latin American countries, the Catholic Church, the left, and traditional political parties are seen as major obstacles to women's empowerment' (1995: 30).

FEMINIST GROUPS IN COLOMBIA Sociologists Diana Medrano and Cristina Escobar (1985: 299) explain that the first Colombian feminist groups were organized during the time of the Liberal (Democratic) republic in 1930–46, founded by elite women. Today, many feminist groups fight for the needs and rights of women. Feminist groups such as Vamos Mujer ('Let's go, women') have developed strong agendas for social change, pressing for women's participation in politics and work, and gender equity (Lavrin 1987; Luna 2001). Amy Lind affirms that Third World feminists still have difficulty in addressing 'gender discrimination [owing to] racial, economic, and religious oppression from an autonomous standpoint' (2003: 227).

In 1975, feminist groups emerged in Colombia with signs of greater strength and visibility than ever to openly criticize patriarchal power. Feminists demanded 'the transformation of women's oppressive condition within society' and the 'freedom to make decisions regarding their bodies and lives' (Villareal Mendez 1995: 184). Unfortunately, political upheaval has created stronger state structures that harm women's interests. War and narco-terrorism have taken control of the country.

Female images and services are intrinsically tied to the peace process. For example, the female presidential candidate, Noemí Sanin, used 'motherhood' to evoke qualities associated with women: renunciation, abnegation, sacrifice and spiritual strength. Because women have 'agreed' with men in their sexual contract, women acquire power through reproduction and/or motherhood. These characteristics are supposedly required to tame men's aggressive behaviour. The idea of maternal instinct is exploited to protect society and its institutions. 'Maternity may not be destiny but it does overshadow women's lives, and motherhood seems to be remarkably resistant as a cultural identity … the commitment to the reproductive arena generally takes precedence over work and careers.'

Box 6.2 Warring females – the guerrilleras

Many women populate the ranks of the two groups of Marxist guerrillas and of the right-wing paramilitary. Approximately 40 per cent of the soldiers in each guerrilla group are females who are never mentioned by their superiors, the Colombian government, or the media. They are ignored by society.

Female participation in drug warfare stems from the surge of overwhelming economic and spiritual poverty caused by the fighting itself. The guerrillas and paramilitary groups give clothes, food, shelter and salaries to their members. At times, women are kidnapped, some as young as twelve years old, and are forced to help the men in their war. Some women who are mistreated by their families decide to try their luck with the guerrillas or paramilitary. Others, who have no opportunities whatsoever, think that the war may bring them some kind of empowerment.

Female soldiers have given testimonies of their situation within these masculine strongholds, which are supervised and controlled with an iron grip by the men. In 2000, Patricia Lara's *Mujeres en la Guerra* (Women at War) earned the Spanish prize for journalism, Planeta, for uncovering these phenomena. Women in the terrorist groups serve the men as cooks and washerwomen, and they clean the barracks (Lara 2000). If they are allowed to fight in the war, women soldiers are placed in front of the ranks, together with the very young soldiers, and serve as shields to prevent adult men from being killed first. Women are tortured and raped more often than killed because they are taken prisoner. If they are killed, they are raped first, and 'their bodies are usually mutilated in an atrocious way, as the paramilitary tend to do' (UNIFEM 2004; Craske 1990: 142).

If the women are allowed to supervise the camps, they do so at night to allow the men to sleep. Further, the men use female soldiers in their groups as their 'comfort women' (UNIFEM 2004: A5) and women are forced either to use birth control devices or to undergo abortions if they become pregnant. Men and women are not allowed to fall in love and form relationships unless the man is a chief in command. If women disobey these rules, they can be and often are punished with death. The 2004 UNIFEM report gives statistics on women's deaths and those who killed them – females comprise 49.60 per cent of the deaths.

Towards gender equality

The importance of bringing equality, sustainable development and peace to Colombian society has special bearing on the well-being of women. As a United Nations report states, 'Health is by no means only a question of curing disease … it also means physical, emotional and mental well-being' (Cottingham 1983: 143). Discrimination is an obstacle to health, since it promotes stress and, therefore, mental and physical illness (Fraser 1987). Reports from the Inter-American Bank (IBD 1985), the UN (1989, 1993) and others demonstrate that violence, discrimination and general mistreatment cause women to suffer chronic lack of respect, ill health, depression and anxiety. Most important, the report issued by Amnesty International (2004) on sexual violence in Colombia pictures the chaotic situation women experience. The study shows how violence towards women is endemic to the country, and calls upon the Colombian government to redress this issue without delay. Women are suffering and their lives and their health are being destroyed. Yet the governments of Latin American nations have done little to tackle the problems. As Charlotte Bunch (1995: 12) emphasizes, 'The lack of understanding of women's rights as human rights is reflected in the fact that few governments are committed, in domestic or foreign policy, to women's equality as a basic human right.'

For feasible development and improved female well-being, gender discrimination must be eradicated. Development is not only a matter of economic efficiency – it can also support equity. Economic efficiency 'shifted the emphasis away from *women* and toward *development* on the assumption that increased economic participation for Third World women is automatically linked with increased equity' (Moser 1989: 813). When considering development and women's human rights, however, there must be a gender perspective and a feminist criticism (Vavrus and Richey 2003: 6). The well-being of women as agents of change must be considered. Women's human rights are based on having a happy and fruitful life free from 'inhuman and degrading treatment concerning the high percentage of maternal mortality' caused by abortion, poor sexual and reproductive health and any other kind of violent or inhuman treatment that threatens their integrity (Cabal et al. 2001: 22–43, 472–84).

A new voice for Colombian women In Colombia, as we have seen, the masculine is 'neutral' or the 'normal' – everything follows from that assumption. Of course, gender roles are learned through socialization. Unfortunately, women who are in charge of family life help transmit the social and cultural codes children learn; thus, they become the 'gatekeepers' of patriarchy within the family unit. According to Lavrin, women are entitled to 'an exploration of the ideology of

153

male supremacy and female subordination ... we must understand the nature and cultural roots of gender role models if we wish to dismantle what has been going on in society against women's well-being' (1987: 110–11). For true social change to occur, the feminine must erupt into the social formula, which has to date been defined by the masculine. The feminine must counterbalance the hegemony of masculine force and contribute to a new definition of a more equal and just society in politics, economics, health and reproductive rights, social and cultural rules and gender roles. A strong feminist standpoint and criticism will modify the masculine, patriarchal and machista perspective that has organized and ruled Colombian society for so many centuries.

Usually, and unfortunately, when women work in government they tend to become assimilated or complacent about the persistence of patriarchal ideology (Eder 2002: 130). Women who attain high political posts tend to say that men have never discriminated against them. Colombia needs many more women politicians who can address women's issues from a feminist standpoint. Such issues as violence, rape, health, reproductive rights, discrimination in the labour force and political participation should be addressed not only from a gender perspective but also with a feminist focus. Female politicians should not be 'dressed as males' and impersonate the male viewpoint, as Florence Thomas (2003: 57) recommends. They should act with the desire to feminize the world and do 'away with the hierarchies of class, gender, race, and ethnicity that have so long subordinated much of the Latin American population, men as well as women' (Safa 1995: 239) as they raise the consciousness of the entire population. Unfortunately, as Donna Murdock explains, feminism in Colombia has been seen as a tool for hating men, and is associated with becoming a 'woman-witch', a lesbian or a libertine (Murdock 2003: 144–7) – all perceived as a threat to society's well-being.

Today, Colombian women are still afraid of speaking out and of participating actively in the political life of the country. It is time they now had a voice of their own. Women must be educated towards agency to decide important matters concerning their lives, bodies and families, and their participation in work, culture and politics. Political ownership will give them economic power and help shape destinies (Sen and Grown 1999: 199). Colombian society is in great need of sustainable peace, equality and justice to make women *and* men free (World Bank 1999). Instead of worshipping the Virgin Mary as a model of passivity and resignation, she should be the model of a real woman who speaks up with a voice full of love, desire, eroticism, poetry and understanding as it interrupts the order of things (Oliver 1993: 34–7) on behalf of women *and* men. As we speak of our wants and ideas, no one will ever say that as Colombian women continue to 'forge our paths as we walk' we have sung too loudly!

References

Acosta-Belén, E. and C. E. Bose (1995) 'Colonialism, structural subordination, and empowerment', in C. E. Bose and E. Acosta-Belén (eds), *Women in the Latin American Development Process*, Philadelphia, PA: Temple University Press

Amnesty International (2004) 'Colombia: cuerpos marcados, crímenes silenciados' [Colombia: wounded bodies, silenced crimes], AI: AMR 23/040/2002

Benería, L. (ed.), (1985) *Women and Development: The Sexual Division of Labour in Rural Societies*, New York: Praeger Special Studies

Blum, C. (2001) Personal communication

Bonilla, E. (ed.) (1985) 'Aproximaciones al estudio de la problemática femenina' [Approximations to the study of feminine problematics], *Mujer y familia en Colombia* [Woman and the Family in Colombia], Bogotá: Plaza y Janés

Bose, C. E. and E. Acosta-Belén (eds) (1995) *Women in the Latin American Development Process*, Philadelphia, PA: Temple University Press

Bunch, C. (1995) 'Transforming human rights from a feminist perspective', in J. Peters and A. Wolper (eds), *Women's Rights are Human Rights*, New York: Routledge

Cabal, L. et al. (eds) (2001) *Cuerpo y derecho legislación y jurisprudencia en América Latina*, Bogotá: Editorial Temis

Chaney, E. (1979) *Supermadre: Women in Politics in Latin America*, Austin: University of Texas Press

Cherpak, E. (1995) 'Las mujeres en la independencia' [Women in the independence movement in Gran Colombia 1780–1830] in M. Velasquez Toro (ed.), *Las mujeres en la historia de Colombia, Tomo I* [Women in Colombian History, Vol. 1], Bogotá: Editorial Norma

Corpoeducación (2002) *Situación de la educación en básica, media y superior en Colombia,* [What is going on in Colombia in basic, median, and superior education], Bogotá: Litocamargo

Cottingham, J. (ed.) (1983) *United Nations Report on Health*, New York: United Nations

Craske, N. (1990) *Women and Politics in Latin America*, Rutgers, NJ: Rutgers University Press

— (1999) *Women and Politics in Latin America*, Rutgers, NJ: Rutgers University Press

CRLP (Centre for Reproductive Law and Policy) (1997, 2000) *Women of the World: Laws and Policies Affecting Their Reproductive Lives, Latin America and the Caribbean*

DANE (Departamento Administrativo Nacional de Estadisticas) (2004) *Proyecciones anuales de poblaciòn por sexo y edad 1985-2015*, Bogotá: DANE

De Beauvoir, S. (1952) *The Second Sex*, New York: Vintage Books

De los Ríos, G. (1995) 'Condición jurídica de las mujeres' [The juridical condition of women], in M. Velásquez Toro (ed.), *Las Mujeres en la Historia de Colombia*, Bogotá: Editorial Norma

DNP (Departamento Nacional de Población) (National Department of Population) (2000) *Boletín no. 29*

Eder, E. Garcés de (1988) 'Outline/report on violence and battering of women', Report for the Pan-American Health Organization (PAHO)

— (2002) *The Construction of Radical Feminist Thought: Women in Colombia as an Example*, doctoral dissertation, George Washington University

Farnsworth-Alvear, A. (2000) *Dulcinea in the Factory: Myths, Morals, Men and Women in Colombia's Industrial Experiment, 1905–1960*, Durham, NC: Duke University Press

Florez, C. E., E. Bonilla and R. Echeverri (1987) *La transición demográfica y la historia de vida de las mujeres en Colombia* [The demographic transition and the history of women's lives in Colombia], New York: United Nations University Press

Fraser, A. S. (1987) *The UN Decade for Women Documents and Dialogue*, Boulder, CO: Westview Press

Gebara, I. (2000) *El rostro oculto del mal* [The Hidden Face of Evil], Madrid: Editorial Trotta

Guhl, M. (1997) 'Las madres de la patria: Antonia Santos y Policarpa Salavarrieta' [Mothers of our nation: Antonia Santos and Policarpa Salavarrieta], in M. M. Jaramillo and B. Osorio de Negret (eds), *Las Desobedientes* [The Disobedients], Bogotá: Editorial Panamericana

Gutierrez, V. P. de (1975) *Familia y cultura en Colombia* [Family and Culture in Colombia], Bogotá: Instituto Colombiano de Cultura

IDB (Inter-American Development Bank) (1985) *Too Close to Home: Domestic Violence in the Americas*, ed. A. R. Morrison and M. L. Biehl, Washington, DC: IDB

— (1990) *Working Women in the Americas,* Washington, DC: IDB

— (1999) *Women in the Americas: Bridging the Gender Gap*, Washington, DC: Johns Hopkins University Press

Inter-American Commission of Women (2004) *Violence in the Americas – a Regional Analysis Including a Review of the Implementation of the Inter-American Convention on the Prevention, Punishment and Eradication of Violence Against Women*, Belem do Pará, Brazil (Executive Summary 7/23/04 1–22)

Lara, P. (2000) *Mujeres en la guerra* [Women at War], Bogotá: Editorial Planeta

La Red de Mujeres (2001) 'Informe presentado al Senado Colombiano, Agosto' [Women's Net – report presented to the Colombian Senate, August], Bogotá

Lavrin, A. (1987) 'Women, the family, and social change in Latin America', *World Affairs,* 150(2): 109–28

Lerner, G. (1986) *The Creation of Patriarchy*, New York: Oxford University Press

Lind, A. (2003) 'Feminist post-development thought: women in development and gendered paradoxes of survival in Bolivia', *Women's Studies Quarterly*, 31(3 and 4): 227–46

Luna, L. (2001) 'Los movimientos de mujeres en América Latina y la renovación de la historia política' [Women's movements in Latin America and the renovation of political history], in *Centro de estudios de género mujer y sociedad*, Cali: Universidad del Valle, Editorial La Manzana de la Discordia

— (2004) 'Cinquenta años del voto femenino en Colombia: compañera, no sierva [Fifty years of the feminine vote in Colombia: partner, not serf], *El Espectador*, Bogotá, August, p. A5

Medrano, D. and C. Escobar (1985) 'Pasado y presente de las organizaciones feministas de Colombia' [Past and present of the feminist organizations of Colombia], in *Mujer y familia en Colombia* [Woman and Family in Colombia], Bogotá: Plaza & Janes

Momsen, J. H. (1991) *Women and Development in the Third World*, London: Routledge

Moser, C. O. (1989) 'Gender planning in the Third World: meeting practical and strategic gender needs', *World Development*, 17(11): 1,799–1,825

Murdock, D. F. (2003) 'Neoliberalism, gender, and development: institutionalizing "post-feminism"', *Women's Studies Quarterly*, 31(3 and 4): 129–53

National Geographic (1999) 'Colombia', *National Geographic Atlas of the World*, 7th edn, Washington, DC: National Geographic Society

NCADV (National Coalition Against Domestic Violence) (1989) *Fact Sheets*, Washington, DC: NCADV

OIM/ANEC (Organización Internacional para las Migraciones, and Asociación Nacional de Enfermeras de Colombia, Secional de Antioquia) (2002) *Colombia Country Report*, Bogotá: Unión de Empleados Bancarios

Oliver, K. (1993) *Reading Kristeva*, Bloomington: Indiana University Press

Pitt-Rivers, J. (ed.) (1966) *Mediterranean Countrymen: Essays in the Social Anthropology of the Mediterranean*, Paris: Mouton

Ranke-Heineman, U. (1990) *Eunuchs for the Kingdom of Heaven: Women, Sexuality and the Catholic Church*, New York: Doubleday

Restrepo, R. (1995) 'Las mujeres en las sociedades prehispánicas' [Women in prehispanic societies], in M. Velásquez Toro (ed.), *Las Mujeres en la Historia de Colombia, Tomo I* [Women in Colombian History, Vol. 1], Bogotá: Editorial Norma

Safa, H. (1995) 'Women's social movements in Latin America', in C. E. Bose and E. Acosta-Belén (eds), in *Women in the Latin American Development Process*, Philadelphia, PA: Temple University Press

Schechter, S. (1982) *Women and Male Violence: The Vision and the Struggles of the Battered Women's Movement*, Boston, MA: South End Press

Schneider, J. (1971) 'Of vigilance and virgins: honor, shame and access to resources in Mediterranean societies', *Ethnology*, 10(3): 1–24

Segura Graiño, C. (1995) 'Las mujeres Castellanas de los siglos XV y XVI y su presencia en América' [Castilian women in the fifteenth and sixteenth centuries and their presence in America], in M. Velásquez Toro (ed.), *Mujeres en la historia de Colombia, Tomo I* [Women in Colombian History, Vol. 1], Bogotá: Editorial Norma

Sen, G. and C. Grown (1999) *Development, Crisis, and Alternative Vision: Third World Perspectives*, New York: Anchor Books

Thomas, F. (1999) 'No! doctora Fanny Kertzman' [No! Doctor Fanny Kertzman], in *La mujer tiene la palabra* [Woman Speaks Up], Bogotá: Aguilar

— (2001) 'La bigamia en Colombia' [Bigamy in Colombia], *El Tiempo*, Bogotá

— (2003) *Palabras en el Tiempo* [Words within Time], Bogotá: Aguilar

Tokatlián, G. (1998) 'Feminismo y geopolítica' [Feminism and geopolitics], *El Tiempo*, Bogotá

UN (United Nations) (1989) *Violence Against Women in the Family*, New York: United Nations

— (1993) *Strategies for Confronting Domestic Violence: A Resource Manual*, New York: United Nations

— (2000) *The World's Women 2000: Trends and Statistics*, New York: United Nations

UNICEF (2003) *The Official Summary of the State of the World's Children 2003*, <www.unicef.org/infobycountry/colombia.html>

UNIFEM (2003) 'Promoting gender equality and empowering women, Colombia',

Women in Colombia

The Millennium Development Goals in Latin America and the Caribbean, New York: United Nations

— (2004) 'Report on women's human rights', *El Espectador*, Bogotá, 21 August

Vavrus, F. and L. A. Richey (2003) 'Women and development: rethinking policy and reconceptualizing practice*', Women's Studies Quarterly*, 31(3 and 4): 6–18

Velásquez Toro, M. (1995) 'La república liberal y la lucha por los derechos civiles y políticos de la mujer' [The liberal republic and the struggle for the civil and political rights of woman], in M. Velásquez Toro (ed.), *Mujeres en la historia de Colombia, Tomo I* [Women in Colombian History, Vol. 1, Bogotá: Editorial Norma

Velásquez Toro, M. and C. C. Reyes (1995) 'Proceso histórico y derechos de las mujeres años 50 y 60' [Historical process and women's rights in the 50s and 60s], in M. Velásquez Toro (ed.), *Mujeres en la historia de Colombia, Tomo I* [Women in Colombian History, Vol. 1], Bogotá: Editorial Norma

Villareal Mendez, N. (1995) 'El camino de la utopia feminista en Colombia 1975–1991' [The road to a utopian feminism in Colombia 1975–1991], in M. Velásquez Toro (ed.), *Mujeres en la historia de Colombia, Tomo I* [Women in Colombian History, Vol.1], Bogotá: Editorial Norma

Warner, M. (1976) *Alone of All Her Sex: The Myth and the Cult of the Virgin Mary*, New York: Alfred A. Knopf

World Bank (1999) *Violence in Colombia: Building Sustainable Peace and Social Capital*, World Bank Country Study, Washington, DC: World Bank

Zuñiga, M. (2004) Personal communication

Websites

CEPAL (2001) <www.eclac.cl/publicaciones>

DNP (Departamento Nacional de Planeacion) (2000), Bogotá

PAHO (1998) *Health in the Americas*, <www.webmaster@paho.org>

UNESCO (2002) Institute for Statistics, <www.uis.unesco.org>

UNICEF (2003) *The Official Summary of the State of the World's Children 2003*, <www.unicef.org/infobycountry/colombia.html>

7 | Women in Croatia: continuity and change

VESNA BARILAR, ŽELJKA JELAVIĆ AND
SANDRA PRLENDA

In the tumultuous history of the twentieth century, Croatia was part of two different multinational states and experienced different political systems, including communism, until it achieved the status of an independent state in 1991. Moreover, the country suffered the harsh consequences of the First World War, was a theatre for occupation, warfare and civil war during the Second World War, and participated in military conflicts again in the course of the disintegration of Yugoslavia in the early 1990s.

The enormous social changes and discontinuities were thus due not only to the general modernization of European countries, with the usual traits of urbanization and industrialization, but also to more specific phenomena such as agrarian reform, internal colonization, nationalization of property, considerable loss of population during the war, the near-extermination and expulsion of certain ethnic groups, and economic and political emigration.

The changes in the way of life of women in Croatia were dramatic. At the beginning of the century, the average Croatian woman was illiterate, lived from agriculture in a small village, gave birth to five children, had limited access to healthcare, and did not have any political rights. Today, the collective portrait is almost completely opposite, although more nuanced. It appears that in many aspects of life the generations of women experienced progressive and linear improvement. A finer analysis, however, enables the identification of factors that especially promoted the advancement of female well-being, as well as the developments that threatened the acquired level of quality of life. The post-Second World War reconstruction of a ravaged country, under the banner of socialism, was a period of rapid modernization and intense social change. The break-up of the socialist system at the end of the century, followed by the war and the 'transition' towards a market economy and Western-style democracy, seemed to affect women's lives in a negative way.

Besides tremendous changes, there is a certain continuity to be discerned when analysing statistical data: the permanent gap between women and men. For example, data on literacy show that during the century women always lagged behind by about twenty years in striving to attain the same level as men. Gender inequality seems to be one of the enduring traits of Croatian society.

The geo-political complexities of Croatia

Until 1918, Croatian lands were part of the Austro-Hungarian empire. Roughly, the northern leg of present-day Croatia (the Kingdom of Croatia and Slavonia) was under the control of the Hungarian half of the empire (with a certain autonomy), while the coastal province of Dalmatia and the north-western peninsula of Istria were provinces of the Austrian part of the monarchy, under Vienna's control.

This history creates methodological problems when organizing and interpreting statistical data. Present-day Croatian borders date from 1945, when the People's Republic of Croatia was proclaimed as a part of the Yugoslav federation. In previous periods, Croatian territory, if it was not being incorporated into neighbouring states (such as Istria into Italy between the two world wars), was divided into different sub-state units, and this is reflected in census and other statistics. Data very often cover either the whole of Yugoslavia or small-scale regions. Consequently, it is not always possible to compare relevant data from different periods precisely. The positive side of this problem, however, is an awareness of the uneven development of major Croatian regions (Croatia, Slavonia, Dalmatia and Istria).

Following the break-up of the monarchy in 1918, Croatian lands and other southern Slavic provinces (Carniola, Bosnia and Herzegovina, and Vojvodina) united with the Kingdom of Serbia to form the Kingdom of Serbs, Croats and Slovenes, which was renamed the Kingdom of Yugoslavia in 1929. Istria was joined to Italy. As part of the unitary politics of Belgrade's political centre, the country was divided into new counties that cross-cut traditional regions; this makes the use of statistical data considerably difficult. In 1939, Croatian politicians concluded an agreement with the central government to form a separate political unit inside Yugoslavia, called Banovina Hrvatska. This included several counties from Bosnia and Herzegovina. Two years later, however, when Yugoslavia was invaded and occupied by the Axis powers, the Yugoslav army capitulated and King Peter II left the country. The right-wing Ustasha proclaimed the Independent State of Croatia, a puppet state that included the whole of Bosnia and Herzegovina, but ceded parts of the coast and islands to Mussolini's Italy. The communist-led resistance movement fought both the German and Italian occupiers and the Ustasha and Chetniks (Serbian monarchists). By 1943, it had laid the foundation for the federal state of Yugoslavia with Croatia as one of its republics. The integration of Istria and Međimurje in 1945 completed the make-up of Croatia within today's internationally recognized borders. Consequently, statistical data from 1945 are generally the most reliable for comparison (the first complete census was conducted in 1953).

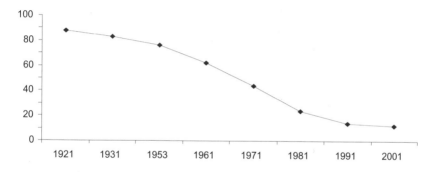

Figure 7.1 Percentage of the active female population engaged in agriculture
Source: CBS (1921 to 2001). Data for 1921 and 1931 were available only
for two counties in today's Croatian territory (the continental part of Croatia
and Slavonia)

A demographic portrait of Croatian women

Urbanization According to a 1910 census, 90.4 per cent of all women above
the age of fourteen lived in rural areas. As plant diseases devastated the vine-
yards, poverty inflicted the majority of the population and caused intensive
emigration (mainly of men) towards the major towns and to South America,
North America and Australia. Women usually remained on family farms or
moved as migrants within the country. The first wave of emigration started
at the end of the nineteenth century. By 1914, approximately 5.5 per cent of
the total population had emigrated. In Lika district alone, the 1910 census
showed that for each 100 men there were 245 women between the ages of
twenty and twenty-nine. This produced an increase in the number of single-
woman households which were supported with occasional financial injections
from emigrants.

This period was characterized by the final phase of dissolution of the *zadruga* – a specific southern Slavic social-economic family unit (see 'Family status',
below). The reason for this disintegration (which ended in the turmoil during
and shortly after the First World War) lies in the gradual industrialization
and monetary economy that took the place of traditional economy and social
organization. The world agrarian crisis that marked the end of the nineteenth
century and lasted more than two decades was initialized by the prosperity of a
growing transport industry. One of the effects of that crisis involved increased
importation of food and lowering of prices of agricultural products. This had
an enormous impact on the dominant occupation of the majority of population. The percentage of women engaged in agriculture has steadily declined
since the beginning of the twentieth century (Figure 7.1).

From a peripheral and completely undeveloped territory of the Austro-

Hungarian empire in 1918, Croatia entered into the new state association of the Kingdom of Serbs, Croats and Slovenes, where it became the most developed area in comparison to the other parts of the newly created state, except for Slovenia. A narrow segment of nouveau riche, who had obtained their wealth in the turmoil of the First World War and were well supported with foreign financial capital, started to invest in certain industries (textiles, tobacco, transport, trade and small financial businesses) using pauperized peasants as an inexhaustible source of cheap labour.

Life expectancy During the twentieth century, healthcare improved for the entire population, not least for women. Diseases such as tuberculosis were successfully eradicated and no longer present a significant health problem for today's population. According to data collected by the National Institute for Public Health, the leading causes of death by the end of the century were circulatory diseases (52.1 per cent), followed by malignant neoplasms (22.3 per cent), injuries and poisonings (5.7 per cent), diseases of the digestive system (5.1 per cent), and respiratory system diseases (4.9 per cent). Among women, the most prevalent cancer is breast cancer, which showed constant growth during the last decade of the century.

Life expectancy for women has increased and is longer by a couple of years than men's. For example, female life expectancy in 1971 was 72.33; in 1991 it was 75.95, and in 2001 it was 78.17 years. Violent deaths among females were rarer than for males. Between 1990 and 1998, the suicide rate grew from 29.7 to 34.9 per 100,000 for males, and from a much lower 9.8 to 13.5 per 100,000 for females.

Population growth, fertility rate and the male–female ratio With a surface area of 56,542 square kilometres, Croatia is a relatively small European country, with a medium population density, ranging from 55.9 inhabitants per square kilometre in 1900 to 78 in 2001. The pattern of population growth is similar to that of other European countries.

New trends of modernization are visible in the move towards smaller families. During the twentieth century, the average number of children per woman (fertility rate) decreased from 5.3 in 1910 to 1.7 in 1997. The birth rate has constantly declined, from 40.34 per 1,000 in 1900 to 18.4 in 1960 and 9.51 in 2001. The mortality rate (per 1,000) varied slightly during the twentieth century and shows no constant decline (27.05 in 1905; 10.0 in 1960; 11.3 in 2001), but in the last decades of the century it has been higher than the birth rate. The population growth rate at the end of the century was in the negative range at −2.4.

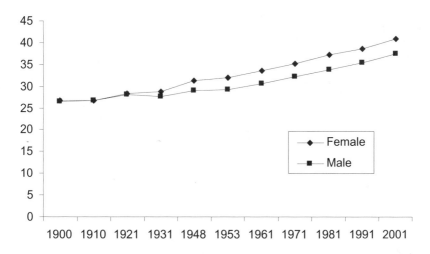

Figure 7.2 Median age of population *Sources:* Gelo (1987: 233); CBS (1991, 2001)

The 2001 census shows a decline in the total population after 1945. In the last decade of the century, because of the war that followed the disintegration of Yugoslavia, the percentage of Serbs in the total population of Croatia declined from 12.16 per cent in 1991 to 4.51 per cent in 2001 (CBS: 2003). The number of persons who emigrated to Western countries for economic reasons is still unknown, but most were young. The country is also becoming more ethnically homogeneous, with 89.6 per cent ethnic Croats and 4.5 per cent Serbs in 2001, while other ethnicities (Bosnians, Hungarians, Slovenes, Roma, Czechs, Italians) constitute less than 0.5 per cent.

The female proportion of the total population increased only after the Second World War, while later it slightly decreased (but it has remained between 51 and 53 per cent of the total) (CBS 1921–2001). Demographic losses during the Second World War are estimated to be half a million (12.4 per cent), including killed combatants and civilians; destroyed ethnicities (Jews, Roma); expelled (Germans); emigrants; and unborn children. The post-war compensational increase in birth rates finished in 1955, followed by a further decline (Gelo 1987: 134).

Age structure of the population Today, Croatia has a predominantly older population. As seen in Figure 7.2, the median age of the population is constantly increasing.

Maternal mortality rate Even though it can be said that the healthcare system advanced during the twentieth century, a more careful analysis shows that from the proclamation of independent Croatia the standard of health has dropped, along with the level of women's healthcare and, above all, that of reproductive health. Under socialism, women had better access to preventive gynaecological exams, and a system of health education and family planning was developed. Primary healthcare was carried out by general practitioners at community health centres and industrial health dispensaries within large factories.

In 1952, 59.6 per cent of all births were medically assisted, while in 1982 almost all births were medically assisted (99.4 per cent). This helps to account for the decline in maternal mortality rates in Croatia in the second half of the century. The rate fluctuates because of the small numbers involved, but Croatia's rate of eighteen deaths per 100,000 live births (in 1995) was similar to the European Union average (WHO 2000). Article 62 of the constitution guarantees state protection of maternity, 'regulates the rights concerning delivery, maternity and care for children', and provides for paid maternity leave, which reduces maternal mortality in the year following childbirth (ibid.).

Infant mortality rate Croatia's infant mortality rate dropped dramatically from 98 per 1,000 live births in 1960 to 16.6 in 1985, 13 in 1990, and 9 in 2000, but it is still 40 per cent over the EU average (UNICEF 2003). War conditions temporarily halted the rate of decline. Infant mortality is most commonly linked with premature birth and consequent immaturity, or with severe malformations. Low birth weight (less than 2,500g) indicates high risk; Croatia's figures are lower than the EU average (WHO 2000).

Contraception and abortion Abortion was one of the more significant indicators of the developed system of women's healthcare and family planning. If we were to observe the decrease in the number of abortions through the prism of increased health education and the use of contraceptive measures, we would see a confusing picture where Croatia is concerned. From the 1970s on, even though contraceptive measures were accessible, abortion was the most widespread method of contraception. In 1987, for example, for every live birth one abortion was carried out. From the time of the declaration of independent Croatia, abortion became inaccessible to a large number of women because of the high cost. The lack of availability of modern contraceptives led to higher rates of induced termination than in western European nations.

In 1951, abortion was still illegal but permitted for justified reasons; a 1960 decree allowed a liberal interpretation of medico-social indications for abortion; a 1969 law proclaimed freedom of woman's individual choice; and a 1978 law allowed abortion on demand up to the first ten weeks (Merunka Golubić 2003). Yet the last decade of the twentieth century was characterized by a very strong neoconservative political trend and strong influence by the Catholic Church that resulted in an inadequate number of prevention programmes for protection and reproductive health education. Abortions decreased in Croatia from 822 recorded in 1985 to 295 in 1997 (WHO 2000); the decline was especially steep among young women. In 1998, the number of abortions in comparison with 1990 was reduced by 67.3 per cent, along with the number of visits to doctors and prescribed contraception. In 1995, there were 44 per cent fewer visits to doctors and 37.6 per cent less prescribed contraception than in 1990 (Petrović 2000). In 1990, more contraceptive measures were used than towards the end of the decade, but at the same time more abortions were performed.

HIV/AIDS In contrast to the many countries throughout the world where HIV infections represent a high risk for women's health, in Croatia this is not the case. Croatia is included among the low-risk countries with an incidence rate of less than four infected per 1 million inhabitants. The first such patients were registered in 1985. Up to 2002, a total of 365 HIV-positive persons were registered. Most of the infected are males of homosexual orientation, and heterosexual persons with promiscuous behaviour (up to 91 per cent of whom were infected abroad). HIV-positive women with steady partners and non-promiscuous behaviour became infected by partners who had travelled abroad. The National HIV/AIDS Prevention Programme began in 1993.

Family status and structure

The turbulent social transformation that marked life in the twentieth-century had its impact on family structure; it was patriarchal, but indicators of that patriarchal nature have been changing throughout the century.

Marriage and divorce Zadruga (as a form of rural cooperative life) in the first two decades of the century existed only as a *residue* of a previously stable way of living, but it provided the context from which twentieth century gender relations emerged. The *zadruga* saw several generations living in the same household under the auspices of a *starješina* (the eldest male in the house); in some regions obedience to him was unconditional. The gender principle had dominance over the age principle; all men in this patrilocal system had a higher status than women, regardless of their age, especially in regions with strong military traditions (Stein Erlich 1971: 345–65). Although the *starješina* had the highest rank in the hierarchy, all married men had the right to participate in the decision-making process.

Obviously, women were excluded from decision-making as their position within the *zadruga* was subordinated; their tasks were to 'ensure the harmony and smooth-working of the household' and to perform work that 'was considered a separate contribution to the home, one of less significance than men's' (Jancar-Webster 1990: 28). Women were sheltered under the protective patriarchal code within their home (Stein Erlich 1971). Their place was traditionally known and unquestioned. They satisfied their needs within the constraints of the situation – sustainability of the household depended on them.

Inheritance According to common law, sons inherited property. The main principle that characterized a *zadruga* was that the male members never left the community. Sons and their male inheritors, in principle, did not abandon the house, whereas daughters, after marriage, became members of their husband's *zadruga*, renouncing their rights to the households of their father. Private property, except personal, did not exist. Differences between regions at the turn of the century were significant and depended on whether disintegration of the *zadruga* was finalized or in process.

The *zadruga* had disappeared by the 1920s and was eventually replaced by the nuclear family. Even though industrialization and migration to the cities brought new family structures, not only in gender roles but also in the relationship between younger members and elderly members, traditional relations were slow to change.

The second half of the twentieth century saw a rise in the number of households, from 1,289,325 in 1971 to 1,544,250 in 1991. Single households and those with up to four members are now increasing while the percentage of households with five or more members is in decline. The average number of household members dropped from 3.94 in 1948 to 3.10 in 1991.

Violence against women Women's well-being was jeopardized because of the verbal abuse women suffered within families, along with various forms of sexual abuse and violence. Unfortunately, there are still no official figures regarding this phenomenon. Feminist groups have been working for the last fifteen years on sensitizing the public, social services and the police to these matters. The public has learned of the visible intensification of domestic violence after the war of the 1990s. Several hotlines and safe houses were set up by feminists, but their number does not come close to meeting the needs of the large number of women who require shelters.

Women's economic participation

The division of labour Women's place was to ensure non-paid reproductive labour in the household (Sklevicky 1996: 95). The disintegration of the *zadruga* caused an increase in small one-family farms with little possibility of economic sustainability. Women started to seek employment in neighbouring towns, occupying mostly undervalued, low-skilled places in industry or working as domestic servants in upper- and middle-class families, analogous to their undervalued place in traditional society. This new women's position undermined their status even more, and it was not uncommon to find women workers active in numerous strikes and wage demonstrations, despite the fact that their number constituted approximately only a quarter of all industrial workers.

Women and children were considered the cheapest labour force of all. Some laws aimed to protect pregnant women (for example, a paid six-week leave before and after childbirth, industrial owners' obligation to provide day-care centres for their workers' children, and women's right to ensured medical treatment); these laws were not enforced. The existence of an unemployed reserve labour force compelled women to work under any conditions in order to keep their jobs. This situation was common despite the fact that, very often, the money they earned was not sufficient even to cover one month's rent in a damp cellar with no running water or plumbing. The number of tuberculosis cases increased significantly.

Women's participation in the labour force

WOMEN'S LEGAL AND ECONOMIC STATUS FROM 1918 TO 1945 The trend during this period was to employ very young women and minors, and to dismiss older persons from employment. Almost 40 per cent of all female workers in the 1930s were in the thirteen-to-twenty-two age-group (in comparison to 27 per cent of men); they received 30 per cent lower wages than men. In spite of the fact that women clerks were working in slightly better conditions, they were subjected to other forms of strict working regulations. The Decree on Personal and Family Allowances of Civil Servants lowered the income of married women in state offices by 50 per cent. Resolving the problem of unemployed male teachers came at the expense of their female colleagues. If a female teacher married a man who was not a teacher himself, she lost her job. As Jovanka Kecman commented (1978), women teachers were submitted to a kind of forced celibacy if they wanted to stay economically independent. Both the domination of younger women among female workers and the attempt to remove married women from paid jobs illustrated the tendency to put women in their 'natural environment' of the home.

Croatia: continuity and change

Obviously, women were not equal to men in the eyes of the law. All legal regulations sanctioned women's inequality, with one significant exception: criminal law. Women were regarded as 'responsible for criminal acts under the same conditions as men' (Kecman 1978: 60). In fact, legal regulations did not include a prohibitive clause referring to specific gender; rather they related to the general and specific capabilities of the persons concerned. Nevertheless, the Appellate Court for Croatia, Slavonia and Međimurje in Zagreb (1925) denied the right of two women adjuncts to vote in criminal matters: 'because you are a woman, who by law cannot be a testament witness ... you cannot be a judge or attorney', according to Nikolić (2000: 243–67). Women were expelled from professions for which they could be educated (at least from 1901, when three women were allowed to study at the Philosophy Faculty in Zagreb). In the process of reducing the female workforce in state institutions, using the Employment Acts of 1931 (continually revised at the expense of women in 1933, 1934 and 1937), women with university degrees were forbidden to work. Highly qualified middle-class women fought for the right to enter the professions, with their own affiliations, as a way of self-realization in search of a new women's identity. Spaces for them were not opened until the end of the Second World War, in the context of a new political environment.

Types of occupation

INSIDE COMMUNIST YUGOSLAVIA (1945–91) During the socialist period of Croatian political history, the status of women radically improved. In a broader framework of various revolutionary changes, obstacles to women's legal and economic equality were abolished by a simple act of political will in accordance with the communist ideology of declarative equality. Two major tasks had to be accomplished: first, to eradicate illiteracy, and second, to rebuild the enormously devastated country. In every village that was liberated during the Second World War, the Anti-Fascist Front of Women began literacy courses. Their motto was 'Death to Illiteracy – Education is a Weapon Against the Enemy'.

Many campaigns were launched in order to 'draw the women's workforce' into the public sphere. The need to reconstruct ruined villages and towns led to industrialization and constant migration towards the cities. The percentage of actively employed women increased slightly (from 24.5 per cent in 1948 to 25 per cent in 1950, 32.8 per cent in 1971 and 37.4 per cent in 1991).

Women were concentrated in certain low-paying industries and professions (textiles, nursing and teaching). In addition, a pyramidal structure was firmly entrenched. In 1971, only 9.2 per cent of management positions were held by women. Women were accepted as employees, but scarcely as those who could make decisions. The proclaimed family concept, in which both parents were employed, had to be accompanied by general social support: affordable children's day-care centres, paid maternity leave, and a guaranteed job after one year of maternal absence. Some legally ensured institutional support eased the burden for women, but running a household and childcare remained primarily a woman's task in the consciousness of the average patriarchal man.

Income and poverty

DECONSTRUCTION AND RECONSTRUCTION – 1991–2004 For women in Croatia, the end of the century meant being faced with another war, another deconstruction of political and ideological systems, and another economic transition. All communist countries relied deeply on the development of heavy industry, but all the industry that was built up in the decades after the Second World War was almost totally destroyed in the process of privatization. 'Transition' in everyday language means unemployment: diminishing of social rights; weakening of the social security system; privatization of the healthcare system, education and pension funds; job insecurity; further pauperization and marginalization of already marginalized social groups (such as women); the domination of men's management in state administration, businesses and unions; inefficiency; and corruption of the judicial system.

Women were subjected to both vertical and horizontal discrimination. Only 6 per cent of women hold executive management positions and they earn less than men; women experts in their fields receive an income 6.8 per cent lower than that of their male colleagues. Women's average income for 2003 was 13 per cent lower than men's. Horizontal discrimination is growing stronger: women are ghettoized in the secondary labour force market with low income and worsening labour conditions. A low valorization of certain previously respected professions is in direct correlation with their feminization (e.g. physicians, teachers). Also, 67.4 per cent of women are part-time workers.

Literacy and education

Literacy rates Statistics show a generally positive trend in female education. In 1900, 35.5 per cent of all women had elementary literacy. There are no data showing which social classes functionally literate women came from, but regional differences were considerable: coastal Dalmatia had a higher percentage of illiterate population than did continental Croatia and Slavonia. Figure 7.3 shows the constant decrease in illiteracy, but also the growing disproportion between illiterate men and women towards the century's end. In 1981,

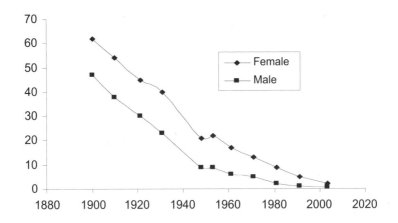

Figure 7.3 Illiteracy rate by gender (per cent) *Sources*: **Steinman (1956);**
<www.geographyiq.com>

78.7 per cent of all illiterate persons were female; in 1991, 81.7 per cent of all illiterate persons were women.

School completion rates

PRIMARY AND SECONDARY In the first half of the century, traditional negative attitudes towards the education of girls were still strong. Girls were considerably less schooled than boys, which is evident from the illiteracy rates. Parents were reluctant to send girls to schools, especially in rural areas. After the Second World War, the socialist state promoted mandatory elementary education for all children, which was extended from four to eight years. As

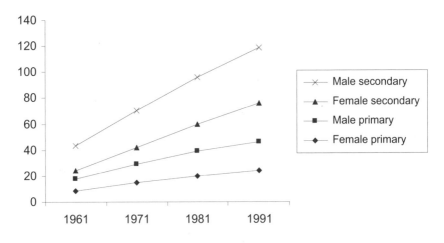

Figure 7.4 Primary and secondary school completion by gender (per cent)
Source: **CBS (1961–91)**

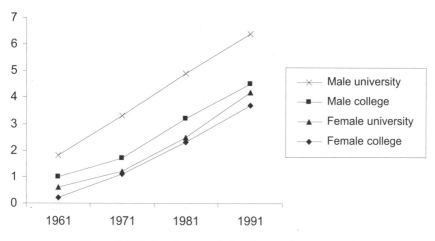

Figure 7.5 University completion by gender (per cent)
Source: CBS (1961-91)

can be seen from Figure 7.4, the educational level of the total population was constantly on the rise throughout the twentieth century.

There is a permanent gap between women and men, however – women are more likely to have below average education. In the last decade, the proportion attending primary and secondary schools for adults was 2.5 times higher for men than for women.

HIGHER EDUCATION Women were not permitted to study at university until 1901. The percentage of enrolled women increased after the Second World War. Female students constituted 1 per cent of all enrolees in the academic year 1905/06 but 53 per cent in 1999/2000. Towards the end of the century, the percentage of graduate female students follows that of women in the entire population (Figure 7.5).

The distribution of women within scientific fields, however, shows that a traditional gender role division remains within disciplinary choices. Women have been more prevalent in the social sciences and humanities; in 1991, 71 per cent of all students enrolled in these fields were women. Although more and more women study scientific and technical disciplines, their percentage is significantly lower than men's. For example, in the technical sciences only 31 per cent of the students are women and in the natural sciences only 38 per cent are women. The exception is the feminization of medical science, where there were 67 per cent women medical students in 1999 compared to 32 per cent in 1953. This does not mean that women are more prevalent within highly valued specializations such as surgery, or that they hold leading positions at clinics. Women occupy specializations such as primary medicine, paediatrics

Croatia: continuity and change

and microbiology, which are not highly valued and are less well paid than other medical specializations (Cerjan-Letica 1987: 94).

In 1997, 52 per cent of all university graduates were women, but at higher scholarly levels the situation is different. The number of women who received MA degrees is lower than that of men, although a small increase was seen from 43 per cent in 1992 to 46 per cent in 1996. The number of women who receive PhD degrees is even smaller, ranging from 32 per cent of all doctoral degrees in 1992 to 36 per cent in 1996 (Zaborski -Cunović 2002).

Fewer women than men are involved in university teaching and research. An analysis of the gender representation of persons employed in higher education shows that the number of women drops the higher the position: there are 47 per cent women in the position of junior assistant lecturers, 46 per cent as assistant lecturers, 45 per cent as senior assistant lecturers, 35 per cent as senior lecturers, 29 per cent as associate professors, and only 19 per cent as full-time professors. The upward mobility of women in sciences and in higher education is less than men's, though it is greater in research institutes.

With the syndrome of double and triple burdens, women's position is not adequately validated within the managerial structure of higher education; women deans and vice-chancellors are rare (Tomić-Koludrović 2003). More women are present at the lower levels of education. Among primary school teachers in 1998/99, 76 per cent were women. In secondary and high schools, this figure was 64 per cent.

Political, educational and cultural leadership

Suffrage: participation in voting and elections At the beginning of the twentieth century, 16 per cent of all men in Croatia and Slavonia had the right to vote. Political debate about universal suffrage did include demands for female suffrage, especially in the light of the experience of the First World War, when men left for the front lines, leaving women to manage the farming on their own in the harsh war economy. The leap from 200,000 to 1 million voters was considered too drastic, however, and the proposition for female suffrage was rejected both in 1917 and in 1920, when the constitution of the new state, the Kingdom of Serbs, Croats and Slovenes, was proclaimed (with 36 votes in favour and 253 against female suffrage).

The principal suffragist organization between 1926 and 1939 was the politically neutral Alliance of the Women's Movement, which campaigned for female suffrage in 1927, 1935, 1937 and 1939, when it organized massive demonstrations throughout the country. The Alliance collaborated with the International Alliance of Women and the International Council of Women, whose congress was held in Dubrovnik in 1936. Croatian (and Yugoslav) women obtained political rights (the right to vote, equality before the law) in 1945, after liberation and establishment of the socialist regime.

The twentieth century can be divided into two periods. The first was the period of struggle for legal and political equality led by women in feminist and leftist organizations, culminating in considerable participation in the partisan liberation movement during the Second World War. The second was the socialist period, when political and social equality was encouraged but also limited by the undemocratic political system marked by patriarchal tradition and official Marxist social theory, both hostile to specific feminist demands. The last decade brought the independence of the Republic of Croatia (25 June 1991), a Western-type democracy marked by political pluralism. The first free multi-party elections were held on 22 April 1990.

Political leadership

1900–18 As in all of the Austro-Hungarian empire, the legal inequality of the two sexes in Croatian lands was the result of the predominant influence of Roman law. The Austrian civil code from 1811 was still in use in Croatia and Slavonia even between the two world wars. Only in Dalmatia (which belonged to the Austrian part of the monarchy) were some amendments introduced in 1914, 1915 and 1916 which enabled women to be testimony witnesses and guardians of their own children after the death of the father. Civil marriage 'by necessity', in addition to the religious union, was another novelty. Women's organized public activities were tied to charity work in small, often religiously defined organizations. Before 1914, there were sixty such groups, with memberships ranging from twenty-five to 350. Women were invited recurrently by political parties to support the nation-building process, mainly as mothers and educators of children, and for the benefit of national culture. In times of political crises, some urban women participated in political demonstrations in public places or from the gallery in the parliament.

1918–41 The Kingdom of Serbs, Croats and Slovenes was a parliamentary monarchy that united the southern Slavic provinces with their very different levels of economic and cultural development. While the northern lands, such as Slovenia and Croatia, had attained a certain level of industrialization, the southern provinces, Bosnia and Herzegovina and Macedonia in particular, were mostly rural countries with a traditional, patriarchal social structure. Owing to internal political discord and the centralizing tendencies of Belgrade's ruling elite, the political system was very unstable. The country changed its name to the Kingdom of Yugoslavia in 1929, and underwent a royal dictatorship from 1929 to 1935.

The period between the two world wars can be considered as the classical period of Western-style women's organizing in the struggle for political and social rights. Already in 1921, the umbrella Women's Union (a pre-war Serbian organization) had amalgamated 205 organizations with 50,000 members across the country, but some conservative religious and Croatian nationalist women's organizations remained independent.

While these organizations rallied mainly urban upper-class and educated women, the majority of rural women remained politically passive. Some of them were attracted to conservative religious organizations; others were targeted by political parties (such as the leading Croatian Peasant Party or the illegal Communist Party) which organized analphabetic (literacy) courses, and cultural and economic development. The overall political activism of women, however, remained relatively modest. In the 1930s, the United Working Trade Union of Yugoslavia had nearly 10 per cent female members (2,639), but that was only a little over 1 per cent of all employed women, much less than the number of female workers participating in strikes and protests. Female membership of the Yugoslav Communist Party rose from 0.8 per cent in 1925 to 6 per cent in 1940 (390 out of 6,500 persons, 4,000 of them from Croatia) (Jancar-Webster 1990: 101). Nevertheless, this small group of mostly young activists would form the core of the important mobilization of women in the anti-fascist movement that would fight for political equality during the Second World War.

1941–45 The war in Yugoslavia was not only waged between the Axis occupiers and the resisters, it also had the characteristics of a civil war between the communist-led partisan movement that sought to liberate the country and carry out the socialist revolution, and the Croatian pro-fascist nationalistic Ustasha and Serbian royalist Chetniks. The two latter movements adopted a very conservative attitude towards women, while the communists promised the emancipation of women within the framework of a general revolutionary project. As a result, the attempt to mobilize women into a separate Ustasha organization failed, while the communists succeeded in attracting many women, mostly peasants, to join the resistance.

According to official (but unreliable) figures, 2 million women participated in the liberation movement in all of Yugoslavia, which is around 24 per cent of the total female population of the country (as opposed to 3.7 million men). Around 5 per cent of them were members of the partisan army; no more than

10 per cent of the troops were women and they were primarily young peasant girls; 42 per cent fought as soldiers and 40 per cent served as medical aides (ibid.: 46, 83). The rest participated in local government in the liberated territory or were active in the Anti-Fascist Front of Women. Women entered the highest political institutions: the first Yugoslav anti-fascist assembly (AVNOJ) in 1942 had one female delegate, Kata Pejnović from Croatia, while the second conference in 1943 included eighteen women (seven full and eleven deputy delegates). The first Croatian wartime assembly (ZAVNOH) had 9.8 per cent female members (eleven out of 112 in 1943).

1945–90 The Yugoslav socialist political system endorsed gender equality, but official Marxist ideology defined emancipation of women as part of the overall emancipation of the working class. The second wave feminism that emerged among sociologists and other intellectuals in Croatia at the end of the 1970s was not welcomed by state women's organizations, which professed that the so-called 'women's question' was resolved during the war and the socialist revolution. Women's social and economic condition had improved compared to pre-war times.

The political breakthrough from the end of the 1950s to the beginning of the 1960s resulted from an increase in female education and employment. Social and cultural changes were not sufficiently deep, however; a more traditional attitude towards politics as a male domain prevailed. From 1974, the new and complicated delegate system, with quotas and an accent on self-management in the workplace, stabilized women's participation but could not foster further attitude changes. The triple burden of workplace, home-making and child-rearing discouraged women from taking a more active part in politics (Leinert Novosel 1990).

1990–2000 The proclamation of Croatian independence and the introduction of a multi-party democratic system in the 1990s were accompanied by ethnic nationalism, war and economic neo-liberalism. The resulting wave of retraditionalization in the discourse of the nationalistic and populist party (the Croatian Democratic Union) was followed by the ever increasing influence of the Catholic Church. Women's political participation in the turning-point year of 1990 was thus at its lowest level ever. The pressure of the newly developed civil society and feminist NGOs, however, seems to have influenced the political establishment. The leftist Social-Democratic Party (in power in a coalition government from 2000 to 2003) is especially concerned with the promotion of women among its membership.

HEADS OF STATE AND GOVERNMENT Savka Dabčević-Kučar was prime minister of the Croatian government from 1967 to 1969, head of the Communist Party in Croatia from 1969 to 1970, and national leader during the nationalistic movement in 1971. Milka Planinc was head of the Communist Party in Croatia from 1971 to 1982 and (the first female) prime minister of Yugoslavia from 1982 to 1986.

MINISTERIAL (CABINET) As of 1945, there was one female minister in Croatia, but the number did not rise significantly in succeeding years. In some periods, women held the highest party and state positions (Figure 7.6). After an exclusively male government during 1990–92, the cabinets always had one or two female members, most often as ministers of traditionally 'female' areas: education, culture, health, social policy, science and tourism. In 2000, however, the government had three women out of twenty-three ministers (13 per cent), including ministers of defence and of justice, while in 2003 the percentage rose to 27 (four out of fifteen ministers).

PARLIAMENTARY Equality was not easily attained, especially in times with less political regulation (Figure 7.7). The proportion of women in the highest political bodies increased only when there was some kind of regulation and affirmative action, as with the introduction of a delegate system in 1974 or at the very end of the century when leftist parties accepted the need for the conscious promotion of female candidates on election lists. The dynamics of women's political representation are more evident in the number of female deputies in the federal assembly in Belgrade, the highest representative body in the state.

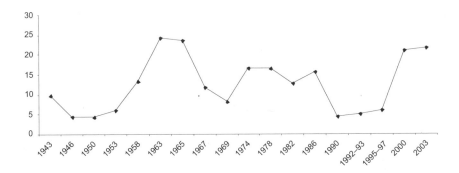

Figure 7.6 Female members of Croatian assemblies (per cent) *Source:* Peric´ **(2000). The number of houses varied from two to five during self-management, so the total is given. From 2000, the parliament was unicameral**

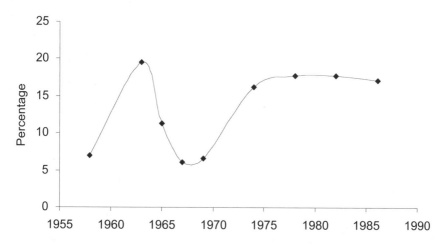

Figure 7.7 Women deputies and assembly delegates (Yugoslavia per cent)
Source: **Leinert Novosel (1990: 29, 33)**

LOCAL GOVERNMENT Today, fourteen out of 123 Croatian cities have female mayors (11 per cent). According to one study, around 88 per cent of women voted in the parliamentary elections in 1990, 1992 and 1995, showing a great degree of politicization among women in Croatian society (Tomić-Koludrović and Kunac 2000: 148).

PARTY LEADERSHIP The highest executive positions in the central committee of the Communist Party of Yugoslavia were always held by men. Progress in this regard has been relatively slow (Figure 7.8).

Participation in religious institutions Croatia is a predominantly Catholic country. The division of labour in the Catholic Church is traditionally strict; priests, theologians, administrators and leaders were always men, while nuns

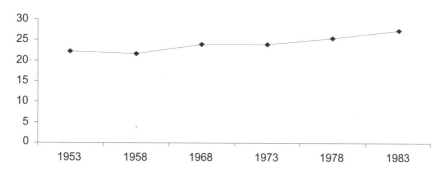

Figure 7.8 Female membership of the Communist Party of Croatia (per cent)
Sources: **Statistički podaci (1959: 20; 1974: 14; 1984: 9)**

and laywomen were active primarily in religious education and social work. In the last decade, considerably more female students have entered theological faculties (up to 52 per cent of students were laywomen in 1997/98), but they are still more attracted to religious education than to theology. Female university professors in Croatia are very rare. The most visible woman in the Catholic Church is the head of the Caritas organization.

Artistic, creative and cultural contributions The participation of women in cultural work, including women artists, and in various cultural institutes can be followed somewhat more precisely from the mid-twentieth century. A noticeably greater presence of women can be seen towards the end of the century, but it should be emphasized that there are disparities between education and the later professional artistic work of women. Very few female students were at the Art Academy for the academic year 1945/46 (26 per cent) and in 1953/54 it was even lower (23 per cent). More women worked in music. At the Music Academy in 1945/46, immediately after the war, females comprised 51 per cent of students; in 1953/54, 54 per cent of all students were women (Steinman 1956: 19).

At the end of the century, 1996/97, 65.9 per cent of all students who graduated from music academies were women; 52.77 per cent from the Academy of Art and 36.3 per cent from the Academy of Dramatic Arts. The number of women lecturers at arts academies is disproportionate in relation to the number of female students. In 1996/97, women constituted 28.3 per cent of all lecturers at arts academies. Women make up only 35 per cent of professional artists.

On the other hand, the number of women who work in various cultural institutions is considerably greater. In 1996, women made up 85.5 per cent of those working in libraries, 60 per cent in museums, 58 per cent in publishing activities, and 58 per cent in archives (Kodrnja 2001: 196). These are activities in which high profits are not realized, however. Even though women are employed in the cultural sector, when it comes to higher-status and management functions, only then does their under-representation become visible (for example, 57 per cent of leading directorial functions in the year 2000 were performed by men). Males are still dominant within this profession in terms of status and symbolic power. The Museum Council of seven members has a male as president; of the remaining six members, only two are women (Franulić 2001: 21).

The absence of women is also noticeable in school resources and textbooks. For instance, in four high-school textbooks on literature, mention is made of one female author for the first, second and fourth years, while the textbook for the third year makes no mention of any female writer. During the four-year span of high-school courses in art history, only two female artists are mentioned; in the history of music, only two female jazz singers are mentioned (Mahalia Jackson and Ella Fitzgerald), and one Croatian musician, Dora Pejačević.

Towards gender equality

As we have seen, in many aspects the quality of life for Croatian women has progressively improved. They benefit from better healthcare, have a better educational level, and live longer than their grandmothers. As a group, however, they still lag behind men. The recurrent inequality of life chances between the two genders is even more emphasized in times of social crisis and transition.

Nevertheless, future prospects are brightened by the joint action of civil society and government in promoting the idea of gender equality and fighting inequality by raising consciousness about the different forms it takes. The most important are measures that reduce androcentric bias in education (textbooks), the economy and human relations. The Croatian population is gradually learning about the different forms of violence against women, including domestic violence, verbal abuse, sexist stereotypes and sexual harassment in the workplace and the academy.

Under pressure from feminist groups, and in order to comply with European Union standards, a number of institutions were created at the threshold of the twenty-first century: the Parliamentary Committee for Gender Equality, the Ombudsperson for Gender Equality (2003) and the Governmental Office for Gender Equality (2004). In 2003, parliament proclaimed the law on gender equality. Women's NGOs actively contribute to the political education of women and cooperate with political parties and local communities in order to bring the proclaimed principles to life. Civil society endeavours to subvert the paradoxes of transition that threaten the highest level of female well-being. Thus, the twentieth century was marked by continuity of certain patriarchal biases while at the same time spawning significant changes that support gender equality in Croatia.

References

CBS (Central Bureau of Statistics) (various years), Zagreb: CBS

Cerjan-Letica, G. (1987) 'Profesija liječnica', *Žena i društvo: kultiviranje dijaloga*, Zagreb: Sociološko društvo Hrvatske, pp. 91–9

Deseti kongres SKJ (1974) *Statistički podaci o Savezu komunista Jugoslavije*, Belgrade: Stručna služba Predsjedništva SKJ

Franulić (2001) 'Muzealci u brojkama (zastupljenost prema spolu)', *Informatica museologica*, 32(1–2): 18–21

Gelo, J. (1987) *Demografske promjene u Hrvatskoj od 1780 do 1981 godine*, Zagreb: Globus

Jancar-Webster, B. (1990) *Women and Revolution in Yugoslavia 1941–1945*, Denver, CO: Arden Press

Kecman, J. (1978) *Žene Jugoslavije u radničkom pokretu i ženskim organizacijama 1918–1941*, Belgrade: Narodna knjiga–Institut za suvremenu historiju

Kodrnja, J. (2001) *Nimfe, Muze, Euronime: društveni položaj umjetnica u Hrvatskoj*, Zagreb: Alinea

Leinert Novosel, S. (1990) *Žene–politička manjina: Perspektive sudjelovanja žena u javnom životu*, Zagreb: NIRO Radničke novine

Merunka Golubić, M. (2003) 'Reprodukcijska prava', *Ženski biografski leksikon*, unpublished manuscript

Nikolić, L. (2000) 'Institucija vlasti muža: historijsko pravni aspekti', in M. Blagojević (ed.), *Mapiranje mizoginije u Srbiji: Diskursi i prakse*, Belgrade: AŽIN, pp. 243–67

Perić, I. (2000) *Hrvatski državni sabor 1848–2000, III*, Zagreb: Hrvatski institut za povijest–Hrvatski državni sabor–Dom i svijet

Petrović, J. (ed.) (2000) *Diskriminacija žena u Hrvatskoj*, Zagreb: ICFTU CEE Women's Network and Ženska sekcija SSSH

Savez komunista (1959) *Statistićki podaci Organizacije Saveza komunista u NR Hrvatskoj za razdoblje od III do IV*, Zagreb: Kongresa SKH

Sklevicky, L. (1996) *Konji, žene, ratovi*, Zagreb: Ženska infoteka

Stein Erlich, V. (1971) 'Jugoslavenska porodica u transformaciji', *Studija u tri stotine sela*, Zagreb: Liber

Steinman, Z. (1956) *Visoko školstvo u NR Hrvatskoj*, Zavod: Zavod za statistiku

Tomić-Koludrović, I. (2003) *Žene u znanosti u Hrvatskoj: današnji položaj i perspektive*, unpublished manuscript

Tomić-Koludrović, I. and S. Kunac (2000) *Rizici modernizacije: Žene u Hrvatskoj devedesetih*, Split: Stope nade

UNICEF (United Nations Children's Fund) (2003) *Progress Since the World Summit for Children: The ChildInfo Statistical Database*, New York: UNICEF

Zaborski-Čunović, K. (2002) 'Feministička epistemologija kao izazov', *Treća*, 2 (IV): 196–205

Websites

WHO (World Health Organization) (2000) *Highlights on Health in Croatia*, <www.euro.who.int/document/E72495.pdf>

<www.geographyiq.com/countries/hr/Croatia_people.htm>

8 | Women in Iceland: strong women – myths and contradictions

THORGERÐUR EINARSDÓTTIR[1]

Women in Iceland, an island in the north Atlantic Ocean that lies between Greenland to the west and Ireland to the east, mounted a strong women's movement during the twentieth century. Women contributed to the economy, entered the paid labour force in high numbers, and engaged in an unusually persistent political struggle. Today, female well-being in Iceland is better than in many other parts of the world. Nevertheless, when compared to that of their Nordic sisters in neighbouring Nordic countries, the situation for women in Iceland today is in many ways weaker. In general, formal and legal equality exists for women in Iceland, but they face much overt and hidden discrimination (Einarsdóttir 2002; Thorgeirsdóttir 2002). A brief glimpse at the life of women in Iceland today reveals a picture of women with more children, longer working hours in paid work, and lower political representation.

The history of twentieth-century Iceland reflects many myths and contradictions that characterize the legacy of Icelandic women's struggle for citizenship and emancipation. During the first decades, women in Iceland were participants in society in many different ways, carving spaces in which to operate despite a multiplicity of structures constraining their potential. Strong liberation movements flourished throughout the century, echoing the Icelandic sagas that featured strong women. Against the background of mythical images of strength and decades of concerted efforts, the socio-political influence of women is more limited in modern Iceland than one might expect. Contradictions and competing ideologies colour gender relations that are simultaneously 'modern' and 'traditional' (Júlíusdóttir 1993). The future task is to identify the mechanisms behind these contradictions and to develop strategies that will overcome barriers to gender equality.

From settlement to independence

People of Nordic and Celtic origin settled in Iceland in the ninth century. In 1262, Iceland came under the Norwegian Crown, and in 1381 under the Danish monarchy. The struggle for independence began in the 1830s. The ancient parliament at Thingvellir, founded in 930, was re-established in Reykjavik in 1845 as a consultative assembly for the nation. In 1874, Iceland received its own constitution and legislative power in internal affairs. The executive power was transferred to Iceland in 1904 when the island nation obtained home rule. Home rule ended in 1918, when Iceland became a separate state under the Danish Crown. Iceland gained full sovereignty in 1944 as the Icelandic Republic.

Geographically and historically, Iceland belongs to the Nordic countries, but it is more isolated than the Scandinavian nations. The population is small compared to that of other Nordic countries and to the other countries in this book. In 1901, the population was 78,000; by the end of 2003, it had increased to over 290,000. Because of isolation and size, the population is relatively homogenous in language, ethnicity and religion.

The historical legacy of Icelandic women

Icelandic sagas and Nordic mythology describe women as being independent and powerful. Inherited sociocultural values shape a continuity from the saga period up to the present, reflected in the interaction patterns and coping strategies of modern families. The situation of women in Iceland is overshadowed by the myth of the 'strong Icelandic woman'. This is a double-edged sword: in private life, women often feel loyal to the historical image, which can result in acceptance of unacceptable situations. To complain is to be defeated (ibid.).

The struggle for independence and nation-building is a deeply gendered process. Historian Sigridur Matthiasdóttir (2004), in analysing the ideological basis of the connection between national identity and social position, 1900–30, showed how the making of the Icelandic nation was entirely masculine. The 'rational' individual's needs for freedom, autonomy and democracy were constructed in hierarchic opposition to female identity. During the same period, women had a strong presence in social life and entered politics with separate lists in local and national elections. After initial success, women suffered a great defeat in the form of strong, growing resistance to women's full participation in public life. By 1930, the 'housewife ideology' became the dominant view of women's role in society, claiming that the future of the Icelandic nation was based on women's role as mothers and housewives (ibid.: 371–4). This ideology persisted for decades. The depression that struck Iceland between 1930 and 1940 (as it did many countries) ended with the Second World War and the post-war economic upswing. Female well-being improved throughout the twentieth century, but the socio-economic situation is still far behind that of other Nordic countries: Icelandic women have a long way to go to full gender equality.

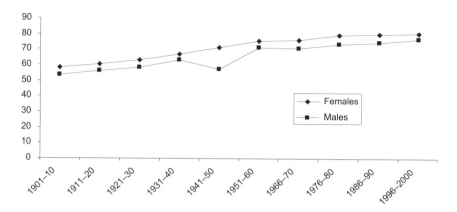

Figure 8.1 Life expectancy by gender at age one *Sources*: Jónsson and Magnússon (1997: Table 2.47); SI (2001: Table 2.41)

A demographic portrait of Icelandic women

Urbanization In the twentieth century Iceland saw extensive urbanization with subsequent changes in social structure and economy. In 1880, more than 90 per cent of the population lived in rural areas and 75 per cent of these were engaged in agriculture. Today, this figure is less than 10 per cent (Gunnlangsson 1993: 107). In 1900, 17 per cent of the population lived in villages with more than two hundred inhabitants. In 2002, this rate was 92 per cent (SI 2003a: Table 2.6). In 1900, the population was evenly distributed over Iceland, with a minority living in the Reykjavik area. There has been a movement from rural areas to urban nuclei or localities, alongside a movement to the Reykjavik area, where more than 60 per cent of the population now live (ibid.: Table 2.5).

Life expectancy Average life expectancy has increased rapidly for both genders (Figure 8.1). In 2000, life expectancy was 77.9 years for men and 81.5 years for women, among the highest rates for Nordic countries (NCM 2003: 82).

Population growth, fertility rate and male–female ratio Iceland's fertility rate (per thousand women) dropped from 3.9 in 1900 to 2.1 in 2000; it peaked in the 1960s and then fell dramatically in the 1970s (Figure 8.2). The country has a high fertility rate compared to other Nordic countries (e.g. 1.5 in Sweden and 1.8 in Norway as of 2000 – NCM 2003: 79).

Age structure of the population Iceland's population is relatively young. In 2000, almost one in four was below the age of fifteen (23 per cent) and 12 per

Women in Iceland

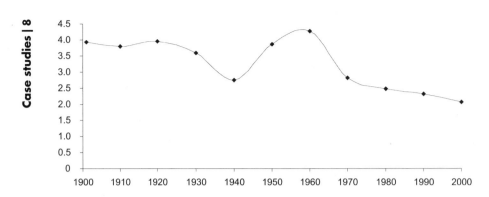

Figure 8.2 Fertility rate, 1900–2000 (per 1,000) *Sources:* **Jónsson and Magnússon (1997: Table 2.38); SI (2003a: Table 2.35)**

cent were sixty-five years or older (SI 2002–2003: 7). In 1960, the figures were 35 and 8 per cent respectively (Jónsson and Magnússon 1997: 125).

Maternal mortality rate Iceland's maternal mortality rate declined dramatic-ally during the first half of the century. For 1911–15, the maternal mortality rate was 3.9 per 1,000 births, but it declined to 1.1 per 1,000 births in 1946–50, mostly because of antibiotics and blood transfusions (Bjarnadóttir 2003). This gain reflects improved material conditions in Iceland, especially from improve-ments in health.

Infant mortality rate Iceland's infant mortality rate (before age one) is among the lowest in the world, although during the early 1800s it was the highest in Europe (Gardarsdóttir 2002). The rate decreased rapidly from 127 per 1,000 live births in 1900 to 3 in 2000. The most dramatic improvement took place between 1920 and 1930 (Figure 8.3). The decline stemmed from a change in how mothers fed their newborns. Midwives played a crucial role in promoting breastfeeding, which many women had abandoned earlier in favour of table food that mothers chewed or cut up for their babies. Breastfed infants had considerably better chances than those who were not. This re-education process depended on improving levels of literacy, since the custom of breastfeeding spread earlier in areas with higher literacy (Gardarsdóttir 2002).

Contraception and abortion The numbers of relatively young and old women giving birth (fifteen to nineteen years and thirty-five to thirty-nine years) is higher than in the other Nordic countries, indicating that the use of contra-

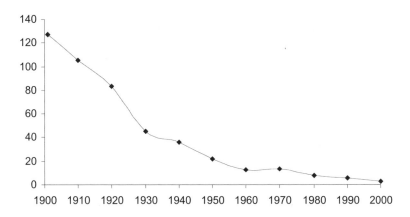

Figure 8.3 Infant mortality rate, 1900–2000 (per 1,000) *Sources:* Jónsson and Magnússon (1997: Table 2.2.c); SI (2001: Table 2.1)

ceptives is less systematic (Heilsufar kvenna 2000). Thus, 6 per cent of all women giving birth in 2000 were fifteen to nineteen years old, and 22 per cent were twenty to twenty-four years old; nearly 3 per cent of the women were forty or older (SI 2003a).

Family status and structure

It is an Icelandic tradition that women normally maintain their original surnames when they marry, as an indication of a certain independence from the husband. At the dawn of the twentieth century, married women were dependent on their husbands and did not enjoy full adult legal rights. In 1900, a new law entitled women to full rights over their own income and property (Pálsdóttir Flygenring 1985). According to a taxation law that was in effect from 1921 until 1978, though, married women were treated as appendages to their husbands. In 1978, a partially individualized taxation system was initiated (Thordardóttir 1985).

Marriage and divorce Marriage rates in Iceland are relatively low, as is the case in the other Nordic countries. Consensual unions have been very common: the man and the woman as an 'engaged' couple, which became a widely accepted and enduring phenomenon (Helgadóttir 2004). This is the Icelandic form of extra-legal family formation, an international phenomenon known in Sweden as 'Stockholm marriage' (Kyle 2002: 51) and as 'common-law marriage' in the United States and Canada. Icelanders are rather liberal when it comes to children born out of wedlock, partly because of the widespread acceptance of consensual unions. Rates of children born out of wedlock have been much

Women in Iceland

higher in Iceland than in other countries, doubling in the 1921–46 period to 26 per cent (Helgadóttir 2004).

During the post-war period, the marriage rates were high because of the economic upswing, with approximately eight or nine marriages per thousand inhabitants. After 1975, the marriage rates went down dramatically, reaching a low in the mid-1990s. The drop could be related to the radical climate of the 1970s and the women's movement, which was very influential in Iceland. In recent years, marriage rates have been rising again; in 2001, the rate was approximately five per thousand.

Divorce rates showed a successive increase during the post-war period, but from 1975 to 2000 the rates were relatively stable at 1.9 per 1,000. In relation to marriage rates, however, the gap is widening. In the 1960s, 10 per cent of all marriages ended in divorce; this figure has increased to 40 per cent in recent years. International data suggest an increasing frequency of marital crises rooted in a deep transformation of modern societies and the patriarchal family (Castells 1997). Marriage has been depicted as an eroding institution (Liljestrom 2002). During the first part of twentieth century, family law aimed to make it easy for people to get married. The emphasis today is on facilitating separation. Thus, the laws on joint custody for divorced parents were enacted in 1992. Table 8.1 reflects clearly the changes that have occurred in family structure since 1960. The biggest change is among cohabiting or married couples with children, a category whose size has decreased dramatically since 1960, while cohabiting or married couples without children have been successively increasing. Single fathers continue to be a very small group, while

TABLE 8.1 Nuclear families, 1965–2000 (%)

	1965	1970	1980	1990	2000
Married without children	26.0	28.8	31.3	34.6	33.6
Cohabiting without children	1.4	1.5	1.6	3.3	4.2
TOTAL	27.4	30.3	32.9	37.9	37.8
Married with children	59.9	56.0	51.1	38.7	34.1
Cohabiting with children	3.4	3.0	5.3	10.8	12.7
TOTAL	63.3	59.0	56.4	49.5	46.8
Single fathers with children	0.6	0.6	0.6	0.9	1.2
Single mothers with children	8.7	10.1	10.1	11.8	14.2

Sources: Jónsson and Magnússon (1997: Table 2.20); SI (2003a: Table 2.12). Age of children is under sixteen for 1965–90; under eighteen for 2000.

single mothers are slowly increasing. Step families are increasing (Júlíusdóttir 1995).

Cohabitation and registered partnerships among gay men and lesbians, who have more legal rights in Iceland than in many other countries, is also on the rise. The law on registered partnerships entered into force in 1996. From 1996 to 2003, forty-eight male couples and fifty-three female couples registered partnerships; twelve male couples and seven female couples are documented as having dissolved (SI 2003b; SI 2004: 3). In 2000, a law was passed that granted gay men and lesbians in registered partnerships the right to step adoptions but not to adoptions (Kristinsson 2000).

Family policies

SOCIAL WELFARE Iceland belongs to the 'family-friendly' Nordic countries, but it departs from them when it comes to public support of families with children. Iceland has a more parsimonious welfare system (Ólafsson 2003), spending considerably less on social welfare (20 per cent of GNP in 2001) than others (26–31 per cent) (NCM 2003: 114).

PARENTAL LEAVE POLICIES In most European countries, national policies that facilitate combining paid work and family responsibilities have developed gradually over a long time. The parental leave system in Iceland, and especially paternity leave, is an exception. Until very recently, it was a highly differentiated and complicated system, distinguishing between different groups of women, depending on whether they were civil servants or employed in the private labour market. Moreover, the system covered certain groups of men while excluding others. The 1946 Act on Social Security guaranteed women a certain amount of money. In 1954, female civil servants won ninety days' fully paid maternity leave; in 1975, unionized working mothers received the same (Einarsdóttir 2004: 19–22).

The 1980 Act on Maternity Leave forbids the dismissal of women on maternity leave. The act did not cover female civil servants, as another law protected their rights. In 1987, maternity leave was extended to six months for both female civil servants and employees in the private labour market. A distinction was made, however, in payments between women in the private and women in the public labour market, leaving women in the private market with limited and insecure leave benefits. Female civil servants had relatively good allowances (ibid.: 19–22).

In 1998, all men were given two independent weeks of paternity leave. In 2000, Iceland passed new laws on parental leave, which are unique in the world. With the new Act on Maternity/Paternity and Parental Leave, men in Iceland were granted a three-month, non-transferable paternity leave, implemented in three steps. The total length of the leave was extended from six to nine months, three months for each of the parents, leaving three months for the parents to divide at their own discretion. The payment is 80 per cent of gross wages, with a fixed minimum amount and an upper limit. This legislation represents a fundamental step in the promotion of gender equality in other areas as well. For example, it is believed that it helps level out gender differences in the labour market and reduce the gender wage gap (Bjartmarz 2003).

DAY CARE POLICIES During the 1960s, children's day care became an increasingly important issue in the social debate. In 1981, 14 per cent of children up to two years old received institutional or family day care; in 1999, it was 42 per cent (Eydal 2001). For children aged three to six years old, public day care was limited until the mid-1990s. In Reykjavik, until 1994 the official care policies were to provide only part-time day care for married couples. In the last decade, there has been an increase in the coverage, along with a rise in the number of full-time placements. In 2002, 70 per cent of children up to five years old had some day care provision (NCM 2003: 117).

Economic participation

Industrialization took place in Iceland at the beginning of the twentieth century. Industrialization started with mechanization of the fishing fleet (Magnússon 1993: 112). The economy of Iceland is unique for its small size and its dependence on fishing, which has been Iceland's basic industry for a long time. During the first decades of the century, fisheries replaced agriculture as the basic economic sector, but during recent decades the importance of fishing has been declining in favour of the service sector (ibid.: 123). Economic growth originated in increasing output of natural resources, fisheries and hydroelectric and geothermal energy. Despite Iceland's small population, the economy is modern, and the standard of living is on a par with that of other European countries. The GDP per capita in 2003 was US$29,800, as measured in terms of PPP (Purchasing Power Parities).

At the beginning of the twenty-first century, information technology, life sciences and related services are important growth areas, in addition to hydroelectric power and aluminium plants. Iceland's economy has been prone to inflation owing to periods of rapid growth and its dependence on just a few key export sectors that can fluctuate significantly. The 1970s oil shocks hit

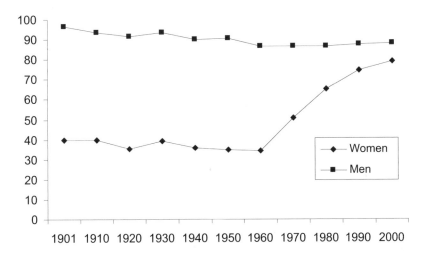

Figure 8.4 Labour force participation rates by gender (per cent) (data for men were not available for 1970, so the 1960 and 1980 figure of 86.6 per cent was used for display purposes *Sources*: Vilhjálmsdóttir (2004, based on Statistics Iceland data)

Iceland hard, contributing to high inflation rates from the 1970s until the 1990s (Andersen and Gudmundsson 1998).

Women in Iceland have contributed significantly to Iceland's economic life, but are few when it comes to economic power and managerial positions. In 2001, women were managers in 18 per cent of registered companies and only 4 per cent of big companies (Efnahagsleg vold kvenna 2004: 21). Women represent only 2.3 per cent of the board members of the fifteen biggest companies on the Icelandic Stock Exchange (Morgunbladid 2004).

Women's participation in the labour force A main characteristic of the Icelandic labour market is its exceptionally high activity rate (SI 2002: 184). In 2000, 79 per cent of women and 88 per cent of men (aged sixteen to seventy-four) were active on the labour market (SI 2002–2003: 8). Women were active throughout the last century (Figure 8.4).

At the beginning of the century, about 40 per cent of women were active on the labour market; that proportion never subsequently fell below one third. A dramatic increase took place in the 1960s, when the proportion of women in paid work rose from 34 to 50 per cent, owing mainly to the entry into the market of married women; until the 1950s, fewer than 10 per cent worked outside the home (Figure 8.5).

Since the 1970s, the numbers of married women in the labour force rose dramatically to surpass that of single women (unmarried, divorced and never-

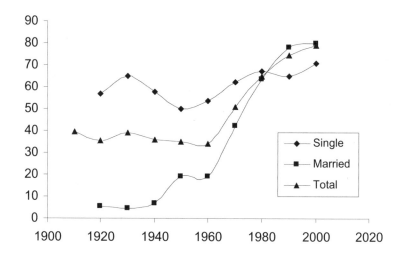

Figure 8.5 Women in the labour force by marital status (per cent)
Source: Vilhjálmsdóttir (2004, based on Statistics Iceland data)

married women). Today, this high labour market participation remains even for women with young children. The housewife ideology applied only to a minority of women and is rapidly disappearing in Iceland.

FULL-/PART-TIME As of 2000, Icelandic women were more likely to work part-time (44 per cent) than were men (11 per cent) (SI 2002: Ch. 2, Table 2.6.12), and were slightly more likely to be unemployed. Icelanders work conspicuously long hours. In 2000, men worked on average fifty-one hours weekly while women worked thirty-six hours. If only those who work full-time are considered, the average working week for men is fifty-four hours, and forty-four hours for women (ibid.: Ch. 2, Table 2.7.11).

TYPES OF OCCUPATION At the end of the nineteenth century almost 80 per cent of Icelanders worked within agriculture, fishing and fish production. Today, the principal employment sectors are services (70 per cent), industry (23 per cent) and agriculture and fishing (7 per cent) (SI 2002–2003: 8; Jónsson and Magnússon 1997). Even with only a minority of the population working in fishing and fish processing throughout the twentieth century, export of fish products continuously represents the greatest proportion of Iceland's exported goods and services. Jobs within this sector were very important for women at the beginning of the twentieth century.

Certainly, in the early 1900s, housekeepers or servants were the biggest occupational group of women working outside of agriculture. These young

TABLE 8.2 Employed persons by occupational group, 1991, 2002 (%)

| | 1991 | | 2002 | |
	Women	Men	Women	Men
Legislators/managers	4.9	11.3	5.0	10.8
Professionals	12.6	11.2	18.6	13.6
Associate professionals	12.0	10.4	16.7	11.4
Clerks	18.2	2.7	14.9	1.9
Service/sales workers	25.6	13.1	27.1	13.1
Agricultural/fishery	4.5	11.7	2.6	8.6
Craft/trades workers	9.9	22.7	4.2	23.4
Machine operators	1.4	10.1	1.5	10.4
Elementary occupations	11.0	6.7	9.3	6.8

Source: SI (2002: Table 2.4.2).

women did housework and caretaking for better-off families in Reykjavik and the larger villages; this was often their first entry into the labour market (Erlendsdóttir 1997: 281). One third of all households had housekeepers (mostly women, but a few men), who constituted approximately 7 per cent of the population in 1910 and 1920. By 1960, housekeepers had fallen to less than 0.5 per cent (Sigurdardóttir 1985: 451; Jónsson and Magnússon 1997: 120). Hence, the decline in the number of housekeepers was the biggest change in women's paid work during the twentieth century (Erlendsdóttir 1997: 281).

Women also supported themselves as free labourers in fish processing. It was common in the early 1900s to be working as a housekeeper during the winter and as a free labourer in fish production during the summer. Women had to work hard in both cases and in harsh conditions. Free labourers were independent, but housekeepers were not (Sigurdardóttir 1985: 416–19).

One of the main features of the Icelandic labour market, as it appears now at the beginning of a new century, is the obvious gender segregation, both by sector and occupation. The vast majority of women (85 per cent) worked in services in 2000, as against 55 per cent of men; 34 per cent of men worked in industry, compared to 11 per cent of women. The gender division within occupations follows that within sectors (SI 2002: Ch. 2, Table 2.3.2). In Table 8.2, employment patterns are displayed by occupational group and gender for 1991 and 2002. The labour market has become more gender segregated in recent years (Mósesdóttir 2004: 31–2).

Women are less likely than men to hold the highest positions: a higher proportion of men are senior officials, managers and legislators. Almost half of all women are employed as clerks, service workers and shop workers (42 per cent versus 15 per cent for men) (SI 2002: Ch. 2, Table 2.4.2). Women are more numerous than are men among the ranks of professionals, clerks and service workers. Many of the female-dominated occupations, such as nursing, teaching and the welfare system, are staffed by professionals who have focused on qualifications and formal education, often without commensurate returns from their education (Einarsdóttir 2000b).

UNEMPLOYMENT Unemployment rates are generally very low in Iceland. Historical data are not available before 1960, but the rate for women is usually slightly higher than for men, with some exceptions. In 2000, the rate for women was 2.9 per cent as against 1.8 per cent for men (SI 2002: Ch. 3, Table 3.1.8).

Income and poverty Women in Iceland struggled for better working conditions and pay from the early 1900s. The first documented women's strike was in 1907 in Hafnarfjordur, a village near Reykjavik. In 1912, women in the same village began a strike that lasted for more than a month (Halldórsdóttir and Jónatansdóttir 1998: 129). The strikes that have gained the most attention historically were in 1926 and 1930 (Sigurdardóttir 1985: 431). The first female trade union was founded in 1914, since women were excluded from the men's unions (Halldórsdóttir and Jónatansdóttir 1998: 108).

Poverty and unemployment characterized the Great Depression. Female well-being was especially vulnerable when so many women earned only half of a man's wage (Helgadóttir 2004). Registration of unemployment and certain employment measures covered only men and boys until 1935. Employers often dismissed women when they married, and the taxation system was disadvantageous to the paid work of married women until 1958 (ibid.). The taxation system reflected clearly the housewife and male breadwinner ideologies, which ignored the fact that more than a third of women were in paid work.

An economic and social upswing swept through Iceland during the post-war period, starting with the British occupation in 1939. In 1940, the British army was replaced by the American army, which is still based at the airport in Keflavik. Occupation meant a heavy injection into the economy, with an improved employment situation, especially for men. The employment rate for women never fell below one third before the 1960s, but after that it increased rapidly.

Wage discrimination against women has been an important social and political issue in Iceland since the first women's associations were founded early in the twentieth century. From 1907, the Icelandic Women's Rights Organization (IWRO) emphasized pay equity. Women's wages were about two-thirds of men's wages until the 1940s (Erlendsdóttir 1997: 280–82). The first clauses on equal pay appeared in a law on civil servants' wages, passed in 1945. The first all-inclusive measure on equal pay was enacted in 1961, but it gave employers five years to adapt. These laws did not eliminate wage discrimination against women. In 1973, a law establishing the Equal Pay Council was passed; since then, all acts regarding gender equality have emphasized equal pay between the sexes (Einarsdóttir and Blondal 2004).

In 1992, almost fifty years after the first laws imposing pay equity were enacted, women's average earnings were still only 55 per cent of men's; this proportion increased to 58 per cent in 2000 (Mósesdóttir 2001: 9). Different hours of paid work explain much of the gap in men and women's average earnings. According to a recent comparative European study, overall gender differences in gross wage rates were 24 per cent in the public sector and 27 per cent in the private sector for 2000, adjusted only for working hours (Barth et al. 2002: 26).

Recent surveys indicate that the so-called adjusted pay gap between men and women is between 12 and 17 per cent, depending on sector and form of compensation. A 2003 survey of service and sales workers found that men in full-time work earned 12 per cent more than women after accounting for occupation, working hours and seniority (Dofradóttir et al. 2003). A new survey among civil servants shows that men earn 17 per cent more than women in comparable occupations, indicating that closing the gender pay gap is a slow process (Jónsdóttir and Blondal 2004).

Literacy and education

Women in Iceland contributed to the economy throughout the twentieth century and were remarkably active on the labour market. The century began with the exclusion of women from education but witnessed a dramatic increase in female education during the last three decades. Women gained formal access to higher education early in the twentieth century; for decades they experienced informal hindrances, but they are now capitalizing on greater educational opportunities. They do not always experience the same returns, however. Recent studies suggest that the gender pay gap may even widen with increased education (Einarsdóttir and Blondal 2004).

Literacy rates The 1907 Education Act made education compulsory for all children from the ages of ten to fourteen. Although the modern school is relatively young, the Icelandic people have traditionally been known for general literacy (Jósepsson 1985). According to a Directive on House Discipline from

1746 (and clarified in 1790), all children were to receive guidance in reading the catechism and in Christian virtues (Halldórsdóttir and Jónatansdóttir 1998: 28). No distinction was made between boys and girls in this directive or in a similar one of 1880 (Gardarsdóttir 2001: 422).

In spite of the gender neutrality of these statements, historical data indicate that parents cared less about the education of their daughters than that of their sons. Girls' writing abilities were thought to be more limited than boys', so only a small minority of women could write by the end of the nineteenth century.

School completion rates

PRIMARY Boys attended school in higher numbers than girls did prior to the 1907 Education Act. This situation was reversed after the act, and when girls entered school, they were more successful in their studies than boys were (ibid.: 422–3).

SECONDARY In 1936, a law made school compulsory for all children from seven to fourteen years old. Before that, education had mainly been the responsibility of parents, even though schools operated around the country. Opportunities continued to be more limited for girls than boys, however, and in the 1930s boys comprised 70 to 80 per cent of all students in Reykjavik's secondary schools (ibid.: 428).

HIGHER EDUCATION Women won equal access to all education and work by virtue of a law enacted in 1911, the same year as the University of Iceland was founded. The IWRO, especially its head, Bríet Bjarnhédinsdóttir, made a major impact when the act was adopted (Erlendsdóttir 1993: 108–13). In these years resistance grew towards the public participation of women. It was assumed that families needed women's emotional and caring abilities. Ironically, as the university opened its doors, there was a great upsurge in schools for home economics, the only accepted education for women at the time (Matthiasdóttir 2004: 319–55).

Formal rights are often only a part of the story. Women had to fight to make use of their legal rights. The first woman, Kristín Ólafsdóttir, graduated (in medicine) from the University of Iceland in 1917. Many years passed before the next one graduated. The first Icelandic woman to receive a PhD, Bjorg Caritas Thorlaksson, who graduated from the Sorbonne in 1926, encountered enormous obstacles in Icelandic society during the first half of the twentieth century (Kristmundsdóttir 2001).

Figure 8.6 shows the proportion of women and men passing the matriculation examination from 1901 to 2000. Fewer than 20 per cent of adults aged

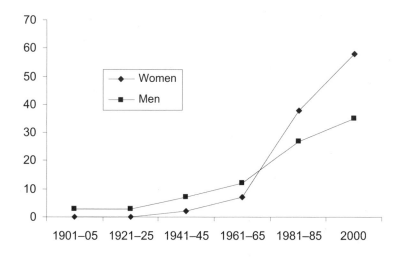

Figure 8.6 Students passing the matriculation exam, 1901–2000 (percentage of 20-year-olds) *Source:* **MESC (2002: 53)**

twenty passed before the 1970s, and far fewer women than men. After 1975, a dramatic increase occurred in women's education. In the last thirty years, the proportion of women passing the examination was increased from 10 to 60 per cent, the figure finally outstripping that of men by the mid-1970s (MESC 2002: 18). The figure also reveals the post-Second World War explosion in education that occurred somewhat later in Iceland than in other countries. Women account for the biggest part of this increase. The number of students at upper secondary level increased threefold from the mid-1960s to the mid-1970s, again because of female enrolments (ibid.).

This trend is not unique for Iceland, even if it is more conspicuous than in other countries (OECD 2004). Women outnumbered men at university level by the 1980s; by 2000, females comprised 60 per cent of those who graduated after a four-year university course. Age differences help explain this phenomenon: 27 per cent of graduating women are aged thirty-five or older as against only 16 per cent of the men (MESC 2002: 53). This might reflect family responsibilities, which represent a bigger obstacle to young women than to men, and the lack of access to education for women in the past.

Figure 8.7 shows education levels for the population from twenty-five to sixty-four years old. Different education routes and age differences reveal gendered patterns. Women are more numerous than men among those who have only compulsory (primary) education, reflecting the fact that in the past girls did not have the same educational opportunities as boys.

Only minor gender differences are found among those with university

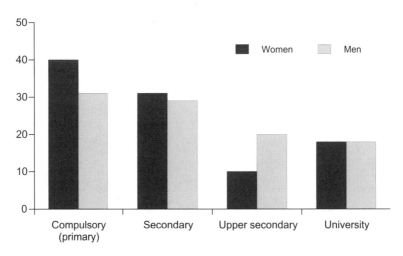

Figure 8.7 Population by education levels, 2000 (percentage of 25–64-year-olds) *Source:* **MESC (2002: 48). Upper secondary includes vocational education and general upper secondary school education**

education, pursued by 17 per cent of women and 19 per cent of men. The gender ratio is almost even in the youngest age groups but, in the older age groups, women fall behind. About 30 per cent of the population have completed vocational and upper-secondary education, the same proportion for women as men. More men than women, 20 per cent versus 9 per cent, have education in vocational programmes (MESC 2002: 48). Iceland is slightly under the OECD average, but the trend of women outnumbering men in higher education is more obvious in Iceland than in other OECD countries (OECD 2003).

Gender disparities in the choice of subject field remain. Iceland follows well-documented patterns of women dominating education sciences, social sciences, arts and humanities, and health, while men constitute the majority in the natural sciences, computer sciences, engineering and mathematics (MESC 2002; OECD 2003). These patterns correspond with the gendered patterns of the labour market.

Public debate in Iceland, reflected in the 1997 conference on boys in school (MESC/OGE 1998), focuses on boys' alleged disadvantages in the school system because the majority of teachers are female. This is supposed to result in a female culture that explains boys' poorer performance and lack of discipline, a view that scholars now contest (Jóhannesson 2004).

Political, educational and cultural leadership
Suffrage: participation in voting and elections Icelandic women reached the first stages of suffrage in 1882 when widows and unmarried women who

paid taxes won the right to vote in local elections – if they had reached the age of twenty-five. The IWRO worked not only for franchise, but also for the rights of women in a wider sense, from education to the founding of women's unions and wage struggles. It had a significant impact on the entire century (Erlendsdóttir 1993).

Women won the right to run for office in 1908 (Halldórsdóttir and Jónatansdóttir 1998), and, after a great struggle, women over forty obtained the right to vote in national elections in 1915. The age limitation was removed in 1920. In the 1970s, a vibrant women's movement emerged. In 1975, the women's 'Day Off' protest in Iceland received international media coverage.

Political leadership Icelandic women made a great impact in the early development of the welfare system. At both ends of the century, the Women's List emphasized humanitarian and welfare issues. These 'maternal politics' are the origins of the modern welfare system (Styrkársdóttir 1997, 1998). Several women's organizations combined in 1926 to found the Mothers' Support Group, which helped single mothers and mothers in hard social conditions (Erlendsdóttir 1993: 179–86).

Women also made an impact on the development of the healthcare system. In 1915, when they won suffrage, women wanted to celebrate their victory. As a sign of gratitude for their rights, nine humanitarian women's associations joined in a remarkable effort to collect money for a hospital, Landspitali, eventually founded in 1926. The money collected by Icelandic women amounted to one third of the total costs (ibid.: 148).

HEADS OF STATE AND GOVERNMENT In 1980, Iceland became the first country to choose a female president in free elections. Icelandic women have had inspiring role models in former President Vigdís Finnbogadóttir (1980–96) and the mayor of the capital, Reykjavik, Ingibjörg Sólrún Gísladóttir (1994–2003). Despite these high-level women, a power gap remains between women and men.

MINISTERIAL (CABINET) Women in Iceland have suffered a backlash when it comes to their participation in the twelve-member cabinet. Women comprised 33 per cent of the cabinet in 2000, a rise from 9 per cent in 1990. This lasted only for a couple of years, however, and in January 2004 the proportion of female ministers was down to 25 per cent. Women comprise 37 per cent of all ministers in Denmark, Norway and Finland, and 44 per cent in Sweden. Reasons given for the high female representations in Nordic countries also shed a light on the

special position of Iceland. The public welfare system, which the Nordic countries introduced in the post-war period, covers diverse human needs from day
care to care of the elderly. The impact of this was twofold: the diverse domestic
and caring tasks for which women had been responsible became socially and
collectively organized by the state and local authorities; this created job opportunities for women within the welfare system (Hernes 1991) and also opened
up women's political and social participation.

When other Nordic countries were introducing measures to increase the
rate of women's political participation in the 1970s (such as quotas in Denmark, Sweden and Norway), primary elections became the Icelandic way of
political selection (Berg 1996: 56). Primaries have proved to disadvantage wom-
en for several reasons, including the fact that women have fewer resources and
opportunities to finance their election campaign (Kristjánsson and Styrkársdóttir 2001).

PARLIAMENTARY Female participation in parliament was very low until the
last two decades of the twentieth century. A significant change occurred in
1983, when the proportion of female MPs rose from 5 to 15 per cent. The
proportion of women candidates in elections is always higher than the proportion of women winners, which reveals a paradoxical process: more women
are becoming members of political parties at the same time as fewer people
are active in political parties in general (Styrkarsdóttir 1999: 18–19). Hence,

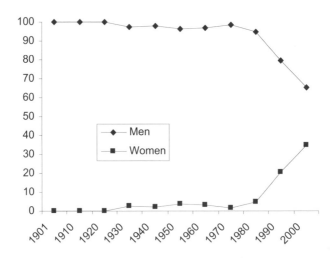

Figure 8.8 Members of parliament (the Althingi) by gender (per cent)
Sources: SI (2003); Vilhjálmsdóttir (2004, based on Statistics Iceland
data); women did not obtain the right to vote until 1915, so could not
have been elected until at least 1920

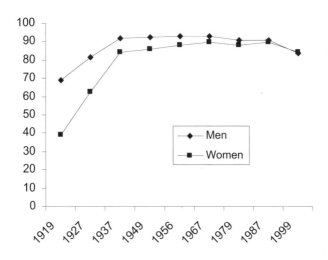

Figure 8.9 Participation in voting in parliamentary elections by gender (per cent)
Sources: SI (2003); Vilhjálmsdóttir (2004, based on Statistics Iceland data)

women's lack of interest does not seem to be the main reason for their insufficient political representation. Women constituted 35 per cent of parliamentary members in 2000 (Figure 8.8). In the elections of 2003, a backlash cut the female proportion to 30 per cent again, showing that progress is far from being linear.

In 1991, female representation in parliament stood at 24 per cent, which was rather low in Nordic terms (Berg 1996: 66). The increase in Iceland did not happen until the Women's List appeared in 1983; this has exerted strong political pressure since then. In the 1999 elections, the Women's List merged with other political parties on the left. It is tempting to link the recent backlash to the disappearance of a separate women's list from the political scene. The proportion of women in public office has increased slowly compared to the other Nordic countries. The claims for political participation were very strong in the 1970s, when the pressure from women's movements resulted in a dramatic rise in female representation *except* in Iceland. Female voting increased dramatically, however (Figure 8.9).

LOCAL GOVERNMENT In local elections, the female proportion of city and county councillors was 6 per cent in 1978; it doubled to 12 per cent in the elections of 1982, when the women's lists ran candidates. By 2002, the number of female city and county councillors had risen to 31 per cent, an increase of less than one percentage point yearly in the period 1986–2002 (Einarsdóttir 2002). In Reykjavik, the Women's List merged into the Reykjavik Alliance in

1994, and Ingibjörg Sólrún Gísladóttir became the mayor of Reykjavik from 1994 to 2003.

PARTY LEADERSHIP In the period 1908–26, women ran their own separate candidate lists for local and national elections. The Women's List in Reykjavik in 1908 received 22 per cent of valid votes cast and all four candidates were elected. The success of the Women's List continued for several mandate periods but ended in 1922 (Styrkársdóttir 1998: 111). Between 1982 and 1996, women ran women's lists again through the Women's Party, in both local and national elections (ibid.). Women in several other countries ran separate lists during the twentieth century, but the most successful were in Iceland (ibid.: 59–60). This presence of women in the political and social life in Iceland can be interpreted as a powerful element against the background of the ideological struggles at the beginning of the century (Box 8.1).

Towards gender equality

The situation of women in Iceland during the twentieth century experienced several phases. The period from 1900 to 1930 was imbued with contradictions and the competing ideologies of a strong women's movement pressing for political participation versus the housewife ideology, which gained ground in the inter-war period and dominated for decades. The IWRO was the backbone of women's organized efforts to improve female well-being.

From 1908 to 1930 the Women's List was a powerful presence in political and social life. Women participated in paid work, and they struggled for social improvements and rights. At the same time, the housewife ideology permeated Icelandic society, proving to be a powerful constraint on women's potential and influences. From 1930 to 1940, the depression placed heavy burdens on many women, which ended in the post-war period. There are strong indications that men gained much more from the post-war upswing than women did, symbolized by the period of stagnation in the women's cause until the 1970s, when the Redstockings and the Women's List emerged. Between 1999 and 2003, no all-inclusive women's movement was operating in Iceland, but many decentralized groups existed. In 2003, the Feminist Association of Iceland was founded. The Association has made a considerable impact on public discourse.

Female well-being in Iceland certainly improved during the twentieth century. Women are highly educated, their labour market participation is exceptionally high, and their social skills are increasingly powerful in the public sphere. Their economic situation, however, is still far behind that of men and

Box 8.1 Ingibjörg Sólrún Gísladóttir

Ingibjörg Sólrún Gísladóttir was born in Reykjavik in 1954. She became prominent during her years as a university student in the 1970s, when she was chair of the Students' Council at the University of Iceland. She graduated in history and literature in 1979 and then studied at the University of Copenhagen for two years.

Ingibjörg Sólrún was a member of the Redstockings, a radical feminist movement founded in Reykjavik in 1970, which dramatically changed the gender discourse in Iceland. They were extremely influential and affected the public agenda as well as general opinion. By the early 1980s, a new mass movement, the Women's List, had replaced the Redstockings. Both were decentralized movements that challenged the patriarchal order, even though their ideologies differed. The Women's List based its ideology on women's culture and maternal politics, in contrast to the Redstockings' radical feminist and, later, Marxist approach.

Ingibjörg Sólrún Gísladóttir was one of the founders of the Women's List, which ran candidates for the local elections in Reykjavik, and became one of two city councillors for the Women's List in 1982–88. She was an editor of the feminist journal *Vera*, and a member of parliament for the Women's List from 1991 to 1994. From the very beginning, Ingibjörg Sólrún Gísladóttir was a strong and promising politician. In 1994, she became the mayor of Reykjavik when she led the Reykjavík List, a coalition of four parties. The right-wing Independence Party had by then held political power almost continuously since the early 1930s, so the victory of the Reykjavik List was an historical event.

With the Reykjavik Alliance, major changes took place in Reykjavik, with a strong emphasis on gender equality and extending day care. Ingibjörg Sólrún Gísladóttir stepped down from her position as mayor in December 2002 in order to run as a prime ministerial candidate for the Social Democratic Alliance in the national elections in 2003. The Alliance showed well in the elections, but not well enough to ensure Ingibjörg Sólrún a place in parliament. She is now the vice-chair of the Social Democratic Alliance.

of women in the other Nordic countries. Women's political representation and economic and political power are not as strong as their education and social participation might indicate. Women are absent from the economic elite and rarely hold high-level decision-making positions. The gender pay gap is stubbornly high.

The legacy of the Icelandic sagas has influenced women in Iceland for good and for bad. The mythical images of strong women featured in the sagas have coloured the self-perception of women and contributed to a contradictory situation. On the one hand, these images have given Icelandic women the strength to fight in public for their rights; on the other, they have created an ideological obstacle.

Women in Iceland still have a long way to go before they can realize gender equality. Gender relations are modern and traditional at the same time. In general, formal and legal equality exists, but women in this small island nation face much overt and hidden discrimination. The future task for women in Iceland is to identify the mechanisms behind this hidden discrimination and to develop strategies for overcoming barriers to gender equality.

Note

1 Some statistical data were collected and coordinated by Sigrídur Vilhjálmsdóttir, Health and Gender Statistics, Statistics Iceland (Hagstofa Íslands). Appreciation is also expressed to Ólöf Garðarsdóttir, Head of Population Statistics at Statistics Iceland, for help in gathering data during the early phase of the project.

References

Andersen, P. S. and M. Gudmundsson (1998) *Inflation and Disinflation in Iceland*, Working Papers no. 1, Reykjavik: Central Bank of Iceland, Economics Department

Barth, E., M. Røed and H. Torp (2002) *Towards a Closing of the Gender Pay Gap: A Comparative Study of Three Occupations in Six European Countries*, Oslo: Institute for Social Research, Norwegian Center for Gender Equality

Berg, S. (1996) *Framganga kvenna í stjórnmálum á Nordurlondum med hlidsjón af Bandaríkjunum, Bretlandi og Frakklandi* [The Progress of Women in Politics in the Nordic Countries in Comparison with the USA, the UK and France], BA-ritgerd: Háskóli Íslands, Félagsvísindadeild

Bjarnadóttir, R. I. (2003) 'Burdarmálsdaudi á Islandi, getum vid enn laekkad tídnina?' [Perinatal death in Iceland: can we still reduce the rate?], *Laeknabladid* [Icelandic Medical Journal], 89: 745–56

Bjartmarz, J. (2003) 'Jafnrétti er réttlaeti' [Equality is fairness], *Morgunbladid*, 9 May

Castells, M. (1997) *The Power of Identity*, Oxford: Blackwell

Dofradóttir, A. G. et al. (2003), *Launakjor félagsmanna í Verzlunarmannafélagi Reykjavíkur árid 2003* [The Wages of the Store and Office Workers Union in Reykjavik], Reykjavik: Félagsvísindastofnun Háskóla Íslands

Efnahagsleg vold kvenna (2004) *Skýrsla nefndar um efnahagsleg vold kvenna. Unnin fyrir forsaetisraduneytid* [Women's Economic Influence in Iceland. A Final Report of the Committee of Women's Economic Influence], Reykjavik: Ministry of the Prime Minister

Einarsdóttir, T. (2000a) *Bryddingar: Um samfélagid sem mannanna verk* [Border. Essays on Society as a Social Construction], Reykjvík, Félagsvísindastofnun, Háskóli Íslands

— (2000b) 'Sérfraedihópar og fagthróun í ljósi kynferdis' [Professions, professionalization and gender], in F. H. Jónsson (ed.), *Rannsóknir í félagsvísindum III*, Félagsvísindastofnun: Háskólaútgáfan

— (2002) 'Jafnrétti án femínisma – pólítik án fraeda: Um tháttaskil í íslenskri jafnréttispólitík' [Gender equality without feminism– politics without theory], *Ritid– Tímarit Hugvísindastofnunar*, 2: 9–36

— (2004) *Culture, Custom and Caring: Men's and Women's Possibilities of Parental Leave* (with G. M. Pétursdóttir), Jafnréttisstofa og Rannsóknastofa í kvenna- og kynjafraedum, Akureyri

Einarsdóttir, T. and K. S. Blondal (2004) 'Kynbundinn launamunur: Umraedan um skýrdan og óútskýrdan launamun kynja í gagnrýnu ljósi' [Pay discrimination: the discussion on adjusted and unadjusted gender pay gap in a critical perspective], in *Kynjafraedi–Kortlagningar, Fléttur II. Rit Rannsóknastofu í kvenna-og kynjafraedum*, Reykjavik: Rannsóknastofa í kvenna-og kynjafraedum og Háskólaútgáfan (forthcoming)

Erlendsdóttir, S. T. (1993) *Verold sem ég vil: Saga Kvenréttindafélags Íslands 1907–1992* [The World I Want: The History of the Icelandic Women's Organization], Reykjavik: Kvenréttindafélag Íslands

— (1997) '"Til faerri fiska metnar". Hlutur Kvenréttindafélags Íslands í kjarabaráttu kvenna 1920–1960' ['"Worth less": the role of the Icelandic Women's Rights Organisation in the wage struggle of Icelandic women 1920–1960'], in H. Kress and R. Traustadóttir (eds), *Íslenskar kvennarannóknir*, Reykjavik: University of Iceland, pp. 279–89

— (1998) 'Til faerri fiska metnar: Hlutur Kvenréttindafélags Íslands í kjarabaráttu kvenna 1920–1960' [Less worth: the impact of the Icelandic Women's Organization in women's wage struggle 1920–1960), in H. Kress and R. Traustadóttir (eds), *Íslenskar kvennarannsóknir, Erindi flutt á rádstefnu í október 1995*, Reykjavik: Háskóli Íslands, Rannsóknastofa í kvennafraedum, pp. 279–89

Eydal, G. (2001) 'Equal rights to parental leave: the case of Iceland', paper presented at the 5th European Conference of Sociology, Helsinki

Flygenring, E. P. (1985) 'Log og adrar réttarheimildir er varda konur' [Laws and other juridical issues relating to women], in J. M. Gudnadóttir (ed.), *Konur hvad nú?*, Reykjavik: 85'nefndin, samstarfsnefnd í lok kvennaáratugar STh og Jafnréttisrád

Gardarsdóttir, Ó. (2001) 'Skóli og kynferdi: Hugleidingar um kynbundinn mun í fraedslu barna og unglinga á fyrri hluta 20. aldar' [School and gender: thoughts on gender differences in the education of children and adolescence in the early 20th century], in A. Agnarsdóttir et al. (eds), *Kvennaslódir: Rit til heidurs Sigrídi Th. Erlendsdóttur*, Reykjavik: Kvennasogusafn Íslands

— (2002) *Saving the Child: Regional, Cultural and Social Aspects of the Infant Mortality Decline in Iceland 1770–1920*, Umeå, Sweden: Umeå University, Report no. 19

Gunnlaugsson, G. Á. (1993) 'Folksfjolda- og byggdathroun 1880–1990', in G. Halfdanarson and S. Kristjansson (eds), *Islensk thjodfelagsthroun 1880–1900. Ritgerdir* [Icelandic Societal Development 1880–1990. Essays], Reykjavik: Social Science Research Institute and Institute of History, University of Iceland, pp. 75–111

Halldórsdóttir, E. H. and G. D. Jónatansdóttir (1998) *Ártol og áfangar í sogu íslenskra kvenna* [Dates and Events in the History of Icelandic Women], Reykjavik: Kvennasogusafn Íslands

Heilbrigdisskýrslur (2002) *Health Reports*, Reykjavik: Landlaeknisembaettid

Heilsufar Kvenna (2000) *Álit og tillogur nefndar um heilsufar kvenna*, Reykjavik: Heil-brigdis-og trygginamálaráduneytid

Helgadóttir, H. (2004) 'Konur í hersetnu landi: Ísland á árunum 1940–1947' [Women in an occupied country: Iceland during 1940–1947], in *Kynjafraedi-Kortlagningar, Fléttur II, Rit Rannsóknastofu í kvenna-og kynjafraedum*, Reykjavík: Rannsóknastofa í kvenna-og kynjafraedum og Háskólaútgáfan (forthcoming)

Hernes, H. M. (1991) *Welfare State and Women Power*, Milan: Vindicacion.

Jóhannesson, I. Á. (2004) *Karlmennska og jafnréttisuppeldi* [Masculinity and Gender Equity Pedagogy], Reykjavik: Centre for Women's Studies and Research

Jónsdóttir, H. H. and K. S. Blondal (2004) *Starfskjarakonnun: Rannsókn á vegum Hagrannsóknastofnunar Samtaka launafólks í almannathjónustu (HASLA)* [Wage Survey on Behalf of the Economic Research Institute of Civil Servants], Reykjavik: Háskóli Íslands, Félagsvísindastofnun

Jónsson, G. and M. S. Magnússon (1997) *Hagskinna: Sogulegar tolur um Ísland* [Icelandic Historical Statistics], Reykjavik: Hagstofa Íslands

Jósepsson, B. (1985) *The Modern Icelandic School System in Historic Perspective*, Reykjavik: National Centre for Educational Materials

Júlíusdóttir, S. (1993) *Den kapabla familjen i det islaendska samhaellet: En studie i lojalitet, aektenskapsdynamik och psykosocial anpassning* [The Capable Family in Icelandic Society: A Study of Loyalty, Marital Dynamics and Psychosocial Adaptation], Göteborg: Göteborg University

— (ed.) (1995) *Barnafjolskyldur: Samfélag, lífsgildi, mótun* [Families with Children: Society, Values, Shaping], Reykjavik: Félagsmálaráduneytid

Kristinsson, T. (2000) 'Misrétti og réttarbaetur: Stuttur annáll' [Discrimination and rights: a brief overview], *Samtokin*, 78

Kristjánsson, S. and A. Styrkársdóttir (2001) *Konur, flokkar og frambod* [Women, Parties and Candidacy], Reykjavik: Háskólaútgáfan

Kristmundsdóttir, S. D. (2001) *Bjorg: Aevisaga Bjargar C. Thorláksson* [The Life of Bjorg C. Thorláksson], Reykjavik: JPV útgáfa

Kyle, G. (2002) 'Married and degraded to legal minority: the Swedish married woman during the emancipation period 1858–1921', in E. Ozdalga and R. Liljestrom (eds), *Autonomy and Dependence in the Family: Turkey and Sweden in a Critical Perspective*, London: Routledge Curzon/Swedish Research Institute in Istanbul

Liljestrom, R. (2002) 'The strongest bond on trial', in E. Ozdalga and R. Liljestrom (eds), *Autonomy and Dependence in the Family: Turkey and Sweden in a Critical Perspective*, London: Routledge Curzon/Swedish Research Institute in Istanbul

Magnússon, M. S. (1993) 'Efnahagsthróun á Íslandi 1880–1990', in G. Hálfdanarson and S. Krisjánsson (eds), *Íslensk thjódfélagsthróun 1880–1990 Ritgerdir* [Icelandic Societal Development 1880–1990 Essays], Reykjavik: Háskóli Íslands

Matthíasdóttir, S. (2004) *Hinn sanni Íslendingur: Thjóderni, kyngervi og vald á Íslandi 1900–1930* [The True Icelander: Nationality, Gender and Power in Iceland 1900–1930], Reykjavik: Háskólaútgáfan

MESC (Ministry of Education, Science and Culture) (2002) *Konur í vísindum á Íslandi* [Women in Science in Iceland], Reykjavik: Menntamálaráduneytid

MESC/OGE (Ministry of Education, Science and Culture and Office of Gender Equality) (1998) *Strákar í skóla* [Boys in School], Erindi frá málthingi Karlanefndar

Jafnréttisráds og menntamálaráduneytisins (conference, 27 November 1997), Reykjavik: Menntamálaráduneytid og Skrifstofa jafnréttismála

Morgunbladid (2004) 'Hlutfall kvenna í stjórnum laekkar i 2.3 per cent' [The proportion of women directors declines to 2.3 per cent], 29 April

Mósesdóttir, L. (2001) 'Evaluating gender equality in the Icelandic labour market', working paper, Reykjavik: Reykjavik University

— (2004) 'Policies shaping employment, skills and gender equality in the Iceland labour market', *National Report: From Welfare to Knowfare, a European Approach to Employment and Gender Mainstreaming in the Knowledge Based Society*, WELL-KNOW-HPSE-CT-2002-00119

NCM (Nordic Council of Ministers) (2003) *Nordic Statistical Yearbook*, Copenhagen: NCM

Nefnd um efnahagsleg vold kvenna (2004) 'Skýrsla nefndar um efnahagsleg vold kvenna: Unnin fyrir forsaetisraduneytid', Reykjavik [Report on women's economic powers in Iceland]

OECD (Organization for Economic Co-operation and Development) (2003) *Education at a Glance: OECD Indicators 2003*, Paris: OECD

— (2004) *Education at a Glance: OECD Indicators 2004*, Paris: OECD

Ólafsson, S. (2003) 'Welfare trends of the 1990s in Iceland', *Scandinavian Journal of Public Health*, 31: 401–4

Pálsdóttir Flygenring, E. (1985) 'Log og adrar réttarheimildir er varda konur', in J. M. Gudnadóttir (ed.), *Konur hvad nú?*: Reykjavik, 85 nefndin, samstarfsnefnd í lok kvennaáratugar STH og Jafnréttisrád

SI (Statistics Iceland) (2001), *Landshagir* [Statistical Yearbook of Iceland], Reykjavik: Hagstofa Íslands

— (2002) *Vinnumarkadur 2002* [Labour Market Statistics], Reykjavik: Hagstofa Íslands

— (2002–2003) *Ísland í tölum* [Iceland in Figures], Reykjavik: Hagstofa Íslands.

— (2003a) *Landshagir* [Statistical Yearbook of Iceland], Reykjavik: Hagstofa Íslands

— (2003b) *Statistical Series, Population: Marriages, Consensual Unions, and Separations*, Reykjavik: Hagstofa Íslands

— (2004) *Marriages, Consensual Unions and Separations 2003*, Reykjavik: Hagstofa Íslands

Sigrún, J. (1997) 'Fjolskyldulíf: Tryggdabond, kvadir og réttlaeti. Erindi um fjolskyldudyg(g)dir og hlutverk fjolskyldustefnu' [Family life: loyalty, duties and justice], in J. Á Kalmansson et al. (eds), *Fjolskyldan og réttlaetid*, Reykjavik: Háskóli Íslands Sidfraedistofnun og Háskólaútgáfan, pp. 171–91

Sigurdardóttir, A. (1985) 'Vinna kvenna á Íslandi í 1100 ár: Úr verold kvenna II' [Women's work in Iceland over 1,100 years: from the world of women II], Reykjavik: Kvennasogusafn Íslands (Women's History Archive)

Styrkársdóttir, A. (1997) 'Maedrahyggja: Frelsisafl eda kúgunartaeki' [Maternal politics: a tool of freedom or oppression?], in H. Kress and R. Traustadóttir (eds), *Íslenskar kvennarannsóknir: Erindi flutt á rádstefnu í október 1995*, Reykjavik: Háskóli Íslands, Rannsóknastofa í kvennafraedum

— (1998) *From Feminism to Class Politics: The Rise and Decline of Women's Politics in Reykjavik, 1908–1922*, Umeå, Sweden: Umeå University, Department of Political Science

— (1999) 'Jafnrétti og lýdraedi? Konur og stjórnmál á Nordurlondum' [Gender equality and democracy? Women and politics in the Nordic countries], *TemaNord*, 566

Thórdardóttir, E. (1985) 'Félagslegar adstaedur kvenna' [Women's social situation], in J. M. Gudnadóttir (ed.), *Konur hvad nú?*, Reykjavik: 85'nefndin, samstarfsnefnd í lok kvennaáratugar STH og Jafnréttisrád

Thorgeirsdóttir, S. (2002) 'Um meintan dauda femínismans' [The alleged death of feminism], in *Ritid–Tímarit Hugvísindastofnunar*, 2: 77–101

Vilhjálmsdóttir, S. (2004) *Health and Gender Statistics*, Reykjavik: Hagstofa Íslands

9 | Women in Japan: change and resistance to change

MASAKO AIUCHI, MAKOTO ICHIMORI, MASAKO INOUE, KEIKO KONDO AND FUSAKO SEKI[1]

The case of Japan is an excellent illustration of the fact that social change is non-linear and complex and that female well-being has to be understood from various points of view, not just in terms of Western standards. During the twentieth century, Japan faced drastic changes of regime, along with reform of legal, political, educational and social institutions. Changing ideas reform society towards increased female well-being, but ideas are easily distorted by political, economic and other social elements. Attempts to change gender relations have met resistance; the legal status of women has advanced, but their status in daily life has not exactly improved. Therefore, in this chapter we pay special attention to the difference between changing ideas and the unchanging realities of everyday life.

The twentieth-century framework in Japan

In terms of female status the twentieth century can be divided into three stages: Period I, from the Meiji Restoration of 1868 to 1946; Period II, from the end of the Second World War to the 1980s; and Period III, from the 1990s to the present. Throughout all periods, the underlying influences of Confucianism shaped the relationship of family members, intensified the concept of maternity, and affected the relationship of women and men in the public sphere.

Period I: 1868–1946 Tokugawa Bakufu (Edo era) occurred before the Meiji Restoration of 1868. The 265 years of Tokugawa Bakufu were dominated by an isolationist policy; Japanese society was relatively free from sex-based division of work in the Western style or the moral notions of sexuality based on Christianity. Then the Meiji government aimed to establish a centralized political system with Tenno (emperor) at the centre of political, military and cultural systems. Within the family, that meant a centralized household with the father at the centre. On the other hand, the Meiji government policy of catching up with Western standards extended the political rights of women to participate in the public sphere. The economic structure changed from a base in peasant farming towards one in light then heavy industry.

Period II: 1946–1980s The transition from Period I to II effectively occurred twice. The first time was in the 1920s, the Taishou democratic era, and the second time in 1946–55, when Japan was coping with defeat in the Second World War and the aftermath of the American atomic bomb attacks on Hiroshima and Nagasaki. After the Second World War, an enlightened constitution promulgated three principles: the protection of fundamental human rights; international pacifism; and sovereignty vested in the people. The constitution reflects feminist assertions of women's political, social and economic rights, and equality. New ideas such as individualism and the essential equality of women and men led to the reform of many institutions, but tradition continued to influence practice. The division of labour did not yet reflect the values of individualism and gender equality. On paper, Japanese women had the same political and social rights as men, but in many ways these were formalities.

Period III: 1990s-2004 After high economic growth in the post-war period, economic slowdown began in the 1990s. Without a drastic change of political regime, a serious social change in the status of women in work and politics transpired. The transition to Period III occurred in the 1980s in response to the second wave of feminism worldwide. Why are Japanese women still experiencing inequalities in spite of realizing their political and economic rights? Feminists criticized the public–private division of labour and the patriarchal power relationship. Feminists also criticized neutral legal provisions that result in the maintenance and intensification of gender inequality, and called for affirmative action to eradicate inequality. This led to complex challenges for female well-being in Japan.

A demographic portrait of Japanese women

Life expectancy Japan has the longest life expectancy in the world at 78.36 years for men and 85.33 years for women as of 2003. The consequences of an ageing population can be recognized as particular problems for women, both those being cared for and the care-givers. Five times more elderly women than men live alone and two-thirds of women over seventy-five years old are widows. An increase in the number of frail elderly, changes in the socio-economic condition and lifestyle of families, and increases in the number of women working outside the home have heightened pressure on women (Seki 2001). Cultural expectations add to the pressure because females have traditionally looked after the elderly. In 1995, 58.9 per cent of the elderly over sixty-five lived with their families – the comparable figure was 22.7 per cent in the United States. In

2001, 42.4 per cent of the frail elderly living with family received care from their children's spouses, or their own children (mainly daughters-in-law and daughters); this was in addition to 25.9 per cent being cared for by their spouses.

The Law for the Welfare of the Elderly (1963) set out the basic welfare policy, followed by the 1982 Health and Medical Service Law for the Elderly, which promoted community health programmes. Three Gold Plans (1989, 1994 and 1999) extended concrete long-term care policies and the Fundamental Law on Measures Responding to the Ageing of Society (1995) outlined the basic philosophy for an ageing society. The New National Long-Term Care Insurance (1997) pays the cost of long-term care. Other laws regulate guardianship for workers' leave for care of the elderly. As society and family changes make traditional familial care increasingly difficult, female well-being will be enhanced if the government and community significantly extend formal elderly care.

Population growth, fertility rate and male–female ratio Japan's fertility rate dropped from 3.65 in 1950 to 1.75 in 1980 and 1.32 in 2002 – one of the lowest in the world – and the birth rate at 10.3 per 1,000 is the lowest in this study. The death rate of 8.3 per 1,000 is relatively high compared to other countries (with an ageing population) but the birth rate is low, so the population growth rate is very low as of 2003. Females constitute 51.1 per cent of the population.

Maternal mortality rate In Japan, surprisingly given its high levels of urbanization and education, the maternal mortality rate had been higher than in other developed countries (176 per 100,000 live births in 1950 and 18 per 100,000 in 1990). By addressing the causes (primarily haemorrhaging after birth and clinics with only one obstetrician on duty), however, the rate was brought down to 10 per 100,000 in 2000. Shifting from home births to hospital or clinic births over the course of the century also contributed significantly to the decline.

Infant mortality rate At the same time, Japan achieved the world's lowest infant mortality rate, which dropped from 60 per 1,000 in 1950 to only 3 in 2002. The low infant mortality rate is a result of early pre-natal care, a low proportion of unmarried mothers (single parents), the favourable age of mothers (most are aged between twenty and thirty-four), a high proportion of clinic or hospital births, a routine stay of one week for both mother and child, and an effective *Maternal and Child Health Handbook*, which details the medical record of every child from conception until age six (Matsuyama 1987).

Urbanization At the end of the nineteenth century, in the midst of the Sino-Japanese War and the Russo-Japanese War, light industry that centred on silk and spinning fostered the Japanese industrial revolution. The transformation of family structure and work patterns occurred rapidly with modernization and urbanization. A demand for educated women rose and was a driving force behind promoting girls' education. In 1900, 64 per cent of factory workers were women, called 'Joko'. Poor farmers sent their daughters to factories in return for advance payment of wages, a practice akin to slave labour. Joko worked fifteen to eighteen hours a day for a small wage and lived in accommodation worse than that for livestock. Women workers were confined to factories, and were subjected to violence and threats from employers.

In 1911, Japan enacted its first Factory Law to protect labourers. The law protected females in a way similar to its treatment of minors, as female workers were presumed to be mentally and physically weaker than men. Because the level of protection was low, and equal treatment was not mandated, women could be employed only at certain jobs. Yet during the Second World War women were mobilized as factory workers to substitute for men. They worked at the front as nurses and comfort women. Female working conditions in urban areas improved significantly after the war.

By 1955, the number of female agricultural workers exceeded that of males by 60 per cent; this pattern continues because the agricultural industry cannot function without women workers. By the end of the century, Japan was 79 per cent urban and only 6 per cent of women and 5 per cent of men still worked in agriculture full time. In agricultural society, old traditions of male-dominated work styles persisted. An evaluation of female work was called for when women started to resist marrying farmers.

Contraception and abortion/average age at first child The number of abortions as a proportion of all pregnancies in Japan in 1997 was 22.1 per cent, which is high compared to other developed countries. The trend can be attributed to the Eugenics Law (1948) and the Protection of Maternity Law (1996), which permit abortion for economic reasons but do not give women the right to abort. Japan's contraception usage rate of about 60 per cent (percentage of currently married women between the ages of fifteen and forty-nine practising some form of contraception) is comparatively low. The use of modern methods (condoms, sterilization, oral contraceptives, IUDs, diaphragms, etc., which can be obtained from medical institutions and pharmacies) is quite low at 53 per cent (GEB 1999).

Family status and structure

During the twentieth century, enactment and renewal of the constitutions, along with that of family laws (the Meiji Constitution of 1889 and the Family Law of 1898, then the Japanese Constitution of 1946 and the Family Law of 1947) affected the status of women in Japan.

After these legal reforms, the image and structure of the family changed with industrial transition. In the late 1950s and early 1960s, high economic growth and urbanization created the 'salary-man family', which is the Japanese archetype of the nuclear family. It consists of a salaried male breadwinner who works very hard, a full-time housewife who manages all the family affairs, and children. Housewives have full responsibility for the household economy, being in charge of how salaries are used, childcare and education, under the supervision of the mother-in law. In the absence of the husbands, housewives acquired relative power and authority in the private sphere. This type of family has been the ideal ever since. Family law, tax regulations and the social welfare system aimed to guarantee the well-being of housewives, intensifying the gendered division of labour. In a high growth period, this was also a suitable policy for Japanese corporations. Companies needed men who could work long hours, devoting their time and energy to the company at the expense of family or community life. A man pledged his loyalty and identified himself by the corporation's name. Companies expected the wife to support such a husband, in return guaranteeing the family's welfare, including housing and leisure. Women functioned as assistants and retired upon marriage or maternity. This is called 'corporate-centred society'.

In the 1970s and early 1980s, the so-called 'new family' emerged, valuing common interests and leisure time. The young new family's idea of companionship and love between spouses influenced middle-aged couples, causing divorces. In the late 1980s and 1990s, the 'parasite single', an adult son or daughter who had graduated from school and found a job but lived with his or her parents, characterized the contemporary family. Many young females enjoying good pocket money become 'parasites', delaying marriage, since life with parents is comfortable and easier.

In Japan, the allocation of authority between the public and private sphere differs from arrangements in some other countries. For example, industrialization is a factor enticing women to enter the labour market in many countries. Except for the period before and during the Second World War, however, high economic growth in Japan kept women at home to support working men. Even in the 1970s, the development of industry did not promote female labour force participation. Rather, employment culture, the tax system and social welfare pushed women into the private sphere. As a result, industrialization enhanced female power at home.

The new Japanese family of today offers contemporary challenges to women in the private sphere. In the 1990s especially, more unmarried persons, late marriages, smaller families and elderly women influenced the relationship between man and woman, husband and wife, and parent and child, building pressures for change.

Marriage and divorce

THE FAMILY LAW OF 1898 – THE IE SYSTEM 'IE' means family or house in Japanese, but the functions of IE under the Family Law of 1898 are different from those of 'family' in English. As the system of status in family and society, IE derives from the relationship between the male head of house (Koshu) and each family member. The Koshu had wide power over other members of his household. For example, without the agreement of the Koshu, no one could marry. The first-born son inherited all property, the homestead and the status of the Koshu. The Meiji government tried to control the people through both the IE system and the Japanese registration system (Koseki) of 1871.

The Family Law of 1898 contained a provision regarding the 'incapability' of a wife. Her husband had the right to manage her properties; she could not inherit property or a house. The Meiji Constitution entrenched unequal status between women and men. Men had rights of sexual access to a public prostitute but adultery on the part of a wife was a criminal offence punishable by two years' penal servitude and was grounds for divorce. In order to have a son as an heir, which was imperative under the IE system, a new provision granted legitimate status to any son born of a concubine or mistress. In practice, family law concerning monogamy was flouted to maintain the concubine system.

In 1925 (the Taisho era), the reformation of Meiji Minpo began under the influence of the women's movement. Some inequality between women and men within the family was abolished. The IE system, the efficient tool used by the Koseki system to control people, was maintained until after the Second World War.

THE FAMILY LAW OF 1947 AND THE CONSTITUTION OF JAPAN The Family Law was drastically reformed under the constitution of 1946, which established the concepts of individual dignity and the essential equality between women and men. The IE system was abolished. The Family Law of 1947, one of the most advanced pieces of legislation for its time, provided for a family of independent persons, husband and wife, parents and children, and other relations, and delineates the rights and obligations among individuals. The law entrenched respect of the individual and the essential equality between women and men as the general basis of civil law. The provision regarding a wife's 'incapability' was abolished and new provisions resolved the inequalities between women and men in terms of divorce, parental authority, distribution of property and inheritance. The Family Law of 1947 guaranteed the autonomy of the family as a private sphere. Family affairs were to be decided by agreement between partners and with the assistance of a family court. Marriage and the choice of a family name for husband and wife became valid simply by agreement between partners.

Divorce law in Japan is especially unique, permitting Japanese to divorce without mediation, assistance, court review or administrative guidance. The divorce rate in 1920 was lower than in 1899 (Figure 9.1). It dropped again in 1935, but increased dramatically in the 1990s.

Reformation of family law appeared to realize formal equality between women and men within the family, but did not address the economic, political or social differentials between the genders. Social custom affects gender inequality. Wives have weaker positions compared to their husbands in terms of social and economic power; they end up divorcing in adverse conditions, for example, without concrete agreement on the cost of childcare. The 1947 law maintains some of the IE system, for example provision of support by relations and inheritance of heirlooms. Thus, reformation of the family law was not complete. Under the 1947 law family is defined as parents and children with the same family name, similar to the nuclear family.

REFORMATION OF FAMILY LAW, 1991–96 In Japan, the nature of the family has changed, but family law has not been fully reformed, with a few minor exceptions, in comparison to Western countries. During 1991–96, the Japanese law council continued to collect opinions from experts and recommended reformation of several points: introducing an optional system of husband and wife retaining separate family names after marriage; setting the conditions for no-fault divorce (five years' separation, no minor children, and no severe consequences for the spouse); abolishing discrimination on inheritance between legitimate and illegitimate children; reducing the waiting period for remarriage for women to 100 days (previously 300 days); and defining a common age for minor status (eighteen for males, sixteen for females).

These reforms aimed to eliminate the remnants of the IE system and the inequality between women and men, and to create equal partnerships in family life. The reforms were not enacted, however. Religious groups opposed the retention of separate family names, mainly because this optional family name system could result in a crisis in the concept of family union. In spite of this deadlock in reformation, the family is continuing to change.

A social welfare system for women The Japanese social welfare system relating to women has developed to protect the welfare of housewives and mothers. A housewife, for example, is exempt from paying insurance premiums; on the other hand, she won her personal pension only in 1986; hitherto a husband's pension was regarded as covering the couple. The phrase 'social welfare' rather than 'social security' signifies *all* the support given by the government for the welfare of the people, including pensions and medical insurance.

A social welfare system that was designed to support the family in a time of a more traditional division of labour can be inconvenient and even discriminatory. Single women or married women with full-time jobs (i.e. not housewives and mothers) have suffered the most. Contrary to the images held internationally, however, this system worked fairly well for many women who chose the role of housewife, which has been highly respected in Japan. Indeed, husbands often find it beneficial to turn over their salary and receive an allowance back from their wives. The term 'housewife' suggests different images from one country to the next. Having control over the home economy makes an important difference to the status of housewife. On the question 'Who holds the decision-making power over the family budget?', a study showed that 79.4 per cent answered 'housewives' in Japan compared to only 11.5 per cent in Germany (Office of the Prime Minister 1983). While discrimination against women in the male-dominated public sphere is well known, the strong status of Japanese housewives in the domestic sphere is under-analysed.

Welfare was managed within the family before the Second World War; the government welfare system developed mainly after the war. Social welfare for women improved during the century, as Japan tried to catch up with the standard obtaining in many developed countries. Problems arose when the lifestyle of women became more diversified.

BEFORE AND AFTER CHILDBIRTH The social welfare system first advanced the status of women by enacting and upgrading welfare measures for mothers. Employees' Health Insurance (1922) and National Health Insurance (1938) for the self-employed provide a lump-sum allowance for childbirth, the amount depending on the type of insurance. For example, 300,000 yen or, if greater, half of her monthly salary is paid to the insured mother. Employees' Health Insurance also offers a maternity allowance of 60 per cent of the working mother's wage during maternity leave. Since 1961, the Universal Health Insurance Plan, which consists of these insurances and others, covers all Japanese people. The Child Welfare Law (1947) and Public Assistance Law (1950) assist mothers who lack the means for childbirth by providing a maternity home and maternity aid. The Maternal and Child Health Law (1965) encourages medical examination and was responsible for the issue of the *Maternal and Child Health Handbook*.

CHILDCARE – NURSING AND INCOME SECURITY Until the 1980s, the 'nursing' of (caring for) children was generally considered the mother's responsibility. Government subsidies to childcare programmes have expanded since the mid-1980s and the Child Care Leave Law of 1991 allowed workers to take leave for a year. The government issued two Angel Plans (1994 and 1999) that instituted basic policies to prevent a decline in the birth rate and to support childcare. The Child Welfare Law underwent a major revision in 1997, as the number of working mothers increased and problems regarding nursing became apparent. After-school programmes were also enhanced in this revision. The Children's Allowance Law (1971) supplies a comparatively small allowance to parents on certain income levels until the child is nine years old.

Welfare support for a single-parent family, especially a 'fatherless family', focuses mainly on securing income, since women earn less than men and alimonies from ex-husbands are not well secured. As of 2002, the typical fatherless family's annual income was about 40 per cent of the average family income. The Child Rearing Allowance Law (1961) supports a low-income fatherless family until a child is eighteen years old. Similar allowance is not provided for a motherless family. The 1981 Law for Maternal and Child Welfare provides loans and many services for fatherless families. Homes for mothers and children are maintained under the Child Welfare Law. They are currently also used as homes for victims of domestic violence. Other measures such as tax cuts help provide for these families. Because of the absence of a well-enforced alimony system, establishing a good legal system is essential. Child rearing allowances stop when the father recognizes the child. The system under which a motherless family and a fatherless family are treated differently is being questioned.

WOMEN'S RIGHT TO AN INDIVIDUAL PENSION AND HEALTH INSURANCE Public pensions provided 65.7 per cent of income for households consisting of persons aged sixty-five or over in 2001. For 59.5 per cent of these households, public pensions were their only income, indicating the importance of such pensions for elderly women. Earlier measures benefiting women, especially housewives, were enacted in the 1944 revision of the first Workers' Pension Law (1941); for example, the survivor's pension became perpetual. In 1959, the National Pension Law enforced a universal pension system. It was optional for a wife who was covered by her husband's pension to join the national pension scheme but her husband's pension would cease to cover her in the event of divorce. About two-thirds of housewives had joined the pension scheme by 1980. Feminists advocated laws that would create a woman's right to her own pension and erase the imbalances between gender, such as age differences in qualifying for the pension and differences in the amount received.

The Basic Pension System (1985) made it *compulsory* for housewives to join the pension scheme. Controversy arose because housewives are exempted from paying a premium – even students over twenty years old, who also do not work, must pay. Some survivors' pensions are given only to mothers, depending on age. Single or working women, whose premiums also contribute to insuring housewives, criticized this system, arguing that mothers, especially house-wives, are over-protected. Nevertheless, along with advances in the welfare of mother and child, obtaining an individualized pension is a great achievement for the feminist movement. Through the pension reform of 2004, a housewife's pension after divorce is at last secured.

Similarly, under the Universal Health Insurance Plan, when a woman does not work and has no insurance of her own, she is covered by the insurance of the head of household, usually her husband or father. Having only one insurance policy card created difficulties for women who lived away from their husbands pending divorce or who were running away from domestic violence. In 2001, the ministerial ordinance gave each individual the right to an insurance policy card. Individualization of health insurance helps improve the well-being of women in Japan, but it also conflicts with the interests of many housewives who benefit from not paying a premium.

Violence against women

According to the Japanese Cabinet Report on Conditions in Domestic Violence Nationally (2002) one out of every two women has suffered psychological brutality; one out of every five has been the object of sexual violence; one out of six has experienced physical violence; and one out of twenty fears at some time for her life. The National Police Agency reports that, on average, once every three days a wife in Japan is killed by her husband.

For generations, society defined violence and abuse as an acceptable way for males to manage and control their wives and children. In the first half of the twentieth century, Japanese women lived under a system of patriarchal hierarchy. The 1947 constitution formed a legal basis for women's rights and from the late 1960s the women's movement brought a new development: increased consciousness about rape, sexual harassment and domestic violence (DV).

The international movement to resist domestic violence The second wave of the feminist movement in Japan received strong support from feminists in Europe and the USA in the fight against domestic violence. The UN Decade of the Woman was a landmark period. As the women's movement in Japan worked against domestic violence, the UN adopted the Anti-Feminine Prejudice Pact of 1979. The international women's conferences added to the support.

The Beijing conference defined violence towards women and adopted its eradication. Women focused on ending the individual level of brutality, along with war between nations and violence on an international level. The Beijing conference also provided an impetus for the rapid increase in the number of support shelters for victims of domestic violence all over Japan. Before Beijing there were only seven shelters; a few years later, there were more than sixty.

A support network to eradicate violence Feminism in Japan came to grips with brutality towards women as a central problem in the early 1990s. Japanese women began to use the words 'sexual harassment' and the Tama Association for Considering Sexual Bias in the Workplace carried out a Ten-Thousand-Person Questionnaire on Sexual Harassment. Japan's first real sexual harassment trial resulted in complete victory for the woman plaintiff in 1992.

'Domestic violence' became a common phrase after the national report on DV by the Research Committee Investigating Violence by Husbands (and male associates), which was initiated by eight feminists (lawyers, researchers and activists). The report highlighted the extent of injury from domestic violence in Japanese society. By labelling gender abuse in the workplace 'sexual harassment' and gender violence in the personal area 'domestic violence', Japanese women began to fight against the long-standing brutal control of husbands and other males.

In the 1980s, Michaela Dormitory in Kanagawa prefecture, Women's House HELP and others pioneered private shelters that provided support for victims of domestic violence. There was also a rapid increase in the number of facilities supporting Asian women, such as Friendship Cosmos in Chiba prefecture, Women's House Sara, and Kanagawa Space 'Mizura' in Kanagawa prefecture. The AKK Shelter in Tokyo targeted support for DV.

Several critical factors contributed to the spread of the private shelter nationally. The women's movement and feminism matured in theory and practice during the latter half of the twentieth century. The number of women activists increased and a national network spread into every corner of Japan. This network crossed local and national boundaries and became an immediately available source of aid to women and children who were facing brutality at home. Feminists began to provide counselling activities in various localities. The work of DV victim support shelters, by its very nature, presupposes very closely coordinated network activities. A woman fleeing from Okinawa is welcomed in Sapporo. The victims of brutality can find a place to live safely in an area where there are no victimizers or relatives. Sometimes it is necessary to cross international boundaries to ensure the safety of the fleeing victim. The support network began in 1998 with the establishment of the National Refuge Shelter Networking for Women Fleeing Brutality (Japan Women's ShelterNet).

THE DV PREVENTION LAW The First Japan Women's Shelter Symposium held in Sapporo in 1998 under the slogan 'Kick up a Storm for the Shelter Movement!' appealed for new legislation to protect victims. Although DV support workers aimed to rebuild victims' lives, they found it difficult to help women recover in a society that did not formally recognize the existence of domestic violence. Solutions do not exist for a problem that does not exist.

The urgent task of prohibiting domestic violence required new legislation that would declare domestic violence to be a crime, punish the perpetrators, protect and provide relief for the victims and support their independence, and build a care system for affected children. Therefore, the National Women's ShelterNet continued to hold annual symposia and conducted a national questionnaire on establishing a DV Prevention Law. Over three years of national activities finally bore fruit in 2001, when the Law Concerning the Prohibition of Violence against One's Mate and the Protection of Victims (DV Prevention Law) was born through the mutual cooperation of women advocates, victims, support groups, Diet members, bureaucrats and professionals – by women and for women.

The law applies only in the area of protection; it is a 'restricted law', having no power to punish the wrongdoer. In order to eliminate crimes of DV, there is an absolute need for punishment and re-education that will point up the responsibility of the perpetrator. The present law lacks teeth. The weakness of simply supplying support for the victim who is attempting to get away from violence, and the present contradictions and limits in the practice, are becoming clearer every day. The goals of a more complete law include providing total support for victims (from safe counselling to independent self-support) and a social system that functions so that women's lives are in no danger from domestic violence.

Even since the law's enactment, crimes of domestic violence have continued unabated. People continued to be murdered, particularly women, children and related family members. On the other hand, women working in the public sphere extend strong support. Female doctors and counsellors take care of their women clients. Female police officers are now in charge of the women victims of sexual assaults, working towards the successful prosecution of assailants. Women judges seem to be more compassionate towards women victims in the courtroom. Women lawyers seem to be more effective in lawsuits involving job discrimination, sexual harassment and domestic violence. All these efforts and stronger legislation will be essential as the battle for female well-being continues.

Economic participation

The division of labour As in other countries, definitions of male/female characteristics affect the educational system and the nature of labour force participation. In Japan, coming out of a deeply patriarchal past, the predominant understanding of 'equality of the sexes' after the war was the 'theory of sex-based character'. This theory emphasized biological differences between women and men. Thus, differences in the subjects females and males were obliged to take were not discriminatory but simply complied with the differences in the role and status of women and men. For example, in 1958 boys and girls took different subjects in primary school: the boys went to a crafts class and the girls to a homemaking class. In 1960, the homemaking class became a required subject only for girls in high school, fixing the notion of a gendered division of labour.

This pattern hindered female entry into the paid labour market. Women who wanted to raise children were also attracted to working conditions that were different from men's. The sexual division of labour was positively adopted as a policy that would meet the needs of an expanding economy. At the same time, other policies improved employment conditions for working women, but the sexual division of labour is still apparent in the family and the workplace.

Women's participation in the labour force Japanese women workers experienced four distinct phases in the twentieth century. First, there was exploitation of women's labour; second, there was special protection for female workers (similar to child labour laws); third, women were protected as mothers; finally, the concept of equal treatment was promoted.

After the Second World War, Article 14 of the new constitution (1946) declared equal rights of protection for all people. Following the constitution, the Labour Standards Law (1947) called for equal treatment and banned sex discrimination in wages. This law protected women as mothers, establishing maternity leave (six weeks before and eight weeks after the birth), nursing hours and menstrual leave. The law also prohibited or limited overtime work, weekend and holiday work, night work, and hazardous or noxious work for women.

The Labour Standards Law in effect prescribed different labour treatment for women and men. Sex-based discrimination was not prohibited under the equal treatment principle, except in terms of wages. Nevertheless, the importance of this law was immeasurable, because it freed women from prior feudalistic labour relations. As mentioned earlier, in 1900, the majority of factory workers were women ('Joko'). These women suffered in terms of long working hours, low compensation and unacceptable living conditions. Although factory life for these young women was deplorable, it took until 1955 for the Supreme Court to invalidate the advance payment of wages, which had created such miserable conditions for factory girls.

EFFECTS OF HIGH ECONOMIC GROWTH From 1966 to 1970, Japan's average annual economic growth was 11.6 per cent. The GNP doubled in six years. This high growth, coupled with technological innovation and women obtaining higher education, changed women's employment situation. Companies that wanted to rationalize their enterprises forced women to retire after marriage or earlier than men. Female workers were used as cheap and dispensable labour. Simultaneously, companies argued that women were over-protected. Greater attention has since been paid to the debate about protection versus equal treatment in guiding social policy.

Women fought for protection of motherhood and equal treatment. Opinions valuing the wife's housework developed after 1955. During the 1960s, private enterprises introduced childcare leave, but only for women. Court cases in 1966 invalidated the system of retirement after marriage. The early 1970s created a new phrase, 'full-time housewife'. The Law for Household Industry (1970) supported housewives doing piecework at home. The Working Women's Welfare Law was enacted in 1972 and the Akita district court held wage differentials to be discriminatory in 1975. Working mothers campaigned to increase the number of day nurseries, but nursing was widely recognized as the responsibility of mothers at home.

EXPANSION OF EQUALITY BETWEEN WOMEN AND MEN In 1985, Japan ratified CEDAW. For the ratification, the Working Women's Welfare Law was renamed the Equal Employment Opportunity Law (EEOL). Simultaneously, Japan amended its Labour Standards Law to lessen the protection of women – in terms of night work, for example. EEOL had limitations: one interpretation was that women could be treated differently unless their welfare was violated. Companies were required only to *aim* for equal treatment in recruitment, employment and promotion. Discrimination was prohibited in education, training, retirement and dismissal, but there were no sanctions for violations.

The 1990s saw many measures establishing the equal treatment of women and men. The shock of the declining fertility rate stimulated enactment of the Child Care Leave Law (1991). Both male and female workers can take leave to care for their child for a year, or request a reduction in working hours or other measures facilitating childcare. Employment insurance provides 40 per cent of the person's wage in financial support, and payment of premiums for both health insurance and pension are suspended. In 1995, the law was revised and renamed the Child Care and Family Care Leave Law, in an effort to stop many female workers quitting their jobs to care for the elderly. With Family Care Leave, both male and female workers can take three months' leave. Again, employment insurance provides 40 per cent of the person's wage, but the premium payments are not suspended.

In a landmark sexual harassment case in 1922, a court ordered that both wrongdoer and employer must pay damages. This case has ignited other lawsuits by women. Backed by court decisions, the EEOL was amended in 1997. The emphasis of Japanese labour laws shifted from welfare law to law for equal treatment. Although the EEOL bans discrimination only against women, not men, the amendment was an enormous step for working women, clearly banning discrimination in recruitment, employment, transfer and promotion. The law now bans special treatment for women, which initially created the difference in job specifications between the sexes. New measures, such as for sexual harassment, were created. The government can support companies introducing positive action to promote gender equality. Simultaneously, the Labour Standards Law was revised and special protection for women against overtime and night work was abolished, except during childcare.

In spite of many legal advances, the reality for women workers is still not

ideal. The slowing down of the economy in the 1990s hindered women graduates in finding jobs; many companies dismissed female part-timers and the
glass ceiling for women remains. In 1997 the government measured the monetary value of unpaid work. The appraised value of unpaid work was 30 to 50
per cent of wages, and women account for 90 per cent of this work. Much
remains to be done in this area.

FULL-/PART-TIME The female labour situation in Japan constitutes an 'M'
or bimodal curve. Many women start work after graduating from school but
retire to have children and then go back to work as part-timers. Since seniority governs pay scales and part-timers are not well paid, the wage differential
between women and men at the end of the twentieth century was still very
high. Even the full-time woman worker's average wage was only 66 per cent of
male wages as of 2000.

In 1961, a Tax Credit for Spouses had allowed a reduction in the husband's
taxes when the wife's income was less than a certain amount. In addition,
her income was exempted from taxation. When a woman's income rose to
the point of her not being dependent on her husband, residence tax, health
insurance, pension and the family allowance provided by companies to husbands were affected. Hence, many female part-timers were discouraged from
earning more. The Tax Credit for Spouses was called the 'wall of one million',
since the income of a family decreased when housewives earned more than a
million yen. In order to solve this problem, a Special Tax Credit for Spouses
was established in 1987 for families whose main income is less than 10 million yen. Tax credits still stand in the way of women's independence, creating
a demand for them to be abolished.

Part-time workers constitute 26.1 per cent of all employees, but 73.5 per
cent of them were female as of 2001. Among *all* female employees, 45.7 per
cent are part-timers; many are middle-aged and older married women. Thanks
to the policies that protect housewives, part-timers contributed to the economic growth of Japan – but at low wages. Among part-timers, 32.3 per cent work
more than seven hours a day, engaging in similar tasks to full-time workers.
Nevertheless, their wages are lower than full-timers', and employers dismiss
them according to business fluctuations. The 1993 Labour Law for Part-timers
fought to establish their equal treatment. The law does not ban discrimination,
however, so many part-timers still suffer from low wages, no bonuses and no
retirement money. The poor working conditions of part-timers generally lower
the status of working women.

TYPES OF OCCUPATION Even in the 1980s, laws allowed companies to create a separate-track employment system, peculiar to Japan, in which workers are channelled into two tracks based on their ambition and abilities. The 'career track' could lead to the top executive level of promotion, but involves duties that males traditionally performed, such as working prolonged hours and enduring company-wide transfers. The 'general track' engages workers in non-discretionary tasks and does not require job transfers that entail change of residence; this track limits the level of promotion. Many women chose the general track to avoid working late hours and succumbing to other demands that compete with family life. This employment system accelerated the wage differential between sexes.

With the enactment of the EEOL in 1985, the number of women workers increased significantly from 15 million in 1985 to 20 million in 1995. The range of jobs for women also expanded. The number of working women exceeded the number of full-time housewives for the first time in 1984. Women bore the dual burden of employed-work and housework, however. Women on the career track especially suffered through working (as men did) until late at night – but were still taking care of household duties.

In 2000, working men on average spent only twenty minutes a day on housework during weekdays, whereas working women spent two hours and fifty-three minutes on average; this figure applies also to part-timers. In the same statistics, the average full-time housewife spent seven hours and twelve minutes on housework (Cabinet Office website). In 2002, 51.3 per cent of men in Japan still thought that men should work outside the home and women should stay at home. Some women currently prefer the general track, since life on the career track is hard for women. Gender equality cannot be achieved without substantial increases in support from men and society in household duties and raising children.

Literacy and education

Literacy rates Literacy rates were 90 per cent in 1900 and stand at virtually 100 per cent today. The Meiji Constitution of 1889 called for a compulsory education system, in which six years of primary education, segregated by sex except during the first two years, was the citizen's obligation under the Tenno system. The Japanese constitution of 1946 extended free compulsory education to nine years of primary and secondary school, not segregated by sex.

Until the end of the Second World War, the 'Ryousai Kennbo' principle (good wives and wise mothers) provided the framework for girls' education to prepare women to support the imperial-patriarchal family system,

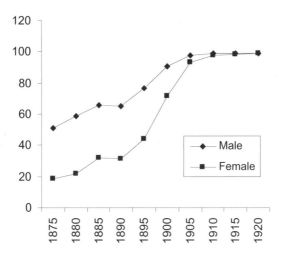

Figure 9.1 Elementary school enrolment, six–to-twelve-year-olds, 1875–1920 (per cent) *Source:* **Statistics Bureau (1999, Table 22–01)**

emphasizing loyalty to the Tenno and duty to one's parents (especially to the father as master). The girls' curriculum in primary and secondary education mirrored this principle. It focused on classes in domestic affairs (sewing and cooking) and did not teach the skills needed for empowerment in the public sphere. Men and women followed different educational systems in the double tracks of secondary and advanced education. Thus, although education often promotes female participation in the workplace, this was not the case in Japan. After 1945, the goals of education shifted towards equal rights for women and men and co-education, expressed in the constitution and the Fundamentals of Education Law. A single-track educational system was adopted to allow females to receive the same secondary education and higher education as men. There were many problems in realizing these goals, however.

School completion rates
PRIMARY Japan developed a modern, public education system in 1872. Women's education was approved but the enrolment rate of females in primary education was low (15.4 per cent in 1873) and remained low given a social trend that resisted female education. Around 1900, primary education attendance rates skyrocketed from 50 to 90 per cent in ten years, as the government shared the cost of compulsory education (Figure 9.1).

SECONDARY Before the Second World War, the principle of separate education based on sex, grounded in the assumption of male superiority, required

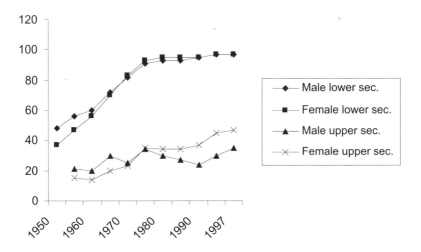

Figure 9.2 Advancement rates from lower and upper secondary schools, by gender, 1950–97 (per cent) *Source:* **Statistics Bureau (various years),** *Japan Statistical Yearbook*

completely separate schools in secondary (junior high and high school) and higher education. The number of years required for graduation for females was apt to be lower than that for males.

The improvement in secondary education followed the Higher Girls' School Law (1899), which corresponded to the Secondary Men's School Law (1894/1918). The number of schools offering secondary education open to females expanded rapidly from thirty-seven in 1899 to 1,272 in 1945. After the war, the percentage of female students going through secondary education rapidly began to equal and then to surpass that of male students (Figure 9.2). Co-education, compulsory education and tuition covered at public expense at primary and junior high-school levels facilitated girls' enrolment. In high school, co-education was recognized as the principal system, but females tended to be concentrated in the cultural sciences, education, medicine and domestic science. The advancement rate to further education was 37 per cent in 1950 and 98 per cent in 1997.

Co-education in homemaking courses was implemented in secondary schools in 1993 and in higher schools in 1994. In reality, the problems of gender-segregated classes remained, and a gender bias continued in teaching materials and textbooks. Poor content remains a problem with respect to resources on women's reproductive heath and rights, as does a persistent emphasis on motherhood and a lack of understanding of sexual diversity. In the 1980s, a civilian educational movement arose to advocate the importance of educational equality of the sexes and gender-neutral lessons.

HIGHER EDUCATION Women's higher education started with teacher training in 1890. The Special School Law of 1903 promoted institutions of higher education: the Women's English Academy, founded by Umeko Tsuda; the Tokyo Women's Medical School, founded by Yayoi Yoshioka; and the Japan Women's Advanced School, founded by Jinzo Naruse. In spite of rapid expansion and support for female education, none of the women's schools was promoted to university status until after the Second World War.

The Fundamentals Law of Education called for co-education and the founding of a women's university. The unique woman's junior college, which requires two years of study in fields such as childcare, originated during this period. The number of co-educational universities increased rapidly. In the latter half of the twentieth century, the sexual division of labour was not as obvious under the compulsory educational system. As children proceed into higher education, however, gender affects the rate of advancement and the major field of study. The turn-around took place in 1989; by 1997, the gender balance stood at 49 per cent for women advancing into higher education and 46 per cent for men. Forty-seven per cent of the women who had decided to advance in 1997 attended junior colleges, however, whereas men's advancement rate to junior colleges was only 4 per cent. Accordingly, women's advancement rate to the four-year university was 26 per cent compared to 43 per cent for men. Extremely few females advance in engineering. These factors have an enormous impact on women graduates in the labour market.

Finally, the system tends to reproduce itself. The number of female teachers decreases as school level rises. Men also dominate the administrative jobs. In 2001, female teachers accounted for 65 per cent of elementary school personnel, but only 17 per cent of heads were female. For junior high schools the proportions were 40 and 4 per cent respectively, and 25 and 4 per cent in high schools. Nine per cent of professors and 8 per cent of deans are female in universities, but females make up 33 per cent of all professors and 14 per cent of heads in junior colleges. Female professors and heads are much more prevalent in junior colleges because males dominate the universities. Progress in gender studies at institutions of higher education has contributed to a shift towards gender-balanced education at lower levels.

Political, educational and cultural leadership

Today, at the start of a new century, Japanese women are increasingly showing their political capabilities by gaining ever larger representation in decision-making bodies at both national and local levels. This would not have been possible a hundred years ago. Exposed to pressures for women's equality from both outside and inside, Japanese society has gradually changed, but politics remains a man's world. The rapid increase in the number of women in politics in the last years of the past century, however, seems to signify a more promising future for women's empowerment in politics.

Suffrage: participation in voting and elections

THE MEIJI RESTORATION AND WOMEN'S POLITICAL RIGHTS After the Meiji Restoration, Japan began to take the road to modernization. The Freedom and People's Rights Movement, influenced by Western concepts, claimed equal rights for women and men. The Meiji Constitution and the Electoral Law of 1889 denied women the right to vote, though, and the Public Order and Police Law of 1900 totally excluded women from politics, forbidding them even to attend political rallies or to join political associations.

THE WOMEN'S SUFFRAGE MOVEMENT The movement first aimed at repealing the 1900 law by establishing women's branches and spearheading women's political rights. Progressive women organized the Shin-Fujin-Kyokai (New Women's Association) in 1920. The organization petitioned the Diet for the repeal of the Public Order and Police Law, and was successful in 1922 in passing an amendment that permitted women to attend political rallies. Suffragist leader Ichikawa Fusae established the Fusen-Kakutoku-Domei (Women's Suffrage League) in 1924, calling for alliances with other groups; they held the Women's Suffrage Rally in 1930. The limited women's suffrage bill would have passed the Diet except for the Manchurian Incident in 1931–33, which triggered the war between China and Japan and made women's rights a dead issue.

THE SECOND WORLD WAR AND THE MOBILIZATION OF WOMEN In the years before the Second World War, women's organizations were established to give moral support to the Japanese military. The Kokubo-Fujinkai (Women's Association for National Defence), formed in 1932, played a leading role in mobilizing women in wartime Japan. Members of the organization wore a uniform-like white apron, and served tea at embarkation points to young men leaving for the front. Their motto was 'Defence from the Kitchen'. As the country plunged into war in 1941, the Kokubo-Fujinkai and other women's associations united under the guidance of government to form the Dainihon-Fujinkai (All Japan Women's Association).

Some progressive women supported the war and cooperated with the government. Ichikawa took this opportunity for women to participate in mainstream politics, and voluntarily disbanded the Women's Suffrage League to show support to the military-run government. Thus, the suffrage movement suffered a setback during the war, and women activists split, according to their different positions regarding the war. Because of disarmament and the democratization process pursued by the Allied powers after the war, Japanese women finally gained suffrage on 17 December 1945, twenty years after universal male suffrage.

Women as voters seem to be more conscientious about their civic duties than men: their voting rate has been higher than the male rate since 1963 for the unified local election, since 1968 for the upper house (House of Councillors) election, and since 1969 for the lower house (House of Representatives) election. Women, however, do not especially vote differently from men, and the so-called 'gender gap' has not been so evident on the Japanese electoral scene, although women voters are slightly more critical than men of their government's performance.

Political leadership Today, women still suffer at workplaces. Increasing domestic violence victimizes women and environmental deterioration endangers maternal health. Women recognize the necessity of empowering women in the decision-making bodies to cope with these problems.

HEADS OF STATE AND GOVERNMENT In the last decade of the twentieth century Japanese women increased their visibility in the public sphere and gained considerable political power. Their empowerment, however, would not have been possible without the strong base that women's movements had prepared. To date, however, no heads of state have been chosen.

MINISTERIAL (CABINET) In the higher echelons of bureaucracy women contribute to formulating policies that address women's problems. Women bureaucrats are likely to concentrate in so-called women's divisions, and not many women are found in more powerful ministries such as the Ministry of Finance. Thus, gender segregation is apparent in the governmental make-up. The number of women appointed to cabinet posts has been very small. The first Koizumi cabinet (2001–2003) included five women; that number is still a record.

PARLIAMENTARY In the first national election after the war ended in 1946, a large number of women stood as candidates and a record thirty-nine women were elected to the lower house (House of Representatives). These women were successful partly because of the large district/multiple ballot that worked advantageously for women. The change in the electoral system to the unique combination of middle-sized district and multi-member/single ballot changed women's fortunes in the following election of 1947. Moreover, the establishment of political parties dominated by male politicians and ideological confrontation between the parties did not offer women a niche in politics. Since then, women have been under-represented in the Diet and local assemblies.

The 'party list' was introduced to the upper house election in 1983, partly to replace the costly national at-large electoral system, with positive effects for women. Parties now assume greater responsibility for the political representation of women. Leftist parties such as the Japan Communist Party and the Social Democratic Party have defended women's candidacies and put women on their slates. In recent national elections, more women from conservative parties ran and succeeded, changing the liberal-leaning landscape among political women and balancing their partisanship.

In addition, after long discussions about political reform, the electoral system for the lower house was changed in 1994 for the first time in nearly fifty years. The new system allows candidates to run both in the districts and on a party list. Women fared better under this system in 1996 and 2000 than under the previous system. More women were elected from the party lists than from the single-member districts, suggesting that the party list based on proportional representation offers women the optimum situation for electoral success. Women comprised 7.5 per cent of the lower house after the 2000 general election and 15.4 per cent of the upper house after the election of 2001.

LOCAL GOVERNMENT In the 1970s and 1980s, women gradually gained political power through various grassroots activities in the suburban areas of central Japan. Women in consumer and environmental protection movements ran for political office, and won seats in city halls and other local decision-making bodies. The Seikatsu Club is a nationwide consumer group whose political division has sent its branch members, mostly housewives, to the local political arenas. Since the club's cause is food safety, environmental protection and the quality of education, it has increasingly gained support from the public, especially in big cities. The Japan Communist Party and the Clean Party also recruited heavily for the local assemblies in 1999, resulting in the highest women's political representation ever (6 per cent) at local level. The women's proportion varies according to the power of decision-making bodies and the districts' level of urbanization. Prefectures tend to have fewer female representatives than cities or villages, and cities have more women than villages, where the 'old-boy network' remains strong. The first woman governor was elected in Osaka in 2000, followed by one in Kumamoto in the same year. The first woman mayor was elected in 1991 in Ashiya, followed by Zushi, Hasuda and Kunitachi in 1999. As of 2004, there are four female governors and seven female mayors in Japan.

PARTY LEADERSHIP – THE JAPANESE VERSION OF THE YEAR OF THE WOMAN In the upper house election of 1989, 'sick and tired' of the constant scandals among male members of the ruling Liberal Democratic Party, and fuelled by anger about the introduction of a sales tax, women voters united under the slogan 'Revolution from the Kitchen'. Angry voters sent twenty-two women to the upper house, bringing the number of women to a record high of thirty-two (13 per cent). Twelve of them were recruited by the Social Democratic Party, the largest opposition force at that time, headed by Doi Takako, the first female chair in the major political parties. Doi played a significant role in recruiting women candidates and fostering their electoral successes. 'The Year of the Woman' effect lasted into the lower house election of 1990; twelve women were elected, bringing the women's proportion to a record high of 5.9 per cent in this powerful chamber.

'WOMEN HELP WOMEN' – EMPOWERMENT FOR THE TWENTY-FIRST CENTURY One of the most remarkable activities in the 1990s was the establishment of women's political organizations that support women running for political office at the local level. One of these organizations is the 'NET', a political division of the Seikatsu Club. The local 'Back-up Schools' also contributed to the success of women in the unified local election of 1999. Their activities include candidate selection, training and fund-raising. As of 1999, there were more than twenty-five such schools founded and run by women all over Japan.

For the national-level election, the 'WINWIN' was founded in 1999 after the well-known US women's political action committee, 'Emily's List'. The WINWIN adopted the Emily's List formula, directing votors towards recommended candidates, and endorsed four women candidates for the first time in the lower house election of 2000. Three of them successfully challenged the male incumbents and defeated them. The 'Women Help Women' strategy has contributed to increased representation of women in politics (Box 9.1).

Towards gender equality and freedom

In the twentieth century Japan saw advances in the status of women and gender equality, particularly with the establishment of legal systems. Yet the attitudes and customs of male-dominated society still remain in the reality

Box 9.1 The Ainu women's group in Hokkaido

The Ainu are Japan's indigenous peoples, who once inhabited the northern part of mainland Japan and other northern islands, but now occupy only the northern island of Hokkaido. As the Ainu constitute a minority group in Japan, Ainu organizations are seeking to establish their rights as Aboriginal people; Ainu women as 'keepers of the culture' have spearheaded the movement (Billson 2005).

The Yay Yukar Academic Society was founded in 1973 with the aim of reclaiming the lost Ainu heritage. In 1992, Yay Yukar no Mori was founded to make Ainu traditions more relevant to contemporary life. The revival of important traditional ceremonies (and greater public awareness) has led to recognition of Aboriginal hunting and fishing rights. The Ainu have also joined with Japan's other minorities – resident Koreans and Chinese – to express their mutual solidarity. The Ainu seek to retain their characteristic culture, rooted in land and sea, and ask that the Japanese government return their ancestral lands. The Ainu Women's Association (AWA) was present at the Beijing Congress and was especially active at the Indigenous Women's Forum, where it sought to establish solidarity with indigenous women around the world. AWA raised questions about what indigenous women should do and how they should raise their children for life in the new millennium. (Adapted from Yamamoto and Keira 1995) (Carolyn Fluehr-Lobban)

of everyday lives. Japanese women are struggling to achieve actual equality between the sexes. The new agenda emerged at the same time as lifestyles were becoming more complicated, with increasing choices and recent female empowerment in career and individual fulfilment. This trend creates diversity among women. For example, having children and enjoying familial life are becoming more difficult when both sexes work outside the home, perhaps in different locales. These problems do not bother some women, who choose to become housewives. Diversity could create policy disagreements between women, but improving the status of one group of women should eventually enrich the lives of the others. People are not ready to support the various lifestyles of both women and men, however. Many complicated challenges shape the agenda for Japanese women.

Legal tasks remain, such as tackling gender differences in family and other laws. Females, especially housewives, have acquired strong status and power at home in daily life, but that status is still dependent on the existence of a husband. Divorced women suffer legally. For example, separate family names are illegal. A woman is often the one who has to retain her ex-husband's name or change back to her pre-marriage name after divorce. Today, 'freedom from gender' is desired beyond 'gender equality'. A diversified family structure, such as a single-parent or composite family that consists of a remarried couple with children from a previous marriage, should be accepted. For this purpose, discrimination relating to legal marriage, which disadvantages non-housewives, needs to be abolished. This includes discrimination in inheritance between legitimate and illegitimate children.

A woman who is dependent on her husband or family is facing an invisible wall. The social welfare system should be reconstructed for individuals, and not support only housewives and mothers. The diversity of women's lifestyles complicates welfare policy decisions. A solution might benefit one group of females but not necessarily another. For example, individualization of health insurance could benefit working and divorced women, but would introduce premium payments for housewives, who are currently covered by their husband's insurance. Many housewives, though, are part-time workers with no employees' insurance. Policies such as enabling more part-timers to obtain employees' health insurance might benefit both housewives and working women. Compromises should be sought.

The employment status of women has advanced legally, but the male/female wage differential and blocked opportunities for women remain. Lower wages can be attributed in large part to burdening women with most of the housework, creating the M-curve. At the same time, working women have the double burden of earning and housekeeping. Gender equality cannot be achieved without decreasing men's working hours, so they can engage in housework and childcare. Working conditions also hinder many women in choosing their career track, eventually lowering female wages. Old customs that supported a male-dominated society still prevail, such as long working hours and company-wide transfers that make it difficult for working couples to live together. Flexible employment conditions with reasonable compensation could promote female well-being.

At this point, schools play a major function in justifying a gender-neutral social and occupational position. Japanese success in providing competition among students based on ability and effort rather than gender tends to mask discrimination in the labour market. Schools have successfully helped students define their future as an independent choice, but they still function as an effective device for reproducing the gender order.

Female well-being in Japan also depends on uprooting violence against women, which requires overturning the structure of gender discrimination grounded in ancient male–female power relations. Eliminating control through gender violence will benefit from ending violence in wars and all relationships among districts, cultures and countries. The fight to end brutality against women will continue until humans achieve a way to solve problems without violence.

At the very last moment of the twentieth century, the idea of 'Women Help Women' was realized. Women have been active at the grass roots and the women's network is expected to link up effectively by establishing women's coalitions. Women in office meet women in grassroots organizations, thereby creating a more woman-friendly society for the coming era.

The transition out of Period III (1990s to today) is occurring. Can we imagine a third wave of feminism? After the 1990s, Japanese women entered a new phase, in which the notion of sexual diversity was incorporated into the Basic Law for a Gender-Equal Society (1999). This law was epoch-making by presenting a new vision of gender relations and calling for 'even greater efforts' towards 'genuine equality between women and men'. It recognizes that the rapid changes occurring in Japan's socio-economic situation make the realization of a gender-equal society a matter of urgent importance in determining the framework of twenty-first-century Japan. Backlashes against this law are also occurring, however, making the road towards gender equality non-linear and complex.

Gender equality should be pursued in consciousness and in everyday life. The significant roles of feminism and gender theory are first to criticize existing notions of human rights and second to present a new *type* of human rights, for example in reproductive health, in order to establish individual self-determination. This foreshadows a new phase, moving from gender equality to gender freedom, which protects diversity. Regendering social theory can help analyse complex social change, but more importantly we hope that it will lead to greater gender equality and freedom in everyday life for women and men in Japan and around the world.

Note

1 The authors gratefully acknowledge the support of Grants in Aid for Scientists (B) (1999–2000, Inoue Masako) from the Japan Ministry of Education. The grant made possible the International Symposium on Family in the New Millennium: Approaches from Foreign Perspectives and Practical Scenes, with Professors Billson and Fluehr-Lobban, held in Nagoya and Sapporo in 2000.

References

Aiuchi, M. (2003a) 'Gender and the American politics', in H. Watanabe (ed.), *Sex and Politics*, Japan Political Science Association, Tokyo: Iwanami Publishing

— (2003b) 'Politics and family life', in H. Amano (ed.), *One Hundred Years in Family Life*, Japan Lifology Association, Tokyo: Domes Publishing

Araki, T. (2002) *Labour and Employment Law in Japan*, Tokyo: Japan Institute of Labour

Asakura, M. (2002) *Rodo to Gender no Horitsugaku* [Gender and Employment Law], Tokyo: Yuhikaku Publishing

Billson, J. M. (2005) *Keepers of the Culture: Women and Power in the Canadian Mosaic*, Boulder, CO: Rowman & Littlefield

Cabinet Statistics Bureau (1943 and earlier) *Statistics Yearbook of Imperial Japan*, Tokyo: Cabinet Statistics Bureau

— (1943 and earlier) *Vital Statistics of Imperial Japan*, Tokyo: Cabinet Statistics Bureau

Educational Research Institute of Women's Education (1965–85) *Series on Women's Education and Research 1–8*, Tokyo: Japan Women's University

Ehara, Y. (2001) *Gender Titsujo* [Gender Order], Tokyo: Keisou Publishing

Fukaya, M. (1966) *Ryosaikennboshugino Kyouiku* [Education for Good Wives and Wise Mothers], Nagoya: Soumei Publishing

Hashimoto, N. (1992) *Danjokyougakuseino Sitekikennkyuu* [Historical Research on Co-Educationalism], Tokyo: Otsuki Publishing

Hisatake, A. et al. (eds) (1997) *Kazoku Data Book* [Data Book on Family], Tokyo: Yuhikaku Publishing

Hounoki, K. (1996) *Jenda-Bunnka to Gakusyuu Rironn to Houhou* [Gender Culture, Learning Theory and Method], Tokyo: Meiji Tosho Publishing

Ichimori, M., M. Tutomu and Y. Jyunosuke (1998) *Nihon Kindaikyouiku to Sabetsu* [Education and Discrimination in Modern Japan], Tokyo: Akashi Publishing

Imamura, E. A. (ed.) (1996) *Re-imaging Japanese Women*, Berkeley: University of California Press

Inoue, M. (1999) 'Significances and tasks of feminism as social theory', *Annual of Legal Philosophy*

— (2001) 'Con-, dis- and re-construction: theory of feminism and civil society', in I. Hiromichi (ed.), *New Theory of Civil Society*, Tokyo: Fukousha

— (2004) 'Domestic violence as violence within the intimate sphere: roles of law', *Studies in Community Policy*, 7

Iwao, S. (1993) *The Japanese Woman: Traditional Image and Changing Reality*, New York: Free Press

JAIWR (Japanese Association of International Women's Rights) (1998) *Josei Kanrenho Data Book* [Women's Rights Resource Book], Tokyo: Yuhikaku Publishing

Kameda, A. and K. Tachi (eds) (2000) *Gakkou Wo Jendafuri Ni* [Make Gender-Free Schools], Tokyo: Akashi Publishing

Kimura, R. (2000) *Gakkoubunnka to Gender* [School Culture and Gender], Tokyo: Keisou Publishing

Koyama, S. (1991) *Ryousaikennbo toiu Kihann* [Standard of Good Wives and Wise Mothers], Tokyo: Keisou Publishing

Matsuyama, E. (1987) 'Japan shows how to save the children', *JOICFP*, 14: 24–9

Ministry of Education (1993) *Gakusei 120 Nennsshi* [120 Years' History of the Educational System], Tokyo: Ministry of Education

Ministry of Health and Welfare (1947 and later) *Vital Statistics of Japan*, Tokyo: Ministry of Health and Welfare

Office of the Prime Minister (1983) *Fujinmondai ni kansuru kokusai hikaku chosa* [Research on an International Comparison of the Problems Women Face], Tokyo: Office of the Prime Minister

Seki, F. (2001) 'The role of the government and the family in taking care of the frail elderly: a comparison of the United States and Japan', in S. Gauthier et al. (eds), *Aging: Caring for Our Elders*, Vol. 11, International Library of Ethics, Law and the New Medicine, Dordrecht: Kluwer Academic Publishers

Shakai Hosho Kenkyusho (National Institute of Population and Social Security Research) (1993) *Josei to Shakai Hosho* [Women and Social Welfare], Tokyo: University of Tokyo Press

Statistics Bureau (various years) *Japan Statistical Yearbook*, Tokyo: Japan Statistics Bureau

Statistics Bureau (Management and Coordination Agency) (1999) *Historical Statistics of Japan on CD-ROM*, Tokyo: Japan Statistics Bureau

Sugeno, K. (1992) *Japanese Labour Law*, trans. L. Kanowitz, Tokyo: University of Tokyo Press

Yamamoto, E. and T. Keira (1995) *Ainu Women: Aboriginal People of Japan – Keeping the Hearts of Our Eldresses Alive Today*, prepared for the World Conference on Women, Beijing

Websites (in English)

Cabinet Office, <www.cao.go.jp>

GEB (Gender Equality Bureau) (1999) Cabinet Office, <www.gender.go.jp>

MHLW (Ministry of Health, Labour and Welfare), <www.mhlw.go.jp>

<www.gender.go.jp/danjyo/english/plan2000/1999>

10 | Women in South Africa: crossing the great divides of race and gender

A. M. (RIA) VAN NIEKERK AND JOPIE VAN ROOYEN

> Freedom cannot be achieved unless women have been emancipated
> from all forms of oppression. Nelson Mandela, 1994

Life for women in South Africa in the twentieth century started with a war at home and continued through two world wars and a socio-political struggle. It concluded with a social revolution culminating in the acceptance of a constitution that abolished all forms of discrimination.

South Africa started out as a halfway station at the Cape of Good Hope for passing ships on their way to the east in 1652. By 1900 the cape had become a British colony, while dissident farmers, mainly Afrikaans-speaking and referred to as Boers, had migrated to the north to start independent republics. The lifestyle of white women in the Cape Colony reflected a prosperous community with strong influences from Britain and the continent of Europe. Pioneer women in the northern areas lived mainly on farms or in mining camps, while the majority of women from indigenous groups continued to live in rural areas. Colonization had a gradual and varying effect on their traditional way of life, the most important consequence being the movement of black men to urban areas in order to earn money.

From the inception of the Union of South Africa in 1910, all governments tended to follow a policy of differentiated development for different population groups (Bureau for Information 1986: 100–204). This culminated in the policy of 'apartheid' from 1948 onwards. The fragmentation of the population resulting from these policies had a direct effect on the lack of comparable statistical information for a large part of the twentieth century.

A demographic portrait of South African women

The Republic of South Africa is one of a small number of sovereign states in which the population is comprised of permanent groups with unique characteristics (Bureau of Information 1987: 1). The population of 44.7 million (53 per cent women) can be divided into four main groups (Behr and MacMillan 1971: 7). Blacks (about 74 per cent) represent a diversity of indigenous groups; whites (14 per cent) are mainly descendants of European immigrants; coloureds (9 per cent) are descendants of Malay slaves and cross-racial relationships; and Asians (2 per cent) are mainly of Indian descent. This 'rainbow nation' also includes minority groups of Chinese, Taiwanese and Japanese. The population mix is unique in that whites and blacks, who form the majority, have their roots in two totally different worlds: the first in a European capitalistic, industrialized society and the second in a mainly pre-industrial way of life (Van Niekerk 1991: 3).

Urbanization South Africa's population at the beginning of the century was mainly rural. Migration to cities increased in 1904 after the destruction of 30,000 rural homesteads, part of the British 'scorched earth' policy during the Anglo-Boer War (1889 to 1902). By 1930 the population had increased to 1.8 million (Joyce 2000: 77). A second wave of migration to urban areas occurred during the 1930s because of the Great Depression, a severe drought and a devastating locust plague. It was only during the last ten years of the century that '... the country "tipped" from being a rural nation to being an urban one' (Star 1999: iii, 9).

The policy of migrant labour utilized by the mines, as well as restrictions placed on the movement of blacks, especially during the apartheid era, meant that '... a smaller percentage of the Black group became urbanized' (Harvey 1994: 84). Black women were barred from joining their husbands in mining hostels or working in 'white' urban areas; they tended to remain in rural areas to fulfil family responsibilities.

At present there are nine provinces (Mallet 2000: i). Population density does not reflect the extent of urbanization of any particular area. KwaZulu-Natal has the highest number of people but only 38.2 per cent live in urban areas while Northern Cape has the lowest number of people but 74.2 per cent are urbanized (Tait et al. 1996: 36, 42).

Life expectancy Between 1970 and 1998, life expectancy in South Africa increased from forty to fifty-one years (Nkau 1998: 30); as of 2002, the negative impact of AIDS had resulted in declining life expectancy: 45.3 years for women and 43.3 years for men (WHO 2004).

Population growth, fertility rate and male–female ratio After the end of the Anglo-Boer War, South Africa's population was unevenly distributed over four provinces. In 1963, as an outflow of the policy of separate development ('apartheid'), ten black national self-governing states were formed; by 1991 five of these had become independent. In 1993, with the birth of a comprehensive

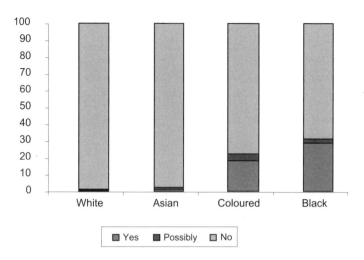

Figure 10.1 Households with extramarital children (per cent)
Source: **Steyn (1994: 43)**

democratic form of government, it was decided to incorporate once again the self-governing and independent states.

South Africa was the first country in sub-Saharan Africa to record a decline in fertility rates. In 1993, fertility rates for blacks varied from 2.8 per 1,000 in urban areas to 3.4 in semi-rural areas and 5.3 in rural areas. In 1994, the average number of children per woman was 4.3 for blacks, 2.3 for coloureds, 2.2 for Asians and 1.6 for whites (Taylor and Conradie 1997: 4). The lower fertility rates in urban areas can be attributed to higher levels of education, higher income, accessibility of health services, and a higher proportion of economically active women (Nkau 1998: 31).

Teenage fertility rates decreased from 1980 to 1986. The number for whites decreased from 6,361 in 1980 (8.2 per cent) to 5,189 (7.1 per cent) in 1986. Asian rates decreased from 2,238 (11.3 per cent) to 1,867 (9.5 per cent), and coloured rates from 12,246 (16.8 per cent) to 11,835 (14.5 per cent). Unfortunately, no figures are available for blacks in this period (Beets 1996: 9). In 1995, the rate of teenage pregnancies, excluding the former independent black national states, was estimated at 330 per 1,000 births (Taylor and Conradie 1997: 4). In 1998, this figure had fallen to 124 per 1,000. Teenage pregnancies often cause girls to leave school; most of them do not return. This has a negative effect on 'the health, education and employability of young women' (Nkau 1998: 32).

Statistics indicate that the incidence of children born out of wedlock was highest for blacks and coloureds (Figure 10.1).

Adoption is strictly regulated in South Africa. Moving children from one population group to another was not allowed during apartheid. Although this

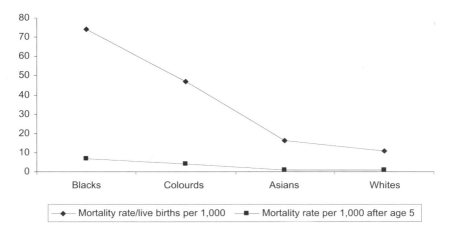

Figure 10.2 Child mortality rates by population group, 1980–89
Source: **Rock (1997: 53)**

restriction is no longer in force, the right of the child to remain within his/her birth culture is taken seriously.

Age structure of the population Age and population group converge with socio-economic status in South Africa. Black women with young children and old people suffer the most, with nearly a million people older than sixty-five living below the poverty line. Households with a female head had a much higher incidence of poverty, while households in rural areas had an even higher incidence of poverty (Whiteford and McGrath 1991: 73–4).

Maternal mortality rate The unequal distribution of state and state-aided health facilities, which tend to be concentrated in urban areas, had far-reaching implications for the health of women and children in rural areas (O'Donovan 1998: 41). Estimates of maternal mortality rates vary greatly, between 0.52 and 0.83 per 1,000 for 1992 (Taylor and Conradie 1997: 4), mainly because data were not always representative of the population as a whole.

Infant mortality rate Although statistics were not quoted, Nkau (1998: 30) indicated that infant mortality rates in South Africa were nearly halved between 1970 and 1998. Differences between the rates for different population groups from 1980 to 1989 are depicted in Figure 10.2, showing the narrowing of the racial gap. Ignorance, lack of education and poor healthcare are direct causes of the high mortality rate for black and coloured infants. As the level of education of mothers increases, the mortality rate decreases (Rock 1997: 53).

Contraception and abortion Lack of access to medical personnel hampered the family planning programmes that began in the 1960s. The use of contraceptives by black women in the latter part of the twentieth century varied between 62.6 and 53.9 per cent, depending on the area concerned (Nkau 1998: 32). Cultural resistance to the use of contraception and lack of knowledge remained problems, especially in rural areas (September 1987: 251). Legal abortions were available only according to very strict prerequisites until 2000. In 1991 only 40 per cent of applications for legal abortions were granted (Taylor and Conradie 1997: 4). Of all legal abortions, 71 per cent were performed on white women. The result was a proliferation of illegal abortions among all racial groups, with an estimated 200,000 to 300,000 performed each year.

HIV/AIDS At the end of the twentieth century, an estimated one in nine South Africans had HIV/AIDS (Joyce 2000: 223). Women and children are in the majority and at greatest risk (WHO: 2001). In a major city hospital, 30 per cent of all patients and 24.5 per cent of pregnant women tested positive. AIDS-related illnesses (50 per cent of all tuberculosis victims, according to Joyce 2000: 223) and resulting deaths increased the number of orphans and abandoned babies. Campaigns launched to prevent further spread of the disease have limited success because of ignorance and cultural biases.

Family status and structure

Family life in South Africa was influenced in an evolutionary fashion by socio-political factors, moving from the colonial phase through '... phases in which the policies of segregation, apartheid and "own" and "general" affairs featured strongly. Throughout, the policy of separateness prevailed' (Harvey 1994: 84). Conflict formed an integral part of social change in South African society, always with the family at its centre.

Marriage age and rate At the beginning of the twentieth century, couples from the Asian, coloured and white communities tended to prefer a religious ceremony. A change to a preference for civil ceremonies during the course of the century was most apparent in the Asian population. In 1940, 91.4 per cent of Asian marriages were religious, compared to 8.6 per cent civil. By 1975, the proportion of civil marriages had risen to 85.3 per cent. In the coloured community, the proportion of civil marriages rose from 21.4 per cent in 1940 to 36.9 per cent in 1984. In the white community, the preference for religious marriages remained relatively constant – 28.3 per cent in 1915 compared to 26.4 per cent in 1984. Ante-nuptial contracts became more common among white couples, with only 29.7 per cent choosing this option in 1925, compared to 54.8 per cent in 1984. Among the Asian and coloured communities, contracts remained the exception (Steyn 1994: 449–51).

The crude marriage rate for Asians, coloureds and whites has remained fairly constant over a number of decades. The rate for whites (1915–85) varied from 8.3 to 13.1 per cent; the rate for coloureds (1935–85) varied from 6.0 to 9.0 per cent; and the rate for Asians (1940–85) varied from 7.2 to 10.8 per cent. The median age for females getting married for the first time was twenty-two (ibid.: 448, 455). In 1996, 46 per cent of women were married, living together with a male, widowed, divorced or separated, while 51.6 per cent had never married (SSA 1999: 2).

Marriage and divorce Traditional family life, especially among black and Asian families, revolved around the extended patrilineal family characterized by patriarchal dominance. The extended family helped to ensure stability through mutual support and inter-dependence among family members. The adoption of the core family as the focal point of government policy had far-reaching effects. Housing policies for non-whites in urban areas made no provision for extended or large families and placed restrictions on accommodation for female-headed single-parent families. Children were often placed under the care of grandmothers in rural areas where, because of the age of the care-giver, lack of education or poverty, children did not always receive adequate stimulation and care (Taylor and Conradie 1997: 43–3). In the migrant labour system, men left their families behind and lived in single quarters. They often started 'second families' in cities (Harvey 1994: 85), which led to less money being sent to families in rural areas and compounded the hardships.

Before 1993, the power of a husband in South Africa formed the cornerstone of all marital relationships, except when excluded by ante-nuptial contract. Even then, the husband remained the legal guardian of any children born from the union, unless specifically changed by order of the court. The General Law Fourth Amendment Act 132 of 1993 abolished all exclusively male marital power, although consent by both parties for important transactions was required. A married woman could, according to the Domicile Act 3 of 1992, acquire her own domicile. This placed the woman on an equal footing for determining the jurisdiction of the court during divorce proceedings. Women were also protected by a system whereby, on the dissolution of marriage through death or divorce, the wife was entitled to half of any assets accrued. Pension benefits and annuities formed part of the estate. Unfortunately,

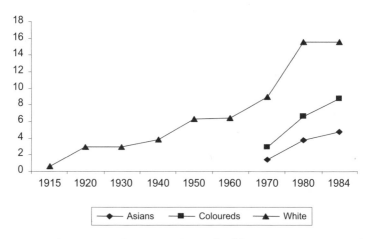

Figure 10.3 Divorce rate in South Africa (per 1,000)
Source: Steyn (1987: 460)

in many cases black married women remained subject to the traditional authority of their husband's family (Taylor and Conradie 1997: 93–4).

An overall increase in the divorce rate took place during the century. Viewing marriage as a lifelong contract gave way to a perception that individual personal rights and welfare are more important (Steyn 1994: 460). Women's increasing economic independence also influenced this tendency. Figure 10.3 shows the divorce rate increase from 1915 to 1984.

One or more minor children were involved in at least 55 per cent of divorce cases (Steyn 1987: 468). Non-payment of maintenance (child support) had a crippling effect on the quality of life of divorcees, with many women having to spend days in a futile effort to have their cases heard in court; many lost their jobs or had wages withheld (Wilson and Ramphele 1989: 179). After 1994 legislation, non-payment of maintenance became a criminal offence entailing a possible jail sentence.

No precise figures on the number of widows in South Africa were available for the twentieth century. Research conducted in particular areas indicated that the proportions of households affected could be as high as 30 per cent. In the case of mine workers, pensions were paid to widows through a local magistrate who decided on a monthly sum. Traditionally, in some black groups, a widow found protection by becoming another wife in her brother-in-law's household. Even when this was not relevant, a male relative, who became the effective custodian of the household, was responsible for handling the estate. If the woman refused, any assets involved could be withheld. Non-white women without a husband forfeited the right to housing in urban areas, while women in rural areas who lost a breadwinner were barred from moving to urban areas to obtain work.

Because of these practices, divorced and deserted wives often found themselves destitute (Wilson and Ramphele 1989: 178).

EXTENDED VERSUS NUCLEAR FAMILIES Traditionally, the survival of the black agricultural and pastoral way of life depended on the availability of labour (Van Niekerk 1991: 3). All the black ethnic groups had a similar tradition of reliance on the extended family to fill their needs. The main factors that influenced the corrosion of the traditional black extended family were urbanization and the adoption of Western ways of living (Nzimande 1987: 43–4). Asian families were less affected because, irrespective of some disruption, many traditional values and mores were retained (Jithoo 1987: 79); coloured families tended to be organized around social networks (Rabie 1987: 102–3).

FEMALE-HEADED HOUSEHOLDS Female-headed households, especially black households, were significantly poorer than average households in South Africa (Taylor and Conradie 1997: 4). Women were barred from moving freely to obtain work where they chose and were burdened by lack of education and prejudices on the part of male managers. Female-headed families in rural areas were '... at the bottom of the economic pyramid in this country' (Wilson and Ramphele 1989: 179). The percentage of single-parent families headed by women reported in 1989 varied between 4.7 for whites, 5.8 for Asians, 9.3 for blacks and 9.6 for coloureds. If multi-generational families with a female head are added, the percentages rise to 6.2 for whites, 11.4 for Asians, 21.4 for coloureds and 25.5 for blacks (Beets 1996: 6). In a Women's Day speech in March 2001, the Minister of Public Service and Administration, Geraldine Fraser-Moloketi, indicated that the overall figure had risen to 38 per cent. According to the Department of Health (1998: 10), 50 per cent of households in non-urban areas are headed by women. The involvement of males in migrant labour is cited as one of the reasons for this phenomenon.

Violence against women

Until the late 1960s and the early 1970s, very little attention was given to family violence. Even in the 1980s, no reliable information was available (Viljoen 1987: 378). 'Despite evidence from an historical perspective that conflict and violence between family members is not uncommon, academics have been slow to undertake studies in this field' (Pretorius 1987: 417), and we can only speculate upon the extent of the problem. Statistics on child abuse indicate that the number of cases reported had risen from 243 in 1982 to 314 in 1983.

In Johannesburg, numbers had risen from 46 in 1983 to 135 in 1984 (Allwood 1987: 407).

Reported cases of rape also increased considerably. In 1992, 4,349 cases were reported, but in 1993 this had risen to 28,318 (Taylor and Conradie 1997: 4). It is not clear whether the increase was in real terms or whether it indicated a stronger willingness on the part of victims to come forward in light of greater support from authorities and the media.

Economic participation

Although South Africa has the strongest economy on the African continent, the World Bank classified it as the eighty-fifth-poorest nation in 1971. Its position improved to ninetieth in 1990, reverting to eighty-fifth in 1993 after ' ... nearly five years of recession, a turbulent political process, a drop in international commodity prices, a world recession, and the combined effects of sanctions and drought' (Spier 1994: 8–9).

The discovery of diamonds and gold in 1870 and 1886 respectively and the outbreak of the Anglo-Boer War (1899–1902) had a devastating effect on the economy and a profound effect on the lives of women in South Africa. The mines, which had provided income to thousands of black workers, were closed down, leaving thousands of families destitute. Agriculture came to a standstill, mainly as a result of the British 'scorched earth' policy. After the end of the war, much of the agricultural community moved to urban areas, giving rise to severe competition for jobs between unskilled whites and blacks. From the start, 'race and ethnicity profoundly influenced the development of industrial relations and a peculiar South African economic culture' (Theron 1990: 1).

The division of labour Many factors impeded women's upward mobility in the employment market. Until 1984, when the Matrimonial Property Act was promulgated, married women were viewed as minors in the eyes of the law in South Africa. A husband had control over his wife's right to negotiate or undertake contractual agreements; fathers were legal guardians of offspring. Black women were still subject to traditional laws that regarded women as subordinate to men, regardless of age or educational status.

Women's participation in the labour force Women's participation in the labour force increased dramatically by 250 per cent between 1969 and 1989, with a particularly large rise in teaching and medicine, and slower movement in law and engineering (Gerdes 1987: 294). The Promotion of Equal Opportunities Bill addressed discrimination on the basis of gender, marital status or pregnancy. The Abolition of Discrimination Bill tabled in parliament in February 1993 did not address discrimination against married women with regard to taxation, medical aid, pensions and subsidies because men were still designated as breadwinners. The judiciary's inherent paternalistic mindset was reflected in the lack of consultation with women's organizations, employer/employee organizations, or political parties during the drafting process (Erwee 1994: 331). Discrimination persisted in customary laws and administrative practices handled by municipalities and local authorities, accessing credit facilities, bank loans and licensing and funding for small businesses (Taylor and Conradie 1997: 83–4).

The legislative barring of discriminatory practices did not prohibit covert discrimination in the form of inadequate career planning, training programmes and promotional opportunities for professional women (Erwee 1994: 332). Exploitation continued through differential salary scales and discriminatory promotional policies. The most exploited categories were domestics and agricultural workers, who worked long hours and were paid the lowest wages. Only recently were these workers provided with more legislative protection (Wilson and Ramphele 1989: 179).

TYPES OF OCCUPATION A change in the balance of the male-dominated world started as early as 1900, during the Anglo-Boer War, when women were 'given permission' to take over post and telegraph services in Pretoria to free men to fight (Marais 1999). In 1907, mention is made of women in South Africa working as secretaries and telephone operators. In 1908, Cecilia Makiwane became the first black woman admitted to the nursing register and in 1914 E. Doidge became the first woman to obtain a doctorate (DSc Botany) in South Africa. The First World War brought about a second wave of emancipation, with women stepping in to do the jobs of men involved in the fighting. In May 1923, Irene Antoinette Geffen of Johannesburg was the first woman admitted to the bar in the Transvaal, followed shortly by Bertha Solomon (Star 1999: 198). In 1924, Anne Manthey became the first full-time female radio announcer (Joyce 2000: 60).

From 1930 to 1939, female role models were breaking ground in traditional male domains, becoming architects (M. Sauer), attorneys (C. Hall), veterinarians (J. Morice), ophthalmic surgeons (E. Franks), physicians (A. van Heerden) and surgeons (Group Democracy and Governance 2000: 267, 246, 204, 196, 206). The Second World War provided women with even greater opportunities, although most were available only to white women. The 1970s are referred to as the decade of the liberated women (Star 1999: 198), with women becoming engineers and crane drivers. Coloured and black women were first appointed

245

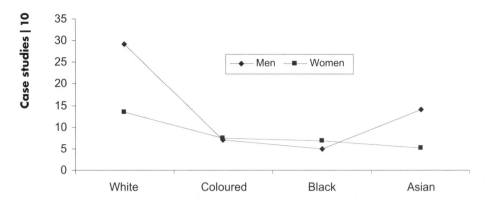

Figure 10.4 Professional women in the labour force (per cent)
Source: Erwee (1994: 326)

as till operators and bank tellers in traditionally white areas. By 1977 discriminatory clauses in labour legislation were removed and ' ... coloured cashiers
became commonplace overnight' (ibid.: 174).

Differences emerged in labour force participation towards the end of the
twentieth century. Overall the rate increased slightly from 1980, with coloured
women employed at a higher rate than others. The low increase in the involvement of black women can be attributed to omission of data from the independent national states, which is a problem with some statistics in South Africa
up to the 1990s (Le Roux 1987: 318). Among married women, white women
have the highest rate of employment and coloureds the lowest. In spite of
their increased participation, women continued working mainly in traditional
positions. Figures 10.4, 10.5 and 10.6 show women's participation at various
occupational levels.

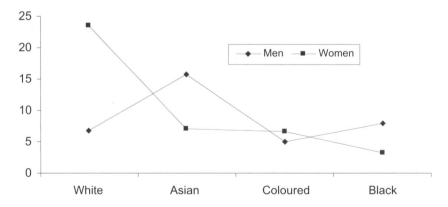

Figure 10.5 Administrative and clerical women in the labour force (per cent)
Source: Erwee (1994: 326)

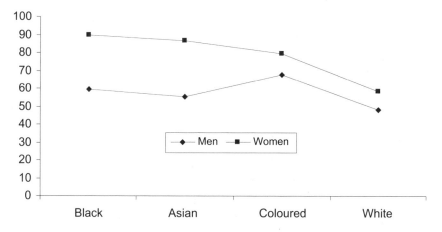

Figure 10.6 All other female occupational types in the labour force (per cent)
Source: **Erwee (1994: 326)**

Virtually all domestics (95 per cent) were women, as were 65 per cent of clerks (SSA 1999: 2). Asian women are more likely to be in the 'housewife' category (73.5 per cent) compared to other women. White males dominate in professional and management positions (Figure 10.7). Coloured and black women do better than their male counterparts.

The proportion of women in management, executive and junior management positions increased from 17 per cent in 1985 to 20 per cent in 1992. Rates for black women showed the greatest change between 1985 and 1992, from 16.5 to 26 per cent (Erwee 1994: 328–9). From 1969 to 1989 there was a consistent increase in women's involvement in higher-level occupations that typically require an academic qualification.

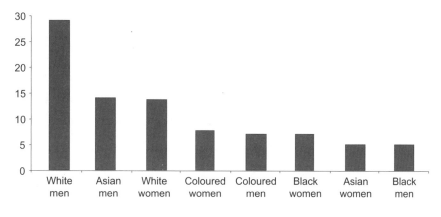

Figure 10.7 Professional and management partcipation by gender and race (per cent) *Source:* **Steyn (1994: 330)**

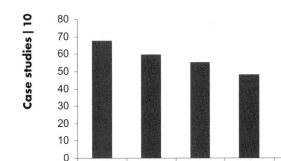

Figure 10.8 Skilled labour, service, agriculture, transport, technical, trade, mining, industrial by gender and race (per cent) *Source:* **Steyn (1994: 330)**

During the last decade of the century, women started to edge up the corporate ladder. The removal of discriminatory legislation, some attitudinal changes and the establishment of multiracial women's groups began to break through the glass ceiling (ibid.: 326). Nevertheless, in 1988, when the South African Federation of Business and Professional Women researched fair employment practices in companies, they found that women were appointed to executive positions primarily in more traditional areas, namely education, retail, travel and utilities.

As in other areas of life in South Africa, the years 1990 to 2000 were characterized by efforts by women to cooperate with each other for economic empowerment. In 1995, the Women's Investment Portfolio Holdings (WHIPHOLD), a women's empowerment group, was created. Gill Marcus became the first woman appointed deputy governor of the Reserve Bank. Bridgette Radeba, founder of Mmajau Mining, was the first black woman to engage in executive management in gold, platinum and diamond mining. Wendy Luhabe was honoured in 1999 as one of the fifty leading women entrepreneurs in the world (Group Democracy and Governance 2000: 286, 294). In contrast, lower-level positions are held by black men and women of all groups (Figure 10.8). These figures do not reflect the growing involvement of women in commerce. From 1961 to 1990, women of all population groups excelled as entrepreneurs (ibid.: 281, 280, 285).

Income and poverty The majority of women in South Africa were subjected to ongoing poverty throughout the twentieth century. The policy on migration labour and the restrictions on black women joining their husbands in the cities meant that women and children were left in rural areas to fend for themselves.

During the early 1930s, poverty became a crisis with 300,000 people (16.7 per cent) classified as 'very poor' (Joyce 2000: 77). In 1994 more than 17 million people (48.9 per cent of households) subsisted below the accepted minimum living level (Whiteford and McGrath 1994: 74). Of these, 11 million lived in rural areas and ' … the remaining six million [are] almost equal to the present number of squatters' informal settlements found around urban areas' (Spier 1994: 9). Two million were children.

Until 1980, the personal income of non-whites was considerably lower than that of whites, and then significant changes began to take place. The share of blacks increased from 24.9 to 27.6 per cent, that of coloureds from 7.2 to 7.3 per cent, and that of Asians from 3.0 to 3.9 per cent, while the white share decreased from 65 to 61.2 per cent. The redistribution of income had little effect in practical terms, however. The increased income accruing to the black population '… flowed to the richest 20% of Black households' (Whiteford and McGrath 1994: 74), while the remaining 80 per cent are poorer than they were in 1975. More than 25 per cent were living on less than half of the minimum living wage.

Women have been paid less than males, which resulted in female-headed households becoming significantly poorer than those headed by men (Taylor and Conradie 1997: 4). In contrast, households headed by men often reaped the benefit of dual incomes. The difference in pay between men and women for 1984, 1988 and 1990 was calculated using the Patterson system, a job evaluation system that takes into account the level of decision-making. These surveys compare the annual salaries of full-time personnel in large South African companies. Depending on racial group, as of 1990 women made between 70 and 100 per cent of white men's pay in lower junior management positions and in upper department head or professional positions. The gap was highest for black and coloured women (Erwee 1994: 333).

The gap between men and women's remuneration narrowed between 1984 and 1990. Women performed jobs previously filled by men, for example supervisory positions, and in certain categories they received practically the same pay. Black women supervisors at times received higher salaries than their male counterparts, as they moved into positions previously occupied by white women.

BENEFITS For the greater part of the century, women, especially married women, were excluded from many of the financial benefits available to men – membership in pension and medical aid schemes, and housing subsidies. Although pregnant women were supposed to receive four months' maternity leave, they were often subject to dismissal or withholding of pay for the time they were unable to work (ibid.: 334). Working mothers had to contend with an acute shortage of pre-school centres and day care facilities, as few companies were willing to commit funding for such facilities.

Literacy and education

One of South Africa's most crucial problems has been the low level of education of most of its population. For most of the century, education for black children was neither compulsory nor free (Star 1999: 176).

Literacy rates Functional literacy (Grade 7) was estimated at 60 per cent in urban areas and as low as 30 per cent in rural areas, indicating a pattern of lower education qualifications for women. Unequal educational opportunity ' ... limits women's capacity to develop and thereby limits the extent to which they can become economically and politically empowered and less dependent' (Taylor and Conradie 1997: 81).

School completion rates

PRIMARY AND SECONDARY At the end of the century, the proportion of children between the ages of six and fourteen not in school varied from 1 to 30 per cent and even 45 per cent in selected areas (Krige 1996: 98; Howes et al. 1997: 2). Table 10.1 reflects the discrepancy between the educational levels of males and females.

TABLE 10.1 Education by gender and population group (%)

Education	White		Coloured		Asian		Black	
	F	M	F	M	F	M	F	M
None	0.3	0.1	8.1	7.0	8.3	1.3	13.9	14.7
1–7 Yrs	0.9	0.5	37.8	30.7	26.9	14.6	35.4	27.1
8–11 Yrs	40.4	31.5	46.2	49.0	49.2	53.2	43.2	46.1
12 Yrs	35.3	33.0	4.3	7.1	7.1	19.6	4.6	7.3

Source: Steyn (1994: 31).

HIGHER EDUCATION As the century progressed, the number of women obtaining degrees steadily increased. In 1947, Mary Malahlele was the first black woman to qualify as a medical doctor. By 1991, women were acquiring 40 per cent of bachelor's degrees awarded, 25 per cent of master's and 23 per cent of doctorates. By 1995, the number of women receiving university degrees

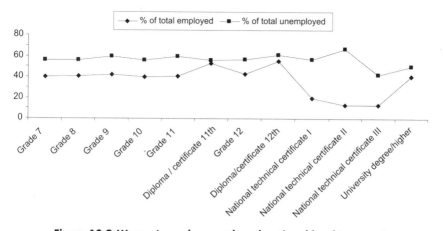

Figure 10.9 Women's employment by educational level (per cent)
Source: **SSA (1999: 2)**

exceeded that of men for the first time (Erwee 1994: 328), but participation levels were much lower for coloured, Asian and black women than they were for white women.

EDUCATIONAL STATUS OF WOMEN IN THE WORKPLACE Women have a lower employment rate than men with the same qualifications, while women with the same qualifications as men have a higher rate of unemployment. Figure 10.9 compares the percentage of functionally literate women employed with that of unemployed women with similar qualifications. The figures clearly show that education for women in South Africa thus far has *not* been able to overcome the entrenched biases against racial and gender groups.

Political, educational and cultural leadership

Turbulence and resistance characterized most of the twentieth century. Women were actively involved in the struggle for independence, dignity and respect.

Suffrage: participation in voting and elections White women over the age of thirty obtained the right to vote in 1930. Despite strong protests, non-white groups were denied direct representation or voting rights; coloureds and Asians were given suffrage in 1984.

Political leadership

1900–39 During the period 1899 to 1902 women experienced a country at war. More than 26,000 women and children died in British concentration

251

Women in South Africa

camps and more than 30,000 homesteads were destroyed in the northern provinces. Some managed to escape internment by hiding in the veldt, while others joined their men in guerrilla warfare (Joyce 2000: 11). Women in the Cape Colony protested against the 'scorched earth' policy of the British and started a South African Conciliation Committee and a Women and Children Distress Fund. Among women who tried to alleviate suffering was British-born Emily Hobhouse, whom Lord Kitchener referred to as ' ... that bloody woman' (ibid.: 68) because of her humane activities in the camps.

In 1903, Charlotte Maxeke, the first black woman to earn a university degree in South Africa, founded the Bantu Women's League (later renamed the African National Congress Women's League). In 1908, women supporting Mohandas Gandhi, a campaigner for Indian rights, burned more than three thousand documents in protest against laws requiring Indians and Chinese to carry registration books bearing their thumbprints. In 1910, the Union of South Africa was established under the guidance of the British government. In 1911, the Mines and Works Act was passed, excluding blacks from most skilled jobs. A new dimension in labour disputes came into being when women took an active part in the tramways strike in Johannesburg in 1911 and the miners' strike in 1913. Mary Fitzgerald ('Mary Pickhandle'), one of the leaders, was taken into custody for inciting miners to riot and leading a militant group of miners' wives in protest rallies. She was later elected as the first female city councillor in Johannesburg (Group Democracy and Governance 2000: 281).

In 1912, the South African Native National Congress (SANNC, later called the African National Congress or ANC) came into being. When passes for women (as required of black men since the end of the nineteenth century) were suggested in 1913, women refused in open defiance. Many women chose to go to jail rather than to carry a pass (Star 1999: 63). In 1918 and 1919, Charlotte Maxeke led vigorous campaigns against passes for black women. In 1935, Maxeke co-founded the All Africa Convention and in 1939 Cissie Gool, a human rights activist, was elected president of the Non-European United Front, inspired by the Communist Party of South Africa. When South Africa joined the Allies during the Second World War, some women joined the war effort while others who remembered the suffering at the hands of the British during the Anglo-Boer War protested (Beyers and Basson 1987: 281-3).

1940-60 This period was characterized by ' ... the stricter application of the existing discriminatory legislation', resulting in a growing polarization between whites and non-whites. The Youth League of the African National Congress was established in 1940. Ellen Hellman became well known for her involvement with the South African Institute of Race Relations, compiling and submitting evidence on sociocultural realities in the country. In 1948, a white nationalist government came to power, which led to the 'parting of the ways' between government and black political organizations. During the 1950s, the government launched a myriad of race laws and regulations aimed at physically, economically and culturally separating whites and non-whites. Blacks were barred from schools and other educational institutions in 'white' areas. In 1949, mixed marriages were banned and in 1950 the Immorality Act placed a complete prohibition on intimate relations between white and non-white (Joyce 2000: 113). Black nationalism gained momentum and international resistance increased.

In 1951, Cissie Gool was involved with other moderate coloureds in starting the Franchise Action Council. Then, in 1952, the ANC, the Coloured People's Congress and the South African Indian Congress cooperated to organize protest actions against the pass laws, the Group Areas Act and other restrictive legislation. The Native Resettlement Bill, providing for the forced removal of blacks from so-called white areas, was passed in 1954 (ibid.: 116–24).

Women played an increasingly important role in black protest politics during the 1950s. A multiracial Federation of South African Women (FSAW) was launched in 1954 to function as a coordinating body for affiliated groups such as the ANC Women's League, South African Congress of Democrats, South African Coloured People's Organization, Indian Congresses and various trade unions. In 1954, white women started the Women's Defence of the Constitution League ('Black Sash') to protest against the apartheid laws. Women from all population groups started working together in protest against the contexts in which they were trapped. In 1956 the first passes for women were distributed in the Free State. A few weeks later, under the leadership of Lilian Ngoyi of the ANC, women marched to the Winburg magistrates' court and burned their passes. Following this demonstration ' ... waves of protest swept the country' (Group Democracy and Governance 2000: 4) with approximately fifty thousand women taking part in thirty-eight demonstrations during 1956.

On 9 August 1956, FSAW organized a gathering of women to meet at the Union Buildings in Pretoria to protest against the pass laws. Twenty thousand women, led by representatives of each of the four population groups (Lilian Ngoyi, Helen Joseph, Rahima Moosa and Sophie Williams), requested an audience with the prime minister to put forward their case; they were refused. A protest song in honour of this occasion asserted: '... you have tampered with the women. You have struck a rock' (ibid.: 6). This ended the period of peaceful resistance in South Africa (Joyce 2000: 139).

Women in South Africa

In December 1956, 156 black front-rank leaders, many of them women, were detained. Among the thirty people brought to trial for treason were Lilian Ngoyi, Helen Joseph, Frances Baard and Annie Silinga. Other significant role models during this period were Helen Suzman, a champion for human rights; Ray Alexander, a prominent trade unionist; Margaret Ballinger, a member of parliament who criticized the government's policy; Ruth First, wife of the Communist Party leader Joe Slovo, who was arrested for treason in 1956 and later died from a letter bomb; and Barbara Hogan, who was jailed for ten years for treason (Group Democracy and Governance 2000: 25; Star 1999: 120, 132, 115, 145; Joyce 2000: 186).

In 1960, the Pan Africanist Congress (PAC) announced: 'There is no freedom without bloodshed' (Grobler 1988: 123). Twenty thousand protesters against the pass laws surrounded the police station in Sharpeville; sixty-nine protesters were wounded and 186 killed (Star 1999: 142). This triggered an escalation in international concern about racial problems in South Africa and led to its isolation. In retaliation, the country moved to become a republic in 1961 (Joyce 2000: 142).

1961–90 Characteristic of this period was an explosion of black political frustration with urban terrorism and counter-reactions by government. There was increased active and passive resistance against discrimination by women, who were detained under house arrest and placed in solitary confinement for their role in 'subversive' activities. It was also a time of increasing solidarity among women, reflected in the creation of the Women's Bureau of South Africa (with its slogan 'If women stand together all things are possible') and the demands of the Federation of South African Women that women become united in common actions for the removal of all political, legal, economic and social disabilities.

The ANC was forced underground in 1961 and the black military organization Umkhonto we Sizwe ('Spear of the Nation') came into being. Police searching for activist Nelson Mandela were refused entry to his home by his wife, Winnie. She was later placed under house arrest after spending seventeen months in solitary confinement (ibid.: 144–6).

An estimated 3.5 million people, mostly black, were subjected to forced removals from 1960 to 1983 (Grobler 1988: 105; Wilson and Ramphele 1989: 216). In 1966, District Six, close to the centre of Cape Town and populated mainly by coloured families, was declared a 'white' area; coloured families were evacuated to 'coloured' areas far from the city. Many restrictions were enforced. Blacks caught without passes on their person were jailed. Non-whites were barred from using 'whites only' facilities. By 1970, indignities continued to influence lives. The Chinese community was shocked when Patricia Tam, thirteen, was forced to withdraw from a tennis tournament and Ava Junkin was barred from the Rhodes University Rag Queen competition. In 1976, black students rioted against the use of Afrikaans in education; hundreds were killed. Violence was becoming an everyday occurrence, with organized work stoppages and school boycotts (Grobler 1988: 172).

From 1978 to 1990, efforts were launched to defuse the possibility of large-scale war in the country. Women actively participated in various attempts to gain recognition and to contribute to political change. By 1978 concerted efforts were under way to dismantle apartheid. Hospitals, theatres and places of worship opened their doors to all races. In 1979 recommendations by the Wiehahn and Riekert Commissions for the abolition of discriminatory labour laws were accepted by government. Restrictions on black workers in 'white' areas were abolished in 1980; in 1981, nearly eight hundred mostly obsolete apartheid laws were scrapped. In 1983, a new constitution that allowed coloureds and Indians to take part in government was approved by referendum. It excluded blacks. Victoria Mxenge, a civil rights attorney, was assassinated in 1985 while defending sixteen people at a treason trial. In 1986, restrictions on mixed marriages and pass laws were abolished. In 1990, President F. W. de Klerk announced the removal of bans on thirty-four organizations, including the ANC, and the freeing of political prisoners. Nelson Mandela was released from prison in February 1990 (Jsoyce 2000: 201).

1990–2000 Characteristic of this period was dramatic transformation. From a political perspective, the most important feature of the national liberation struggle was the creation of a non-sexist democracy. On 5 May 1990, representatives of the National Party and the ANC met to discuss the future. Among the ANC delegates were Ruth Mompati and Cheryl Carolus. In 1991, the National Women's Coalition (NWC) was launched and ninety organizations came together by 1994, coordinating women from diverse socio-economic and educational backgrounds, as well as radically different political perspectives. A gender committee was established to advise the Convention for a Democratic South Africa (CODESA) on gender issues. In 1994, people from all population groups voted for a democratic government and Nelson Mandela became the first state president (ibid.: 178–208).

HEADS OF STATE AND GOVERNMENT In 2004, President Thabo Mbeki established a Women's Working Group to advise the government and help with the challenges facing South African women. To date, a woman has not held the country's highest political position, but South Africa ranks eighth in the world for women's representation in government.

MINISTERIAL (CABINET) Appointments following the 1999 elections resulted in eight women out of twenty-nine cabinet ministers and eight out of thirteen deputy ministers (Group Democracy and Governance 2000: 81).

PARLIAMENTARY In 1933 Bertha Solomon claimed her seat in parliament – the first woman to do so. Mabel Malherbe, a well-known figure in various women's organizations, became the first female mayor of Pretoria in 1931 and in 1934 she became the second woman in parliament. At a conference on the status of women in 1963, black speakers appealed to black women to enter public life. Lilian Twetwa became the first woman to be elected to the Transkeian Legislative Assembly ' ... in the face of stern masculine opposition' (Star 1999: 173). Before 1994, only 2.7 per cent of parliamentarians were women. After 1994, women filled 112 (29.8 per cent) seats in the National Assembly, and 119 (27.6 per cent) in the provincial legislatures (Group Democracy and Governance 2000: 81).

Educational and social welfare leadership Initially, women leaders in South Africa focused on alleviating the ravages of the war, poverty and lack of education. During the 1900–39 period, Emily Hobhouse assisted in creating training in homemaking skills for girls from impoverished districts after the Anglo-Boer War, while Anna Bliss, born in the United States, established a college for young women where they could learn ' ... to use their heads, hearts and hands' (De Kock and Krüger 1986: 65).

Women's efforts at this time were primarily focused on dealing with social issues such as misuse of alcohol, and welfare work among women prisoners, prostitutes and the blind. Emilie Solomon from Britain became involved in the Temperance Union, the Young Women's Christian Association (YWCA) and the Salvation Army. She was the first chairperson of the Congregational Women's Federation of South Africa and later vice-president of the South African National Council of Women (Krüger and Beyers 1977: 4). Anna Tempo (Sister Nannie), daughter of a freed slave in the Cape, assisted Henriette Schneider with welfare work among non-white population groups. In 1914 she received help from the Dutch Reformed Church to fund a shelter ('Nannie House') for destitute women. In 1937 she received the King George Coronation Medal in recognition of her work with prostitutes (Group Democracy and Governance 2000: 269).

Women of note during the 1961–90 period were Fatima Meer, an activist and freedom fighter in the liberation movement; Mamphele Ramphele, an academic and human rights activist who became vice-chancellor of the University of Cape Town, and then managing director of the World Bank; and Erika Theron, a sociologist and former Chancellor of the University of the Western Cape, who campaigned for the rights of coloured people (ibid.: 266, 270).

Participation in religious institutions Approximately 70 per cent of the South African population belong to a Christian church. Just over 1 per cent are Hindus, 0.86 per cent Muslims, 0.17 per cent Jewish, and 0.16 per cent observe other non-Christian religions (Tait et al. 1996: 228). Reverence for their ancestors and traditional beliefs remain an integral part of the belief system in the black culture.

Women were always involved in assisting people in need and in doing missionary work by creating and maintaining schools, clinics and hospitals. Of particular note are Cheryl Allen, pastor of a Baptist church, who created the 'Door of Hope' to care for unwanted babies who could be placed in a box fitted in a church wall (Group Democracy and Governance 2000: 235). Another prominent woman is Brigalia Bam, who has served as general secretary of the South African Council of Churches (ibid.: 237).

Artistic, creative and cultural contributions Political upheaval and socio-political changes during the twentieth century did not keep women from achieving recognition in many fields. V. Mizrah won the UNESCO Women in Sciences Award for Africa in 2000 for her medical research on AIDS and tuberculosis; H. Soodyari undertook ground-breaking research in molecular biology and DNA, finding that southern Africa was '... the most likely geographic region for the origin of our species' (ibid.: 205).

Women have also excelled in the arts. Irma Stern and Maggie Laubser became internationally famous for their unconventional paintings; Olive Schreiner published *Women in Labour* (1911), voicing her concern for the status of women and their struggle for emancipation; and M. E. Rothman (M.E.R.), one of the first women to obtain a bachelor's degree, was editor of an Afrikaans daily newspaper and a well-known author. Two women became legends in their own time for pioneering theatre, namely Taubie Kuschlik and Anna Neethling-Pohl. Bertha Slosberg became the first white female impresario to present black artists (ibid.: 112, 113, 123, 125, 177, 185).

Other cultural contributors are Yvonne Bryceland, an internationally known actress; Poppy Frames, who pioneered classical ballet in South Africa;

Juliet Prowse, an internationally acclaimed dancer; and Helen Southern-Holt, accredited as the initiator of the Eoan Group of coloured performers. International acclaim was received by Mimi Coertze, who performed with the Vienna State Opera; Miriam Makeba, also known as 'Mother of the Nation' and 'Empress of African Song'; and Dolly Rathebe, who was equally at home in Soweto or Westminster Cathedral, where she sang for Queen Elizabeth (ibid.: 119, 132, 136, 142, 155, 167).

Women continued to excel in cultural activities between 1961 and 1990. For example, Gcina Mhlophe, a feminist writer, storyteller and actress was actively involved in fighting illiteracy; actress Janet Suzman joined the Royal Shakespeare Company in London; Nadine Gordimer won the Nobel Prize for Literature in 1991; Kathleen Lindsay published extensively under different pseudonyms; and Miriam Tlalu was the first black woman to have a novel published (ibid.: 111, 129, 103, 167; Joyce 2000: 171). Monica Wilson, one of the most important anthropologists of her time, commented on issues relating to racism, discrimination, migrant labour, family life and the creation of black homelands (Beyers and Basson 1987: 945–6).

Towards gender equality

Although great strides have been made in female well-being in the last two decades, much more needs to be achieved. Women differ in how they deal with the barriers that keep them from developing their skills and full potential. Such barriers are both external (discrimination, home-care responsibilities, marriage partner expectations) and internal to each individual. Internal barriers reflect a lack of inner direction, leading to failure to challenge or overrule societal and cultural expectations. Women tend to isolate themselves in typically female areas of work and personal development. Personal independence needs to become '... a central life interest' (Van Rooyen 1981: 239) if women are to take their rightful place in the twenty-first century.

It will be important to strengthen women's studies to determine the implications of historical differences and conflict. This includes engaging in practical and strategic planning to consolidate gains regarding gender equality, and creating a new vision of female development. Female well-being will benefit from recognizing the personal aspects of women's experiences and learning processes, and taking both life experiences and individual personality preferences into account. Forming alliances and using existing female associations to create a lobby for speaking with one voice on gender issues will foster well-being. It will be critical to focus on female leadership as valuable in the workplace, but also to engage the involvement of men in the processes of changing attitudes (Taylor and Conradie 1997: 121–4; Van Rooyen 1981: 229–39).

South African women, like women everywhere, need support in realizing that they are not powerless in dealing with their environments, nor are they completely free to do as they choose. They need to accept responsibility to carve their own destiny with the awareness that '… the curve of this destiny is much more uneven, more discontinuous than the masculine curve' (De Beauvoir 1965: 541).

Of course, the fate of South African women in the twenty-first century will depend in part on whether the end of apartheid will eventually lead to deeper social transformations which diminish class and gender stratifications that have emanated from racial differences throughout the country's history.

References

Allwood, C. W. (1987) 'Child abuse in South Africa', in A. F. Steyn et al. (eds), *Marriage and Family Life in South Africa*, Pretoria: HSRC

Beets, H. M. (1996) *Pastoraat van die Enkelouergesin*, RGN Verslag HG/MF 30, Pretoria: RGN

Behr, A. L. and R. G. MacMillan (1971) *Education in South Africa*, Pretoria: Van Schaik

Beyers, C. J. and J. L. Basson (eds) (1987) *Suid-Afrikaanse Biografiese Woordeboek*, vol. V (1st edn), Pretoria: Creda Press

Bureau for Information (1986) *South Africa 1986*, Pretoria: Direktoraat Navorsings-inligting

— (1987) *Profiel: die Ses Selfregerende Gebiede binne Suid-Afrika*, Pretoria: Direktoraat vir Navorsingsinligting

De Beauvoir, S. (1965) *The Second Sex*, Harmondsworth: Penguin

De Kock, W. T. and D. W. Krüger (eds) (1986) *Suid-Afrikaanse Biografiese Woordeboek*, vol. II (2nd edn), Cape Town: Nasionale Boek Drukkery

Department of Health (1998) *South African Demographic and Health Survey*, Pretoria: Government Printer

Erwee, R. (1994) 'South African women: changing career patterns', in N. J. Adler and D. N. Izraeli (eds), *Competitive Frontiers: Women Managers in a Global Economy*, Oxford: Basil Blackwell

Gerdes, L. C. (1987) 'Family relationships: general perspective', in A. F. Steyn et al. (eds), *Marriage and Family Life in South Africa*, Pretoria: HSRC

Grobler, J. (1988) *A Decisive Clash: A Short History of Black Protest Politics in South Africa*, Pretoria: Acacia Books

Group Democracy and Governance (2000) *Women Marching into the 21st Century*, Pretoria: HSRC

Harvey, E. W. (1994) *Social Change and Family Policy in South Africa*, HSRC Report HG/MF2, Pretoria: HSRC

Howes, F., S. Green and L. van Zyl (1997) *Buite-egtelike Moederskap in die Paarl-Wellington-gebied: die Tienermoeder se Versorgingspotensiaal en Steunstelsel*, HSRC Report HG/MF32, Pretoria: HSRC

Jithoo, S. (1987) 'Family structure and support systems in Indian communities', in A. F. Steyn et al. (eds), *Marriage and Family Life in South Africa*, Pretoria: HSRC.

Joyce, P. (2000) *South Africa in the 20th Century: Chronicles of an Era*, Cape Town: Struik Publishers

Krige, D. (1996) 'Education priorities under a government of national unity', in N. Tait et al. (eds), *A Socio-economic Atlas of South Africa: A Demographic, Socio-economic and Cultural Profile of South Africa*, Pretoria: HSRC

Krüger, D. W. and C. J. Beyers (eds) (1977) *Suid-Afrikaanse Biografiese Woordeboek*, vol. III, Cape Town: Tafelberg Uitgewers

Le Roux, T. (1987) 'The economically active married woman and dual income couples', in A. F. Steyn et al. (eds), *Marriage and Family Life in South Africa*, Pretoria: HSRC

Le Roux, W. L. du P. (1987) 'Attitudes and practices pertaining to premarital and extramarital sex and cohabitation among Whites in South Africa', in A. F. Steyn et al. (eds), *Marriage and Family Life in South Africa*, Pretoria: HSRC

Mallet, V. (2000) 'Rainbow nation in search of self-assurance', in *Financial Times Survey: South Africa*, 6 October, Johannesburg: Financial Times

Mandela, N. (1994) Opening of Parliament speech

Marais, P. (1999) *Die Vrou in die Anglo-Boere Oorlog 1899–1902*, Pretoria: J. P. van der Walt

Nkau, D. J. (1998) 'How fertility rates vary in different parts of South Africa: the use of GIS in Demography', in *Focus Forum*, 5(3): 30–32

Nzimande, S. V. (1987) 'Family structure and support systems in black communities', in A. F. Steyn et al. (eds), *Marriage and Family Life in South Africa*, Pretoria: HSRC

O'Donovan, M. (1998) 'Baragwanath: one bed to every 100 people?', *Focus Forum*, 5(3): 41–2

Pretorius, R. (1987) 'Research on family violence in the Republic of South Africa', in A. F. Steyn et al. (eds), *Marriage and Family Life in South Africa*, HSRC: Pretoria

Rabie, P. J. (1987) 'Family structure and support systems in coloured communities', in A. F. Steyn et al. (eds), *Marriage and Family Life in South Africa*, Pretoria: HSRC

Rocha-Silva, L. (1998) 'Substance use on the rise in South Africa', *Focus Forum*, 5(3): 51–3

Rock, ß. (ed.) (1997) *Spirals of Suffering: Public Violence and Children*, Pretoria: HSRC

September, W. J. (1987) 'Attitudes and practices pertaining to premarital and extra-marital sex and cohabitation among Coloureds', in A. F. Steyn et al. (eds), *Marriage and Family Life in South Africa*, Pretoria: HSRC

South African Institute of Race Relations (1989/90) *Race Relations Survey*, Johannesburg: SA Institute of Race Relations

Spier, A. (1994) *Poverty, Employment and Wealth Distribution*, Pretoria: HSRC

SSA (Statistics South Africa) (1999) *October 1999 Household Survey*, Pretoria: SSA.

Star, the (1999) 'An extraordinary 20th century', Johannesburg: Independent Newspapers

Steyn, A. F. (1987) *Family Structures in the Republic of South Africa*, HSRC Report: HG/MF-4, Pretoria: HSRC

Steyn, H. G. (1994) 'Analyses of South African marriage and divorce statistics', in A. F. Steyn et al. (eds), *Marriage and Family Life in South Africa*, Pretoria: HSRC

Tait, N. G. (1998) 'Using census data to develop a socio-economic database for South Africa', *Focus Forum*, 5(3): 36–42

Tait, N. G. et al. (1996) *Socio-economic Atlas of South Africa,* Pretoria: HSRC

Taylor, V. and I. Conradie (1997) *We Have Been Taught by Life Itself: Empowering Women as Leaders – the Role of Development Education,* Pretoria: HSRC

Theron, S. W. (1990) *Race Prejudice and Discrimination in Industry and Organization,* Pretoria: University of Pretoria

Van Niekerk, A. M. (1991) *'n Konseptuele Raamwerk vir Organisasie-aanpassing in Onafhanklike en Selfregerende State in Suider-Afrika,* unpublished doctoral dissertation, Johannesburg: Rand Afrikaans University

Van Rooyen, J. (1981) *Female Career Commitment – a Life-Span Perspective,* unpublished doctoral dissertation, Pretoria: University of South Africa

Viljoen, S. (1987) 'Violence in the family: situating the theme theoretically and empirically within the South African context', in A. F. Steyn et al. (eds), *Marriage and Family Life in South Africa,* Pretoria: HSRC

Whiteford, A. and M. McGrath (1994) *The Distribution of Income in South Africa,* Pretoria: HSRC

WHO (World Health Organization) (2001) *Fact Sheet 10: Women and HIV and Mother to Child Transmission,* Geneva: World Health Organization

— (2004) 'Core health indicators from the latest World Health Report, South Africa 2002', WHO Statistical Information System (WHOSIS) online

Wilson, F. and M. Ramphele (1989) *Uprooting Poverty: The South African Challenge,* Cape Town: David Philip

World Bank (2002) *World Development Indicators 2002,* Washington, DC: World Bank

11 | Women in Sudan: resistance and survival

CAROLYN FLUEHR-LOBBAN[1]

Sudan experienced deep political and human rights crises in the twentieth century, resulting from decades of colonialism, civil war and Islamist policies that have affected women throughout the country. During the century, women in Sudan experienced colonialism, participated in movements for independence and national liberation, benefited slightly from brief periods of state feminism, and were most severely affected by decades of chronic civil war and displacement of ethnic populations.

Sudan ranks among the world's poorest countries, with low GNP and high rates of adult illiteracy and fertility, and relatively low life expectancy. Yet Sudan made significant political advances as a result of female participation in the anti-colonial struggles of the 1940s which improved the formal legal status of women, especially after independence in 1956. An important movement – the Republican Brothers – significantly involved 'Republican Sisters', thus pioneering Islamic reform of women's status well in advance of other parts of the Muslim world in this century.

In the last two decades of the century, Sudan became a human rights disaster as the chronic war waged against the south by the central government in Khartoum revived slavery and created a group of refugees known as 'the lost boys', begging the question as to what happened to refugee women and girls. Some southern women and girls were kidnapped and enslaved or indentured, but a majority suffered the effects of war in broken families and many became effective heads of households. Women in refugee communities are living in a state of dependency with their children. Sudan must be understood on its own terms, but it can also serve as an analogous example to nations that have experienced chronic civil war and serious challenges to human rights entitlement.

The geopolitical complexities of Sudan

Sudan is Africa's largest nation, bordering nine other African nations and comprising over a million square miles. The vast regions of Sudan are mainly desert, arid or semi-arid in the northern region, and savannah and rainforest in the southern third. The Blue and the White Nile shape the geography and history of the country. Central Sudan, known as al-Jazeerah or 'island', is the fertile region between the two Niles. Cotton-growing schemes during the colonial era made this a more economically developed region which began to employ women as informal-sector day labourers in the post-independence period. The popularity of synthetic fabrics and a failure to retain a measure of the global cotton market have decimated this cash crop production.

Eastern Sudan is geographically marked by the Red Sea littoral and the hills along the coast with the major outlet to the sea, Port Sudan. Pastoral peoples such as the Beja and Hadendowa, marked by patrilineality and a sharply gendered division of labour, traditionally occupied these hills. The other major eastern city is Kassala on the Ethiopian border.

Western Sudan includes Kordofan and Darfur, which has connected Sudan with Saharan West Africa from the time of the medieval Islamic African kingdoms. In the early twenty-first century, it became a focus of world attention for the ethnic cleansing and displacement of population that government-backed militias wrought upon the local population, resulting in another human rights crisis.

These regions, northern riverain, southern, central, eastern and western, are geographic mental maps constituting the main indigenous ideas about national identity. These ideas are subject to much discussion and negotiation as a mature, unified national identity has yet to be achieved.

From antiquity to the twenty-first century

As in many parts of the world, women played a more significant role in the ancient histories of their societies than in the colonial and post-independence periods of the modern era. In the ancient civilization of Kush, women held high positions as queen mother or queen consort. When Nubians ruled pharaonic Egypt in the 25th Dynasty (664–270 BCE), a female relative of the king traditionally held the position of God's Wife of Amun at Thebes, the southern capital of Egypt. In Meroë, an exclusively Nubian civilization, during five centuries (between 260 BCE and AD 320), eight queens ruled in their own right. These regnant queens, known to the classical European world as 'Candaces' or 'Kendakes' (Amanitore and Amanashkhtete are two examples), ruled alone or were co-regents with their brothers, marking this exceptional period of African history. In the Nubian Christian period (sixth to ninth centuries AD), the queens and queen mothers were active in government affairs, and were still referred to by the title 'Kandake' (Fluehr-Lobban 2004). Matrilineality was common in pre-Islamic and pre-colonial Sudan, and prevalent in Nubia, in Darfur, in some eastern Beja peoples who still display matrilineal remnants, and in the first of the Islamic sultanates, the Funj.

In Darfur, the West African medieval kingship pattern of brother-sister rule prevailed with a long line of sultan co-rulers. The title of the ruling sister was 'Iya Bassi'; after her brother, she was above all other male officials and all women. The most famous was Sultana Taja or Tajodj, who, with her brother Ali Dinar, resisted the onslaught of British imperialism until 1916, giving the region the colonial name Anglo-Egyptian Sudan (Muhammad 2002: 140). The founder of the pre-Islamic city of Soba was a woman named Ajuba.

The colonial period Great Britain wanted to control the entire Nile valley, where they rivalled and eventually replaced Ottoman Turkish rule from Egypt south to Sudan. England ruled for fifty-eight years with a governor general, anglicizing and westernizing basic institutions of law, education and commerce. The British laid out their colonial city of Khartoum in the shape of the Union Jack. Capitalism and wage labour were introduced as the last vestiges of the slave trade were suppressed. The British ruled Sudan from 1898 until 1956.

The colonial institutions had lasting effects until the beginning of the Islamist political movement in the late 1970s and early 1980s. The English sought to eliminate child betrothal, to reduce the power of the male marriage guardian, and to increase the importance of women's consent in marriage, and they initiated a process whereby judicial divorce for women became legal on the grounds of abuse, neglect or desertion. They also sought to outlaw certain 'harmful' customs, such as female circumcision and child betrothal, and were more successful in the latter than the former. At the time of the growing influence of the nationalist movement, however, abolition of female circumcision in 1946 was rejected by the masses of northern Sudanese as colonialist interference and served only to drive the practice underground.

Independence and beyond In the post-independence period, family law developed in a progressive way by combining the indigenous heritage of Islamic and customary law and selectively retaining elements of English law. After Islamic law, shariah, was made state law in 1983, however, Islamization of civil and family law and basic institutions became the norm. This move ignored the non-Muslim, increasingly Christian orientation of a third of Sudan's population in the south. Islamization sought to restore the authentic Islamic institutions of shariah law and to establish new ones, such as Islamic banks and insurance companies. In 1989, a military coup led by Omer al-Bashir (backed by the founder of the Muslim Brotherhood, Hasan al-Turabi) seized power and in effect created an Islamic state which has held power ever since. Arabic was instituted as the language of study in the universities and Arabization and Islamization proceeded at an accelerated pace.

Diversity With its more than five hundred languages and ethnic groups, it is impossible to classify the immense geo-political complexity of Sudan. The major northern ethnic groups follow the course of the River Nile north to south and include Fadija- and Mahas-speaking Nubians (historically matrilineal, converting to patriliny after the introduction of Islam), Arabic-speaking Nubians, the Shayqiya and Ja'aliin, from whose ranks most of the post-independence elites have been drawn, and other riverain groups referred to as 'northerners'. Major southern ethnic groups include the Nilotic pastoralists, the Dinka and Nuer, and the Shilluk and central African linguistic groups such as the Azande. The Nilotic societies have been most profoundly affected by the civil war.

Racial and ethnic heterogeneity in Sudan have received much attention in world news for the long-standing wars between various governments in Khartoum and the southern regions (of so-called black Africans) and the politically dominant 'Arabs' of the north, as well as ethnic cleansing of the Nuba mountains and Darfur region waged by militias supported by the Khartoum regime. Officially the country is divided by religion between the majority Sunni Muslim of the northern regions (65 per cent), minority Christian (10–15 per cent) and animist believers from the southern third of the nation (about 20 per cent).

Much of popular Islam in Sudan is Sufi, with prominent African religious brotherhoods maintaining religious traditions without government interest or intervention. Christianity was introduced into the Nuba mountains and southern region during the five colonial decades of the twentieth century. Christian missionary work continued until the proselytizers were expelled shortly after independence. The Catholic missionaries most active during colonialism were Italian, so many southerners educated during this time bear Christian names of Italian origin. The suffering southern Catholic population witnessed a historic moment in 2000 when Mother Josephine Bakhita was canonized. Although a native of Darfur, she is revered by southerners for her enslavement as a child and her conversion to Catholicism. She entered a convent in Italy, where she lived out her life.

A demographic portrait of Sudanese women

Sudan is multi-ethnic, multiracial and multi-religious. Its estimated population in 1999 was 34.5 million with a growth rate of 2.7 per cent (USCIA 2003) while UNICEF's population estimate is 28.3 million. Accurate population statistics are problematical since no official census has been conducted since the end of colonialism and millions of Sudanese have died, been forced into exile or otherwise been displaced by the chronic civil war, especially since 1983.

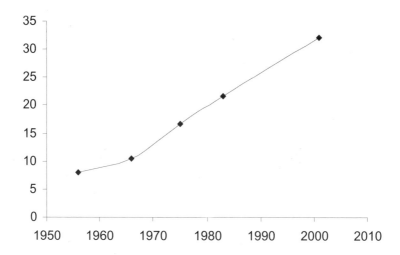

Figure 11.1 Population, 1950–2000 (millions)
Source: <www.countrystudies.us>

Refugees and displaced families The number of displaced or utterly destroyed families in the southern war regions is incalculable, but estimates range as high as 2 million dead or displaced persons. Perhaps as many as 4 million southerners are internal refugees in the nation's capital. The plight of the 'lost boys' from southern Sudan, who have walked to Kenya or Ethiopia from war-torn regions of the south (their mothers, fathers and sisters having presumably been killed or enslaved) is by now well known. Many have been resettled in the USA by American relief agencies.

Urbanization The shift to urban or suburban residence from rural, agrarian residence has been witnessed in the dramatic growth in size and density of Sudan's major cities, especially Khartoum, which swelled from 0.5 million in 1970 to approximately 7 million in 2004. Its projected urban population growth by 2015 is 48 per cent. Although still predominantly agrarian (80 per cent of the labour force), Sudan is rapidly urbanizing.

Life expectancy Life expectancy is fifty-six years for Sudanese women and fifty-five for men; it has not improved much since independence. This probably reflects the effects of chronic civil war, static non-development and a low standard of living and healthcare.

Population growth, fertility rate and male–female ratio Sudan has witnessed a dramatic rate of population growth throughout the second half of the twentieth century, the period for which statistics are available. The average household size of 5.1 reflects the continuing strength of the extended family. The population growth rate increased from a low 2.6 per cent (1960–70) to 3.3 per cent (1980–90), but dipped again in 2000 to 2.8 per cent.

The total fertility rate for Sudanese women is 5.47 children. The government conducted a major research initiative, the Sudan Demographic and Health Survey of 1989/90, which indicated a higher fertility rate of 5.5, which conforms to the relatively high fertility rates for African women.

Infant mortality rates The infant mortality rate was 73 per 1,000 live births as of 2000, with an under-five-year-old mortality rate of 115 per 1,000 live births. Male and female infant mortality are virtually identical, but the probability at birth of surviving to age sixty as of 2000 was only 42 per cent. The relatively high rates both of fertility and infant mortality reflect the agrarian pattern of large families with poor healthcare delivery, especially in the rural areas, but also in the increasingly impoverished urban areas with refugees from the civil war. The rates are consistent with Sudan's standing as one of the world's poorest countries.

Age structure of the population As in other predominantly agrarian countries throughout the world, the Sudanese population pyramid is the reverse of the situation in industrial nations, with a preponderance of the young and very young over the older segments of the population. The population under age fifteen in 2001 stood at 40 per cent; only 3.5 per cent were over sixty-five.

Contraception and abortion Contraception is generally available in cities and mid-sized towns, with the significant limitation that in northern Muslim regions it is not available to single women, following Islamic social and religious codes. Birth control has not otherwise been limited by Islam or any other religious ideology.

Public health issues In 1998–2000, 21 per cent of Sudanese were undernourished, with 17 per cent of children under age five underweight in 1995–2001. In 1991, 7.8 million people were at risk of famine because of drought and conflict. The rate of malaria is very high at 13,934 per 100,000, with a malaria mortality rate of 408 cases per 100,000 for children under four in 2000. The tuberculosis-related mortality rate was 50 per 100,000 in 2001. An extremely low rate of 16 physicians per 100,000 in 1990–2002 reflects not only pervasive underdevelopment but also the high cost of warfare and displacement over the last decades of the century. It also points to one of the highest priorities for the eventual post-peace nation-building and rebuilding of the nation. Survival and family health depend upon class and access to healthcare providers in urban areas or isolated rural locales.

HIV/AIDS An estimated 2.6 per cent of Sudanese were infected with HIV/AIDS in 2001. The power of the Islamic code forbidding illicit heterosexual and homosexual acts (and strict enforcement of morality through its police patrols and courts, which deliver prompt justice for moral code offenders) underlies official denial that infection rates are significant. Muslim Sudan, like much of Islamic Africa, has been less affected by the AIDS epidemic than other countries on the continent. More stringent controls over sexual behaviour and promiscuity have helped to keep the rates of HIV infection relatively low in Sudan. One must view the statistics with some scepticism, as the Islamist government prides itself on its imposed moral code. If the AIDS infection rate is not intentionally suppressed, it is certainly underestimated.

Chronic warfare and ethnic cleansing, displacement of populations and the resulting impoverishment make women vulnerable to rape and sexual assault, through which AIDS can spread. Rape has been used as a systematic feature of the ethnic cleansing that occurred in Darfur in 2003–2004. A new trend against the marriage of very young girls in the south has apparently slowed the HIV/AIDS infection rate there.

Family status and structure
Marriage and divorce
PATRIARCHY AND PATRILINY Sudanese society is framed by African culture and the Arabic language, and by a pre-eminence of egalitarian values rooted in collective rural, ethnically based ways of life. Its patriarchy is shaped by original African faiths and by the introduction of Islam. Family life has been resistant to the modernizing forces of the twentieth century, and remains one of the stabilizing forces in Sudanese life.

The patrilineal principle means not only that descent and inheritance are traced through men but that a core of related males constitutes the key decision-makers of the family. These core males are responsible for family order, marriages and control over family property and inheritance outside of the strict parameters of Islamic law. Women's position is defined in relation to the core. A woman is known as the daughter of her father, from whom she has the greatest inheritance rights; she does not take the name of her husband, nor will her children take her name.

Southern Nilotic patrilineal families exchange women between clans and lineages through the use of cattle as bridewealth. That marriage property belongs to the father and the patrilineal males, while women maintain usufruct rights over the dairying of cows. Polygyny is unrestricted and a wealthy man or powerful chief may have dozens of wives and hundreds of children. Islamic law limits the number of wives to four, while few men can afford the cost of marriage and maintenance of multiple households that must be equitably maintained. Although polygyny is legal and customary, it is declining in all Sudanese regions owing to the increasing cost of marriage and a more educated population that has come to view polygamy as an old custom. The civil war has displaced millions of Nilotic peoples, destroyed their cattle-based economy, and disrupted family, perhaps to the point of no return.

The majority of Muslim marriages are still formally arranged by the senior male members of the patrilineage but they are strongly influenced by the female members of the kin group. Increasingly, couples are selecting each other in 'love marriages', having met at university or their place of employment, but the permission of the male marriage guardian is still needed for the family blessing and negotiation of the requisite dower. The consent of the bride is required by Islamic law; no arranged marriage can be imposed upon her against her will.

Non-Muslim marriage is regulated by customary law based upon the necessity of bridewealth exchange. Despite the ravages of civil war, marriages are still arranged with the demand for a dower of cows by the woman's family, thus keeping women dependent upon tradition. Upholding these customs in the face of chronic wartime conditions among southerners has been difficult – the essential cattle bridewealth payments have been nearly impossible, given cattle and slave raiding.

MATRILINY Although matriliny (descent through the female line) was probably more widespread in the past, especially among Nubians and some eastern and western ethnic groups, the coming of Islam and the traditional pastoralism of many societies render patriliny the predominant type of kinship system.

Divorce is permissible in Islamic law, but there are two forms: traditional unilateral declarations by men and judicial divorce initiated by women. This was studied by Fluehr-Lobban (1987) in the capital city of Khartoum, with tentative estimates of a rate of about 20 per cent in the major urban area.

FAMILY LAW REFORM Significant family law reform occurred during the late 1960s and 1970s, before Islamization in 1983. This shift took place during coalescence between activism on the part of the Sudanese Women's Union (SWU) and a liberal, enlightened Grand Qadi. An overhaul of family law was an early priority of the National Islamic Front (NIF) in 1990, with the most significant conservative move being the reinstitution of the concept of male guardianship over women in marriage, requiring them to seek permission to work outside the home for wages, and permission to travel alone outside the country.

The Sudan was once a leader in legal reform of marriage and divorce laws in shariah (ibid.). Judicial divorce for women on the ground of harm or abuse was innovated in Sudan in 1915, years before such reform was undertaken in Egypt and elsewhere in the Muslim world. In the 1970s, Sudan continued its path of legal innovation under the leadership of Sheikh Muhammad al-Gizouli, who appointed women judges to the shariah courts and expanded legal divorce for women using the concept of ransom, whereby a woman could use her dower to obtain her release from a harmful marriage.

The Permanent Constitution of 1973, another significant document, provides for equal rights of all citizens irrespective of gender. Since 1989, however, with an Islamist regime under the political control of the NIF, questions of citizenship and human rights of women have been raised in the following areas: making the wearing of the hijab in public mandatory; empowering morals protection police and courts to enforce public morality; bringing cases of lashing for immoral public behaviour to international attention by human rights groups; purging of non-NIF women from government employment; and application of the harsh *hadd* punishment of stoning to women for adultery or fornication.

According to feminist critics, constitutional equality for women has had little impact since women lack full equality in a number of respects, for example in the debated right of a woman to become head of state or in rights to inheritance. Nevertheless, reforms in Islamic family law were achieved through feminist agitation, presidential decree and judicial interpretation. The enforced obedience of wives, whereby wives who fled from their husbands' abuse were forcibly returned by court-ordered police action, was abolished in 1970. The limitations of state feminism noted elsewhere in this book are evident in Sudan as well. Throughout the decades since independence, political and military regimes have offered rhetorical support for women's rights, but this has resulted in little structural or transformational change favouring female well-being.

Inheritance In Muslim law, women are entitled to inherit from their fathers, other patrilineal kin and their husbands. Their inheritance is half that of their brothers and less for a wife than for her children. This patriarchal general rule must be tempered with another rule, which requires that men provide all basic support to their female kin and wives. Any property a woman inherits, or any wages she earns, are hers alone to keep and control. Men have no legal right to women's property or independent sources of wealth.

In other mixed Muslim and non-Muslim regions, inheritance may be more strictly patrilineal and patriarchal than the moderate reforms Islamic law provides; women may hold no entitlement to inheritance. The eastern Beja and northern Nubians, with prior matrilineal descent, have special customs that ameliorate strict patrilineal rules.

Violence against women

Effects of chronic civil war It is estimated that as many as 2 million people died or were displaced by the civil war between 1983 and 2004, when a peace agreement was signed between the government of Sudan and the southern Sudan People's Liberation Movement (SPLM). The promise of peace was shattered with the outbreak of conflict in the Darfur region, where the emphasis shifted to concerns over violence against women (Box 11.1).

Once again, the waging of war by men has cruel and devastating effects upon women and their young children who survive the attacks. Chronic war removes men from the household and displaced families become immigrant squatters, creating the dramatic rise in matrifocal or female-headed families. For the southern refugees, the refugee camp becomes home. The connections among family members may be maintained via the Internet, mobile phone

---

Box 11.1 Darfur 2003–2004 – ethnic cleansing and alleged genocide hurts women and children most

Ironically, violence erupted in Darfur just as the Sudan government was on the verge of signing a peace agreement with leaders of the southern resistance in the spring of 2003. While the origins of the conflict are disputed, the effects of 'janjaweed' (men on horse or camel back) attacks on sedentary villagers fell most heavily upon women and children, who constituted 90 per cent of the refugees in camps in border areas and in Chad. The destruction of villages and their meagre resources; the terrorist tactic of rape (also employed against Muslim women in Bosnia), leaving young victims shamed and unmarriageable; and the scorched earth policy all exert some of the worst conditions affecting female well-being.

networks or small self-help groups of refugees. Many of the 'lost boys' were expatriated to the USA from Kakuma. For the purposes of female well-being, it is important to note that 'lost girls' did not attract comparable media attention, because of their lesser numbers and the typical patriarchy of the media and relief agencies.

Zeinab Eyega, director of the Sauti Yetu Center for African Women in New York City, speaks of 'dreaming of equality from the margins'. Owing to years of chronic warfare, women in southern Sudan have not been adequately studied and have been conspicuously absent from the formal peace negotiations between the SPLM and the government of Sudan (GOS), and between the National Democratic Alliance (NDA) and GOS. Demands for inclusion fell on deaf ears.

Women waging peace Towards the end of the twentieth century, Sudan attracted international attention for its violations of numerous human rights standards, including the revival of slavery during the civil war with the south; detention and torture of government opponents; ethnic cleansing in the Nuba mountains and Darfur regions; sexual assaults and rape as part of wars waged against ethnic populations; and harassment and lashing of women for improper dress or behaviour in northern cities, according to strict interpretations of Islamic law. Women inside the country and exiles outside have vigorously opposed these measures and have provided a powerful voice for peace.

The Secretariat for Peace, a union of Sudanese women's organizations, was formed after the Sudanese General SWU began in 1990 to promote a culture of peace, working towards narrowing the gap among groups in Sudan, building a women's cadre in the peace process and in political decision-making, promoting seminars, conferences, symposia and conventions on peace, organizing demonstrations for peace, developing relief programmes for displaced people, creating contact with Sudanese women refugees abroad and leading tour teams to take relief aid to the war zones (Badri and Abdel Sadig 1998: 53–4).

This group recognizes the unique role of women in spreading a culture of peace through their function of socializing children. For example, the cultural tradition of 'Hakkamat' – women provocateurs and tribal war poets – can be used for waging peace rather than providing support for war and ethnic cleansing. The feminist peace activists also encourage the mass media to cultivate compassion and forgiveness through music and drama within the context of the development of a national culture of democracy in the post-war phase. They define a 'culture of peace' as moral, spiritual, scientific and practical efforts to protect against and prevent outbreak of conflicts and war, and a global movement for sustainable development, human rights and democracy.

SPECIAL CONSIDERATION FOR SOUTHERN WOMEN The average southern woman has as her immediate concern continued survival. Although she is desperate for peace, the effects of extreme underdevelopment after twenty years of the worst phase of the civil war are her primary concern. The death rate of 865 per 100,000 as compared with 550 for all of Sudan, and a literacy rate as low as 10 per cent according to a UNICEF study (Chawla 2003), make southern women the most in need of the Sudanese populations. Many southern men joined the armed struggle, while others left the country, becoming refugees in Kenya or Uganda, leaving the home front to women. According to the same UNICEF report, the population of the Bahr el-Ghazal southern region was only about 25 per cent of its pre-war total in 2001. The women left behind suffer from low status, poor access to income generation, little or no education, and no political voice; about half of the households are headed by women.

The limited education available in the south is for males. As an unsteady peace looms, the lack of an educated female population in the south brings a critical need for doctors, lawyers, and teachers. UNICEF opened twenty-six schools in the southern region, but in order to ensure regular attendance for girls, families must live within fifteen minutes' walk of the school.

RAPE AND DOMESTIC VIOLENCE As with other countries for which official statistics for domestic violence and child abuse are not available, the picture must be drawn indirectly. My own studies of the family courts in the early 1980s (Fluehr-Lobban 1987, 2004) show that the most frequent ground for a woman requesting a judicial divorce is her claim of abuse and economic neglect. Both of these are considered as harm to the woman and her children, and are grounds for divorce. The implied abuse is suspected but not confirmed; when a woman flees the conjugal home, however, it is more certain that the direct cause is abuse.

Economic participation

Sudan's GDP was US$1,387 per capita for 2002 (<www.nationmaster.com>), which is not keeping pace with population growth. The proportion of women in the formal labour force was 20 per cent as of 1990. Including women in the informal economic sector would probably double this figure, however. Sudan has a low unemployment rate, mainly because its labour force is still mainly agricultural (USCIA 2003). Major pan-Saharan droughts in the 1970s and 1990s undermined food production and caused environmental degradation and deforestation.

The division of labour As with the division of labour in any 'Third World' family, the economic stresses of daily life can be overwhelming and result in fractures or breakdown. Economic demands have forced many men to migrate to the cities; urban husbands and fathers have had to work at two or three jobs – one in the formal sector and others in the informal sector, such as taxi driving. The rising costs of marriage have made it difficult for young men to secure enough money to marry at home, so many migrate to the oil-rich states of the Gulf to work until they earn enough to marry. Many, once married, return to the Gulf region for several more years to support their families at a higher standard than is possible in Sudan, producing the usual effect of matrifocal families and extended households of older relatives and children headed by women. An increasing number of judicial divorces initiated by women stem from a migrant husband's failure to support his wife and children. On the other hand, men working abroad constitute a huge source of revenue. This cash influx in many ways keeps the Sudanese economy from collapse.

With expanded male economic activity, women also became active in the formal and informal sectors, expanding their economic contribution outside the domestic realm. Salaried women workers are active in the educational, healthcare, commercial, communications and government ministries sectors. Since the establishment of political Islamism, married Muslim women need to obtain the permission of their husbands to work outside the home, and unmarried women need their father's permission.

Women's participation in the labour force The number of women working in salaried positions has grown to 20–25 per cent of the total workforce. Traditional Islamic values of female seclusion and since 1989 Islamist policies that officially discourage women from working in public places negatively affect these relatively low numbers. Women's increased participation in informal economic activities has probably doubled in the last decades of the twentieth century, however, in response to economic stresses on the family.

THE IMPACT OF ISLAMISM Female participation in the formal workforce increased by 13 per cent during Sudan's Islamist phase, 1990–2000. This increase seems counter-intuitive to those unfamiliar with the dynamics of Islamism. There is a tendency to view all Islamist-inclined governments as disadvantageous to women in all respects. In fact, the Islamist movement did little to slow the trend towards the greater participation of women in the formal workforce, especially as the populations of the major cities swelled, where wage labour for all is the primary means of survival. Before the current Islamist regime, the proportion of women in the workforce rose to about 15 per cent. With the advent of official Islamism in 1989, however, women were discouraged from working outside the home unless their economic contribution was vital. This late-twentieth-century trend should not be interpreted as an amelioration or delegitimization of historical patriarchy throughout Sudan (Hale 1996); it is undeniably the case that these economic forces have brought more women into public sector jobs and activities from their traditional domestic seclusion.

TYPES OF OCCUPATION The proportions of women in the professions are relatively low. Post-independence, women were first employed as teachers and nurses; later the numbers of female physicians, lawyers and judges increased. Unlike other majority Muslim countries, Sudan appointed women as judges, first in the civil courts in the 1960s, and in the Islamic courts in the 1970s. In 1970, Sayeda Nagua Kemal Farid was among the first women judges to be appointed to the shariah court system (Fluehr-Lobban 1987). The historically female profession of nursing remains at 91.6 per cent female-dominated.

Literacy and education

Literacy rates The overall literacy rate total for Sudan was 46 per cent in 1995, and in 2000 it was 57 per cent for males and 34.6 per cent for females, reflecting both the level of the country's development and a dramatic male–female discrepancy. Low female literacy reflects patriarchal traditions regarding education and the still predominantly agrarian nature of Sudan. The extremely low literacy rate of 10 per cent for southern females reflects both these factors, as well as the effects of chronic civil war. For example, in 1990 public expenditure on education as a percentage of GDP was 1.4 per cent as compared to 2.5 per cent for the Sudanese military.

Thus, at 65.4 per cent, Sudan has among the highest illiteracy rates for females aged fifteen and over in the world, while overall male illiteracy is also high at 42.3 per cent. The first literacy programme in Sudan was not launched until 1949, as colonialism was nearing its end. After independence, civil war from 1955 to 1972 and again from 1983 to 2004 drained Sudan's economic resources, making basic education a privilege of urban residents outside war-torn areas. The civil war destroyed many schools.

School completion rates

PRIMARY AND SECONDARY At the height of British colonialism in 1920, there were only five elementary schools for girls, and until 1940 there were *only* elementary schools for girls. In 1940, the Omdurman Intermediate School for Girls was opened (<www.countrystudies.us/Sudan>), and from it the first secondary school grew, providing the base for the first generation of female activists who participated in the anti-colonial struggles of the late 1940s and early 1950s. As of 1991, 94 per cent of Sudanese children completed the fifth grade; the ratio of girls to boys was .75, showing that females were lagging behind significantly even in primary education, compared with other countries in this study and in the world. By 2001, the ratio had increased to .82. Girls are tracked into certain types of educational institutions at secondary level, and thus into certain types of occupations, such as nursing and teaching.

HIGHER EDUCATION In the usual African colonial pattern, females lagged behind males, but once Sudanese women gained education, they formed the heart of the women's and nationalist movements. Late in the century, higher education expanded with new universities in such secondary cities as Wad Medani, Shendi and Juba. New universities opened in the capital city (for example, the private Ahlia University, founded by Mohamed Omer Beshir, and Omdurman Islamic University).

Ahfad University for Women in Omdurman established one of the earliest women's studies programmes in Africa in the 1970s. It is one of the few remaining English-language universities that attract women from all over Africa and the *only* university exclusively for women on the African continent. Founded by Sheikh Babiker Badri, Ahfad University houses a women's studies programme that emphasizes research on women and development issues. Ahfad women activists challenged the fundamentalist al-Bashir regime after 1989 by protesting against the imposed Islamic dress code and other restrictions on workplace and public behaviour. The faculty have pitted their research on women and family life, especially in rural areas, against government positions; they have succeeded in keeping a vigorous research agenda alive in spite of many struggles.

Political, educational and cultural leadership

Suffrage: participation in voting and elections Women won suffrage, not at the time of independence, but after the 1964 popular revolution against the Abboud military government, when women openly and enthusiastically demonstrated for popular democracy.

Political leadership

THE SUDANESE WOMEN'S UNION (SWU) The struggle for Sudanese women's rights was an integral part of the larger nationalist movement. The SWU was formed in 1946 as an outgrowth of the Sudanese Communist Party, with an eye on the creation of the new Sudanese woman in an independent Sudan. The SWU focused its early activities on organizing trade unions in female-dominated economic sectors such as teaching and nursing, as well as on nationalist activities.

Throughout the 1950s and 1960s, SWU published its *Voice of Women* (*Sawt al-Mara*), raising social and legal issues regarding polygamy, divorce reform and female circumcision. The SWU was influential in agitating for reforms in the shariah law of marriage and divorce in the 1960s and early 1970s. In 1994, Fatma Ahmed Ibrahim accepted a United Nations Human Rights Award on behalf of the SWU for its consistent work in support of women's rights since the 1940s.

With the coming to power of Ja'far Nimeiri in 1969, the women's movement achieved new gains and higher visibility as the government promulgated a moderate state feminist agenda of reform. The gains for women lay primarily in the appointment of northern Sudanese women to ministerial, judicial and other official posts; southern and other marginalized women were not included. Eventually, the original autonomy and effectiveness of the SWU were lost and attempts to construct a national organization for women through President Nimeiri's Sudanese Socialist Union (SSU) foundered, as the regime drifted to the Islamist right. The historically secular women's movement and Sudanese feminists have been critical of the ensuing Islamization, which they view as negatively affecting the status of women.

PARLIAMENTARY Fatma Ahmed Ibrahim was the first woman elected to parliament (1964). As a founder and leader of the women's movement, she is synonymous with the struggle for Sudanese women's rights. Women held a low 10 per cent of parliamentary seats in the Constituent Assembly of the military al-Bashir government in 2003. These women, like their male counterparts, are the party faithful who do little to challenge the status quo.

BREAKING INTO PATRIARCHAL POLITICS The main problem with the lack of female participation is the virtual lack of electoral politics since 1956, with only twelve years of democracy in nearly fifty years of independence that have been dominated by military regimes. The overwhelmingly masculine nature of military governments is a barrier to the advancement of women in state and society beyond the usual patriarchal politics. Sudan has historically had a low rate of female appointments to cabinet posts and public political participation. Some Sudanese women, though, have held responsible positions as government ministers and judges.

THE NATIONAL DEMOCRATIC ALLIANCE (NDA) Since the Islamist regime came to power in 1989, a national opposition movement has attempted to build the politics of a 'new Sudan'. The NDA came into being to challenge the undemocratic nature of the Islamist military regime of General 'Umar al-Bashir, who was allied with National Islamic Front founder Hasan al-Turabi. It represents the largest grouping of oppositional parties from all regions of Sudan as well as from the trade unions. The NDA includes the historical parties, such as the Umma, Democratic Unionist and Communist parties, as well as the southern resistance movement, the SPLM. Attitudes and practices of the Sudanese government in relation to women's issues are admittedly negative and regressive, but little is known about the situation of women within the NDA. The NDA perceives itself as progressive; it adheres to secularism, and it has repeatedly claimed that it is committed to guaranteeing the equal rights of women, yet not much has been achieved.

Despite much inclusive rhetoric in the NDA, women were once again left out of the process. Amel Gorani's analysis of why this happened rests primarily on the 'ghettoization' of women's issues in all political parties. The first NDA Declaration in Asmara contradicted itself as women's rights were allocated to the religious domain. According to Gorani, there was insufficient lobbying from women resulting from their inexperience, lack of political training and conditioned tendency to yield power (Box 11.2). She argues for a network of women politicians and activists. She also favours the continuation of strong international pressure for greater female representation in these organizations as a condition for their continued support.

Amel Gorani argues that this situation for women applies to Sudanese politics in general because politics revolves around individuals and powerful personalities rather than institutions. Women leaders would benefit from the creation and consolidation of institutions and structures that can ensure continuous communication, dialogue, participation and reflection on the challenges facing Sudanese women. They would also benefit greatly from creating alliances, both horizontally and vertically, for a genuine women's agenda that sets the interests of women first and takes into consideration the sources of women's suppression, including religious extremism, class, ethnicity and language. This would boost their credibility and power and would add substantial strength to the Sudanese women's movement.

Box 11.2 Women and the National Democratic Alliance (NDA)

From the first congress of the NDA in 1995, the rights of women were compromised by the introduction of Article 5 of the Conference on Fundamental Issues, held in Asmara. It stated that the NDA commits itself to guaranteeing women equal rights *as long as they do not contradict religions.* This is a clear contradiction of the NDA commitment to secularism and the agreement that citizenship alone will form the basis for equal rights and obligations, regardless of religion, language, ethnicity or sex. Women have made many efforts to delete the reference to religion in Article 5 and to acquire a firm commitment to guaranteeing the equal rights of women according to international human rights conventions, including CEDAW (which the government of Sudan still opposes).

Most NDA parties are not opposed to CEDAW or the deletion of the reference to religion. Opposition comes mainly from the Democratic Unionist Party (DUP), whose leader is chairman of the NDA. The marginalization of women and their absence from all important decision-making positions and bodies within the NDA are also to blame for sidelining women's issues. Women have been subjected to serious harassment, persecution and gross violations of their rights under the current regime. They have championed many acts of resistance and have fought diligently against the excesses and violations of the regime. The NDA Women's Alliance, operating in Khartoum and the larger cities, has played a prominent role in the struggle against the ruling regime, but this activism and energetic advocacy were not reciprocated by the NDA leadership council, which is entrusted with ensuring representation of women at the highest decision-making levels.

Fatma Ahmed Ibrahim lobbied relentlessly for the representation of Sudanese women in the NDA leadership council. She was granted observer status. The intensive lobbying by some women representatives at the second NDA congress in Massawa in 2000 focused on the reformulation of Article 5 and the representation of women in the NDA leadership council. Again, there was considerable argument from the DUP, not least from their women representatives, as to what should be the priorities, issues and strategies for achieving change for women. The conference ended without any solutions to the 'woman question', but with a promise that an NDA Women's Conference would be held within six months to put forward a comprehensive strategy for the advancement of women in Sudan. Four years later the conference has still not taken place. The attitude (and

Women in Sudan

practice) of many NDA leaders is at best one of complacency, indifference and apparent total lack of commitment to ensuring the equal rights and full participation of women.

Clearly, the relative weakness of the Sudanese women's movement and the lack of a strong base at the grassroots level reduce the possibility that Sudanese women leaders can win more ground and acquire more power or better representation in decision-making bodies.

The women's movement in Sudan remains largely elitist. There is a definite lack of strong institutions and structures that connect women leaders and representatives to the enormous number of marginalized and subordinated women groups which they claim to or are meant to represent. (Amel Gorani)

HUMAN RIGHTS VIOLATIONS Since the National Islamic Front (NIF) regime came to power in 1989 there have been reports of human rights violations against non-NIF women, who were alleged to have lost government positions, while women in public were harassed for improper, non-Islamic dress. Female NIF supporters had greater opportunities and defended the regime's policies towards women internally and in the media. Sudanese Islamist feminists were especially active at the 1995 Fourth International Congress on Women held in Beijing, raising challenges to the human rights criticism of Islamic regimes. They argued that Islam and shariah provide comprehensive legal, political and religious rights for women. Their critics, especially the Republican Brothers and Muslim liberal secularists, argue that the ban some Muslim countries impose on women as heads of state and the lack of equal legal rights in divorce and inheritance amount to a violation of women's rights as human rights.

The United Nations has singled out the following special concerns for the rights of women in Sudan: the high maternal mortality rate; the practice of female genital mutilation (FGM); women's consent in marriage mediated by a guardian with no recourse to the courts for redress; no legal minimum age for marriage; slavery, disappearances and child abductions; arbitrary requests for proof of male guardian consent to travel; and the strict dress code for women in public places (UN 2002).

FEMALE CIRCUMCISION AND UNIVERSAL HUMAN RIGHTS The most severe form of female circumcision, infibulation, is practised in Sudan among Muslims, but not among the non-Muslim third of the country. It is estimated

The UN recommends abolition of flogging of men and women for morals offences, amputation of male limbs for theft, and stoning for adultery or illicit sex. The report recommends the equalization of women's rights in marriage and the appointment of women and minorities as judges.

The public behaviour of women has been regulated further with NIF rule, including: enforced segregation in transportation and shops; insisting that women should be accompanied by a male at night; and prohibition of co-education. Of 200 media personnel who lost jobs in June 1996, 150 were women, including some of Sudan's most renowned journalists. (UN 2002)

that over 90 per cent of northern Muslim women in Sudan are infibulated. Many in the West associate female circumcision with Islam, which is true demographically but not religiously. Some Sudanese and Western writers prefer the term female genital mutilation (FGM) (Toubia 1993), while others prefer the folk classification 'female circumcision' (Gruenbaum 2001). The movement to ameliorate or eradicate FGM has been both indigenous and global. Sudanese women doctors have led the way, along with activists from the educational and healthcare sectors. Although outlawed in 1946, and not required by Islam or any other religion, female circumcision remains a widespread practice. International human rights organizations have called for the elimination of FGM on the grounds that it violates the human rights of women and girls (Fluehr-Lobban 1996).

In some of the urban centres of the Muslim north, 'lighter' forms of circumcision, such as 'simple' clitoridectomy, are gradually replacing the most severe infibulation, in which the clitoris and labia are excised and a small opening for both urine and menses is all that remains of the external female genitalia. This practice is entirely in the hands of women, leaving many Western feminists puzzled as to why such drastic and oppressive surgery is practised by women on their female kin. The reasons for the maintenance of FGM in Sudan are much the same as in other parts of Africa where the practice continues: control of female sexuality, marriageability, and a belief that it *is* commanded by religion, promotes cleanliness and hygiene, and is a long-standing cultural custom that should be observed.

The global women's rights movement has asserted that female circumcision is in a category with other human rights violations, such as domestic violence and honour killings. An international human rights campaign against

Women in Sudan

281

FGM has advocated banning or at least ameliorating the practice as a violation of the rights of children and women. The Vienna Human Rights Conference (1993) and the Beijing International Women's Conference (1995) passed resolutions against FGM and called for state-supported and international educational and public health campaigns to eradicate or ameliorate FGM. FGM has been criminalized in Egypt only when performed outside of a hospital by a person without medical credentials.

EDUCATIONAL LEADERSHIP The Babiker Bedri Scientific Association for Women's Studies at Ahfad University for Women, in collaboration with UNESCO, has pioneered the development of a new culture of peace through sports, music and drama. A pilot training package was delivered to sixty teachers in 2002 (El-Hussein 2003). Since independence in 1956, the movement for women's rights has been dominated by northern Muslim women and their supporters while the rights of southern women were left out of the process, or offered merely lip-service. Rural women have also all but been forgotten, especially in education.

ARTISTIC, CREATIVE AND CULTURAL CONTRIBUTIONS Women as creative artists and public performers have been constrained culturally in the north owing to traditions of modesty and the association of such performers with low morals. With the explosion of the mass media, however, and the presence of radios and televisions in the majority of homes, the appearance of female singers and news announcers is more acceptable (thanks to the degree of separation from public scrutiny that mass media afford). In other regions, similar cultural constraints operate, and chronic conflict has disrupted every public service, including radio and television broadcasts. An ancient cultural institution of women 'hakkamat', songstresses and poets who exhort men to courageous acts in battle, has provided many legends and popular stories of such cultural heroines as Mihera bint Abboud, whose name the author carries in Sudan. This cultural tradition has, however, been scrutinized and criticized in 2004 for its revival in the war-torn areas of Darfur. Government-backed 'Arab' militias are supported by female hakkamat who are alleged to have used this tradition to encourage men's attacks and to sing racist insults. The Women's Programme for Peace has recommended that the hakkamat tradition be re-interpreted to utilize women as 'wagers of peace' and not of war.

Towards gender equality

Peace is the essential basis for nation-building – and achievement of female well-being – in Africa's largest country. The development of Sudan awaits this long-overdue peace. The strengthening of families will occur only in the context of peace. The ideology of family life remains strong in Sudan, although many families have been torn apart by the war or forced to live in exile in neighbouring African countries, Europe and North America. The revival of slavery in the context of the civil war and the plight of Sudan's refugees, who have been separated from their families by war and instability, are urgent problems. The growing impoverishment of all regions of the nation with protracted war and its drain on the Sudanese economy portends a difficult immediate future. The long-term picture is brighter. Sudan has abundant physical and human resources to sustain a prolonged period of peace with equitable resource distribution and development. Women, men and children throughout Sudan will rapidly improve their overall status and well-being under long-overdue conditions of peace and stability.

With peace, a basic ethnography of the country's hundreds of different ethnic and linguistic groups will be possible. Scholars will be able to explore Sudanese antiquity, from the possible origins of agriculture in the Nile valley through the rise of the state, examining the changes in women's status. An examination of cultural traditions across the Sahel in Sudanic Africa will highlight the role of women in pastoral and farming societies.

While equal rights for women are formally protected in the constitution, much needs to be addressed in practice, including paying urgent attention to women and children harmed by chronic civil war, ethnic cleansing and displacement in the southern and western regions of the country. In the longer term, the well-being of Sudanese women requires an approach to national family law that moves beyond the Islamization of the early 1980s to the increased political participation of women at all levels, and a concerted effort to include women in development planning and economic development.

With the severe disruption and displacement of peoples stemming from the protracted civil war, AIDS infection rates are probably higher than official claims and deserve future study. Research on the effects of protracted war on families will be a priority in the post-war period. Ahfad University researchers are examining ideas about intermarriage between northerners and southerners (perceived as problematical because of racial, religious and ethnic differences) that might be helpful in a peaceful Sudan. Studying the effects of rapid urbanization on families – which has accompanied the displacement of millions of Sudanese resulting from the civil war – will be essential to improved services and well-being.

This daunting research, activist and policy agenda calls for the training of applied social scientists, development specialists, educators and other change agents to meet the many demands required by the new post-war Sudan.

Note

1 I wish to express my gratitude to Amel Gorani, Sudan Future Care, Asmara, Eritrea, who contributed a special section on women in the National Democratic Alliance.

References

Ali, I. M. (2002) 'Culture of peace in African perspective', paper presented at the Regional Seminar on the Role of Women in the Promotion of a Culture of Peace and Conflict Resolution, 25–26 March, Khartoum

Ali, N. M. M. (1998) 'The invisible economy, survival, and empowerment: five cases from Atbara, Sudan', in R. Lobban (ed.), *Women in the Informal Sector in the Middle East*, Gainesville: University Press of Florida

Badri, A. E. and I. I. Abdel Sadig (1998) 'Sudan, between peace and war: internally displaced women in Khartoum and South and West Kordofan', Nairobi: UNIFEM

Chawla, N. (2003) 'From survival to thrival: children and women in the southern part of Sudan', *UN Human Development Report*, New York: United Nations

El-Hussein, D. M. (2003) 'Building "a culture of peace": the concept within the Sudanese context', *Ahfad Journal, Women and Change*, 20(2): 26–37

Fluehr-Lobban, C. (1987) *Islamic Law and Society in the Sudan*, London: Frank Cass (trans. into Arabic by Jameel Mahbouli (2004), *Al-Shari'a wa al-Mujtemaa fi al-Sudan*, Cairo: Three Apples Press

— (1996) 'Cultural relativism and universal rights', *Chronicle of Higher Education*, 9 June

— (2004) 'Nubian queens in Nile Valley and Afro-Asiatic culture history', proceedings of the 9th Conference of Nubian Studies, 1998, ed. T. Kendall, Boston, MA: Northeastern University Press

Gruenbaum, E. (2001) *The Female Circumcision Controversy: An Anthropological Perspective*, Philadelphia: University of Pennsylvania Press

Hale, S. (1996) *Gender Politics in Sudan*, Boulder, CO: Westview Press

Muhammad, B. B. (2002) Entry on 'Iya Bassi', in R. Lobban, R. Kramer and C. Fluehr-Lobban (eds), *Historical Dictionary of the Sudan*, 3rd edn, Lanham, MD: Scarecrow Press

Omer, A. (2002) 'Culture of peace, the concept', paper presented at the Regional Seminar on the Role of Women in the Promotion of a Culture of Peace and Conflict Resolution, 25–26 March, Khartoum

Toubia, N. (1993) *Female Genital Mutilation: A Call for Global Action*, New York: Women Ink

UN (United Nations) (2002) *Fourth Periodic Report on Sudan Civil and Political Rights*, 16 June, New York: United Nations

USCIA (United States Central Intelligence Agency) (2003) *The CIA World Fact Book*, Washington, DC: USCIA

Websites

<www.countrystudies.us/Sudan>

12 | Women in Thailand: changing the paradigm of female well-being

FARUNG MEE-UDON AND RANEE ITARAT[1]

Women are buffaloes. Men are humans. (Traditional Thai saying)

Back in 1994, I met one of my long-lost friends at a party organized by local politicians. We had come to the party for different reasons. I was invited as an academic while my friend was invited as an escort for a politician. At first I did not recognize her, as she was so beautiful. She told me she was doing very well but later she admitted that she had undergone plastic surgery and become a high-class sex worker. When I recall my friend's life, a number of questions come into my head: Is she happy with her life? Am I happier than she is? How do we define well-being? What differences exist between male and female well-being in Thailand? These questions touch on contemporary academic debate about whether development promotes human well-being. (Farung Mee-Udon)

Major influences on Thai female well-being in the twentieth century include the country's gendered sociocultural context, continuing processes of modernization and globalization, and three defining episodes: the period of constitutional monarchy, the Second World War, and the post-war period of the National Plan.

The Kingdom of Thailand, previously known as Siam, is in central South-East Asia, bounded by the Andaman Sea, Myanmar, Laos, Cambodia and Malaysia and the Gulf of Thailand. Consisting of seventy-six provinces, the country comprises 513,960 square kilometres; the population in 2002 was approximately 63.2 million, with slightly more females than males; the sex ratio is 99.28 males to 100 females. Thailand is a multi-ethnic, multi-religious society. The majority of its population, however, are Thai; they speak Thai and 95 per cent are of the Theravada Buddhism faith. A minority of Chinese origin follow Buddhism, Taoism or Confucianism. A significant minority in the south are Muslim. Indigenous tribal peoples still practise traditional beliefs.

The gendered sociocultural context of Thailand

Evidence exists of female oppression in previous eras. For example, in the Ayudhaya period (1350–1767) this oppression was characterized by the saying

'Women are buffaloes. Men are humans' (Suriyasarn 1993). Women suffered their lowest status in the early nineteenth century. In 1804, women were the legal property of men and could be bought and sold in the marketplace. At the time the law classified a 'wife' in three categories: 1) a major wife, a woman who becomes the wife of a man through parental agreement; 2) a minor wife, a woman who becomes the wife of a man upon the request of the latter; and 3) a slave wife, a woman who is bought by a man to become his wife (ibid.: 1).

According to Vella (1978: 153–4), King Rama VI (1910-25) enumerated the restrictions on Thai women: limited freedom to socialize with men on equal terms; sanctioning of the practice of polygamy; and limited access of females to education. Buddhism, the state religion, views men as superior to women, which has had a significant impact on female status and well-being in Thailand.

The transformation brought by the modernization process has affected gender relations in Thailand. According to Muscat (1990), Thailand's late-nineteenth-century economic and security relationships with the industrialized world have strongly influenced the country's modern economic development policy, which, in turn, has altered Thai society's outlook on female well-being.

From modernization to mobilization The main reason for change in the first half of the twentieth century was economic and social development, while in the second half change was driven by modernization and globalization. Capitalism replaced feudalism, as machines replaced men and animals. Agriculture is still a major employer today, but the service sector has grown significantly in line with other economies. This has encouraged greater female participation in the formal economy. Consumption is slowly replacing production.

In the late twentieth century, globalization affected Thailand; the term was translated into the Thai language in the Seventh National Plan (1992–96). For Thailand, globalization entails technological advancement and the importance of addressing a wide range of social issues through information technology, as outlined in the 1995 plan entitled *Towards Social Equity and Prosperity: Thailand IT Policy into the 21st Century*. The plan addresses the importance of developing 'a well educated population and a well-being society', as well as correcting the imbalance in social and economic development that exists between urban and rural areas (because of preferential provision in urban areas). The issue of social equality is central, with emphasis given to human development (TNITC 2000). Globalization can have positive effects.

For example, information and communications technologies brought Thai women closer to women around the world, which helps make contemporary females less isolated. Women, however, have less opportunity than men to access this new resource.

Constitutional monarchy Thailand changed from an absolute to a constitutional monarchy in 1932. Under Field Marshal Phibun's government from 1947 onwards, the status of Thai females at lower social levels improved. The present king (Bhumibol – the ninth Rama) was educated in the West and has supported modernization. Female organizations (both governmental and non-governmental) were established (for example, the Association for the Promotion of the Status of Females). This NGO pressured the government into amending Section 28 of the constitution, concerning the equal rights of Thai females (<www.apsw-thailand.org>).

In 1979, a Sub-Committee for the Development of Female Roles and Status under the National Economic and Social Development Board (NESDB) was formed. Ten years later, the government's Thai National Commission on Women's Affairs approved the establishment of a state organization for females to formulate policies and plans for the promotion of Thai female roles and status (NCWA 1996).

The Second World War The war affected all aspects of female and male well-being in Thailand. The Thai government came to an agreement in 1941 with the Japanese, whose presence was seen by the Thai people more and more as an occupation. Trade and the economy were adversely affected. The Japanese military became a drain on domestic resources as they requisitioned supplies; Allied bombing raids damaged Bangkok and caused extensive loss of life.

The post-war period In the immediate post-war period, the government actively promoted population growth with economic incentives for families. This had a mixed impact on women's well-being. As in many other developing countries in the post-war period, social and economic policy was dominated by national plans launched in 1961. From 1972 on, the National Plan promoted family planning, which had a clear impact on female quality of life, especially in reducing the maternal mortality rate. Widespread support for contraceptive use has prevented many unwanted pregnancies, which has affected Thailand's demography. Care for females was institutionalized. Laws were passed to prosecute rape and abuse. Rape within marriage is not illegal. There has been more recognition of maternal care and child support needs.

A demographic portrait of Thai women

Urbanization During the second half of the twentieth century, the status of Thai females changed drastically in response to the country's economic and social development policy. Thailand has witnessed widespread urbanization. A large proportion of the rural population has migrated to urban areas for better-paid jobs, especially to Bangkok and its peripheries. Cities in Thailand have a minimum population of 50,000 and a density not less than 3,000 people/sq. km. The population in municipal areas increased from 12.2 per cent in 1960 to 31.85 per cent in 2000 (NSO 2000 [1960]).

Urban migration has had a significant impact on social structure. Statistics on migrants show that slightly more females than males are migrating to urban areas (930,200 females compared to 918,800 males in 2000 – GDRI 2000). Urbanization and modernization can bring females both positive and negative opportunities: they earn more than they can in rural areas but working in what are still low-paid jobs or falling into the sex industry can create serious risks to female well-being.

Life expectancy Life expectancy increased throughout the twentieth century for both sexes (Figure 12.1). As in most societies, Thai females live longer than males by approximately four years, reflecting improved healthcare service (NSO 2000). Improved healthcare in Thailand, eradication of diseases such as malaria, and better sanitation contributed to the rise in the Thai population. Female life expectancy at birth was 53.5 in 1940 (UN 1948) and increased to 71 in 2000 (UN 2004). The differences between female and male life expectancy

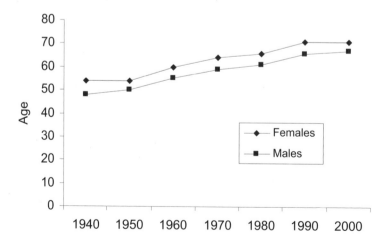

Figure 12.1 Life expectancy by gender (years)
Source: **UN (1948, 2004)**

are related to factors such as differential consumption of alcohol, tobacco and drug use, and HIV/AIDS infection. Statistics document these declines and the improvements in Thai female well-being through improved healthcare services.

Population growth, fertility rate and male–female ratio After the Second World War ended in 1945, Thai population growth decreased from 25.7 to 20.6 per cent (NSO 2000 [1950]). In 1960 the population growth dramatically increased, as it did in many other countries adversely affected by the war. The country began the first stage of the demographic transition. Mortality had fallen considerably but fertility was still high. In 1956, the government offered bonuses for large families, which may have contributed to a 50 per cent increase in the population growth rate in 1960 (NSO 1983). In the 1950s, the total population was around 17 million; it increased to 26 million in 1960. In 1970, however, the government launched the National Family Planning Programme (NFPP) to control population (NSO 1973).

Low mortality and high fertility were significant goals in order to increase the population. More recently, however, rapid declines in fertility and mortality have had a significant effect on female well-being; the fertility rate dropped from 3.5 in 1980 to 2.2 in 1990 and to 1.9 in 1999 (ADB 2004). There were approximately six children to every woman in 1960, but in 2000 there were fewer than two (NSO 1973, 2000). The status of females improved over the course of the twentieth century in this regard. The gender ratio is exactly equal.

Age structure of the population The crude birth rate dropped from 28 per 1,000 in 1980 to 17 per 1,000 in 1999. Because people are having fewer children than before, and males and females are living longer than ever, the population is becoming a predominantly older (and more female) population, with more citizens in need of formal and informal healthcare to treat illness and disabilities (e.g. blindness, immobility, etc.). Most people who look after others in the ageing population are female.

Maternal mortality rate The statistics indicate better survival of children and women by the end of the century. The fertility transition from high to low and the decline in infant and maternal mortality rates have increased female well-being. Moreover, this has been one of the most rapid transitions among developing countries in Asia (Prachuabmoh and Mithranon 2003).

One reason for longer female life expectancy is that the Thai Department of Health has placed a high priority on the reduction of maternal and infant

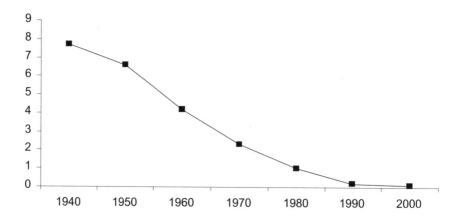

Figure 12.2 Maternal mortality rates (per 1,000 live births)
Source: **NSO (2000 [1950, 1960, 1970, 1980, 1990])**

mortality. The maternal mortality rate fell from almost 8 women per 1,000 live births to 0.2 in 1991–2000 – (44 per 100,000 births in 2000) (Figure 12.2).

Infant mortality rate The infant mortality rate (per 1,000 live births) is higher for males; the overall rate decreased from 103.8 in 1940 to 26 in 1999 (Figure 12.3).

Contraception and abortion Feminists have argued that the policy on population growth has always focused on females, and thus the responsibility of Thai population control has largely been a female one. This policy adversely affects women more than men, in particular in terms of responsibility for contraception and personal choice. The rate of contraceptive use has increased from about 66 per cent in 1990 to 72 per cent in 1999 (ADB 2004). About 90 per cent of women use the pill, female sterilization or injections (GDRI 2000).

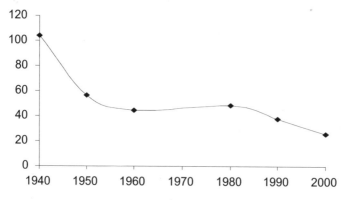

Figure 12.3 Infant mortality rate (per 1,000 live births)
Source: **NSO (1973); ADB (2004)**

HIV/AIDS Since the 1980s, HIV has spread rapidly throughout Thailand, but with government policies to encourage contraception use, the rate of infection is decreasing (Ministry of Education n.d.). The UN reports that life expectancy in Thailand has fallen from 70.3 to 68.9 years owing to the number of young people dying of AIDS (Agence France-Press 2003).

In 1990, there were almost four times as many males as females with HIV. In 2000 both rates had declined, with about 40,000 fewer HIV-positive males (56,454 down to 15,887) and 5,000 fewer HIV-positive females (12,489 down to 7,465) (NSO 2000 [1990]). The risk for females of being an AIDS patient, however, has increased. Among AIDS patients, the proportion of females steadily increased from 1994 to 1998 –from 11.4 per cent of all AIDS patients in 1994 to 21.7 per cent in 1998 (MPH n.d.).

Suicide In 1991–97, the suicide rate in Thailand was about three times higher for males than for females. Male behaviour seems to be more violent than that of females. When males attempt to commit suicide, they are more successful. From 1992 to 1996 the suicide rate among male adolescents (fifteen to twenty-nine) was much greater than among males aged forty-five and over (ibid.). Also, because most men are responsible for family income, they may suffer from pressure as the primary breadwinner.

According to the Mental Health Department of Thailand, the main reasons for suicide are domestic pressure, financial despair and AIDS (Thai Government 2000). One of the main reasons for suicide put forward by the Mental Health Department was domestic pressure, which could explain the higher suicide rates among married females. Statistics show that more married females committed suicide from 1993 to 1997 than single females (MPH n.d.), indicating a disadvantage to marriage for at least some Thai women. Between single and married men the rates were similar, perhaps because of the positive effect marriage has on males. It could be argued from this that males are affected less by marriage than females, hence the similar figures for both single and married men. That AIDS was also listed as a major reason for suicide, helps account for the higher rates among males.

Family status and structure

Marriage age With urbanization, the family structure changed from a predominantly extended model to a nuclear family model. Now females are delaying marriage compared to the situation thirty years ago. In 1970, the average age at first marriage was twenty-two; this had increased to twenty-four by 2000. Furthermore, the number of children per thousand females has decreased in line with first marriage age. Later marriage is one of the consequences of education; the longer females spend in school, the more likely they are to continue in higher education and marry at a later age.

Gender roles in Thai rural households Studies of gender relations in Thai families regularly show that women and girls are expected to be responsible primarily for family rather than their own well-being. The continuation of these cultural attitudes towards gender roles in contemporary Thai families means that there is little evidence of a significant improvement in female well-being on this score.

. Traditional Thai rural culture holds strong beliefs about favour and obligation between parents and their children. Sons are responsible for the spiritual well-being of the family and thus become monks, while daughters are responsible for the economic well-being of the family and become workers alongside males. Vantanee and Sunee (1998) concluded that males are considered superior to females; similarly, daughters are expected to help their families and to work more than sons. Although work obligations can give Thai women a certain financial independence, they often send wages back to their family.

In a predominantly Buddhist society, religion has an important influence on family relationships and social structure. Gendered family expectations derived from Buddhist theology have a tangible impact on gender roles and patterns of family economic activity. Buddhism influences the lower status of Thai females in religious life by promulgating the belief that males are superior to females. For example, Buddhist ideology places females in a lower position: 'Men and women live their everyday lives as Buddhists under very different circumstances: men are the "first-class" citizens, and women are "second-class"' (Thitsa 1990: 16). Kirsch (1975) agrees, but he particularly emphasizes the fact that Buddhism underpins the control of men in polity while women are active in the economy. The control of polity gives men prestige, rights and authority more than control over the household.

Violence against women

According to the UNIFEM Biennial Report, in 1993 20 per cent of women in Thailand were subjected to assault by their intimate partner. Although the criminal code covers spousal and child abuse, victims may not call police and police may not make arrests, since both victims and authorities tend to see domestic violence as a personal matter (true in most countries). Also, evidence rules make it difficult to prosecute perpetrators (UNDP and UNIFEM 2000).

Economic participation

The division of labour Females in Thailand have played a significant role in Thai society, especially in the economic arena (Yoddumnern-Attig 1992). Although Thai society is usually considered to be predominantly patriarchal, the role of Thai females has never been restricted solely to the household sphere. They have worked side by side with males in agriculture, industry, commerce and services for generations. Females are economically active in the informal sector. Still, the traditional model of relationships between husband and wife in Thailand portrays females as inferior. Thitsa (1990: 17) gives the example of a typical Thai woman, who reflects, 'We [women] will always be grateful to our husbands for everything they give us, whether children, home or simply [the] satisfaction of seeing them.'

In the past, Thai boys were educated as apprentices in the monasteries and were individually educated by a particular monk, usually a friend or relative of the family. Thai girls received education at home and were trained to do household work (Sonakul 1959: 15–16). As a result, Thai men have tended to take responsibility for activities outside the home – particularly social and political activities – and women became more responsible for household activities and for finances once money entered the household sphere. This led to a gendered distribution of decision-making power that still influences gender roles in Thailand.

Migration and modernity have brought about a change in the division of labour between the sexes; family structure has shifted from the traditional extended model to a more nuclear type among rural migrants to Bangkok. These changes may give women more opportunity to work outside the household, which could contribute to increased female emancipation. Sopchokchai et al. (1991) argue that most households still follow traditional divisions, meaning that almost all activities requiring external contact or negotiation outside the home are considered a man's responsibility.

Women's participation in the labour force The percentage of females who work outside the household increased to around 46 per cent in 2000. They have been especially involved in the industrial sector, which should contribute to improved economic development and free females to seek more educational opportunities and independence; the income thus generated will raise their importance within the household and society.

TYPES OF OCCUPATION Thailand was an agricultural country for many centuries; in 1940, for example, 93.4 per cent of the female labour force was engaged

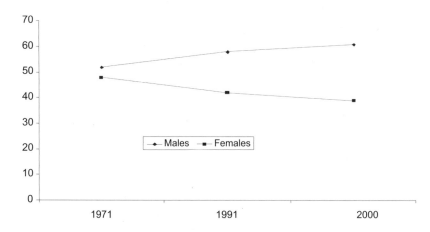

Figure 12.4 Male and female participation in agriculture (per cent)
Source: GDRI (2000); authors' calculations

in agriculture (NSO 2000 [1940]). Only a few women were engaged in the commercial and service sectors. In 1971, 52 per cent of farmers were male. Twenty years later 58 per cent of farmers were male and 42 per cent were female. In 2000, only 47.6 per cent of the female workforce and 50.19 per cent of males were in the agricultural sector (NSO 2000). The agricultural labour force has declined continually because of the country's industrialization policy, but females have left agriculture at a faster rate than have males (GDRI 2000) (Figure 12.4).

During the second half of the twentieth century there was a remarkable increase in female participation in the sales, service and professional sectors. Females have moved into industrial and commercial work. Since 1986, they have become the main workforce in the labour-intensive industries driving the Thai economic boom (Phongpaichit and Baker 1998). Moreover, about 80 per cent of the labour force consists of women who work in the production of leading exported industrial goods (NCWA 1996).

The proportion of females participating in the labour force was very high in 1950 (81.7 per cent). This percentage is continually changing, however, and is linked to Thailand's economic performance. During times of economic slowdown (such as in 1980 and 2000), female labour force participation has reached its lowest levels, about 60 per cent (NSO 2000 [1950, 1980]). There has also been, however, an observable downward trend in female labour participation over the last six decades, which may be related to an increasing proportion of females in education.

FEMALES AND PROSTITUTION Tourism and the sex industry are among Thailand's biggest sources of income (Phongpaichit 1987: 11–14). According to a study on migration and gender in Thailand, the reasons why females migrate to the sex sector are intimately linked to their family roles: 'Young females migrate to work in prostitution because they perceive a family need for the money that they earn. This gives them a great deal of responsibility, especially since, in many cases, they are responsible for how their families spend the money' (IPSR 1995: 1). This responsibility represents an important dimension of female economic agency.

The official number of prostitutes decreased from 85,126 in 1989 to 61,135 in 1998 (MPH n.d.), but (as in all countries) the exact number of prostitutes is thought to be far greater than that officially recorded. In addition, the number of girls at risk of child prostitution has declined over the last two decades, according to Baker (2000), who studied child prostitution in northern Thailand. The reasons for this changing situation are fertility reduction, increased educational opportunities, the impact of HIV/AIDS, and such changes in Thai law as the 1996 Prostitution Prevention and Suppression Act. The act has several important elements, including: 1) the penalty for prostitution has been much reduced, with police activity now focused on the client; 2) A client using the sexual services of a child prostitute under eighteen years of age will be punished with imprisonment; and 3) anyone who procures or detains another person for prostitution will be severely punished; if the victim is a child under eighteen years of age, the offender will be punished more severely; and if the child victim suffers grievous bodily harm or is killed, the offender will be punished with life imprisonment or with the death penalty (GT 1996).

These provisions are designed to some extent to protect females under the law, but the treatment of prostitution as a crime varies greatly, relative to time and place. Prostitutes and sex workers are vulnerable to abuse and rape behind closed doors, and are at the mercy of customers with regard to contraception and sexually transmitted infections. Recent revelations in the press from massage parlour owners highlighted a culture of bribery in the relationship between the sex industry and the police. Earnings are not high for most sex workers; the major beneficiaries are brothel and parlour owners, pimps and the police.

Unemployment The 1997 economic crisis that swept through South-East Asia affected much of Thailand's population, but poorer communities suffered the biggest impact (Box 12.1). As in most parts of the world, females are disproportionately represented among the poor. Thus, females experienced greater job insecurity, unemployment and old-age poverty during the downturn (World Bank 1998).

> ### Box 12.1 *The economic crisis in Thailand*
>
> Between 1985 and 1994, Thailand experienced an impressive economic growth rate of 8.2 per cent per annum, the highest in the world at that time. In early 1996, Thailand was considered a model of developmental success. In mid-1997, however, an economic crisis erupted, starting in the financial sector. The Bank of Thailand announced flotation of the currency and the level of foreign exchange moved immediately from 25 baht per US dollar to 30 baht. Since then, the baht price has fluctuated (40 baht per dollar in September 2000).
>
> The economic crisis has profoundly affected Thai livelihoods in both urban and rural areas. Hundreds of thousands of workers who had migrated to urban areas (in order to find work) lost their jobs. in February 1998, unemployment was estimated at 8.8 per cent of the workforce, or 2.8 million people (NCWA 1996; Warr 1998).

The economic crisis affected both females and households generally. A large number of unemployed workers returned to their villages, disrupting local economies, social relations and intra-household relationships. Females were severely affected. For example, the World Bank's *Road to Recovery* report states that: 'Women and girls may be disproportionately hurt by the financial crisis. Women lost their jobs first, and families pulled their daughters out of school before their sons ... ' (1998: 81).

In Thailand, laid-off workers tend to be family members rather than heads of households. A report from Thai NGOs states that there are now more females, children and elderly in the labour force, but also that child labour, child beggars and child prostitution are on the increase. In north-east Thailand, 'females were justifiably angry because they had to send their children to the garbage site every day to support the family' (Robb in ibid.: 83). As unemployment increased sharply, it caused psychological problems, including domestic violence that affected females and children.

Income and poverty Currently, Thai females are becoming increasingly important as family income earners. In 1999, there were more female workers than male workers in the important export industries (GDRI 1999). There are, however, more females than males in unpaid work (such as housework) and more females in low-income groups. Over 90 per cent of people in the lowest income bracket (less than 6,501 baht per month) are female. Men dominate the middle and higher income brackets, with males accounting for 60 per cent of those earning between 6,501 and 10,000 baht per month and 68 per cent of those earning over 10,000 baht per month (GDRI 2001). Thus, more males than females appear in the middle and high-income groups.

Females were the driving force behind the high economic growth rates. In fact, during the economic crisis, a higher proportion of the unemployed were males – 58 per cent compared to 42 per cent females (DOLA 1999). It is simplistic to conclude that males were affected more than females by using only this one indicator (ibid.). As Baden points out, 'While joblessness may affect men and women, women may find it harder than men to regain employment or become self-employed, due to relative lack of education and skill' (1999: 7). In some occupations, it is very difficult for women to juggle marriage and work or to re-enter the labour force after childbirth.

Many Thai females make decisions in the household and have more economic power than men do in controlling financial income and other household economic resources. While facing new challenges and adjustments in urban areas, young females rarely spend much of their own money on themselves; often, large portions of income are sent back to their families. Family structure facilitates and encourages this. With little disposable income of their own, it could be argued that the quality of life of young urban females is limited.

The north-eastern region is the poorest part of rural Thailand, and has always been dryer and less fertile than other regions. Drought is now a regular feature of this area and constantly pushes a number of villagers into a cycle of debt. Many view it as the most 'traditional' part of Thailand (Ekachai 1990: 11–19).

According to Promphakping (2000) and Blumberg and Mee-Udon (2002), particularly in rural areas and the north-eastern region, women have always enjoyed a certain amount of economic power both inside and outside the household in small-scale economic activities such as handicrafts. This is because women control income and other economic resources, especially land, and husbands often turned much of the family income over to women. Although this power is often not readily apparent, it should be taken into account when considering the economic power of women, and should not be seen merely as a recent phenomenon.

Literacy and education

The Buddhist temples provided Thai public education in earlier times. In the mid-1800s modernization influenced Thai society with the coming of

Western missionaries. Since England was more powerful, King Rama IV realized that the kind of education provided by the monasteries was not adequate for future government officials. This drove modernization and Westernization in the 1900s.

From 1868 to 1910, King Rama V ruled Thailand. Since neighbouring countries had been colonized by Britain or France, he tried to modernize in order to maintain the country's sovereignty. He realized the importance of education. The first school for Thai females was established in 1897. His son, King Rama VI, who was educated in England, followed his father's modernization policy; he also wanted to improve female status because of Western influence. He first improved the status of high-level females so that other females would follow. Although there was not much improvement in female education at the lower level, this period saw the true beginning of female education in Thailand.

Literacy rates Female literacy rates have risen from 10 per cent of the male figure in 1910 to almost equal proportions. In 2000, 89.2 per cent of females above the age of ten were literate (NSO 2000). Figure 12.5 shows the illiteracy rates for males and females.

School completion rates The gross enrolment ratio for boys and girls is virtually at parity: about 81 per cent in primary schools, 47 per cent in secondary schools and 11 per cent in university (ESCAP 1998), according to the National Statistical Office.

PRIMARY In the past, only a small number of females received education because of the traditional Thai social structure. In general, Thai boys had a

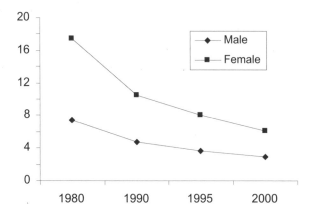

Figure 12.5 Illiteracy rate by gender, 1980–2000 (per cent)
Source: **CIDA (2001)**

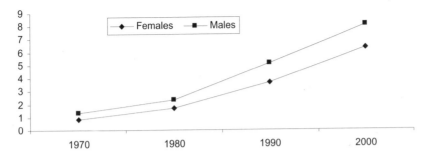

Figure 12.6 Female and male participation in high school education (per cent)
Source: **NSO various years**

chance to be educated at the temples, while girls were not allowed to benefit. Most educated females were from the royal family or the upper class. The important change for female education came in 1932, when King Rama VI revolutionized the education system by introducing four years of compulsory education for every Thai child (Ministry of Education n.d.).

SECONDARY From 1940 to 1950, the percentage of students completing higher grades fell dramatically for both boys and girls. This can be attributed to the Second World War, when students had to stay away from colleges and universities. From 1970 onwards, female participation rates doubled, perhaps owing to the influence of the global progression of female rights and changing attitudes within Thailand. Female participation has doubled every decade since, from 0.86 per cent in 1970 to 6.34 per cent in 2000. This growth is greater than the increase in male education rates (Figure 12.6).

HIGHER EDUCATION At university level, female participation increased significantly between 1920 and 2000. The ratio of men to women completing university education in 1920 was 3:1 (202 males to 61 females), whereas by 2000 a higher proportion of women (5.3 per cent) than men (4.5 per cent) were completing university (NSO 2000 [1920]). This change was most noticeable in the ten years from 1990 to 2000, when females overtook males in university education attendance (NSO 2000 [1990]) (Figure 12.7). Educational opportunity levels reflect the growth in participation of females, especially at university level, but girls tend to concentrate in fields that command lower wages: at university women study social sciences, nursing and education (as is true in most countries); increasingly, women are entering medicine but not law, science or engineering in any appreciable numbers (ADB 2004). In some disciplines, quotas are set by gender, which tends to hold female rates down; the only field that has a higher quota for females than males is nursing.

Women in Thailand

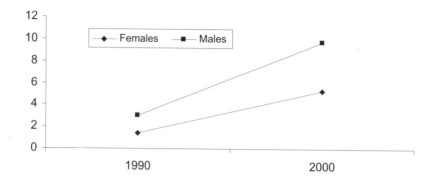

Figure 12.7 University enrolment by gender (per cent)
Source: **NSO various years**

Various studies have shown that female participation in education leads to an increase in their status (Costa 1997; Knodel 1994; Keyes 1991), which is likely to improve female well-being in certain ways. Further, an increase in female education has slowly but steadily brought about an increase in the number of women in formal politics, which arguably improves Thai female well-being (Costa 1997).

In addition, Thai people generally assume that more education means better employment opportunities and increased social mobility (ibid.), which leads to an increase in women's pay. Improvements in women's pay mean an increase in family wealth, since daughters in Thailand give the money they earn to their families. This increase in wealth inevitably leads to certain improvements in family well-being. In other words, parents gain from the education of daughters more than from the education of sons.

Political, educational and cultural leadership

Thai society is currently undergoing widespread social and economic changes that have expanded female well-being. For example, there are more females pursuing higher education, in paid employment and in good occupational positions. Wider benefits of education accrue to Thai females when they can 'visualize a world very different from that known by their grandmother' (Keyes, cited in Costa 1997). Women play key roles as social change agents in society and, through their education, Thai women are exploring new ideas and creating the possibility of new worlds for their children.

Suffrage Thai women won the right to vote in 1932.

Political leadership Although female political participation in Thai society has broadened in recent years, women are rarely visible in the 'formal' national

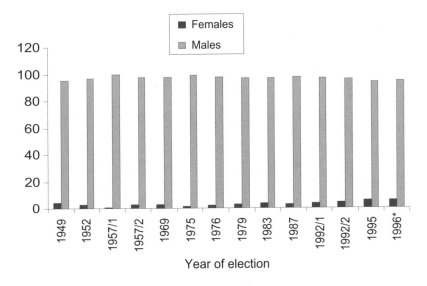

Figure 12.8 Members of parliament by gender, 1949–96 (per cent); *author's calculations Sources: Thomson and Bhongsvej (1995: 8); NSO (1997)

political arena. Defining politics is an elusive undertaking because it is subject to varying definitions. Political participation is essentially about participation in decision-making, power-sharing, collective bargaining, and negotiating all issues affecting society – formal and informal, public and private. The definition of women's political participation should go beyond participation in the parliamentary system and should refer to the effectiveness of women's representation. Little research has been conducted on Thai women in this regard, however.

Parliamentary Presently, fewer than 10 per cent of Thai females participate in the national parliament and state legislatures. In Thailand, women and men have had the right to stand for election since 1932, but the first female was elected to parliament in 1949. Thus, data in Figure 12.8 begin in 1949.

In 1996, the proportion of female politicians was only 5.6 per cent, one of the lowest in Asia. In other Asian countries, comparable figures for female representation in the national assemblies are higher than Thailand's – e.g. India, 8 per cent, Malaysia, 11 per cent, China, 21 per cent (UNDP 1996: 23).

LOCAL GOVERNMENT The number of female politicians at local level has increased. For example, the proportion of positions occupied by females at the Sub-district Administration Organization (SAO) gradually changed from 7.9 per cent in 1996 to 9.14 per cent in 1999 (Ministry of Interior 1999). Thai

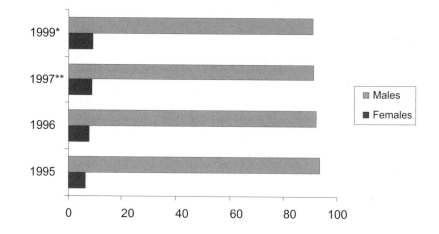

Figure 12.9 Members of SAO by gender (per cent) *Sources:* Ministry of Interior;
*Phongngam (1998: 193); ** The result of the latest national election to the
SAO from the Ministry of Interior (18 July 1999)

local politics may be about to go through an important transformation. While
progress is still slow, females have become more visible in the local political
arena. The change has taken place in the context of decentralization, which is
in line with the restructuring of the SAO, female networking, the new constitution and globalization trends (Figure 12.9) (Mee-Udon 2000).

The major barriers that females still encounter are deeply rooted traditional
practices that cannot be changed merely by raising the number of females
in formal politics. The level of female political participation might be much
higher if all-female movements challenged the status quo, as their actions
would then be regarded by the critical mass as political. The need to involve
females in politics is not only in order to change power relations between
females and males but also to foster democracy, human rights, transparency,
accountability, good governance and female well-being.

The increasing number of female politicians does not imply that female
well-being will automatically be enhanced. Females entering the political
arena do not necessarily make a difference, because many do not have a broad
enough gender perspective to appreciate overarching gender issues. Indeed,
more politically active gender-sensitive people are a necessary condition for
improvements in female well-being.

PARTY LEADERSHIP Promoting female well-being in Thai society requires
sensitizing males to the importance of female involvement, and gaining their
support. When females enter the political arena they should do so with the

intent of addressing matters that are traditionally the province of (male-dominated) politics, as well as championing gender issues. If female politicians harbour these intentions, they should make them known to their potential colleagues. Politicians versed in gender policy alone would find it difficult to tackle the problems of social class, age, race, religion and economics that are endemic problems for Thailand. This has implications for women's involvement in party leadership.

Educational leadership Somswasdi (2003) links women's studies programmes in Thailand to the country's democratization movement in 1973, which ended in a coup d'état in 1976. The Marxist approach that emphasized class struggle and oppression moved towards gender equality and women's participation in development after the UN-sponsored International Women's Year in 1975. At the same time, the Thai government began to pay attention to women's issues in its national plans, which led to a new emphasis on Women in Development (WiD). Eight women's studies programmes have sprung up around the country, and a major international conference is slated for Bangkok in 2005 (Association for Women's Rights in Development, 10th International Forum).

PARTICIPATION IN RELIGIOUS INSTITUTIONS Certain Buddhists believe that bad luck in life is the result of bad karma in the last life. The notion of karma relates fortunes in the present life to deeds from a previous life. To improve one's next life, karma can be accrued in the present; if people want to have a better next life, they have to achieve merit. This belief system largely excludes females from monkhood, because of the historical lack of female Buddhist priestesses.

In Thailand, it is illegal for females to serve as female monks or *Bhikkuni*, so the only way that they can accrue this merit is through their sons. Daughters contribute to their parents' lives less in terms of improving karma than in terms of material or economic benefit. Thai sons can pay back their debt to their parents by becoming monks while daughters have to pay their parents back financially or by taking care of them. Consequently, one of the most important ways in which women achieve karma is through a son's work as a monk.

Kabinlasing (1998), who later became the first *Bhikkuni* in Thailand, points out that Buddhist ideology gives females some prestige and values. According to the Tripitaka (equivalent to the Bible), no valid reasons exist for not allowing females to become *Bhikkuni*. When asked whether a female could enter monkhood, the Buddha said, 'Please do not ask so,' and repeated it three times before He allowed the existence of the first female monk. Thai females were forbidden to enter monkhood long after the enfranchisement of the Tripitaka: a group of male monks in Thailand created this new 'rule' in 1928 (Buddhist Era 2471). To conclude, there is nothing written in the Tripitaka about restricting the monkhood to males.

Towards gender equality

In Thai, 'well-being' is *kin dee yoo dee*, meaning 'eat well, live well'. Thailand is in the period of the ninth National Plan (2002–2006). Since the eighth plan (1997–2001), more stress has been placed on 'people-centred' rather than economic development, and the meaning of well-being has changed slightly to *yoo dee mee sook* or 'live well, be happy' (NESDB 1997). Well-being as defined by the NESDB comprises seven key aspects: health, education, employment, income and income distribution, family life, environment, and good governance. The health component is possibly the most significant category in Thai society. A traditional Thai proverb which represents the importance of good health is *'Kwam mai mee rok pen lap an prasert'* ('no disease is precious luck'). This is because most people would agree that health is the foundation of human well-being.

The twentieth century witnessed transformations in Thai female well-being in terms of quality of life, reduction of poverty, and lessening of inequality. In terms of the economic, health and family spheres, the well-being of Thai females has improved substantially, particularly in its demographic and health aspects. This does not necessarily represent a higher quality of life for females, however, because when males contract HIV, quality of life decreases for both sexes – traditionally, females are responsible for the well-being of their family and others. Similarly, when males commit suicide, females bear most of the brunt as family care falls solely on their shoulders. Poor, unskilled, widowed females have to turn to low-status, low-paid work for survival (for example, the risky massage and personal service industry). When this happens to young females, education may have to be sacrificed.

The most important factor affecting the well-being of Thai females is the dramatic increase in their participation in education, especially university education. The female literacy rate has improved, although there are still more females than males unable to read or write. Most illiterate are elderly, and the prospects for the younger generation look better.

Linked to the higher participation of females in education are two other factors: a decrease in the fertility level and later marriage, both of which contribute to improved female well-being. More females are participating in politics and administration. It seems that overall the political arena in Thailand is not for females, however – fewer than 10 per cent of politicians are females, which means that female interests are probably not well represented in the decision-making process at the national level.

The process of economic development renders females vulnerable to increased economic exploitation by subjecting them to gender biases. The traditional gender roles remain unchanged; for example, most females are still engaged in unpaid work, such as being homemakers and assisting with family businesses. In addition, female workers receive lower pay than do males. Therefore, there is a need for appropriate institutions to safeguard female well-being.

In terms of religion, female monks remain a controversial issue in Thai society. We suggest that the lack of female monks is not because of Buddhist injunctions. Interpretation of rules is heavily dependent on the expertise and personal prejudice of the interpreters, who are often males who reinforce the patriarchy of a socio-religious country. In 2003, Monk Prayom and S. Siwaluk, an outspoken social activist, spoke in favour of the existence of female monks in Thailand. It is also noteworthy that, with patriarchy pervading society, some women join in the debate, opposed to the idea of monks of their own gender. It is simply inappropriate to some that females should be elevated to the same status of respectability as that belonging to male monks.

The ultimate challenge for Thai female well-being is not simply to put females into the mainstream but to change the mainstream to reflect the well-being of females. This requires a practical change from national to local level. At the national level, the active participation of the government, political parties, pressure groups and the media is required in an effort to increase the number of women and men who are committed to addressing female well-being. There should be a more equal participation of females in many spheres of national development. Improvements need to be made for females in access to credit and technology; subordinate female roles need to be abolished and negative stereotypes lifted; and gender bias in the legislature needs to end.

Recently, there has been much discourse about the ideas of gender equality and female well-being. At the same time, many critics claim that these ideas are too Westernized. Rather, a practical knowledge of the everyday life of people is required. The integration of ideas generated by local wisdom and those of experts can change power relations at all levels of Thai society. This will be the challenge for twenty-first-century Thai females.

I have not encountered my female friend again, the one I referred to at the beginning of this chapter, but I hope that she enjoys the benefits of positive social change in Thailand in her own life. Throughout the last century, Thai females increased their visibility in the development process and advanced in well-being. (Farung Mee-Don)

Note

1 The authors express their gratitude to Dan Feng Qin, former fellow at WeD, University of Bath, for her diligent compilation of many of the statistical data for this chapter.

References

Sources in English

Baden, S. (1999) 'Economic reform and poverty: a gender analysis', briefing paper prepared for the Gender Equality Office, Swedish International Development Agency (SIDA)

Baker, S. (2000) *The Changing Situation of Child Prostitution in Northern Thailand: A Case Study of Changwat Chiang Rai*, Bangkok: Population Council

Blumberg, R. and F. Mee-Udon (2002) 'A "natural experiment" for gender stratification theory? The Lao of northeast Thailand and Laos', paper presented at the annual meeting of the American Sociological Association, Chicago

Costa, L. (1997) 'Exploring the history of women's education and activism in Thailand', *Journal of Asian Studies Student Association*, 1(1)

Ekachai, S. (1990) 'Voices from Isan', in *Behind the Smile: Voices from Thailand*, Bangkok: Post Publishing

ESCAP (Economic and Social Commission for Asia and the Pacific) (1998) *Women in Thailand: A Country Profile*, New York: ESCAP

GDRI (Gender and Development Research Institute) (1999) *GDRI Pamphlet*, Bangkok: GDRI

Keyes, C. F. (1991) 'The proposed world of the school', in *Reshaping Local Worlds: Formal Education and Cultural Change in Rural Southeast Asia*, New Haven, CT: Yale University Press

Kirsch, T. A. (1975) 'Economy, polity and religion in Thailand', in T. A. Sharp et al. (eds), *Change and Persistence in Thai Society*, Ithaca, NY: Cornell University Press

Knodel, J. (1994) 'Gender and schooling in Thailand', <www.popcouncil.org/publications/wp/prd/60.html>

Mee-Udon, F. (2000) *Thai Women's Participation in Local Politics*, PhD dissertation, Brighton: University of Sussex

— (2003) 'Gender roles in local politics in the northeast of Thailand', paper presented at the workshop 'Socio-economics and Political Transitions in Northeast Thailand', May, Kyoto University, Japan

Muscat, R. J. (1990) *Thailand and the United States: Development, Security, and Foreign Aid*, New York: Columbia University Press

NCWA (National Commission on Women's Affairs) (1996) *The National Commission on Women's Affairs*, Bangkok: Amarin Printing Group

NESDB (National Economic and Social Development Board) (1997) *The Eighth National Economic and Social Development Plan* (1997–2001), Bangkok: NESDB

NSO (National Statistical Office) (1973) *1970 Population and Housing Census*, Whole Kingdom, Bangkok: National Statistical Office

— (1980) *1978 Agricultural Census Report, Thailand. Whole Kingdom*, Bangkok: National Statistical Office

— (1983) *1980 Population and Housing Census: Whole Kingdom*, Bangkok: National Statistical Office

— (1997) *Report on the 1995–1996 Survey of Population Change*, Bangkok: National Statistical Office

— (2000) *Statistical Year Book* nos 15 (1920), 21 (1940), 22 (1950), 24 (1960), 29 (1970), 33 (1980), 39 (1990) and 48 (2002), Bangkok: National Statistical Office

Phongpaichit, P. (1987) 'The last resort to tourism', *Thai Development Newsletter*, 20: 11–14

Phongpaichit, P. and C. Baker (1995) *Thailand: Economics and Politics,* New York: Oxford University Press

— (1998) *Thailand's Boom and Bust*, Chiang Mai: Silkworm Books

Promphakping, B. (2000) *Rural Transformation and Gender Relations in the Northeast of Thailand*, PhD thesis, University of Bath

Somswasdi, V. (2003) 'Women's studies in Thailand', paper presented at UNESCO conference, Bangkok, December

Sonakul, S. (1959) 'The role of women in the development of Thailand', in W. Siwasari-yanon (ed.), *Aspects and Facets of Thailand*, Bangkok: Public Relations Department

Sopchokchai, O. et al. (1991) *Report on Women's Organizing Abilities: A Case Study of Sixteen Northeastern Villages in Thailand*, Bangkok: Thailand Development Research Institute Foundation

Thitsa, K. (1990) *Providence and Prostitution: Women in Buddhist Thailand*, London: Calverts Press

Thomson, S. and M. Bhongsvej (1995) *Putting Women's Concerns on the Political Agenda,* Bangkok: GDRI

UN (United Nations) (1948) *UN Demographic Year Book*, New York: United Nations

UNDP (United Nations Development Programme) (1996) *Human Development Report*, New York: Oxford University Press

UNDP and UNIFEM (United Nations Development Programme and United Nations Development Fund for Women) (2000) *Gender and Development: Facts and Figures*, Bangkok and London: Calverts Press

Vella, W. F. (1978) *Chaiyo! King Vajiravudh and the Development of Thai Nationalism*, Honolulu: University Press of Hawaii

Warr, P. G. (1998) 'Thailand: the troubled economies', in H. M. Ross and G. Ross (eds), *East Asia in Crisis: From Being a Miracle to Needing One?* London: Routledge

World Bank (1998) *East Asia: The Road to Recovery*, Washington, DC: World Bank

Yoddumnern-Attig et al. (1992) *Changing Roles and Statuses of Women in Thailand: A Documentary Assessment*, Bangkok: Institute for Population and Social Research, Mahidol University

Sources in Thai

Kabinlasing, C. (1998) 'Women and Buddhism', in NCWA, *Women Studies I: Women's Issues*, Bangkok: Khu Ru Sa Pha

Mee-Udon, F. (1997) 'Princess Diana, Queen of our hearts, and Mother Teresa, our angel', *Journal of Women's Studies*, 3(2)

— (1998) 'The constitution and new election system', training manual for female members of administrative sub-district

— (2003) 'Equality and inequality', paper presented at Workshop on Well-being in Developing Countries, Bangkok

Ministry of Interior (1999) 'The result of the 18 July 1999 National Election SAO', *Journal of SAOs*, 4(19): 1

Vantanee, W. and H. Sunee (1998) 'Value and attitudes of Thai society that affect the institution of the family and society', in *What Thai Society Expects from Women*, Bangkok: Thai Khadi Research Institute

Websites

Agence France-Press (2003) *Thailand-AIDS-UN: Life Expectancy in Thailand Drops as AIDS Takes Heavy Toll*, <www.aegis.com/ news/afp/2003>

Asian Development Bank (ADB) (2004) 'Demographic indicators, table 2', *Key Indicators of Developing Asian and Pacific Countries*, <www.adb.org>

Association for the Promotion of the Status of Females, www.apsw-thailand.org>

CIDA (Canadian International Development Agency) (2001) *Gender Profile: Thaïland*, <www.cida.gc.ca>

DOLA (Department of Local Administration) (1999), <www.dola.go.th.

GDRI (Gender and Development Research Institute) (2000–2001), <www.gdri.org>

GT (Government of Thailand) (1996) *Prostitution Prevention and Suppression Act*, <www.tat.or.th/visitor/prostit.htm>

IPSR (Institute for Population and Social Research) (1995) 'Prostitution and migration', <www.seameo.org/vl/migrate/migrate1.htm>

Ministry of Education (n.d.) *History of Thai Education*, <www.moe.go.th>

MPH (Ministry of Public Health) (n.d.), <www.moph.go.th>

NCFA (National Commission on Female Affairs) (n.d.), <www.inet.co.th/org/tncwa>

Prachuabmoh, V. and P. Mithranon (2003) *Below-Replacement Fertility in Thailand and Its Policy Implications,* <www.articles.findarticles.com>

Suriyasarn, B. (1993) 'Roles and status of Thai women: from past to present', <www.busakorn.addr.com/women>

Thaibhikkunis (2002) <www.thaibhikkhunis.org/english>

Thai Government (2000) *Suicide Rate in Thailand Rising,* <www.aegis.com/news>

TNITC (Thailand National Information Technology Committee) (2000) *IT2000*, <www.nitc.go.th/it-2000>

UN (United Nations) (2004) *Statistics and Indicators on Women and Men*, <www.unstats.un.org/unsd>

<www.avert.org/aidsthai.htm>

13 | Women in the United Kingdom: the impacts of immigration, 1900–2000

ERICA HALVORSEN AND HEATHER EGGINS

Like every other industrialized country, the United Kingdom (UK) changed beyond recognition in the twentieth century. Change is reflected in the proportion of women in the workplace, the ethnic composition of the population, and the effects of educational achievement. From 'foreigners' making up less than 1 per cent of the population in 1900, to 'visible ethnic minorities' comprising almost 8 per cent in 2000, the century has marked an irreversible shift in what it is to be British and live in the UK. There has been official recognition that the nation is no longer composed of a white, homogenous group. While the UK census still records those who were born overseas ('foreigners'), in 1991 the form requested the first information on ethnicity, followed by religion in 2001. Immigration from the former colonies has had an impact on many aspects of British life, including the nation's favourite food – chicken tikka masala.

In 1901, very few women entered the workforce from anything other than economic necessity. Careers tended to be incompatible with marriage. A century later, the majority of women work and professional women accommodate childbearing within their career aspirations. The change in the nature of work and the introduction of new technologies decreased the requirement for physical strength, which opened many occupational doors to women. Traditional concepts of men's and women's work are dissolving.

In this chapter, we examine the impact of immigration on life in the UK, especially as it applies to changes in the roles and work of the country's women. Immigration has been an aspect of mainland British life for thousands of years and is generally divided into four periods leading up to 1900: first, the age of invasions until the eleventh century; second, continental (European) tradesmen, craftsmen and Jews during the high and late Middle Ages; third, religious refugees, economic newcomers and slaves, c.1500–1650; and fourth, a significant take-off in a variety of groups from the mid-seventeenth century until 1815 (Panayi 1994: 10).

The largest immigrant group to Britain during the mid- and late 1800s was from Ireland, largely owing to poverty and famine. Even though many different nationalities and ethnicities lived in Britain at the end of the nineteenth century, they were a very small minority presence. During the first half of the twentieth century, the majority of immigrants came as political and religious refugees from mainland Europe. Immigration in the last fifty years was mainly from the countries of the British Commonwealth.

The first year of the century

Victoria, Queen of the United Kingdom of Great Britain and Ireland, and Empress of India, who died in 1901, was the descendant of relatively recent German immigrants on her father's side; her mother was also German. At the time of Victoria's death, there were no immigration restrictions in Britain, and 'foreigners', who were defined as people born outside the UK, were recorded in the 1901 census.

In 1901, 247,758 foreigners were living in England and Wales. The exact number of countries from which they emigrated is unknown. The majority came from continental Europe and were identified by country, but continental origin absorbed the national identity of the small number who arrived from Africa, the Americas (other than the United States) and Asia (other than China or Japan). The 1901 census did not record the foreigners' ethnicity or religion.

Religious belief was in large part responsible for the migration of at least some settlers in the UK. Many more passed through the UK on their way to a new life in the United States. For example, the assassination of Alexander II of Russia in 1881 resulted in pogroms in southern Russia against the Jewish community, many of whom fled. The greatest number of foreigners residing in England and Wales in 1901 came from Russia, the majority of them Jewish (Panayi 1994). Many Russian Jews made their homes in the East End of London and either established or took up employment in the garment trade: 'The London tailoring trade was divided into two sections – the production of ladies' outerwear (dominated by male workers) and the production of men's and boys' outerwear (where women were an increasing proportion of the workforce)' (Morris 1986: 10). In 1901, 4 per cent of all female workers in the garment industry were foreign born. Men predominated in skilled tailoring, while women were consigned to work as machinists, hand sewers and finishers.

The majority of foreign women workers aged ten and over, including students, were employed in private homes as domestic indoor servants or were not employed at all. Many of them were the wives of male immigrants and, probably in a much smaller proportion, UK nationals. For example, there were about 30,000 Russian, Polish and German married women in England and Wales compared to 40,000 married men of the same national origin, indicating that these foreign men were more likely to marry a UK national than their countrywomen. Skilled female employment in the form of teaching was undertaken primarily by French, German and Swiss women, which may explain why France is the only country to have a greater number of unmarried female than male immigrants to the UK. In the first years of the century, the impact that female immigration had on British society overall was minimal; most worked in domestic and office services, and the numbers were small, according to the Census for England and Wales of 1901. Within immigrant communities, the impact was undoubtedly larger.

Restrictions on immigration

In direct reaction to the influx of Jews into the country, the first immigration restrictions were introduced in the Aliens Act (1905) against 'undesirable aliens', who were defined as paupers, lunatics, vagrants and prostitutes. Asylum seekers were not affected by the act, but the diseased and criminal could be refused entry. The Aliens Restriction Act imposed further immigration controls at the outbreak of the First World War in 1914. Designed to prevent the entry of enemy aliens into the UK, this act was reinforced post-war by the Aliens Act (1919) and was supplemented by the Home Secretary's Order of Council (1920). Under the order, a work permit was a prerequisite for entry to the UK, and those who could not support themselves were forbidden to enter the country. The legislation was applied selectively; labour shortages enabled the entry of Belgian refugees during the First World War and West Indian workers were actively recruited during the Second World War. The rules were relaxed somewhat just before the Second World War, when the British government acknowledged the persecution of Jews by the Nazis and allowed 55,000 to seek refuge in the UK. In the six previous years, the law had been strictly applied and only 11,000 refugees had been admitted.

Admitting Commonwealth citizens to the UK

The Victorian legacy of the British Empire evolved to become the Commonwealth of Nations in the third decade of the twentieth century. Members of the Commonwealth included India, Australia, the British West Indies, Canada, Nigeria, Uganda, Pakistan, Ceylon (now Sri Lanka), Malta and Malaysia. In 1948, the British Nationality Act conferred the status of British subject on all Commonwealth citizens, enabling their migration to the UK. Jamaican immigrants arrived on HMS *Windrush* in the same year the act was passed, but immigration from the West Indies was initially only a trickle until the early 1950s; by 1961 it had risen to over 74,000. Between 1952 and 1961, almost

290,000 people came from the islands of the Caribbean to settle in Britain. In subsequent years, both the absolute and relative volume of West Indian immigration decreased (Tranter 1996: 30). At the same time, immigration from the Indian sub-continent was increasing.

Britain had been regarded as a liberal country during unsettled periods in Europe, but it had not been devoid of prejudice and intolerance. Anti-Semitism had featured over the centuries and Jews were stereotyped as Faginesque figures. Even though attacks against Jews had never taken on the proportions of those perpetrated by the Nazis, there had been significant anti-Semitic feeling in the 1930s. In 1958, Britain experienced its first race riots in Notting Hill, London, and in the Midlands. This manifest increase in racial tension, and growing unemployment, resulted in the ending of the open-door policy for former British colonial subjects by the passing of the Commonwealth and Immigration Act (1962). Subsequently, Commonwealth citizens were required to apply to enter the country under the same conditions as any other foreign national (except those who had a work permit or were dependants of British citizens).

Immigration controls became more stringent as the century progressed, in response to specific changes in the former colonies. For example, the British Nationality Act (1990) limited immigration from Hong Kong to 50,000 key workers and their dependants. Generally speaking, the majority of immigrants in the first half of the twentieth century came to the UK because conditions in their own countries were intolerable. Persecution drove Jews to Britain and the Second World War saw a considerable increase in the number of non-Jewish Poles in the UK. The Polish government was re-established in London in 1939, after Poland fell to the Germans, and the Polish armed forces used Britain as a base to regroup and re-form. In the immediate post-war period, the Polish presence grew with the arrival of thousands of prisoners of war, political prisoners, members of Polish military families and European Volunteer Workers (Peach et al. 1988). Though migration to Britain from mainland Europe because of the war was not confined to Poles, they comprised the largest single national group. Effectively, both the Jews and the Poles were refugees forced from their homelands and pushed towards other countries, in this case Britain. Before the influx of asylum seekers from central Europe and the Middle East at the end of the century, East African Asians and Vietnamese were the two most significant groups to come to Britain as refugees.

The second half of the century saw a surge in immigration for economic reasons. Initially, targeted recruitment in the New Commonwealth countries to combat labour shortages in Britain encouraged immigration.

The last year of the century

At the end of the twentieth century it could no longer be said that immigrant women had no impact on British society overall. Ethnic minorities have changed the demographic profile of the country, and their influence has permeated almost every level of society. Post-war immigration transformed Britain into a multiracial, multi-cultural society. The fastest-growing ethnic group in the UK is mixed race. In the 1990s the number of mixed race people grew by more than 75 per cent, making mixed race people 10 per cent of the total ethnic minority population in the UK (John 2002), but they are still less numerous than the other ethnic groups considered here, except Chinese. By 2000, nearly 8 per cent of the population was non-white. 'The number of people who came from an ethnic group other than White grew by 53% between 1991 and 2001, from 3 million in 1991 to 4.6 million in 2001' (ONS 2004). About half of the non-white population was of Asian origin, a quarter was black, 15 per cent were of mixed race, and the remaining 10 per cent were from Chinese and 'other' ethnic groups.

The present queen, Elizabeth, a direct descendant of Queen Victoria, is regarded as British. In 2000, the majority of ethnic minority people living in Britain were born in the UK. The questions being asked now do not revolve around the effects of immigration assimilation.

Economic participation

The division of labour It would be facilely dismissive, and incorrect, to homo-genize the immigrant groups. Each has brought elements of its own culture to Britain and each has defined the role of women and the division of labour within its own as well as wider British society. The implications of gendered expectations within some of these cultures have affected society in a number of different ways. For example, they have influenced achievement and aspiration among British-born blacks; created cultural diasporas; and perpetuated the traditional roles of women from within their societies. Other ethnic groups have encouraged both boy and girl children to dispense with traditional expectations and promote themselves within British culture.

Women's participation in the labour force

TYPES OF OCCUPATION 'At the beginning of the 20th century, around five million women worked, making up 29% of the total workforce. By 2000, the figure had risen to 13 million, 46 percent of the total workforce [in Great Britain]' (Lindsay 2003: 133). Many reasons exist for this increase, including economic necessity, changing social attitudes towards women working outside the home, availability of contraception, and increased levels of female education. The decline in industry and the switch to a service-based culture provided women with the most opportunities: ' ... one major change over the last century was the shift in industrial composition, with the decline of agriculture and manufacturing's share of total employment and the rise of services. In the UK, manufacturing's share fell from 28 to 14% of employment, and agriculture's share from 11 to 2% ... service sector employment increase[d] from 21 to 32%' (ibid.: 137). These estimates exclude transport, communications, commerce and finance sectors, which could increase the proportions employed in services from 34 per cent in 1901 to 70 per cent in 1991.

There is near equality of representation between the two sexes in the workplace across all ethnic groups. Overall, men still outnumber women by just over 1.5 million, and obviously do so within most of the ethnic groups. The exception is the black community. It is the only ethnic group in which more women than men work. For the purposes of the English and Welsh census returns, black encompasses Black Caribbean, Black African and Other Black. Black Caribbean is the majority group and its members make up 55 per cent of the total; followed by Black African, 38 per cent; and Other Black, 7 per cent.

As Black Caribbeans are the most numerous group within the black community, one of the reasons why more black women than men work might be the legacy of slavery: 'The West Indian population had never absorbed the ethos of the male breadwinner. Under colonial rule, the slave master took responsibility for meeting material needs, rather than individual male slaves' (Bruley 1999: 175). In some cases, this pattern appears to have had a detrimental effect on the educational and occupational attainment levels of the black community. Both black working women and men are the least likely of any of the broad ethnic groups to be employed in a managerial capacity. Black men are the most likely group to be engaged in the lowest of the Standard Occupational Categories (SOCS) – elementary occupations. Even though black women are unlikely to be in the top two categories, over 60 per cent of them are represented in the top four categories. They have the highest proportional representation in associate professional and technical occupations, as well as administrative and secretarial ones.

Chinese people make up only 0.4 per cent of the working population in England and Wales, yet if a Chinese woman works, then she is more likely than her white, Asian, black or mixed race sisters to be a manager or senior official. If she is not a manager, then she is still more likely than a female member of any other ethnic group to be in a professional or technical occupation. In fact, nearly half of all Chinese working women are employed in the top three

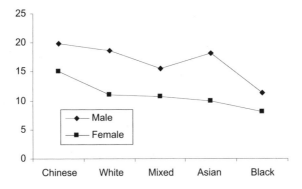

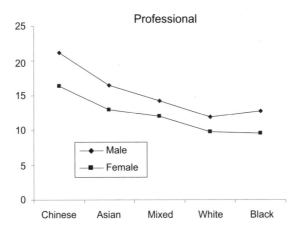

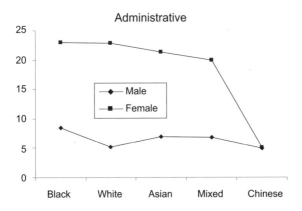

Figure 13.1 Employment level by ethnic group and gender, 2001 (per cent)
Source: **ONS (2001)**

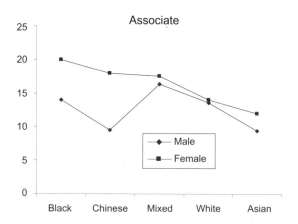

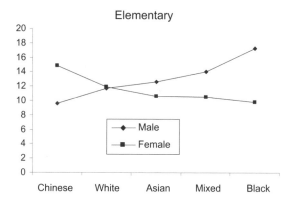

Figure 13.1 Employment level by ethnic group and gender, 2001 (per cent) (cont.)

SOCs. Chinese men do equally well, though there are proportionally slightly more of them in the top two categories, managerial and professional, than there are women. Figure 13.1 shows employment classifications for 2001, by gender and ethnic group, ordered left to right by highest female percentage in each classification.

Women's level of representation in some of the major occupational groups is illustrative of the advances they have made, particularly in the professional occupations, which include science and technology, health, teaching and research, and business and public services. It is from this pool that the next generation of managers and senior officials will be drawn.

Given the growth in women's representation at this level, it is likely that in 2011 (the next UK census date) women's representation at the top of the professions will have increased further (Table 13.1).

TABLE 13.1 Women in major occupational groups, 1911–2001 (%)

	1911	1931	1951	1961	1981	2001
Managers and senior officials	19.8	13	15.2	15.5	21.4	34
Professionals	6	7.5	8.3	9.7	13	41
Associate professional and technical	62.9	58.8	53.5	50.8	55	47
Administrative and secretarial	21.4	46	60.2	65.2	78.1	78
Sales	35.2	37.2	51.6	54.9	77.8	71

Sources: Peach et al. (1988); ONS (2001).

In England and Wales in 2000, 3.1 per cent of the workforce was made up of non-white women and 42.8 per cent were white women. If levels of representation in the whole workforce are taken as the benchmark against which under- or over-representation in each occupation is measured, then it would appear that it is sex, rather than ethnicity, which is the more discriminatory factor (Table 13.2).

TABLE 13.2 Women in the workforce by occupation, 2000 (%)

Occupation	Women in occupation	White women in occupation	Non-white women in occupation	Proportion of total workforce in occupation
Managers and senior officials	34	31.7	2.3	15.1
Professionals	41	37.8	3.1	11.1
Associate professional and technical	47	43.4	3.6	13.8
Administrative and secretarial	78	73.1	4.8	13.3
Skilled trade occupations	10	9	1	11.6
Personal service occupations	84	79.3	4.7	6.9
Sales and customer service occupations	71	66.1	4.9	7.7
Process, plant and machine operatives	17	15.2	1.8	8.5
Elementary occupations	46	43	3	11.9

Source: ONS (2001).

UNEMPLOYMENT The converse of what is seemingly a success story for certain groups of immigrants in the UK is that a disproportionate number of people from ethnic groups other than white are unemployed. In the broad

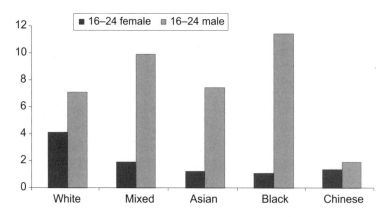

Figure 13.2 Unemployment by gender and race, 16-24 years old (per cent)
Source: **CEW (2001)**

ethnic categories, of people aged twenty-five and over, black women and black men are the most likely to be unemployed, followed by mixed race men and women (Figures 13.2 and 13.3). White men and women are the least likely to be unemployed. Being unemployed in Census 2001 terms is different from being economically inactive. It does not include those who are permanently sick or disabled, or people looking after a home or family.

Income and poverty Women's place within hierarchies is still somewhat resistant to change, as is the amount they are paid compared to men.

Literacy and education

The level of occupation appears to reflect the level of educational attainment. In the mid-1990s, nearly half of sixteen-to-twenty-four–year-old ethnic

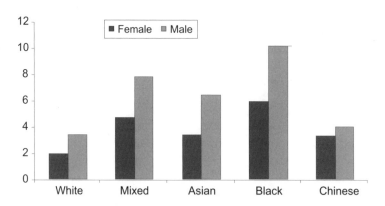

Figure 13.3 Unemployment by gender and race, over 25 years old (per cent)
Source: **CEW (2001)**

minority women were in full- or part-time education, compared with about a third of white women. Chinese women had the highest participation rate at 66 per cent and Black Caribbean women the lowest, just slightly lower than white women (CRE 1997).

Literacy, school completion and employment In 1900, compulsory full-time education ended at the age of twelve, when children were allowed to work half-time. The statutory leaving age was raised to fourteen in 1921, fifteen in 1947, and sixteen in 1972–73. In 1900–1901 there were 25,000 students in full-time higher education, and in 1923 women students obtained 23 per cent of all first degrees. By 2000, women were as likely as men were to obtain a first degree. In the first years of the twenty-first century, more women than men are graduating from Britain's universities and colleges of higher education.

The high proportion of Chinese women in tertiary education is a relatively recent phenomenon. In the mid-1980s, the vast majority were employed in the family business – the Chinese takeaway or restaurant. In 1985, a British government report 'estimated that about 90% of Britain's Chinese were employed in the catering industry and that of these, perhaps 60% were employed in small family shops' (Baxter and Raw 1988: 58). Such an occupation was isolating for immigrant women, who often spoke little English. There was no incentive for them to venture outside the Chinese community. Their British-born children, however, shunned the family businesses. Fluency in the language and assimilation into British culture through schooling, at least, provided them with the broader horizons that can be attained through education.

The selective nature of the Hong Kong Act 1990 also contributed to the raising of the level of educational attainment within the community, as only those who fell within four distinct categories were admitted to the UK. Not surprisingly, the four classes that were identified as being eligible by the British government contained those from professional backgrounds, entrepreneurs, essential workers (police, fire and prison officers), and those who might be vulnerable owing to the nature of the work they had been engaged in under the British regime.

The Chinese population of England and Wales has demonstrated that in a thirty-year period the educational attainment levels within an immigrant community can be absolutely reversed. Forty-five per cent of Chinese people aged between fifty and fifty-nine have no academic qualifications whatsoever. Of those aged between twenty-five and thirty-four, 63 per cent have a first degree, or higher, or equivalent professional qualification. The result is that fifteen years after the government report (ibid.), family-owned Chinese businesses are finding it difficult to continue. Second- and third-generation British Chinese people have made opportunities outside the home, with women almost as numerous as men in the workplace and achieving near-parity of status.

Like the Chinese population, most black people who have no educational qualification are in the fifty-to-fifty-nine age group. Proportionally fewer blacks than Chinese, however, are in this position. While the proportion of Chinese without qualifications drops the younger they are, the proportion of blacks does not show such a consistent decline. Fifteen per cent of those in the thirty-five-to-forty-nine age group have no qualifications, about the same proportion as those in the sixteen-to-twenty-four age group; just over 10 per cent of those in between have no qualification. Between the ages of twenty-five and fifty-nine, about a third have a degree, degree equivalent or higher qualification. Black Africans are more likely to have a degree in every age grouping than Black Caribbeans.

ETHNICITY AND EDUCATION Asians are defined as being of Indian, Pakistani, Bangladeshi or Other Asian origin. A complicating factor of their integration into British society has been religious belief. Great Britain is historically a Christian country and its official holidays are scheduled around the Christian calendar. Its official places of worship were all churches and chapels until 1657, when the first synagogue was built after Oliver Cromwell readmitted Jews to the country. Over two centuries later, the first mosque was opened in Liverpool, in 1889. In 2000, there were nearly a million Pakistani and Bangladeshi Muslims living in England and Wales, and a quarter of a million white Jews (ONS 2003). (There were also nearly half a million Indian Hindus and a third of a million Indian Sikhs.) It is Muslims, however, who have been the subject of most debate, and about whom there are possibly the most misconceptions, particularly regarding the education of young women. Polly Toynbee, social commentator and journalist, argued against state-funded Muslim schools because they could unwittingly support educating children to believe that females are inferior. This claim was refuted by the Ugandan Asian author and journalist, Yasmin Alibhai-Brown: ' ... in my Muslim community, way back in 1951, our Imam issued an edict, which was immediately followed, that every family should educate their daughters first and then their sons because the world was male and boys would find a way of making it. [...] in some Muslim communities, the proportion of university-educated women is significantly higher than the national average' (Alibhai-Brown 2001: 14–15). Neither is wholly right or wholly wrong. Alibhai-Brown goes on to discuss *inter alia* arranged marriages and the 'place' of the Muslim women within some homes; she intends her writing to provoke wider debate about the nature of New Britain and Britishness. Her claims for the achievements of Asian Muslim women are not entirely corroborated, at least in the workplace.

Including Hindus and Sikhs, Asian women are almost as likely to be employed as managers as white women. When the figures are broken down, however, Indian women are more likely to be managers than white women are, while Pakistanis and Bangladeshis are less so. Both groups are more likely to be found in professional occupations than are white women. Asian men have the same level of proportional representation as managers as white men, but again, when the figures are investigated a little more, the same result emerges: Indian men are more likely to be managers than white men are; Pakistanis and Bangladeshis are less likely. Pakistani and Bangladeshi men, however, are less likely to be in professional occupations than are white men. Indian men are more likely to be employed thus. Like the Chinese, Asians have consistently raised their level of educational attainment, with the highest proportion of any ethnic group having no qualification in the fifty-to-fifty-nine age range, at 46 per cent, to the second-highest proportion with a first degree, higher or equivalent among those aged twenty-five to thirty-four (Table 13.3).

TABLE 13.3 Ethnic group with no qualifications versus those with a degree (%)

Age	White None	White Degree	Mixed None	Mixed Degree	Asian None	Asian Degree	Black None	Black Degree	Chinese None	Chinese Degree
16–24	16	11	18	10	17	15	15	11	9	25
25–35	11.7	28	12	31	27	42	11	35.9	11.2	63

Source: ONS (2001). 'Degree' = Level 4/5: first degree, higher degree, NVQ levels 4–5, HNC, HND, qualified teacher status, qualified medical doctor, qualified dentist, qualified nurse, midwife, health visitor, or equivalent.

Towards gender equality

Other explanations emerge beyond educational achievement for the relative positions held by women in the workplace. Since the arrival of the non-white immigrant population in Britain, there have been many examples of overt and subtle discrimination by employers. Discrimination has probably had the effect of limiting opportunities for at least some non-whites, and they are generally under-represented in positions that are more senior. Britain now has among the most comprehensive race laws in Europe, which were bolstered in the Race Relations (Amendment) Act of 2001. This act was passed in response to the racist murder of the black teenager Stephen Lawrence and the ensuing inquiry into institutional racism in the police force. One of its main provisions is that it imposes a 'positive duty' on public sector employers to promote good race relations. These employers are now required to monitor their workforces and assess the potential impact of all their policies and practices on all staff to ensure that they are not being unwittingly, or otherwise, discriminatory to any ethnic group.

As discussed above, the proportion of non-white people (primarily second- and third-generation immigrants to the UK) with a degree-level qualification is higher in some age groups, most notably the twenty-five-to-thirty-five category. This has obvious implications for the representation of non-whites in the professions, and also for their position within them. Non-white women face the possibility of being doubly discriminated against – for their sex and their ethnicity. Thus, even though women from different ethnic backgrounds may not experience the same cultural pressures within the home, once they are in the workplace their situation is broadly the same. There are marked occupational gender divisions; women predominate in administrative and secretarial roles, personal service occupations, and sales. Gender neutrality is creeping up the occupational ladder, however, and the higher professions are edging towards parity of male/female representation. As a measure of the extent to which immigrant communities are integrated into British society, it can be expected in future that non-white women will become leaders and enter the professions at roughly the same rate as white women. Progression appears to be slowed by sexism but, when that is overcome, the impact of immigration on the UK and on women's lives during the twentieth century will become more apparent.

References

Alibhai-Brown, Y. (2001) *Who Do We Think We are?*, London: Penguin

Baxter, S and G. Raw (1988) 'Fast food, fettered work: Chinese women in the catering industry', in S. Westwood and P. Bhachu (eds), *Enterprising Women*, London: Routledge

Bruley, S. (1999) *Women in Britain Since 1900*, Basingstoke: Macmillan

CRE (Commission for Racial Equality) (1997) *Ethnic Minority Women*, CRE factsheet, London: CRE

Lindsay, C. (2003) 'A century of labour market change: 1900 to 2000', in *Labour Market Trends*, London: Office for National Statistics

Morris, J. (1986) 'The characteristics of sweating: the late 19th-century London and Leeds tailoring trade', in A. V. John (ed.), *Unequal Opportunities, Women's Employment in England 1800-1918*, Oxford: Basil Blackwell

ONS (Office for National Statistics) (2001) Census for England and Wales, London: Office for National Statistics

Panayi, P. (1994) *Immigration, Ethnicity and Racism in Britain 1915–1945*, Manchester: Manchester University Press

Peach, C. et al. (1988) 'Immigration and ethnicity', in A. H. Halsey (ed.), *British Social Trends Since 1900*, Basingstoke: Macmillan

Tranter, N. L. (1996) *British Population in the 20th Century*, Basingstoke: Macmillan

Websites

CEW (Census for England and Wales) (2001), <www.statistics.gov.uk/census2001/>

John, C. (2002) *Changing Face of Britain: Britain's Blurring Ethnic Mix*, BBC Online <www.news.bbc.co.uk>

ONS (Office for National Statistics) (2003) *Ethnicity and Religion*, National Statistics Online, <www.statistics.gov.uk>

— (2004) *People and Migration*, National Statistics Online, <www.statistics.gov.uk>

Women in the UK

14 | Women in the United States of America: the struggle for economic citizenship

LAURA KHOURY

> Woman is the gate of the devil, the path of wickedness, the sting of the serpent, in a word, a perilous object. (St Jerome, fourth-century Latin Church father)

The past century

This chapter demonstrates how over the past century women in the United States have made some advances – economic, educational and political – but their gains were accompanied by shortfalls. American women are far from attaining equality. We address gender and power in American politics, education and women's changing contributions to the labour force, in order to understand which socio-economic and political factors have interacted over time to produce positive or negative change in female well-being over the century. A historical context will assist in this analysis.

1900–40 Women's history in the early-twentieth-century USA was marked by the growing participation of women in the labour force, especially among married women after the Second World War. The evolution occurred independently of any organized women's movement, and resulted in a gradual shift in women's role from 'stay-at-home mom' and homemaker to working mother in the formal labour force. The seeds for this shift were planted at the beginning of the century, starting with a reform impulse on the part of Theodore Roosevelt (president 1901–1909), followed by William H. Taft (1909–13) and Woodrow Wilson (1913–21).

Indeed, the early 1900s were marked by continuing industrialization led by the 'robber barons', technological development, the consolidation of corporations and trusts, and rapid urbanization. About three hundred new industrial trusts began making vast accumulations of capital by consolidating industries. This made the burgeoning cities the centre of activity. New industries invited increased women's participation in paid labour in the cities – and sometimes opposition in the form of strikes. In support of women wage earners, a strike in 1909 in New York was followed by others in which women participated, for example, the 1912 strike in Lawrence, Massachusetts.

During the First World War, 16,000 women were mobilized for the first time to serve in the armed forces with the American Expeditionary Force, 1917–19. The Women in Industry Service, originally a governmental office, was established in 1920 and developed the first standards for employing women workers. What came to be the Women's Bureau was a war agency for the Department of Labor. Unskilled women worked as servants in the homes of the rising 'nouveau riche' and in factories, food processing and textiles. Educated women were able to work as teachers and nurses, both emphasizing traditionally female roles. On the other hand, farmers shared least in the increased well-being, although mechanization changed farming. Droves of men and women left the farms during the Depression.

The progressive reform early in the century aimed at privatizing the nuclear family by imposing middle-class norms. The 'welfare system aimed to relieve single mothers of the need to work full-time ... Mothers' Pensions, similarly, were made contingent on a woman's display of middle-class norms about privacy and domesticity' (Coontz 1992: 135–7).

Coming out of the First World War, an explosion of affluence for the middle class, with the popularization of automobiles and electric appliances, gave women more leisure, as illustrated by women's fashion. The beginning of the century was marked by the Jazz Age – exemplified in the 'flapper', a young woman who was often thought of as sexually liberated, opposing the older generation, with short hair, baggy dresses exposing her arms and knees, and wearing make-up. Though the International Women's Day originated in the first decade of the twentieth century, it resulted in few advances for American women. The views of suffragists in the 1920s, predominantly middle-class women, influenced women's opportunities.

During the 1930s, the Depression (which began in 1929) forced many more married women into employment as men were laid off or experienced wage cuts. The federal government mandated, however, that married women should be the first to be fired in cutbacks; twenty-six states passed laws prohibiting their employment. Coontz contends that the Great Depression 'temporarily expanded the value and amount of women's household work, reducing the relative returns of full time employment' (ibid.: 159). In the 1930s, only single, lower-class women were allowed to work. A powerful campaign against women in public life was evident; as soon as they married, they were automatically fired. This was true even in the profession of teaching.

The New Deal, a collection of 'social cushion' acts championed by President Franklin D. Roosevelt and passed by the US Congress in the famous '100 days' of 1933, and the Social Security Act of 1935, 'related to men as if they were all independent wage earners in the market and to women as if they were all dependent caregivers in the family' (ibid.: 138). The Social Security Act specifically redefined the recipient as the worker and 'his' family. Most women received benefits only through their husbands – and many discovered later that if the relationship lasted less than twenty years, they ended up with no benefits at all. Kessler-Harris (2003) traced the impact of a gender bias in the unemployment insurance policies, the fair labour standards, federal income tax policy, and in the new discussion of women's rights that emerged after the Second World War.

The Second World War (1941–45) The Japanese attack on Pearl Harbor on 7 December 1941 brought the USA into the Second World War (which started in Europe in 1939) and transformed the lives and roles of American women. Men joined or were drafted into the armed forces, so war industries demanded new workers to replace them. Women's employment became a necessity as they became the family breadwinners. The image of 'Rosie the Riveter' – the woman working in the steel industry, making weapons and tanks – became a familiar one on posters and in magazines. Through the Selective Training and Service Act of 1940, women took on male jobs such as welding, aircraft assembly-line work and shipbuilding. Married and middle-class women joined the labour force with alacrity. Millions of women were also recruited into the Women's Land Army (WLA) to provide a steady labour supply for American farms. More Americans considered themselves part of the middle class.

After the Second World War and the 1950s Though the war gave many women some upward occupational mobility, many married women pulled back following the war. Against all expectations, however, many women wanted to stay in their jobs. The 'cold war' between the USA and the Union of Soviet Socialist Republics that unfolded after the war brought prosperity when the USA consolidated its position as the world's richest country. The gross national product jumped dramatically.

The 1950s proved to be a friendlier economic and social environment, an easier climate in which to feel hope for the family. The media, politicians and historians all contributed to sensationalizing the 'golden era' that followed the Great Depression of the 1930s and the disruptions of the Second World War. Not until the 1950s did employers begin to accommodate married women in their hiring practices. Rising real wages led more and more women into the public sphere.

The 1960s and 1970s In the 1960s, women continued to enter the labour force – before the rise of feminism. Certainly, working-class women have always worked. Aspirations for a higher standard of living led many lower-class women to delay marriage and financial necessity brought many into the labour market. The second wave feminist movement, which was percolating during the 1960s and crystallized in the early 1970s, appeared *after* the entry of women into the labour force, but it brought new attitudes towards such middle-class institutions as monogamy, marriage and the church. In fact, one of the principal mechanisms of the women's movement was the proliferation of 'consciousness raising' and support groups that challenged the myths of male dominance and female inferiority. The feminist movement spurred opportunities for middle-class white women, but did little to help women of colour or low-income women.

Maternal employment rose during this period, especially among single women with children under fifteen years old. The rationale after the Second World War was that a woman could work outside the home to help the family: the 'little woman' brought in 'pin money' and helped with the grocery bill. In the 1970s, however, the feminist movement inspired a critical step towards female independence and autonomy through the concept of work for women as intrinsically valuable for female self-actualization.

The 1980s and 1990s A recession marked the 1980s. The national debt almost tripled (partly because of cold war military spending on the arms race). This culminated in a major stock market crash on 19 October 1987, known as 'Black Monday'. Although the situation was the outcome of two decades of decline in real incomes, women's participation in the labour market increased dramatically. President Ronald Reagan committed himself to tax cuts, but the tax burden was shifted to more regressive payroll taxes and created severe cutbacks in public support programmes. This policy shift threw many middle- and lower-class families into poverty and cut services to those who were already in need of government assistance. The crash had differential effects according to social class.

In the last decade of the twentieth century, the government became more and more captive to the needs of corporate capitalism; power was concentrated in the hands of the few. The living standards of the American people were no better in the late 1990s than in the late 1980s, despite the increase in the productive capacity indicated by the growth in gross domestic product (Dye 1995).

A demographic portrait of American women[1]

All academic works inherently carry within them their specific weaknesses. This chapter is designed to mesh the heterogeneous female population under the label of 'American females', but women in the twentieth-century USA were far from being a homogeneous group. Rather, the fate of women in the USA during the twentieth century must be explored within the context of four main historical streams that pre-dated 1900 and set the stage for an extremely heterogeneous society in the twentieth century.

Numerous Native American tribes existed throughout the land for thousands of years; in most cases, their female economic citizenship was closer to equal than it was for their descendants or for the colonists and immigrants who came to America later. Many studies have documented the unique gender roles and status of Native American women in pre-contact times (e.g. Albers and Medicine 1983; Bales 1996; Bonvillain 1989; DeMallie 1983; Perdue 1998; Shoemaker 2001, 2002). Then the colonizing period of the 1600s and 1700s saw white British (and some Spanish or French) staking their claim in the 'New World', which resulted in conflict with and decimation of the Native Americans (see, e.g., Hubbard 1990). The colonists brought with them patriarchal values and a presumption of male superiority (Berkin 1997; Brown 1996; Norton 1997; Ulrich 1991).

The practice of slavery from colonial days through the Civil War in the 1860s had an enormous effect on the fate of black or African-American women during the twentieth century (Collins 1990). It also influenced subsequent race relations and patterns of racial and class discrimination. Additionally, massive waves of immigration from all over the world flooded American shores from the mid-1800s onwards (Daniels 1990; Ewen 1985; Gabaccia 1994; Leach 1995; Tanner 1995; Weatherford 1995).

In addition to Native Americans and the historical inclusion of African-Americans and Hispanics with the majority of white Europeans, starting in 1890 immigrants of other than white Western or northern European origins began to arrive. Slavs, Greeks, Russian Jews, eastern European Jews and Italians were trying to fit into an amalgam referred to in the first decades of the twentieth century as the 'melting pot'. Later in the century, immigrants came from Latin America, Asia, Africa and the former Soviet states, further complicating the ethnic, racial, cultural, religious, linguistic and political backgrounds of the country's citizenry. (The Census Bureau sets a limitation on comparing white women with black, Hispanic or Asian women. In 1910, the census divided the races into black, white and a third category that combined all others. Not until 1970 did the Census Bureau begin collecting information on Hispanics and some Asian groups. For the 2000 census, individuals could identify themselves as belonging to more than one race.)

Thus, by the beginning of the twentieth century, women were living the daily life of distinct cultural enclaves, on Indian reservations, in small towns, and especially in such bustling East Coast cities as Boston, New York and Philadelphia, and 'old' Midwestern cities such as Buffalo, Detroit, Cleveland and Chicago. To present data for American females from 1900 to 2000 is to mask the impressive ethnic diversity that lies at the very heart of this country. While all women in twentieth-century America suffered from gender oppression, certainly women of colour and poor women lived in a world of greater risk and less opportunity. As Patricia Hill Collins has argued in her analysis of African-American women, 'interlocking race, class, and gender oppression expands the focus of analysis from merely describing the similarities and differences distinguishing these systems of oppression and focuses greater attention on how they interconnect' (Collins 1990: 221). This is true for all women who live in a multi-ethnic, multiracial and/or multicultural society such as the USA. Nevertheless, our task in this chapter requires merging the socio-economic and political history of each sub-group of women and looking at the data for females in general – compared to males in general – which allows us the opportunity to capture the big picture of how women in the USA fared during the century.

IN SEARCH OF ECONOMIC CITIZENSHIP Another prominent thread that winds its way through the story of American women is the remarkable rise in their formal labour force participation during the twentieth century – and the fact that they were still not viewed as equal contributors to the economy or given full access to political power.

Women in the USA have gone from being persecuted as 'witches' in colonial days to fighting for economic equality throughout the twentieth century. When their labour has been indispensable, as during shortages of male labour during the world wars, the labour of American women was 'equal' in value to that of men. When the crisis receded, the general expectation was that women would leave the factory floor and return to the kitchen. Alice Kessler-Harris (2003) argues that women are historically limited by restrictions on economic opportunities, which then blocks their ability to attain full political status. It may be fair to say that American women, in general, left the twentieth century without full economic citizenship and entered the twenty-first century with less political influence than their education and numbers would suggest.

Urbanization Throughout the twentieth century, the US population became predominantly urban. The Census Bureau defined metropolitan for the first time in 1910, when 26.1 million people lived in nineteen metropolitan districts (urban and suburban), leaving 65.9 million people living in non-metropolitan areas (rural). By 1950, the US population had become predominantly metropolitan for the first time (USBC 2000: 32).

Metropolitan concentrations grew because of births and in-migration, as well as territorial expansion in the early part of the century. The cities grew with industrialization. After the Second World War, urbanization extended to suburbanization, as countless families took part in the 'white flight' to the suburbs in search of a small piece of land, a single-family home and fresh air. This movement was spurred by the construction of the interstate highway system under President Dwight D. Eisenhower in the early 1950s, increasing affluence, the GI bill for returning veterans (which included low-cost, no-down-payment home loans), the decline of the older central cities, and the general return to female domesticity. In 1950, there was a large gap between the metropolitan and non-metropolitan sex ratios, which steadily narrowed from 1950 to 1990 as females moved into urban areas.

Life expectancy The gap between female and male life expectancy increased significantly in every decade (Figure 14.1). Life expectancy for the female population, however, has been higher than that for the male population; the gap in life expectancy increased from 2.2 years in 1900 to 5.6 years in 2000, reflecting a steady widening since the beginning of the century.

The population aged sixty-five and older increased more than tenfold between 1900 and 2000. In the century's last decade, however, the proportion of the population aged sixty-five and older declined because of the low fertility of the late 1920s and early 1930s. Interestingly, the predominance of women

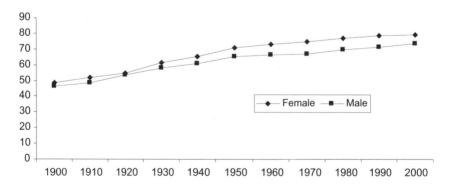

Figure 14.1 **Life expectancy (years)** *Source:* **USBC, decennial census of population, 1950 to 2000**

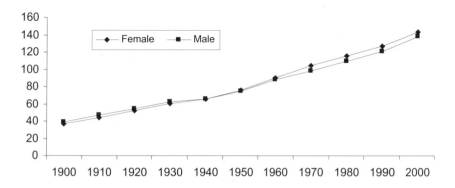

Figure 14.2 Proportion of males and females in the total population (millions) *Source:* **USBC (2000)**

is most pronounced among the elderly, especially among those eighty-five and older (ibid.).

Improvements in the quality of life of women, namely in health, were the most dramatic improvement of the twentieth century for all Americans, but gender-based differences in healthcare access persist. Women are still under-represented in federally funded clinical trials; they fall behind men in the probability of receiving major therapeutic procedures, proper diagnosis and appropriate treatment of disease. Many working women remain under-insured. It was not until 1993 that the Family and Medical Leave Act was finally passed by Congress, enabling women (and men) to take up to three months off in a twelve-month period to take care of family matters (such as childbirth) without losing their jobs.

Population growth, fertility rate and male–female ratio The US population tripled from 76 million in 1900 to 281 million in 2000, with females out-numbering males: out of 281.4 million people, 50.9 per cent were female and 49.1 per cent were male (Figure 14.2). In 1900, there was little or no variance between males and females. In the first fifty years of the century, the male population was slightly higher than the female population. The female population outgrew the male population around 1960. The change in the male–female ratio until 1980 resulted from the decline in female mortality rates, but 'the male–female ratio reversed its downward trend between 1980 and 1990 as male death rates declined faster than female rates and as immigration brought in more men' (USBC 2001: 1).

We can infer that the foremost reason for the reversal described above is demographic – the influx of male immigrants to the USA at the turn of the century exceeded the influx of female immigrants. That is, the foremost reason

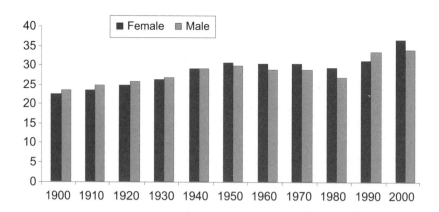

Figure 14.3 Median age of population (years)
Source: USBC

for males outnumbering females until the middle of the century was medical technology – changes in the mortality rate – as well as about 600,000 war dead among males during the 1940s.

Age structure of the population The median age steadily increased from 22.4 (females) and 23.3 years (males) in 1900 to 36.5 and 34.0 years respectively in 2000 (Figure 14.3). The median age for females in the first five decades was lower than that of the male population. In the second five decades, the median age of the female population was higher than that of the male population. In 1900, the age group one to five represents the largest five-year age group, but in 2000, people aged thirty-five to thirty-nine years outnumbered all other age groups (USBC 2000: 53) because of the post-Second World War baby boom.

The sizeable decline in fertility that continued through the Great Depression (caused by the stock market crash of 1929) changed the age composition (ibid.). In 1950, the group under age five was again the largest. One can imagine an age–sex pyramid with a large base but pinched in for both males and females because of the low fertility rate of the Depression years, as people born during the 1930s became ten to nineteen years old. By 2000, the so-called 'greying of America' resulted in part from sustained low fertility levels and from relatively larger declines in mortality at older ages that stemmed from technological developments in medicine. The pyramid is not even because the female proportion of the population became slightly larger, as more and more men were not returning from wars.

Maternal mortality rate The steady increase in female median age may be

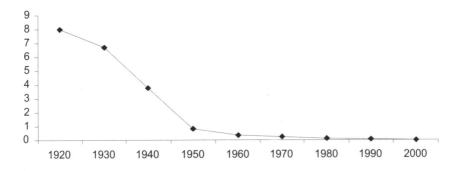

Figure 14.4 Maternal mortality rate (per 1,000 births)
Source: **USBC**

due, among many things, to the increase in life expectancy (Figure 14.1), and ageing of both individuals and the population. Another contribution, however, was the significant decline in maternal mortality rate from 80 per 1,000 in 1920 to 8 per 1,000 in 2000 (Figure 14.4), brought about by medical technology improvements and discoveries (such as antibiotics, safe Caesarean sections for difficult births, blood pressure medications, and better fetal monitoring), improved pre-natal and post-natal care, and an increasing proportion of mothers delivering their babies with the help of trained healthcare professionals.

Infant mortality rate The US infant mortality rate has declined significantly since the beginning of the century for the total population (Figure 14.5). The numbers declined from 171,000 in 1920 to 28,000 in 2000. The infant mortality rate for females was lower than for males in 2001 (6.3 per cent to 7.6 per cent) and lower than the rate for the total population by the end of the century (<www.cdc.gov/hiv/pubs/facts/women.htm>).

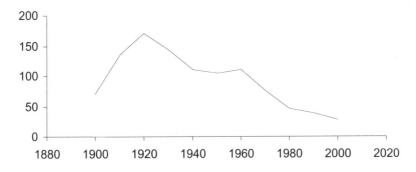

Figure 14.5 Infant mortality rate (per 1,000 live births)
Source: **USBC (2001)**

Women in the USA

333

Contraception and abortion/average age at first child Contraceptive use among sexually active high-school youths in the year 2003 was 63 per cent (use of condoms during most recent sex). In 1991, it was only 46 per cent. That shows a significant increase even from the 1990s. Interestingly, African-American high-school students in 2003 were more likely than white or Latino students to report using condoms (73 per cent African-Americans, 63 per cent whites and 57 per cent Latinos). The use of contraceptives is rising because of local and state government involvement in family planning. Estimates show that publicly funded contraceptive services help to prevent 1.3 million un-intended pregnancies a year (Littman 1998: 49). For women, the increase in contraceptive use is very much a result of education. Nine out of ten sexually active women (aged fifteen to forty-four) in the year 1990 reported using some contraceptive method.

The landmark abortion decision of *Roe v. Wade* of 1972 has also affected the abortion rate, which steadily increased between 1973 and 1990 for women under twenty-four years old, and declined in 2000. The abortion rate for US females less than twenty years of age increased steadily between 1973 (32.9 per 1,000 women) and 1990 (42.0 per 1,000) and declined to 24.8 in 2000. As for women twenty to twenty-four years of age, the rate doubled between 1973 (26.2 per 1,000 women) and 1990 (56.7 per 1,000). Similarly, the rate declined to 45.9 per 1,000 for this category in 2000, but the drop was not as significant as the decline in the first category.

The mean age of mother at first birth steadily increased from 21.4 in 1970 to 24.9 in 2000, reflecting the rise in both contraceptive use and abortion. The increase in the mean age of mother at first birth was 1.3 years between 1970 and 1980, 1.5 years between 1980 and 1990, and 0.7 years between 1990 and 2000.

According to a US Center for Disease Control and Prevention (CDC) estimate, 384,906 persons were living with AIDS in America at the end of December 2002. According to this estimate, 298,248 of them were males over thirteen years old and 82,764 were females. The CDC estimated the total number of AIDS cases in 2002 in the USA at 886,575. Adult and adolescent AIDS cases totalled 877,273, with 718,002 male cases and 159,271 female cases. Through the same time period, 9,300 AIDS cases were estimated in children under age thirteen.

Although 76,507 US women died of AIDS up to December 2002, and although more women have been living with the infection since 1993 (up from 26,868 in 1993 to 82,764 in 2002), the number of deaths has been declining (from 6,190 in 1993 to 4,226 in 2001). According to the CDC, however, women with AIDS are constituting an increasing part of the epidemic. In 1992, the CDC estimated that women accounted for 14 per cent of adults and adolescents living with AIDS. By the end of 2003, this percentage had grown to 22. Moreover, the CDC estimated that 'from 1999 through 2003, the annual number of estimated AIDS diagnoses increased 15 per cent among women and increased 1 per cent among men', showing an alarming rise in risks for women and girls, as is true also for other countries (CDC n.d.).

Family status and structure

Marriage age The marriage age patterns for both males and females were similar during the twentieth century. The average age at first marriage for both sexes declined steadily until the 1950s (from 21.9 years to 20.3 years for women and from 25.9 to 22.8 years for men), and reversed course after that. Between the 1960s and 2000, the average marriage age for males and females steadily increased (from 20.3 years to 25.1 years for females and from 22.8 years to 26.8 for males). The increase might be related to the increase in the percentage of women completing higher education.

Marriage and divorce Although the marriage rate for both females and males at the end of the century was the same as it was at the beginning of the century (45 per cent), it declined steadily in the first fifty years (from 45 per cent in 1900 to 34 per cent in 1950), and bounced back in the second half of the century (from 34 per cent in 1960 to 45 per cent in 2000). The most notable decline in the marriage rate for both men and women took place in the 1950s and 1960s (Figure 14.6). It is notable that the marriage rates actually declined during the 1950s and 1960s – the time of glorification of the 'suburban housewife', afflu-

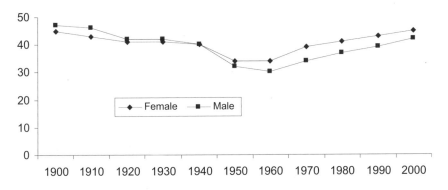

Figure 14.6 Proportion of married American females and males (per cent)
Source: USBC (1975 for 1900–1970, 2001 for 1980–2000)

Women in the USA

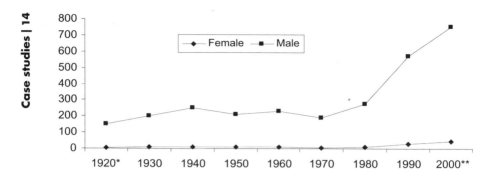

Figure 14.7 Prisoners in state and federal institutions by gender (per 100,000);
***the data represent prisoners sentenced to more than one year, the earliest found was 1925 **1994 data used for 2000** *Source*: USDJ (1996: Table 21)**

ence and relatively high marital stability. After the emergence of the second wave of the women's movement in the early 1970s, marriage as a social institution was no longer assumed to be benign for women. By the late 1970s and early 1980s, many marriages were second or third marriages (a reflection of the higher divorce rate and changing gender relations and marital power during that period).

Female social status underwent steady changes throughout the century. Except for widowhood, all other statuses (married, divorced and never married) changed. The proportion of females who were never married has increased since the 1950s from 20 per cent to 23.5 per cent in 2000. Similarly, 9.8 per cent were divorced women in 2000, up from 0.6 per cent in 1910. The percentage of married women declined from 65.8 in 1950 to 56.2 in 2000.

Violence against women

As early as the colonial era, signs of the suppression of powerful women were evident. The hysteria of hanging witches in colonial New England reflects a struggle for political power by the new commercial class as the colonies were undergoing economic and political transitions from an agrarian to a more commercial society. To exert control over women in colonial America, the label 'witches' – which originated in the home colonial country of England – was applied. Interestingly, the women who were charged with witchcraft in puritan New England often owned property and were of independent means. They exerted a level of authority or showed strength in their communities, which proved too threatening for some males (Karlsen 1987). The Salem, Massachusetts, witch hunts left an indelible image of women as dangerous, unpredictable, capable of luring men into illicit behaviours, and immoral – expressions of which can still be heard in rape and sexual harassment cases today.

Crime and deviant behaviour The rate of sentenced female prisoners in US state and federal institutions increased significantly in the last three decades of the century. Although the rate of imprisonment fluctuated between 1920 and 1970, it doubled in the 1980s, tripled in the 1990s, and continued upwards in the 2000s (Figure 14.7). An even more dramatic increase over the last three decades can be seen for males, possibly because of the 'zero tolerance' policy on drug use, possession and selling that was introduced in the 1980s. African-American and Native American males and females are vastly over-represented in the prisons.

Economic participation

The division of labour Historically, the labour of Native American women was of equal value to men's labour during the hunting and gathering period that ended only in the late 1870s. On the Great Plains of the west, for example, Blackfoot women expertly picked and dried berries and were the main producers of processed buffalo robes (Billson 2005; Albers and Medicine 1983). In Alaska, Inuit (Eskimo) women contributed equally to the survival of their families through berry-picking, fishing, sewing and processing food (Burch 1975; Billson and Reis 2005). Women maintained a level of relative equality in early horticultural societies (for example, among the Native Americans of the south-west), when their technical expertise in pottery and basketry, so essential to food storage, made them an economic necessity. Colonization, immigration, the move west, technology and urbanization changed women's power in the economic system.

Coontz describes the division of labour in terms of the nineteenth-century separation of women from the productive system. The factory system 'established a more rigid division of labour and location than had previously existed between household production and production for the market. Middle-class families put men in the public side and women in the private, working-class families assigned only married women to the household side, sending men, unmarried women into paid work' (1992: 155). The ideological transformation of domesticity was connected to changes in the organization and technology of production in both the home and the economy. These changes laid the groundwork for the increasing entry of women into paid employment during the twentieth century. This phenomenon was largely independent of either the suffrage movement of the early 1900s or the women's liberation movement of

337

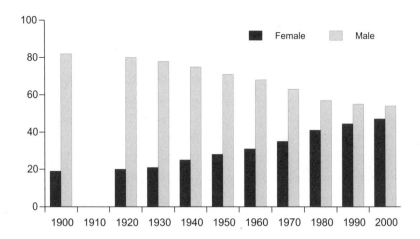

Figure 14.8 Participation in the labour force by gender (per cent); data not available for 1910; 1998 data used for 2000 *Source:* **BLS (1999)**

the early 1960s: 'The revival of feminism in the 1960s was more a response than impetus to women's integration into the labour force ... certainly feminism changed the terms in which women understood their work and confronted its conditions' (ibid.: 154).

Women's participation in the labour force The most dramatic change in American labour in the past few decades has been the influx of women into the labour force, expanding from 20.4 per cent in the 1920s to 46.3 per cent in 2000. At the same time, men reduced their participation in the labour force from 79.6 per cent in the 1920s to 57.5 per cent in the 1980s. The decline in male participation was overshadowed by the sustained increase in female participation, and resulted in a general rise in labour force participation in the 1990s (Figure 14.8).

The reasons for women's sustained increase are the expansion in the proportion of women aged sixteen years and over, marrying at a later age, postponing childbirth to later ages, and/or placing young children in day-care centres, nursery schools and after-school care programmes. Important variations exist by age group among the female working population. The Bureau of Labor Statistics (BLS 2000) found that labour participation doubled for women in the twenty-five-to-thirty-four age bracket (from 34 per cent in 1950 to 76.3 per cent in 1998), as females delayed marriage and child bearing and completed higher levels of education, which prepared them for better job opportunities. The phrase 'the biological clock is ticking' emanated from this career-minded group during the 1980s and 1990s, as they held on to their jobs long enough

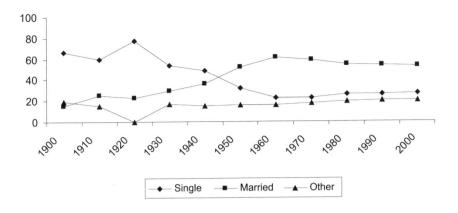

Figure 14.9 Female labour force by marital status (per cent); single includes widowed or divorced *Source:* **USBC (1999: Table 6.1431, p. 879)**

to develop some seniority and security before having children (or choosing not to do so at all).

Littman suggests that 'the fact that women have developed ever stronger attachment to their jobs, with many having also attained relatively high-paying positions, may be one of the driving forces leading to the slight persistent decline in the labour force participation among men of prime working age' (1998: 59). Especially between 1970 and 1990, another factor was 'the changing age distribution of the population stemming from the baby-boom phenomenon' (Fullerton 1999: 3). Early retirement and living longer after retirement explain the slight decline in the male rate of participation; also, some couples found that the wife's earning power was superior to the husband's, so 'house-husbands' became more prevalent. This trend contributed to the decline in the fertility rate in the USA, spurred the growth in day care, and contributed to the shift towards cohabitation rather than marriage.

Figure 14.9 shows that participation of single women decreased as a proportion of employed women over the century, while the category of married women increased. Medical technology, bottled formulas, increased access to childcare, expansion of the super-highways linking the growing suburbs back to the cities in the 1950s, and greater educational attainment made it easier for mothers to join the labour force. It is fascinating how, in spite of the absence of affordable government-sponsored childcare services, women developed strong attachment to their jobs.

FULL-/PART-TIME Women hold the majority of low-paying jobs and are often restricted to part-time or seasonal jobs that lack security or benefits. Women

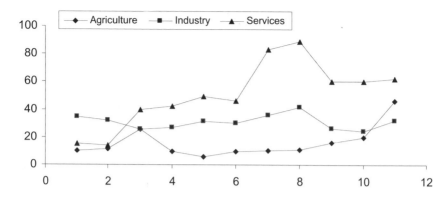

Figure 14.10 Female labour as percentage of male labour (per cent)
Source: USBLS (1999: Table 675, p. 421)

have been discouraged from applying for full-time, high-paying jobs: two or more women covering a full-time position part-time is cheaper and more convenient for the employer. For example, labour laws require employers to pay benefits to employees who work more than nineteen hours a week – so many jobs are posted at eighteen hours in order to avoid having to pay for pension plans, health insurance and paid sick leave. This pattern, backed up by formal social policy and law, contributes to female economic insecurity and slow or blocked upward mobility.

TYPES OF OCCUPATION Increasing female labour force participation has not necessarily meant equal access to opportunity for American women, who have found themselves concentrated in certain industries, sectors and traditionally female jobs. The 'glass ceiling' (inability to gain promotion to the highest positions in an organization) and occupational segregation persist. Women are often denied access to top managerial jobs and are still paid less than the male population, on average.

Women's participation in the labour force throughout the century increased, from 15.4 per cent of male labour in 1900 to 62 per cent in 2000 (Figure 14.10). In terms of ratio, however, women's participation was most significant in the service sector, which usually pays the lowest income (most secretaries and commercial sector service workers are women). When war produced a shortage of male industrial labour, a relative increase in the demand for female participation occurred, raising the percentage in the 1940s.

UNEMPLOYMENT The biggest gap between the sexes in unemployment was in the 1970s (4.4 per cent for males and 5.9 per cent for females), but unemployment reached its highest level in the 1980s for both males and females.

Unemployment rises when economic growth falls but because it is cyclical: as soon as the economy recovers, the rates go down again. Women are more likely than men to leave and re-enter the labour force in response to changes in the demand for surplus labour or changes in their family situations, so the female population generally has a higher unemployment rate than men. In the 1990s, the unemployment rate for the male population was higher, but we find the smallest gap in 2000 (USBC 1998: Table 680, p. 424).

Income and poverty Historically, women have had lower income than men despite the slight shrinking in the margin between their earnings. Throughout the 1960s, 1970s and 1980s, women's earnings as a proportion of men's earnings remained fairly constant at around 60 per cent. During the 1990s, women made progress in narrowing the gap between men's earnings and their own (partly because of legal and policy changes discouraging pay discrimination). Yet thirty-seven years after equal pay became law, women in 2000 were still paid only 73.6 cents for every dollar men received; by 2004, women earned 76 cents. The persistence of a wage gap is not unusual under patriarchal, capitalist systems and in industrialized market economies. Women are over-represented among the poor but under-represented in political office.

No one disputes the existence of a wage gap based on gender but there is disagreement on its causes. One explanation is that women and men tend to work in different industries and professions, and hold different types of jobs. For example, 80 per cent of all women in 1990 were in 5 per cent of all jobs, 'essentially the service jobs, the dead end jobs, the ones that have minimum wage ... so they were caught up in the cycle of poverty' (Chafe 1992).

In addition, gender-related differences in occupational choice, educational attainment and prior work experience – some of which are based on institutionalized sex discrimination – shape the nature and timing of career paths. The latter is a much weaker argument, although clearly some women choose to remain out of the workforce to stay at home with children until they reach school age or finish school, if they are financially able to do so, which then puts them into the market later and in lower positions. Improvements in the earnings ratio often result from decreases in men's real earnings, but studies that control for education, experience and seniority within the same occupation still find gender-based disparities. Jellison (1993) explored how women in rural America chose to work in the period between the First World War and the Vietnam War (1913–63). In contrast to the myths about women, Jellison proved that women chose where to work based on where money was to be made.

Women in the USA

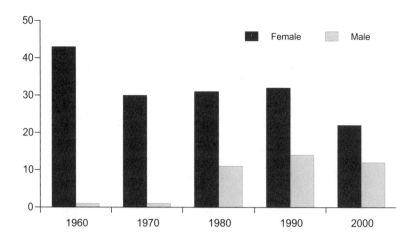

Figure 14.11 Living below poverty level by gender (per cent)
Source: BLS (1999: Table 675, p. 421)

Since the 1960s, the percentage of poor women has declined from 42.6 per cent of all women to 24.7 per cent in 2000. The percentage of poor women, however, is still higher than that of men in all decades (Figure 14.11). It seems that 'poverty has a woman's face' (UNDP 1995). For most households, except for single-parent households, research recently found an apparent advantage of welfare over work (USBC n.d.). The percentage of women living on welfare increased from 37.7 in 1960 to 57.7 per cent in 1990. Since 2000, after the Welfare Reform Act initiated by President Bill Clinton, there have been rigid requirements for employment and leaving welfare.

Literacy and education

Literacy rates At the time of writing, the literacy rate for both females and males in the US was 97 per cent, continuing a tradition of universal public education (operated through states and local districts) that was conceived by Thomas Jefferson in the 1700s and brought to life in the 1800s by educators such as Horace Mann. The US system differs from that of other Western countries in that Americans are more inclined to view education as a solution to social problems (especially in the late twentieth century); Americans have provided more years of schooling for a higher proportion of the population (although schools were racially segregated until the 1960s). The system serves huge numbers of students.

Progressively fewer adults have limited their education to completion of the eighth grade, which was typical in the early part of the century. As of 1940, more than half of the US population had completed no more than an eighth-

Box 14.1 The rise of education in the United States

During the 1940s and 1950s, the more highly educated younger cohorts began to make their mark on the average for the entire adult population. More than half of the young adults of the 1940s and 1950s completed high school and the median educational attainment of 25 to 29-year-olds rose to 12 years. By 1960, 42 percent of males, aged 25 years old and over, still had completed no more than the eighth grade, but 40 percent had completed high school and 10 percent had completed 4 years of college. The corresponding proportion for women completing high school was about the same, but the proportion completing college was somewhat lower.

During the 1960s, there was a rise in the educational attainment of young adults, particularly for blacks. Between 1960 and 1970, the median years of school completed by black males, aged 25 to 29, rose from 10.5 to 12.2. From the middle 1970s to 1991, the educational attainment for all young adults remained very stable, with virtually no change among whites, blacks, males or females. The educational attainment average for the entire population continued to rise as the more highly educated younger cohorts replaced older Americans who had fewer educational opportunities. In 1991, about 70 percent of black and other races males and 69 percent of black and other races females had completed high school. This is lower than the corresponding figures for white males and females (80 percent). However, the differences in these percentages have narrowed appreciably in recent years. Other data corroborate the rapid increase in the education level of the minority population. The proportion of black and other races males with 4 or more years of college rose from 12 percent in 1980 to 18 percent in 1991, with a similar rise for black and other races females. (Snyder 1993)

grade education and only 6 per cent of males and 4 per cent of females had completed college. The median years of school attained by the adult population, aged twenty-five and over, had risen imperceptibly from 8.1 to 8.6 years between 1910 and 1940, probably because of the First World War and the Great Depression. Box 14.1 describes this pattern in detail.

School completion rates The female school completion rate as of 2004 was 86 per cent, while the male rate was 84.5 per cent. It is lower for minority females

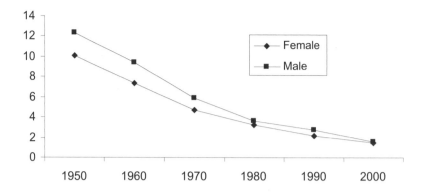

**Figure 14.12 Elementary educational attainment by gender, 25 years +
(per cent)** *Source:* **USBC**

and males. Overall, female educational attainment was slightly lower than male attainment during the twentieth century. Even though there is a steady increase in the percentages of females completing high school and college, male percentages were higher if we exclude the period 1940–60.

PRIMARY Figure 14.12 indicates that the percentage of both males and females aged twenty-five or older with less than five years of elementary school has been declining, from 12.3 to 1.6 per cent for males and from 10.1 to 1.5 per cent for females between 1950 and 2000. The percentage of females who had less than five years of elementary school has steadily declined, while the percentage of females with four years of high school or more and four or more years of college steadily increased.

The 1960s brought a revolutionary way of thinking which influenced education, especially regarding the plight of inner-city schools, ending racial segregation and the forced busing that attempted to break down racial barriers during the 1960s and 1970s. In turn, this affected the attendance levels of minority students in high schools and universities.

SECONDARY The percentage of those who finished four years of high school or more increased significantly between 1950 and 2000. As for high school, there was a steady increase in female completion from 26.3 per cent in 1940 to 84 per cent in 2000 (Figure 14.13). Female and male data converged, so that in 2000 the percentages were almost the same (84 per cent) for high-school completion among the population aged twenty-five and older.

HIGHER EDUCATION Historians of education have argued that, originally, women's education was a mere contribution to a male-defined history. That is,

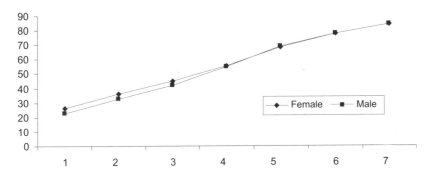

Figure 14.13 Completion of four years of high school by gender (per cent)
Source: USBC

women were to be educated for domestic roles – especially to become better teachers of their children at home (Schwager 1987). Education became available, however, to anyone who qualified for college or university entrance by the last third of the century – as long as one could find money for tuition and other expenses.

Female enrolment peaked towards the end of the century, but male enrolment did not (Figure 14.14). The male decline may be due to unemployment and recession in the 1980s, but also higher female education rates towards the end of the century may be due to immigration, determination to be educated, and changing age composition. In an environment of persistent sex discrimination and the glass ceiling, women have discovered that additional degrees may help them move up the professional ladder and yield slightly higher incomes.

After the 1930s depression, the government attempted to re-employ the

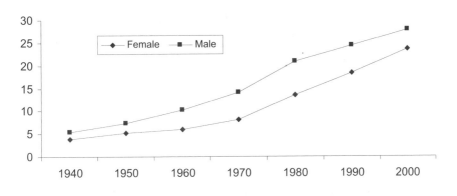

Figure 14.14 Completion of four years of college/university by gender (per cent)
Source: USBC

Women in the USA

population through adult education programmes. On the heels of the Second World War, the GI Bill of Rights meant that veterans were paid to go to school for the first time. American colleges and universities mushroomed and higher education became the desired standard of achievement for both men and women. Males and females diverged in 2000 (23.6 per cent female, 27.8 per cent male).

Political, educational and cultural leadership

THE POWER OF GENDER MYTHS For American women the twentieth century was marked by legal segregation, alienation and conservatism. Civil rights legislation of the 1960s made it more difficult to deny women their rights as economic citizens, but sex discrimination persisted throughout the century. The situation inspired the suffragettes of the 1920s, who fought for women's right to vote in a democracy, and the second wave of the women's movement during the 1970s. As Wallerstein (1996) demonstrated, capitalism begets sexism, since these discriminatory discourses meet the objectives of capital accumulation. That is, sexism and male chauvinism – expressed in subtle and overt forms of discrimination – thrive on gender myths designed to prevent or discourage women from trying to compete in the labour market or to wield political power.

These male inventions, which declare the natural inferiority of women, have held the American imagination in check since colonial times, causing the status of women in law to lag behind male status. For example, the myth of natural female inferiority was expressed in the nineteenth-century common law that precluded a married woman from owning property, entering into a contract, suing or being sued. Myths such as these have been very powerful in distorting the American memory. Historians have used materials such as diaries, personal letters and albums or catalogues to argue that American women 'choose' to be in the kitchen. The myth of the miserable working woman, disseminated by the media, is countered by the fact that working women do not experience high depression and anxiety (Barnett and Rivers 1998). Another myth portrays the 'correct' family as a nuclear family consisting of a breadwinner dad, homemaker mom and two kids.

Gender myths carved out the worlds of machinery and productivity as male spheres; it was said that maternal employment outside the home affected children negatively. Americans held and still hold many of the so-called 'traditional family values' that reject those who do not constitute a model family structure. A distorted family portrait of perfection goes back to the Victorian era, according to Gillis (1997) and Coontz (1989, 1992), and specifically to the creation of a public-versus-private-sphere paradigm by middle-class, Protestant, Victorian women.

THE PERSISTENCE OF SEX DISCRIMINATION Revisionist historians have exposed many of these myths, but sex discrimination persists into the twenty-first century. Recently, the US Civil Rights Commission charged that schools deny equal opportunity in maths and science to girls: 'From fighting for the right to vote to fighting for economic parity, women have had to struggle to achieve equal opportunity and access to the fruits of democracy,' said Commission chairperson Mary Frances Berry (USDJ 1995). The persistence of discrimination in education is just one indicator of the disadvantaged position American women are in today.

Suffrage: participation in voting and elections Political participation of women in the USA is a good measure of the lack of equity. The right to vote was won only after the First World War when the 19th Amendment to the Constitution was approved by Congress in 1919 and became law in 1920, partly in recognition of women's war contributions.

There is a gender gap in presidential elections among voters. The classic measure of political participation is voter registration. In 1872, Susan B. Anthony was the first American woman to register to vote and subsequently became the first to cast her ballot – for which she was arrested. Following the 19th Amendment, 8 million out of 51.8 million women voted for the first time. African-American women and other minority women were denied the right to vote in many states until the Voting Rights Act of 1965 was passed during the era of civil rights legislation. The Center for American Women and Politics

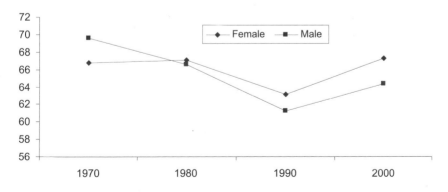

Figure 14.15 Voter registration for presidential elections by gender (per cent)
Source: USBC (1996), Series P20, No. 466

(CAWP) reports that women's votes were never taken seriously; men assumed that women would simply follow the political preferences of their husbands, fathers or brothers.

As Figure 14.15 shows, since 1980 there has been a higher registration and voter turnout rate for women than men. It was highest in 2000 (67.3 per cent for females and 64.4 for males). Similar to that of men, the percentage of females voting declined from 76 per cent in 1960 to 55.5 per cent in 2000. Nevertheless, female voter turnout was higher than men's between 1960 and 2000 (excluding 1970) (Littman 1998).

Political leadership

HEADS OF STATE AND GOVERNMENT The number of women among state government officials, including women governors, has increased, but progress has slowed at the state-wide elective and state legislative levels. The USA has not had a female vice-president or president.

MINISTERIAL (CABINET) Several women have served as cabinet members, starting in 1933, with Frances Perkins, who was appointed Secretary of Labor by President Franklin D. Roosevelt. She was instrumental in reforming labour laws after the disastrous Triangle Shirtwaist Company fire in New York City, which killed over one hundred women. Perkins is considered the architect of the Social Security Act, which (in spite of its weaknesses) helped cushion the negative impacts of the Great Depression. Madeleine Albright served as Secretary of State under President Bill Clinton in the 1990s, and Condoleezza Rice was appointed to that position by President George W. Bush in 2004. Other cabinet posts have also gone to women.

LEGISLATIVE Women still constitute a tiny minority in elected offices at both national and state levels. Since 1917, several women have succeeded their husbands in their positions as governors and congressmen, but American women have found it difficult to be elected to the highest political offices.

The presence of women in elected offices grew over the century but remained small. In the 106th Congress, the last of the century, women held sixty-five (12.1 per cent) of the 535 seats in the US Congress (9 per cent of the 100 seats in the US Senate, and 12.8 per cent of the 435 seats in the House of Representatives). Even though these numbers show that women are underrepresented in both the Senate and the House, the seats held by women more than doubled in the last decade of the twentieth century (from thirty-one seats in 1991 to sixty-five seats in 2001). It took sixty years for women to hold twenty-five seats in Congress (1919–89). After women held twenty seats in 1961–63, the number dropped for the following two decades. Although overall the century showed an increase from only one seat in 1917–19 to sixty-five seats in 1999–2001, according to CAWP (2004) women are still vastly under-represented.

LOCAL GOVERNMENT Women have increasingly filled positions on town or city councils and school boards, and a few have become mayors or town administrators.

Educational leadership The Title IX enactment of 1972, a landmark law that banned sex discrimination in education, seems to have had little effect on the rate of women's progression into the higher ranks of university profes-sors. Women remain under-represented on college/university faculty and in higher education administrative leadership. Women's numbers 'tend to decrease as the rank in the career ladder or the prestige of the education in-stitution increases', according to a progress report by the National Coalition for Women and Girls in Education. Times have been changing in this regard, especially during the last decade of the twentieth century and the first few years of the twenty-first. An American Council on Education report released in 2002 showed that in 2001 women were presidents at 22 per cent of the nation's approximately 3,888 colleges and universities, up from 19 per cent in 1999 and only 9.5 per cent in 1987. As of 1990, women constituted 27 per cent of full-time college/university faculty. The American Association of University Professors has taken a stand on this issue (Box 14.2).

Participation in religious institutions Even though women make up the majority of nearly every religious group, they are still usually excluded from leadership positions (Braude 1999). Historically, Christianity, Islam and Juda-ism barred women from ordained ministry, except for the Society of Friends (Quakers), which permitted women to serve as ministers since their inception in seventeenth-century England.

In the USA, the Church of God sanctioned the ordination of women by 1876, as did the Christian Church (Disciples of Christ) in 1888. AME Zion began ordaining women in the 1890s and the American Baptist Convention allowed women to serve as lay ministers in 1894. Most women, however, were still prohibited from holding positions of church-wide authority, let alone entering the ministry. In 1930, the United Presbyterian Church voted to ordain women as ruling elders but not until 1959 did it agree to the ordination of female clergy. Methodists accepted the ordination of women in 1959, but Lutherans and Episcopalians waited until the 1970s; Unitarians have been progressive

Box 14.2 *The American Association of University Professors (AAUP):
Statement of Principles on Family Responsibilities and Academic Work*

Since 1974, significant demographic and legal changes have affected the academic profession. Notably, the percentage of women faculty has increased. In 1975, women made up 22.5 per cent of full-time faculty while in 2000–2001, women constituted 36 per cent of full-time faculty, according to AAUP's annual salary survey.

Although increasing numbers of women have entered academia, their academic status has been slow to improve. Women remain disproportionately represented as instructors, lecturers and in unranked positions: more than 57 per cent of those holding such positions are women. In contrast, among full professors only 26 per cent are women; 74 per cent are men. Women remain significantly under-represented at research institutions; this is in stark contrast to their significant representation at community colleges. The proportion of full-time women at two-year institutions increased from 38 per cent to approximately 50 per cent in 2000. At the same time, among full professors at doctoral institutions, the proportion of faculty members who are women is only 19 per cent.

on this count. Similar patterns emerged in most of the mainstream historical African-American churches and in Judaism.

Towards gender equality

Thus far, women have achieved two main advances in the USA: access to opportunity through improved access to education and employment, and the right to vote. According to the law, American women have achieved some of their rights. In fact, however, social, economic and political equality with men still needs to be achieved. American women lag behind men in the highest levels of political, academic, corporate, government and science positions. They are still paid around 76 cents for each dollar men earn. Work is a term that describes wage labour and still undermines women's second-shift and unpaid productive labour.

Women are historically limited by restrictions on economic opportunities, so without full economic citizenship American women will be unable to attain full political status. To be a real citizen, one must be able to earn, if necessary or if one chooses, and even be the major breadwinner, if preferred. During the twentieth century American women did not reach these goals. The 'gendered imagination' that Kessler-Harris (2003) explores has wielded an influence on the minds of Americans that makes sexism by institutions conceivable. Full equality will not be achieved until sexism is 'inconceivable'.

This chapter shows that, in spite of women's changing roles and the increased participation of females in the labour force, the qualitative change in attaining equality with their male counterparts has yet to materialize. We can identify two unfortunate moments in women's history. The first was the writing of history that represented a minority of elitist women. The second was the middle-class origin and social agenda that the mainstream women's movement projected. In many cases, a change in women's roles occurred before the initiation or revival of the feminist movement. It makes no difference how many women are represented in local or national political offices if these women are proponents of elitist agendas.

Ironically, in one of the most affluent countries in the world, it was necessary to declare women a legally recognized 'minority' – in a policy and affirmative action sense – in order to help redress institutionalized sexism and gender discrimination. Being half the population is not an indicator that women have equal power. On the contrary, American women are still a minority group in that they are often denied access to top managerial jobs, are discouraged from entering male-dominated occupations, and continue to be inhibited by unpaid work in the home.

We suggest that the needs of working women, who never reached equality before the 1960s and remained disadvantaged thereafter, must be better represented in the political institutions so that they set their agenda and shape policies to ensure that all areas of the economy reflect the needs of wage earners (especially poor and/or single-mother wage earners). This would have significant ramifications for childcare and healthcare insurance policies in the USA, which for the present leave women in a precarious position – regardless of their social class, race or ethnicity. This is the challenge facing women in the United States for the next decades of this century.

Note

1 This chapter draws on data mainly from the United States Census Bureau (USCB). Although the first census was conducted in the United States in 1790, the present USBC was established as part of the Department of Commerce and Labor in 1902. All data that come from sources other than the official census will be cited separately.

References

Albers, P. and B. Medicine (eds) (1983) *The Hidden Half: Studies of Plains Indian Women*, Lanham, MD: University Press of America

Aye, H. V. (1997) 'Developments in women's labor force participation', *Monthly Labor Review*, 120(9) (September)

Bales, R. (1996) 'Native American women: living with landscape', *OAH Magazine of History*, 10 (winter)

Barnett, R. C. and C. Rivers (1998) *She Works/He Works: How Two Income Families are Happy, Healthy and Thriving*, Boston, MA: Harvard University Press

Berkin, C. (1997) *First Generations: Women in Colonial America*, New York: Farrar Straus & Giroux

Billson, J. M. (2005) *Keepers of the Culture: Women and Power in the Canadian Mosaic*, Boulder, CO: Rowman & Littlefield

Billson, J. M. and K. M. Reis (2005) *Inuit Women: Their Powerful Spirit in a Century of Change*, Boulder, CO: Rowman & Littlefield

Bonvillain, N. (1989) 'Gender relations in Native North America', *American Indian Culture and Research Journal*, 13(2)

Braude, A. (1999) *Women and Religion in America*, London: Oxford University Press

Brown, K. M. (1996) *Good Wives, Nasty Wenches, and Anxious Patriarchs: Gender, Race, and Power in Colonial Virginia*, Chapel Hill: University of North Carolina Press

Burch, E. S. (1975) *Eskimo Kinsmen: Changing Family Relations in Northwest Alaska*, New York: West

Chafe, W. (1992) *The Paradox of Change: American Women in the 20th Century*, London: Oxford University Press

Collins, P. H. (1990) *Black Feminist Thought: Knowledge, Consciousness, and the Politics of Empowerment*, Boston, MA: Unwin Hyman

Coontz, S. (1989) 'In search of a golden age', *Context IC*, 12 (spring)

— (1992) *The Way We Never were: American Families and the Nostalgic Trap*, New York: HarperCollins

Daniels, R. (1990) *Coming to America: A History of Immigration and Ethnicity in American Life*, New York: HarperCollins

DeMallie, R. J. (1983) 'Male and female in traditional Lakota culture', in P. Albers and B. Medicine (eds), *The Hidden Half: Studies of Plains Indian Women*, Lanham, MD: University Press of America

Dye, T. (1995) *Who's Running America: The Clinton Years*, Englewood Cliffs, NJ: Prentice Hall

Ewen, E. (1985) 'Immigrant women in the land of dollars: life and culture on the Lower East Side 1890–1925', *Monthly Review Press*

Fullerton, H. N. (1999) 'Labor force participation: 75 years of change 1950–1997 and 1998–2025', *Monthly Labor Review*, 122(12): 3

Gabaccia, D. (1994) 'Bibliographical essay', in *From the Other Side: Women, Gender, and Immigrant Life in the US, 1820–1990*, Bloomington and Indianapolis: Indiana University Press

Gillis, J. R. (1997) *A World of Their Own Making: Myth, Ritual, and the Quest for Family Values*, Cambridge, MA: Harvard University Press.

Hubbard, W. (1990) *The History of the Indian Wars in New England*, 2 vols, Bowie, MD: Heritage Books

Jellison, K. (1993) *Entitled to Power: Farm Women and Technology, 1913–1963*, Chapel Hill: University of North Carolina Press

Karlsen, C. F. (1987) *The Devil in the Shape of a Woman*, New York: Norton

Kessler-Harris, A. (2003) *In Pursuit of Equity: Women, Men and the Quest for Economic Citizenship in 20th-century America*, London: Oxford University Press

Khoury, L. (1999) 'Development, dependency, population pressure, and human rights performance: the cross-national evidence', *Human Ecology Journal*, 6(1)

— (2001) 'The rise and demise of Oslo: globalization and the Middle East', *Middle East Affairs*, 7(1–2) (winter/spring)

— (2004) 'History and race consciousness', in C. Fluehr-Lobban (ed.), *Race and Identity in the Nile Valley*, New Jersey: Red Sea Press

Leach, K. (1995) *In Search of a Common Ground: Nineteenth and Twentieth Century Immigrant Women in America*, San Francisco, CA: Austin & Winfield

Littman, M. S. (1998) *A Statistical Portrait of the United States: Social Conditions and Trends*, Lanham, MD: Bernan Press

Norton, M. B. (1997) *Founding Mothers and Fathers: Gendered Power and the Forming of American Society*, New York: Random House

Perdue, T. (1998) *Cherokee Women: Gender and Culture Change, 1700–1835*, Lincoln: University of Nebraska Press

Schwager, S. (1987) 'Educating women in America', *Signs*, 12

Shoemaker, N. (ed.) (2001) *Blackwell Readers in American Social and Cultural History: American Indians*, Malden, MA: Blackwell

— (ed.) (2002) *Clearing a Path: Theorizing the Past in Native American Studies*, New York: Routledge

Snyder, T. (ed.) (1993) *120 Years of American Education: A Statistical Portrait*, Washington, DC: National Center for Education Statistics

Tanner, H. H. (ed.) (1995) *The Settling of North America: The Atlas of the Great Migrations into North America from the Ice Age to the Present*, New York: Macmillan Press

Ulrich, L. T. (1991) *Good Wives: Image and Reality in the Lives of Women in Northern New England, 1650–1750*, New York: Random House

UNDP (United Nations Development Programme) (1995) *Human Development Report*, New York: UNDP

USBC (United States Bureau of the Census) (1975) *Historical Statistics of the United States: Colonial Times to 1970*, bicentennial edn, Washington, DC: USBC

— (1996, 1998, 1999) *Statistical Abstracts of the United States*, Washington, DC: USBC

— (2000) *Demographic Trends in the 20th Century: Census 2000 Special Reports*, Washington, DC: USBC

— (2001) *Census 2000 Brief: Gender 2000*, Washington, DC: US Department of Commerce, Economics and Statistics Administration

Wallerstein, I. (1996) 'The ideological tensions of capitalism: universalism versus racism and sexism', in E. Balibar and I. Wallerstein (eds), *Race, Nation, Class: Ambiguous Identities*, New York: Verso

Weatherford, D. (1995) *Foreign and Female: Immigrant Women in America, 1840–1930*, New York: Facts on File

Websites

BLS (Bureau of Labor Statistics) (2000) Monthly Labor Review, <www.bls.gov /opub/ted/2000/Feb/wk3/art03.htm>

CAWP (Center for American Women and Politics) (2004), <www.cawp.rutgers.edu>

CDC (United States Centers for Disease Control and Prevention) (n.d.), <www.cdc.gov/nchs/data/nvsr/nvsr53/nvsr53_05.pdf>.

IWPR (Institute for Women's Policy Research) Reports (2002, 2003), (<www.iwpr.org/states/pdf/national.pdf>)

PBS (Public Broadcasting System) (2000) Interview with William Chafe, Duke University, <www.pbs.org/fmc/interviews/chafe.htm>

United States Department of Justice (USDJ) (1996) 'Commission celebrates National Women's History Month', <www.usccr.gov/press/prsndx.htm>

USBC (United States Bureau of the Census) (n.d.) <www.census.gov/population/www.documentation/twps0046.html>

<www.avert.org/womstata.htm>

THREE | **New theory for a new century**

15 | Common challenges: factors that enhance or detract from female well-being

JANET MANCINI BILLSON AND
CAROLYN FLUEHR-LOBBAN

We have seen that women in some countries have more power and greater well-being than women in other countries. Yet common threads run through their lives, threads that have more to do with being a woman than with living in a particular society or culture. Recognizing differences is essential, but recognizing the common patterns in the tapestry of women's oppression is equally important. We have identified several key patterns that serve as sources of oppression and detract from female well-being. At the same time, patterns that serve to enhance female well-being emerge from the case studies. The transformation to equal relations and improved female well-being rests on our understanding all these patterns.

The impact of international movements

All countries in our sample have benefited from several international movements that set new agendas and challenged old myths during the twentieth century:

- international human rights movements;
- the international women's movement and conferences;
- ratification of CEDAW (all but Sudan).

The international human rights movement – beginning in the West in the wake of the Second World War with the Universal Declaration of Human Rights and reaching a plateau with the United Nations Convention on the Elimination of All Forms of Discrimination Against Women (CEDAW) – has profoundly affected the enhancement of female well-being worldwide.

Another sea change in consciousness came with recognition of human rights violations regarding women and girls through domestic violence, warfare, militarism and harmful cultural traditions. This is a continuation of the historic trends emanating from the French Revolution in 1791 and the Seneca Falls (US) Declaration of Women's Rights in 1848. Women's participation in countless national liberation movements in the twentieth century colonies of Africa, Asia and Latin America brought women into the public sphere in meaningful ways. The international women's peace movements, with local, national and international agendas, and the mobilization of women in trade unions to resist predatory global capitalist exploitation of their labour, all contributed to the crowning achievement of the twentieth century: enhanced women's rights and female well-being.

Much work remains to be done in women's rights and human rights, as is apparent from our case studies. In this chapter, we explore both the 'factors that enhance female well-being' and the 'factors that detract from female well-being'. Based on our reading of the cases, we elucidate several factors that seem important for future efforts towards achieving gender equality.

Demographic factors

The impacts of urbanization and industrialization Together with globalization and immigration, urbanization and industrialization resulted in mixed outcomes for female well-being, depending on their extent. All were significant trends in the twentieth century. In one sense, urbanization produced favourable conditions for female well-being through reduction of fertility, improved access to education, and greater formal employment opportunities. Urbanization disproportionately attracted males to cities (in most cases), however, leaving women alone in rural areas, fully responsible for the economic, physical and social security of their families.

Divided families tended to deepen impoverishment of women and their dependent children when migration to urban areas occurred within countries. In contrast, in countries that experienced high rates of immigration from abroad (Canada, the USA and the UK), millions of immigrant women improved their education, health and occupational mobility. In Canada, for example, women from Jamaica and Trinidad often immigrated first, taking the responsibility for settling themselves in the new country and earning enough money to bring their families in later (Billson 2005). In the UK, the daughters of twentieth-century immigrants have competed well at the managerial level, in spite of racial discrimination.

Industrialization and urbanization have also had positive consequences for health (in the long run, though not at first) as medical technology and knowledge mushroomed with specialization and better sanitation. Counter-intuitively, while female life expectancy outpaces that of males across the board, the gap is greater in the richer, industrialized nations than in the poorer, agrarian ones (although humans, irrespective of gender, live longer in the richer nations). This has occurred in spite of urban crowding (especially early in the century) and insufficient programmes addressing women's health needs.

Data from our cases suggest why women are living longer lives. In Thailand, the differential in male/female life expectancy was a result of alcohol, drug and tobacco use by males, plus HIV/AIDS. In Japan, where women enjoy the longest life expectancy of any humans on earth, protective legislation enacted for female workers and the protective individual pensions applying to elderly women may have supported their longevity. Patriarchy itself is a major factor in lower male life expectancies (male near-monopoly of warfare; dangerous and stressful male employment patterns and responsibilities; higher numbers of male homicide victims; and less seeking of medical care, even when available). There is a 115 per cent male mortality rate (compared to females) in the first year of life around the world (Beaujot and Kerr 2004: 54–5), supporting what biologists suggest may be a genetic female propensity for survival enhancement. Patriarchal values seem to make men more likely to engage in risk-taking behaviour. The Canadian data reveal that 20 per cent of men versus 60 per cent of women had never smoked, resulting in a possible overall health benefit to women, since smoking is a well-known detractor from well-being. Women have generally been employed in less dangerous occupations than men have.

Availability of contraception is a powerful indicator that straddles less-developed countries and developed countries. As a major advance of the twentieth century, contraception is widely used by women even in countries and regions where it is illegal, or where it contravenes religious teachings (such as Colombia, Quebec, Italy and much of South America). Declining fertility promotes better maternal health. The overall twentieth-century trend of enhanced educational access for females, together with contraceptive use, formed a powerful combination. Rising rates of child immunization reduced infant mortality, contributing to lower fertility rates, which in turn enhanced female well-being as women cease having supernumerary children to replace those lost to unchecked infectious and communicable diseases.

Common factors that enhance female well-being
- Concerted government and NGO programmes targeting maternal and infant mortality (increased female life expectancy).
- Liberalization of contraception and/or abortion laws.
- High use of contraception (regardless of laws) (lower fertility rates).
- Education and contraceptive use in combination.
- The industrial revolution in agrarian nations and concomitant urbanization (involvement of women in the formal workforce).
- Urbanization (lower fertility rates, lower maternal mortality rates, better access to education and general healthcare).

Common factors that detract from female well-being

- Relatively high HIV/AIDS infection rates.
- State control of reproductive rights with denial of rights of sexual freedom, exemplified in female circumcision, barriers to contraception and abortion, and state-defined fetus viability definitions.
- Disproportionate blame of women for high HIV/AIDS infection rates.
- Male migration to cities, leaving women alone and responsible for their families, often without inadequate resources (poverty or deepening of existing poverty).

Family status and structure factors

The pattern of family entrapment and the persistence of patriarchy Patriarchy literally means the 'rule of the father' but expands to mean the rule of men who are taught, by socialization and ideology, to be dominant and are allowed to use force when they consider it necessary. Patriarchy cuts across the fates of women in all the cases in this volume – across social classes, ethnic and racial groups, epochs and societies. This pattern, perhaps the most complex of all, may be the most difficult to unravel. Across cultures, tightly knotted economic and religious patterns define a woman's role in the family, but the intensely emotional climate of family life further complicates that role. Whether she takes her place in a male/female family system as daughter, wife or senior mother – or heads her own single-parent household – people react negatively and sometimes violently to a woman's attempts to be assertive, challenge authority, or choose reproductive, sexual and financial freedoms.

Families form the key connective tissue of social life. As we have seen, cultures vary on how they view women in the family, but all families raise common issues for women. Perhaps most importantly, families frame the context in which woman's 'proper role' is debated. Families are the home of the forced choice: children or work outside the home; family or career; domesticity or public achievement. Many women feel forced to choose the domestic sphere because of inadequate day care and the reluctance of many males to take on their fair share of childcare and housework.

Women are united by the invisibility of several important aspects of their lives, including motherhood, invisible household work, double shifts in informal/formal labour, rape, intra-family violence, and discrimination, regardless of social class or extent of economic development. These issues affect women's health and well-being, as has been confirmed by international organizations such as UNIFEM and WHO. Colombia chapter author Elena Garcés de Eder observes that Latin American women are at a double disadvantage under the ideologies of machismo and marianismo that permeate the Catholic Church and the political, military, social and cultural arenas. She concludes that everything starts and continues with patriarchy. Frederick Engels observed that the organization of agrarian communities heralded the demise of female power and the beginning of patriarchy as men took over the rule of women. Patriarchy repeats specific domination patterns of men over women and men over men.

Entrenched patriarchy has been challenged in words, but ineffectively in action (Bangladesh, Canada, Colombia, the USA and the UK). As the Bangladesh team said, 'Women have multiple identities in the life cycle which strongly influence their authority and autonomy, preferences and household status. In general, women are [still] treated as an easy apparatus for the ends of others as reproducers, care-givers, sexual outlets, and as agents of a family's general prosperity.'

The average age of marriage for women doubled or nearly doubled in several of our predominantly agrarian or transitional sample countries over the course of the twentieth century – Bangladesh, Thailand – or it dramatically increased in the predominantly industrial countries – the USA, the UK, Canada and Japan. The effects of delayed marriage on lower fertility rates are obvious, as is the important connection between increased educational access and contraceptive use. Explanations for the trend in rising marriage age are varied. Colonial governments in the twentieth century outlawed child marriage and post-independence nations raised the legal age of marriage for women and men to eighteen or twenty-one years. As we know from other customs that are subject to legal regulation, they are capable of continuing unabated, as was the case with FGM in Sudan. The rising education trend for females is surely a significant factor in delayed marriage.

The second wave of feminist consciousness-raising contributed to higher divorce rates in the industrial nations (as high as 50 per cent in some cases) and may have spawned caution against entering into formal marriage. Informal consensual ties between couples increased in the industrial nations, but not in the agrarian ones. In the latter case, there is evidence of women's resistance to arranged marriages (e.g. Sudan). Although not as yet a dominant trend, this is an area of social change to watch in the next decades.

Patrilineal descent systems remained strong in our sample, continuing to result in a strong cross-cultural preference for sons, which we know forms the foundation for discrimination against women in all spheres. Around the world, the birth of a girl is still often an event of sorrow. As the Chinese proverbs say, the birth of a girl is a 'small happiness' – or 'a family without a boy is like a day without sun'. In China and India, male–female ratios have become imbalanced from female feticide and infanticide rooted in the low value placed on females. Anthropologists have studied patriliny for a hundred years, but have failed to assess fully the outcomes of male preference on female well-being.

Nevertheless, the continued strength of patriarchy and patriliny does not minimize the importance of the twentieth-century trend towards matrifocal families in both industrial and agrarian societies. Matrifocal families have increased dramatically in the USA, the UK, Canada, Colombia, Iceland, South Africa, Sudan and Thailand. Increasing matrifocality occurs when males migrate from rural to urban areas for work, or to more favourable labour markets in expatriate countries. In countries where chronic conflict and war are present, such as Sudan, matrifocal families have resulted from the death, long-term absence or exile of men as soldiers. The variable and largely unstudied conditions underlying matrifocality make it difficult to construct an explanatory theory. We can observe its effects, however: increasing responsibility and agency for women, such as in the management of financial affairs; lower rates of male abuse; women assuming multiple non-traditional social roles; and new collective associations among women in similar households. Thus, matrifocality may enhance a capability for female well-being that moves away from present models of social pathology. The major downside of such families in industrial and agrarian nations is financial insecurity.

The rise of female-headed households in industrial nations stems more from higher proportions of divorced or never-married women, the delay of marriage into the twenties and thirties, and women's higher life expectancy. When nuclear or joint families split because of the absence of males in historically patriarchal families, the remaining females become de facto heads of households on a temporary basis with the underlying assumption that male authority will resume once the male(s) return. In other cases, the arrangement is permanent.

In Japan, entrenched patriarchal values and stability of the nuclear family have mitigated against a notable increase in matrifocal families. We predict that the trend towards matrifocality will continue unabated as the forces of globalization and post-industrialism intensify. Given the refusal of women to accept living in abusive relationships with men, matrifocal families may emerge as a positive, conscious choice for women. Nevertheless, patriarchal families are still a powerful norm worldwide and are unlikely to disappear in this century, although they may not survive in present, accepted forms.

Common factors that enhance female well-being

- Legal protections of women's economic and hereditary rights.
- Redefinition of the family away from patriarchal norms.
- Equal treatment of boys and girls in families and schools.
- Maternity leave; paternity or parental leave.
- Questioning absolute power and authority of various religions and belief systems.
- Baby bonuses that support women's role as homemaker/mother.
- Cohabitation, 'registered partners' or marriage legislation for gays and lesbians.

Common factors that detract from female well-being

- Strong, rigid, open patriarchal value systems.
- Hidden patriarchy.
- Legal definitions of men and women as unequal partners in marriage, divorce and inheritance.
- Tax laws that make women 'dependants' of husbands.
- Acceptance of bigamy for males (Colombia) and polygyny (Muslims in Bangladesh, Thailand, Sudan).
- Lower value placed on female infants; preference for males.
- Preferential treatment of boys in families and schools.
- High rates of matrifocal families (when leading to impoverishment).
- Cultural practices that harm women (female circumcision, infibulation in Sudan; Islamic polygamy tied to dowry system, making women vulnerable to divorce or abuse in serial marriages).
- Dissolution of communal family farm system, leaving small, one-family farms with less sustainability.

Violence against women factors

The pattern of personal victimization For the most part, women fall victim to rape and battery because they are women, not because they happen to be wealthy or impoverished, Thai or Colombian, educated or illiterate. Everywhere, rape crisis centres, shelters for battered women and protective services for abused children stand out as visibly important symbols of women's victimization. Women have been bitten, beaten, raped and verbally assaulted – even burned at the stake – in order to keep them 'in their place'. Such patterns originated in ancient times, but echo through more contemporary manifestations of control and abuse. Systems of authority (police and courts) tend to minimize brutality against women as 'a family matter', so that most violence against women goes unpunished.

363

Global consciousness regarding domestic violence intensified towards the end of the twentieth century. Feminist research documenting the issue and the rise of the shelter movement had a radiating effect worldwide. Gender violence as a violation of women's rights and human rights was placed on the global agenda, first acknowledged at the historic UN World Conference on Human Rights in Vienna in 1993. In preparation for the conference, world-wide hearings were held and 500,000 signatures were collected on a petition demanding that women's rights be placed on the main agenda, not just discussed in small groups. Women requested a special rapporteur on violence against women and a tribunal on crimes against women (which evolved to crimes against humanity).

The linkage was made again at the Beijing Women's Congress in 1995, which resulted in the Declaration on Elimination of Violence Against Women. The declaration addresses the physical, sexual and psychological dimensions of violence, including battery, sexual abuse of female children, dowry-related violence, marital rape, FMG, other traditional practices harmful to women, and non-spousal violence related to exploitation (Merry 2001). Since 1995, such acts are prosecutable under the Inter-American Convention on the Prevention, Punishment and Eradication of Violence Against Women, as well as under local and state laws in some countries.

The movement to eradicate violence against women was worldwide. Local women activists in Croatia, Bosnia-Herzegovina and Serbia regularly held peace vigils; women in Serbia ran rape crisis centres for the women of Bosnia-Herzegovina (Mertus 2000). Women in India protested against bride

---

Box 15.1 Domestic violence in China

Spousal abuse occurs in one in three Chinese families. In response, police most often recommend mediation. The marriage law of 2001 gives victims the right to official protection and orders punishment for abusers. In divorce cases, victims of abuse can also sue for damages. The media are playing a positive role in dramatizing domestic abuse and courts are beginning to become more sensitive. Enforcement of the law varies widely across China, however, and the country's first battered women's shelters were forced to close because of lack of funding and protection. The government-affiliated All China Federation of Women is agitating for more specific definitions of abuse to help with prosecution. (Adapted from The Royal Gazette 2003: 13)

burning and intervened to protect women who were threatened by domestic violence. Women in the USA and Canada held candlelight vigils called 'Women Take Back the Night'. As the authors of the Japan chapter said, 'When international society recognizes a universal goal of uprooting acts of violence against women, it supports local and national efforts.'

Common factors that enhance female well-being
- Mandatory reporting of domestic violence by police.
- Codification in law of domestic violence as a violation of basic human rights.
- Activism that defines violence against women as unacceptable.

Common factors that detract from female well-being
- Warfare, chronic civil war or imperial war; wartime rapes.
- Disproportionate number of women and children refugees in times of conflict.
- The 'war on women', fuelled by unrestricted pornography, prostitution, sex tourism and sex traffic that exploit women and girls.

Economic factors

The pattern of economic subordination Female labour super-exploitation has been bolstered by patriarchal values, both in the countries where the multinationals are based as well as in the countries where cheap female labour is in high demand. Patriarchal laws or policies have prevented females from achieving economic security. While not all women have been relegated to the weak and fragile feminine role pressed upon them in the Victorian era, and in fact many have traditionally been held in high esteem for their economic contributions to family and community, men generally get the best jobs, receive more pay than women for the same work, and make the major decisions for community and state. Women remain at the lower end of a segregated labour market in many countries, concentrated in a few 'pink ghetto' occupations, and hold positions of little or no authority. Wherever women have moved upward economically, as delineated by our case studies, equality under the law and strong political will have supported that movement.

Common factors that enhance female well-being
- High female literacy rates.
- Constitutional equality with prohibition of sex discrimination; affirmative action.
- Overall economic growth.

- History of strong female identity and heroines.
- Strong social cushion (day care, socialized medicine and social services, adequate maternity leave).
- Paternity or parental leave in addition to maternity leave.
- Women spacing and/or limiting number of children, legally or despite bans.

Common factors that detract from female well-being

- Persistence of male domination at higher ranks in the workforce.
- Differential hiring of men in core and better-paid positions.
- Disproportionate hiring of women in peripheral, insecure, less-valued jobs including home-based, casual and temporary work.
- Disproportionate exiting of women from paid work in times of economic crisis (often forced to enter the informal economy).
- Ghettoization of females into seasonal, casual, informal or home-based work, with little access to social protections.
- Persistence of lower pay (females earn 20–30 per cent less than men).
- Persistence of unpaid household labour (about one third of the world's economic production).
- In developing countries, long female work hours exceeding men's by 30 per cent.
- Prohibitions against females working outside the home.
- Burdens for women who work outside the home: 'double role, double burden'.
- Education and career paths that push females towards a narrow range of occupational choices.
- Extreme economic underdevelopment (as in Bangladesh, Sudan).
- Warfare, chronic civil war, aggression, imperial war (diverting resources away from education, health and general well-being).
- Occupation by a foreign power.
- Cuts in social cushion, health and education spending.
- Globalization and feminization of labour markets (female labour exploitation by multinationals).

Education and literacy factors

The pattern of educational disadvantage We could call the twentieth century the 'Education Century for Women', as access to schooling was the most momentous catalyst behind upward mobility and opportunity for females. Education shows a positive trend line in all the case study countries, but equal access to education (as with state citizenship and legal rights for women) has not improved commensurately. The long-standing and pervasive pattern of male privilege in this arena cut across cultures, often reflecting assumptions of male superiority. By early in the century, countries such as Canada, the United States, Iceland, Thailand, Sudan and Colombia had brought girls fully into the mass public educational systems (at least at primary level), but many others denied or restricted their access until mid-century, forcing female literacy levels to lag behind male levels until after the Second World War. When females were finally allowed to enter educational systems, they often surpassed males in university attendance and completion.

As the teams reported, the pattern of educating males first and females second (if at all) came from the cultural assumption that males would provide for a wife, children and ageing parents. This assumption kept females out of schools for decades after males were being educated in many countries. In all cases, education for girls lagged behind that for boys – even education just to the point of literacy – until late in the century for most. For some countries, especially in Africa and Asia, girls' education still lags seriously behind.

Education is recognized universally as a primary means of social mobility for all humans, but it is especially relevant for female well-being. An additional one to three years of a mother's schooling correlates with a 20 per cent decline in childhood deaths. A cross-cultural study of sixty-three countries found that gains in women's education made the single greatest contribution to overall declines in malnutrition from 1970 to 1995. Educated women marry later, have fewer children and better pre-natal care. Their children have higher survival rates, superior health and nutrition, and fare better in school. Gains in education correlate closely with life expectancy for women and their societies at large. In a World Bank study of seventeen African and four Latin American countries, education had a significant effect on lowering HIV infection rates. In South Asia, where women have lower levels of education, maternal mortality rates are ten times as high as in East Asia. Female education is also associated with greater political participation. In Nepal, after a nine-month literacy course, over half the women said they would feel comfortable expressing their views to the community (Philadelphia Inquirer 2004: C7).

By the 1990s, international development agencies had concluded that girls' education was the linchpin of sustainable development. Once women have achieved this education, however, they have not reaped the full rewards. Unfortunately, feminization of education appears to result in a degrading of the value of education, just as feminization of the professions has led to their devaluing. The dominant group holds up a barrier that cannot be crossed;

when a rights movement breaks through the barrier (e.g. educational access or suffrage), the goalposts are moved. This is the patriarchal assumption of privilege at work.

Common factors that enhance female well-being
- Improvement of school completion rates through strong public policy and law, and enforcement of law; the use of affirmative action, or set-asides.
- Changing cultural norms towards support of female education.
- Positive role of international development agencies in girls' education programmes.
- Positive emphasis placed on multi-culturalism (opening access to all groups).
- Growth of strong women's studies programmes in universities.
- Existence of quality girls' schools and women's universities.

Common factors that detract from female well-being
- Lack of enforcement of universal education policies.
- Distance from schools and universities.
- Dearth of female teachers (for example in Bangladesh).
- Failure of women's studies programmes to be well developed.

Political factors

The pattern of political exclusion By defining women historically as property or as childlike beings who could not make a decision, men have prevented women from finding their political voice. That changed considerably but not universally in the twentieth century, and only after decades of mobilization on behalf of suffrage. Attaining high political office has been even more difficult for women everywhere.

In all our cases, suffrage for women was achieved in the twentieth century, but females were barred from entering the highest bastions of male power, with few exceptions. The participation of women in the electoral process and in politics remained low in all countries – even in those that had female heads of state (Bangladesh, Canada, the UK and Iceland). Obtaining the right to vote is not sufficient to raise the participation of women in the inner sanctums of political power. Low levels of female involvement in politics provide few role models for women or girls to emulate, which then feeds back into low participation of women in politics.

A minimal, pro forma acceptance of female improvement was granted as barriers fell, but equal power and access were fundamentally withheld – in both the industrial and the agrarian nations. Women who rise to higher positions are often co-opted by the dominant group, as in Sudan, and do not necessarily support women's rights or female well-being; in fact, if they work for women, they will be removed (e.g. Amel Gorani in Sudan). For many women, the only way to penetrate the bastions of power was through co-optation or tokenism.

When women have penetrated these barriers to political power, the indisputable agents of change have been women candidates and parties that helped women enter and win elections. Women candidates in Japan were supported by special 'Back-up Schools' that prepared them for the exigencies of campaigning and supported them in multiple ways; they won when they ran on issues that the general population could relate to, such as health and education. When women's representation in parliament is 30 per cent or higher, it has been the result of specific practices in nations such as Rwanda, Mozambique and Tanzania, where citizens have decided that female participation in politics is a priority that cannot wait.

State feminism was a new phenomenon witnessed in the twentieth century, notably as an offshoot of the socialist states influenced by Marxism-Leninism and Maoism. As an approach to female emancipation, state feminism can be critiqued for its assertion of a female equality that produces token change and little lasting effect, but having laws and legal rights for women, and female appointments to influential positions, was transformational in some cases.

The list of women who have been heads of state in world history is not a long one. In 2004, there were more women in Europe as titular heads of nations (queens) than as presidents or prime ministers. In the same year, despite the stereotype, there were more women heads of Muslim nations than of Western countries – Prime Minister Khalida Zia of Bangladesh and President Megawati Sukarnoputri, elected head of Indonesia, the world's largest Muslim nation. The Asian continent leads the rest of the world in female heads of state with women ruling repetitively in Sri Lanka, the Philippines and Bangladesh. Women have also had a consistent presence at the highest levels of government in Costa Rica, San Marino and Panama.

It is a mistake, though, to view nations as having done away with or even seriously undermined patriarchal models of governance. Political gains can be lost if structural change is not made. Economic development that does not encompass women can result in having a female president or prime minister without significant structural change. The UK (17.2 per cent) and the USA (13.8 per cent) are at the lower end of this scale of democracy and political involvement of women. In nations where predominantly male rule has not been seriously challenged, women who enter politics may not be empowered to agitate openly for women's issues. The 'women's caucus' of the US House and Senate has been able to play this role in a limited fashion and only when they have acted in concert – often over retention of reproductive rights for women. In Indonesia and Bangladesh, the percentage of women in parliamentary seats declined before and during female periods of rule (Table 15.1).

TABLE 15.1 Political leadership (% of women)

	Lowest	Highest
Parliamentarians	Bangladesh 2	Sweden 42.7
	Kenya 3.6	Iceland 34.9
	Thailand 9.6	Mozambique 30 +
	Sudan 9.8	Tanzania 30 +
	Japan 10	South Africa 29.8
	Colombia 12.2	Canada 23.6
	USA 13.8	Senegal 19.2
Ministers	Japan 6.5	Belgium 55
	Sudan 7.1	Colombia 31
	US 7.1	–

Source: UNIFEM (2002).

Recasting of female roles is needed by all groups. Much work has been done to propel women into the political arena, but much remains to be done to elevate examples of competent women in politics. The same is true for the women's movement: it began as a massive critique of patriarchy, and has also been marked by strategic validation of female contributions and significant historical roles, but has alienated many women around the world who are looking for more inclusive leadership.

Common factors that enhance female well-being
- Female suffrage, a product of nineteenth-century activism, throughout the world (except in Saudi Arabia and Kuwait).
- Legal recognition of women as full citizens with 'personhood'.
- A history of strong women's movements.
- Female heads of state who serve as symbols and role models (but may not necessarily be allowed access to the most politically powerful positions).
- Constitutional equality with prohibition of sex discrimination.
- A women's party with 'women's lists' of candidates to encourage grass-roots female participation in political affairs.

- State feminism.
- Feminist activism grounded in broad-based social activism.
- Women leaders emerging to fight civil disorder, war, drug wars.

Common factors that detract from female well-being
- Patriarchal laws that do not recognize females as full legal 'persons'.
- Assumption that females should have limited or no power in formal political circles (except through hereditary claim).
- Low participation of women in politics at all levels (at or below 10 per cent in Sudan, Bangladesh, Thailand, Colombia, Japan, the USA), promoting disengagement, indifference or deference to male leadership.
- Periodic or chronic militarism, promoting a hyper-masculinized culture that renders women invisible.
- Extended male-dominated colonialism.
- Legacy of racism from apartheid (e.g. South Africa) or slavery (e.g. the USA), polarizing women by racial group.
- Governments failing to deliver the basic elements of female emancipation, even after suffrage has been granted.
- Tokenism.
- Religious and other ideological superstructures that under-gird entrenched patriarchy, blocking female participation in positions of power and decision-making.

Another pattern of political power we found was resistance through unexpected and sometimes secret means, as with the Chinese women who invented 'Nushu' (Box 15.2). In other countries, this might take the form of 'underground meetings' in preparation for a targeted women's movement initiative.

Towards gender equality

A number of major trends recast women into roles as active agents rather than passive receivers of male power and influence. Women increasingly choose to be single heads of households and independent agents. They have contributed to anti-colonialism and movements of national liberation, and have advanced feminist agendas. Doors are opening and times, indeed, are changing.

At the same time, women suffer from diminished options because their cultures either approve of male dominance and violence or look the other way. Because cultures contain much that is worth keeping, women often lead efforts to protect and preserve them. Because culture includes everything from

> ## Box 15.2 *Resisting patriarchy with a secret language: 'Nushu'*
>
> In Confucian thought, a woman owes three obediences in her life – to her father, her husband and her son. 'Nushu', meaning 'women's script', was developed by women in Hunan province in central China, perhaps as long as 2,000 years ago, to resist obedience to patriarchy. Women relatives and friends used this secret language in speech and written form exclusively, as 'sworn sisters', to allow them to communicate freely without the knowledge of husbands and fathers.
>
> Chinese women also used this unique form of communication to write poetry and songs that expressed their deepest emotions and feelings. Scholars did not study the language, discovered in the nineteenth century, until after the Maoist Cultural Revolution nearly extinguished it as a 'feudal' vestige and destroyed many texts. The last few remaining speakers were elderly women; the need to preserve the language was vital. Yang Huanyi, the last Nushu speaker and believed to be in her nineties, died in September 2004 in Jiangyong, Hunan. The UN Congress on Women in Beijing invited Yang as a special guest. In the last year of her life, she was visited by many scholars and journalists.
>
> Nushu consisted of about 2,000 characters, in contrast to the 50,000 characters in Mandarin Chinese. The characters, described as curvy, wispy and relatively simple, have been compared to the ancient scratching on Chinese oracle bones. Many of the extant texts are special compilations presented to a bride by the women of her family. These clothbound booklets contain songs and poems that lament the departure of the bride from her childhood home. Other Nushu letters tell of unhappy marriages, share gossip or satirize local politicians. One twentieth-century song criticizes the Chinese government for drafting too many sons into the army. (Carolyn Fluehr-Lobban, adapted from Chu 2004: A18c)

dancing to the rules for sharing wealth and power, however, preserving the more visible elements of culture cannot be separated from preserving the invisible elements, including age-old gender power equations. By perpetuating cultures that support male dominance, women may simultaneously perpetuate their subordination.

In a very real sense, the history of the century can be viewed as the history of women's attack on patriarchy across the globe – and of men's attempts to come to grips with changing values. Although the task of fashioning societies that are closer to the equalist rather than the patriarchal end of the continuum is not yet finished, women in the last century made significant headway. The relatively slow pace of social change enhancing female equality and well-being must be considered in the light of the mere century and a half since the Women's Declaration of Rights was launched in Seneca Falls, New York. This recent assault on perhaps five thousand years of patriarchal rule set the stage for the twentieth century, which saw the critique and eventual dismantling of patriarchy.

References

Beaujot, R. and D. Kerr (2004) *Population Change in Canada*, Toronto: Oxford University Press

Bella Center (1980) 'Conclusions of the World Conference of the United Nations Decade for Women: equality, development and peace', 14–30 July, Copenhagen: Bella Center

Billson, J. M. (2005) *Keepers of the Culture: Women and Power in the Canadian Mosaic*, Boulder, CO: Rowman and Littlefield

Chu, H. (2004) 'With the last "sisters", a language dies', *Philadelphia Inquirer*, 3 October, p. A18c

Merry, S. E. (2001) 'Women, violence, and the human rights system', in M. Agosín (ed.), *Women, Gender, and Human Rights: A Global Perspective*, New Brunswick, NJ: Rutgers University Press

Mertus, J. A. (2000) *War's Offensive on Women: The Humanitarian Challenge in Bosnia, Kosovo and Afghanistan* (for the Humanitarianism and War project), Bloomfield, CT: Kumarian Press

Philadelphia Inquirer, the (2004) 'Women's gains linked to education', 18 March

Royal Gazette, the (Hamilton, Bermuda) (2003) 'Chinese stir the debate about domestic violence', 7 January

UNIFEM (The United Nations Development Fund for Women) (2002) *Progress of the World's Women: Gender Equality and the Millennium Development Goals*, New York: UNIFEM

16 | Towards a gendered theory of social change

CAROLYN FLUEHR-LOBBAN AND
JANET MANCINI BILLSON

The twentieth century was an incubator or 'hothouse' for social change that fundamentally affected female well-being in all aspects of life. All countries in our sample acknowledged profound change in an era that witnessed the maturing effects of the Industrial Revolution, mass public education, and civil rights and social legislation. This 'hothouse effect' – fuelled by sophisticated technology, international travel and telecommunications – simply could not have happened in previous centuries. Moreover, the hothouse effect has had a multiplier effect on women and men worldwide through the spread of female suffrage; access to contraception and reproductive knowledge; and an established global agenda for women's rights via world conferences. The authors of the Japan, Croatia, Iceland, UK and Colombia chapters specifically mentioned the vital influence of the second wave of the women's movement, but it is clear that women in the other countries were also affected deeply by international feminist conferences, writing and research. This is in itself an important finding: global feminism was a key agent of change towards female well-being in the twentieth century.

Principles of change emerging from the case studies

After sifting through the data presented in our case study chapters, we identified several principles that contribute to a new, gendered theory of social change. Our theory-building is grounded in empirical data, so it is both synthetic regarding the past and predictive of the factors that will most likely foster female well-being in the future. Our essential purpose is to bring into sharper relief the significant markers and obstacles on the path towards gender equality so that change in the twenty-first century can improve female well-being everywhere. The processes of social change need to be understood in terms of how they shape *female* well-being as well as well-being for all citizens of the world.

Economic participation and female well-being The effects of the Industrial Revolution matured and diffused in the last century. The labour source was female at the beginning of the Industrial Revolution in the nineteenth-century countries of the North, and we continue to find super-exploited feminine labour in the poorest countries of the South. Capitalism's endless search for the cheapest source of labour has also meant that women around the world have earned greater independence and personal autonomy as they have entered the formal labour force. Asian and Latin American countries especially are facing this contradiction, especially in the garment industry, as illustrated in the Thailand and Bangladesh chapters.

PRINCIPLE 1 Official economic and labour force participation data do not fully or accurately reflect female contributions to the gross domestic product.

- Because women engage in such extensive work in the informal and household economies, analysis of change without reference to the full picture of women's contributions is flawed.
- This both reflects and contributes to devaluing of the work women and girls do in their societies on behalf of families and communities.
- Data that do not distinguish between male and female rates of poverty, labour force participation, occupational type, income levels and pensions mask inequities between males and females.

Lessons for activism: Measurement of economic well-being for societies and communities must distinguish between female and male rates and must include female work in the informal economy. Although this has been an agreed-upon goal at major international conferences, compliance must be monitored and ensured through instruments such as CEDAW.

PRINCIPLE 2 The Industrial Revolution (and accompanying technology) continues to be a significant source of social change.

- The Industrial Revolution is both an emancipator and an exploiter of women.
- Capitalist systems continue to seek new markets for consumption and for cheap labour, which can both enhance female well-being and feed exploitation of women and girls.
- Urbanization and entrepreneurship have opened doors to new modes of female expression, self-sustenance, autonomy and control as women become agents of their own change (for example, Asian, Latin American and African women play a pivotal role in small markets; Nigerian women are instrumental in the country's oil companies; and several American women are now heads of Fortune 500 companies).

A gendered theory of social change

- Urbanization and industrialization also leave women at home in villages without adequate resources as men flow into cities for work.
- Women who go to cities for work may find it difficult to return to rural areas because their families may consider them 'spoiled' (e.g. in Bangladesh and Thailand).

Lessons for activism: International feminists and labour activists have not responded adequately to the new economic order that emerged in the wake of the Second World War and the post-colonial world. Women as workers are divided between the secure and the insecure – the well-paid, full-time, trained professionals and the poorly paid, seasonal, part-time, untrained workers. Women at the bottom of the economic scale are in need of a global movement to protect those who are most vulnerable to exploitation in the labour market – females, especially those in developing countries.

Global knowledge and female well-being Because they were restricted in their movement, silenced and removed from instruments of power, women in the past were not entirely effective in organizing to protect their rights and enhance their well-being. The case studies suggest that global communications – especially the Internet – have the potential to revolutionize the international struggle for women's rights within and across borders.

Women in the last two decades of the century created a cyberspace community, a global feminist nation without borders, an invisible chorus of voices that fostered exchange of ideas, creativity and courage to keep fighting for well-being. 'The Global Gag Rule' works against the international voices of women by promulgating a Christian right-wing view of sexuality and reproductive rights. In addition, as powerful as it is, the Internet has so far remained affordable and available to literate people around the globe, but only to those with access to computers, telephone lines and electricity. Global telecommunications and air travel leave out the poorest of the poor; women in isolated, rural areas; and women in countries that have not embraced technology for primarily economic reasons.

PRINCIPLE 3 Technological advances in communication such as the Internet serve as a significant source of social change to spread rising consciousness, knowledge and ideas around the globe.

- Conversely, technological advances also accentuate the gap between richer and poorer nations, communities and individual women.

Lessons for activism: International women's organizations need to address the issue of establishing readily accessible centres that offer women computers, telephone lines and electricity, especially in Africa and Latin American countries.

Educational attainment and female well-being In all the case countries, female literacy and school completion rates skyrocketed during the twentieth century – in most cases to near-parity with male literacy and school achievement. In some cases, females are even outstripping males in completing school and higher education. Ghettoization of females into traditionally female courses of study (and then jobs and careers), however, has persisted in every country we studied. In addition, the earning power of females is elevated less dramatically by education than it is for males, on average. The glass ceiling is a common phenomenon, as are informal economy survival strategies.

Furthermore, education has been used to promulgate assumptions about females as inferior citizens, or to prepare girls for homemaking and child-rearing roles. In the poorest of countries, girls are still left behind boys in significant proportions as families struggle to survive, and persist in valuing male contributions over female contributions. This is also true in areas dominated by religious or cultural beliefs that define girls' public-sphere participation as inappropriate or immoral. Entry of females into historically male-dominated fields of study takes longer than entry into educational systems in general, especially in higher education.

According to Helliwell, the 'protection of high standards of health care and education is worth whatever it takes to do well' (2002: 55). OECD (2001) research shows that educational level is one of the best predictors of well-being. The probability that education of females will ultimately improve well-being for an entire community has not been lost on international development agencies, which have recently stressed girls' education as a priority. Many have documented the far-reaching effects in improved well-being, especially in fertility rates, health and welfare, for communities that supported the education of girls (such as Thailand, Bangladesh, Sudan and Iceland in our study).

Education, then, is both a route to better community functioning and to higher individual, subjective ratings of well-being. This Helliwell refers to as a 'community-level variable' (2002: 44), even though it flows through the individual girl or young woman for whom the school doors have opened. The integrative link joining these higher-level variables to individual, specific measures (such as income or health) is provided by subjective measures of well-being, such as rising educational levels, later marriage and lower fertility rates, and increasing life expectancy.

PRINCIPLE 4 Comprehensive, publicly supported education for females is a necessary condition for social change that favours well-being.

• Basic female literacy is essential for female well-being in both domestic and public spheres, and facilitates efforts towards social change.

Lessons for activism: Basic literacy and school completion are significant catalysts for improving female opportunity and well-being, and should be supported strenuously wherever girls are left out or left behind.

PRINCIPLE 5 Comprehensive, publicly supported education for females is not a sufficient condition for social change that favours well-being.

• Education alone does not guarantee equal treatment, pay equity, upward mobility, agency, or equal participation in institutions that direct social change.
• The greater the proportion of females (over males) who enter a profession or workplace, the more likely its value and remuneration is to decline over time.

Lessons for activism: Programmes for girls' education (to ensure access and improve quality) are critical to female well-being, but the task does not end there. Strong, enforceable legal instruments are essential for ensuring that occupational and political doors are open wide for females whose educational attainment matches or surpasses that of males. Social change agents must work diligently to train their staff in how to make practices, policies and programmes work towards equal opportunity for females (rather than assuming that interventions will automatically be open to females) and challenge gender-biased practices and policies.

PRINCIPLE 6 Education in general and health education in particular have a dramatic impact on lowering fertility rates, birth rates, infant mortality and maternal mortality rates; on completing the demographic transition (from high birth and death rates to low birth rates and slower population growth); and on elevating economic status (for individuals and for societies).

• Education and information relating to maternal and infant health significantly raise female well-being.

Lessons for activism: Efforts to train literate women with low education levels as health educators should be intensified, especially among low-income rural and urban women who are at greatest risk of early pregnancy, have poor pre- and antenatal care, or restricted access to medical care.

PRINCIPLE 7 Gender segregation is a knife that cuts both ways: it can be used to empower females or to disempower and isolate them.

- Girls' schools and women's colleges can help females focus on their own interests and achieve in a context that does not set up false gender competition; they also exempt women temporarily from the tendency of instructors to favour males in the classroom.

Social movements, legislation and female well-being The struggle for women's rights in the local, state, national and international domains was a major thrust of the twentieth century. Women (and their supporters) made significant gains in legislating for maternity leave, day care, pay equity, access to education and work, and equal pensions. In Canada, Iceland and Japan, reformers mounted multiple legislative initiatives to secure women's rights through educational opportunities, economic access and political participation, but those initiatives have not necessarily or immediately transformed underlying sexist attitudes (held by men and also by some women).

PRINCIPLE 8 Legal reforms, compensatory legislation, policy documents and international conventions are a necessary condition for the realization of social change.

- Law and policy documents are powerful sources of social change.
- Legislation is critical for crystallizing emerging changes in consciousness, public opinion and underlying attitudes and values.
- Conversely, many highly visible social reform movements raise consciousness but fail to change lives until rights have become codified in law and formal policy statements.

PRINCIPLE 9 Legal reforms, compensatory legislation, policy documents and international conventions are not a sufficient condition for the realization of social change.

- Law embodies the will of those who desire change but does not necessarily result in immediate attitudinal shifts among those who resist change.
- Legislation favouring gender equity does not necessarily eradicate chauvinism, sexism or the persistence of patriarchal value systems.
- Social change requires a period of acclimatization to legislation, during which attitudinal shifts may occur across a broader spectrum of the population.
- Early legislation on behalf of women will pave the way for change and reflects changing attitudes, but may have to be rewritten in later stages.

Lessons for activism: Attitudinal and behavioural lags may result in spite of efforts to create change through legislatures and courts. Some who support change may do so for reasons other than full support of the change; others oppose change. Therefore, campaigns to raise consciousness and foster gender equality and tolerance must continue long after rights and other gains have been won. This contributes to 'consolidation' so that the agenda can be set for the next plateau of activism for gender equity.

PRINCIPLE 10 Social change is uneven whether affecting gender, class, race or other iniquitous power relations because those with privilege and power try to keep them (which requires legal or physical force) unless they can be convinced to relinquish them (which requires attitudinal change).

- Social change that improves the well-being of one group may in fact (or in perception) detract from the well-being of another group (e.g. affirmative action to increase women's access to university or jobs may reduce male access).
- Efforts to equalize access or power for one population segment may reduce access or power for another segment.
- The more dramatic the social change, the more likely it is that it will occur either in a revolutionary manner, as in Rwanda, where women's leadership significantly increased, prompting an explanation by Acquaro and Landesman (2003) that a matriarchy had grown from the 'madness' of genocide, or in an incremental manner (as in the Millennium Development Goal of achieving 30 per cent female political participation on the way to the more equitable goal of 50 per cent).

Lessons for activism: Social change agents need to evaluate the extent to which change will result in loss of power for opposing or threatened population segments. Creating change in a 'zero-sum' situation, in which everyone wins and no one loses, will most likely be met with the least resistance. Dramatic change for women can occur out of disasters such as that in Rwanda or in times of critical need for female labour during war, but sustaining change and using it for leverage for the next stage of building gender equity is the most difficult challenge.

PRINCIPLE 11 Legislated social change may result in backlash rather than forward movement.

- Access and equity granted by law may be accompanied by efforts to subvert or reverse social change (for example, affirmative action laws designed to enhance female upward mobility often produce sexual harassment in the workplace, the 'chilly climate' in the classroom, and 'back door' policies that restrict access).

- Backlash may then serve as inspiration for renewed reform efforts to consolidate gains and to prevent their erosion.

Lessons for activism: Social change agents should anticipate backlash and be prepared for attempts to reverse progress through back-door mechanisms.

PRINCIPLE 12 Legislative and policy instruments may reflect changing attitudes among the privileged groups (e.g. male leaders), but change that supports female well-being will not happen unless there is sufficient organizing to reach a 'tipping point' in general public willingness to accept the legislation.

- Even when they apparently are not successful in the short term, social movements may effect eventual change by engaging in relentless efforts to build public awareness and sway public opinion over the long term.
- Social movements may achieve desired changes by manipulating messages to appeal more broadly to resistant population segments.

Lessons for activism: Failure of a movement to effect change is not necessarily reason to disband; rather, it may be reason to renew efforts or to shift to a slightly different (or differently defined) platform in order to bring new support to the cause.

Political participation and female well-being

PRINCIPLE 13 The political arena may be the last door to open fully for women.

- Especially at the highest level of political office or public responsibility (e.g. presidents, governors, parliamentarians, legislators, cabinet members or mayors), women's participation is blocked until the latest stages of liberation and gender equalization.
- Even when women achieve the highest positions (e.g. in Bangladesh, Iceland), those positions may entail relatively little concrete, formal power; the positions are likely to be figurehead rather than truly powerful positions with far-reaching decision-making responsibilities.
- When women hold high office, it is likely to be gained through inheritance or appointment, rather than election.

PRINCIPLE 14 Women in leadership positions may not be motivated to or able to create positive social change for women (for example, Margaret

Thatcher, who had real power as prime minister of the UK, did not launch a major programme to stop domestic violence).

PRINCIPLE 15 Social change is dialectical in that it emerges out of existing structures and social, political and economic arrangements that are not working for at least one segment of the population (e.g. women, poor people or ethnic minorities).

- Reversing the Marxist dialectic that the seeds of destruction are present in each social formation, feminist perspective views present formations as containing the seeds of a new social order, preparing the way for positive social change.
- Conversely, when broad segments of the population are satisfied with existing structures and elites, social change benefiting less powerful segments will be difficult and slow, if not impossible.
- In times of scarcity, recession or depression, extracting cooperation favouring female well-being from the privileged segments will be particularly difficult.

Lessons for activism: Efforts to create beneficial change for those who suffer from present structures and social formations will fare better if they can be shown to benefit as well those who benefit from those structures and arrangements.

PRINCIPLE 16 Women as members of the minority group may hold negative attitudes towards their own group which retard or block social change, the political participation of women (especially at the highest levels) and general progress in gender equity.

- Conversely, members of the overwhelmingly male dominant group may be instrumental in leveraging sufficient public opinion among the dominant group and the resistant minority group in order to pass cutting-edge legislation (for example, suffrage, extended maternity/paternity leave, or pay equity).

Lessons for activism: Campaigns to open doors, change roles or gain equity must be directed towards members of the less privileged group (on whose behalf these efforts are made) as well as towards the privileged group.

PRINCIPLE 17 As with education, gender segregation may inspire and facilitate female activism or block women from full participation in political processes.

- Female-only spaces can help develop autonomy and identity for individuals, groups and movements (for example, sexual segregation facilitates solidarity among Muslim women; the global women's movement has depended on international conferences during which women withdraw temporarily from the male-dominated mainstream to reflect on identity, goals and strategies for change).
- Similarly, women's groups and girls' clubs can help females set goals and create a base for making or sustaining positive change.

Lessons for activism: At the local, national and international levels, it continues to be important for women to organize meetings and other venues at which females can build solidarity, share ideas and garner support.

Violence against women and female well-being A major advance for female well-being occurred when domestic violence was placed on the international agenda of human rights in the last third of the twentieth century. The safety and well-being of children in violent homes were added, as were other forms of violence against women, including sexual assault. Initially, the shelters and safe houses that were provided in some countries in response to male abuse were critical for protecting women and children. This approach cast women as victims, however, and inadvertently stripped them of their right to remain in their own home. We hope the twenty-first century will reverse this process and strip the right of the perpetrator to remain in his home ('a man's home is his castle'), which leaves the situation of men unchanged while the lives of women and children are disrupted.

We acknowledge that the shelter movement was more adapted to Western nuclear families, and not to the extended family life so prevalent in non-Western societies. Other strategies appropriate to local cultural circumstances need to be explored in these nations, such as the successful 'women's police stations' in Brazil and India that have been set up to respond primarily to male violence against women. Women police officers train other community women in how to respond to incidents of domestic violence that they witness or experience. Female police have the power of arrest in response to a woman's complaint. The anonymity and potential disappearance of the abusing male are far less prevalent in extended families, and appropriate strategies to contend with these offenders can be creatively developed. A fundamental paradigm shift needs to occur in this area.

PRINCIPLE 18 The more powerful and independent women become, the more likely it is that powerful males will abuse, ignore, ridicule or physically harm them – as a way to regain their real or perceived lost power.

- The unrelenting problem of violence against women reveals the still-unreconstructed patriarchy underlying gender relations.
- Social change in economic, political and educational institutions depends in part on the ability to change unbalanced, male-dominated gender regimes in family and intimate relations.

Lessons for activism: Existing programmatic and policy responses, while helpful in reducing the effects of male abuse, remain inadequate to the scope of the problem and fail to address its underlying causes. In the case of domestic violence or sexual harassment, explicit attention should be paid to the power relations between perpetrators and victims in areas such as educational level, job level and income level; efforts to improve women's status should be accompanied by particular vigilance when they are in relationships with relatively disenfranchised, powerless males.

PRINCIPLE 19 To the extent that legislation and policies focus on women as 'victims' or 'welfare recipients', rather than fully human, autonomous agents, they tend to be piecemeal and to entrench inequitable treatment, intimidation or human rights violations.

Lessons for activism: Laws and policies that protect women from domestic violence (for example, through the provision of safe houses and shelters) need to be rethought. Defining women (and their children) as victims who must be removed from their homes and communities for their own protection actually doubly victimizes women and detracts from female well-being. Rather, laws and policies should remove the perpetrator from circulation in order to protect his victims.

Warfare and female well-being The twentieth century was one of the most conflict-ridden eras in history. Not only were there more wars than hitherto, but the conflicts also tended to last longer. For example, in 1995 approximately one third of the world's countries engaged in some form of warfare. How does this affect female well-being? Nordstrom (2004) identifies two key points. First, the vast majority (75 per cent) of refugees are women and children and 90 per cent of casualties are civilians. Women are targeted because they are perceived as strong – or as weak and vulnerable – or because they are related to targeted males. In Taliban-controlled Afghanistan, war created 50,000 widows who were not permitted to work outside the home and 2.5 million refugees;

76 per cent of female deaths were due to aerial bombings. Second, life for women is extensively damaged by the collateral damage of political violence, state-sponsored terror, violence against refugees, campaigns against street children, and the invariable intensification of domestic violence during war or chronic conflict.

These patterns require special attention by international women's and human rights organizations. As Nordstrom argues, gender-based violence complicates the picture of well-being for females in time of war *or* in societies that allow gender violence even in peacetime. For example, women's flight may result from the threat of FGM, bride-burning, forced sterilization or abortion, forced prostitution, or legal domestic violence. Such examples of abuse should entitle victims to international protection and, if necessary, asylum. While all uprooted people are more vulnerable to abuse, displaced women and girls are particularly susceptible to gender-based violence in refugee camps; women need protection in all stages of flight. Finally, uprooted men and women have different needs which stem from the inequitable gender relations embedded in their pre-war society.

Consciousness about the devastating impacts of warfare, civil unrest and chronic insurgency on women was raised to unprecedented levels in the twentieth century. Women are left to manage homes, children, institutions and communities by themselves; women and children make up the majority of refugees; and women are exposed to great danger, dislocation and sexual crimes committed in the context of war and chronic conflict. For example, for the first time in human history the rape of women during wartime became a crime against humanity, especially after the strategic use of rape was revealed in the Bosnian war, and was reaffirmed in the crises in Rwanda and Darfur, Sudan. Wartime rapes were common as Croatian women were raped by Serbian men; the number of women raped in Bosnia during the war is put at between 30,000 and 50,000. The United Nations estimates that in Rwanda at least a quarter of a million women were raped; 70 per cent of those who survived now have AIDS. In Burma, as in other countries, women refugees are vulnerable to terrorist tactics of rape but continue as self-sufficient heads of households wherever they are.

PRINCIPLE 20 War and chronic conflict contribute to fundamental social changes in female well-being, including impoverishment, dislocation and vulnerability to sexual violence.

- Women and children suffer disproportionately among refugees and the homeless during (and after) war; this impoverishes but can also radicalize women.

385

- Insurgency and guerrilla warfare may lead to militarization of children and co-optation of women, who see no other avenue to security during prolonged conflict.
- A strong connection exists between militarism and war and rising levels of domestic violence. Returning soldiers inured to violence in battle are more likely to beat their wives.

Lessons for activism: Recognizing the relationship between warfare and domestic violence can lead to important policy decisions regarding female safety and well-being. Governments and NGOs should expect women and children to suffer disproportionately in times of war or chronic conflict, and should anticipate strategies for managing refugees. Many creative, ameliorative responses have been developed to protect women under these circumstances but, as the case of ethnic cleansing in Darfur has shown, words are insufficient to alleviate suffering. It is critical to establish that violations of human rights during conflict are still violations of human rights, and that females of all ages and situations are particularly vulnerable.

PRINCIPLE 21 Assessment of social change should be made during war, crisis or chronic conflict to pinpoint the level of impact on female well-being.

- Often it is women who work diligently behind the scenes to end armed conflict.
- Women continue to manage families, communities and basic institutions in the face of great adversity as in Rwanda.

Lessons for activism: Women arrange for medicines, food and scarce commodities, and demand public accounting of relations who have 'disappeared'. For example, women in Kosovo and Albania organized and effectively worked with NGOs, established humanitarian programmes, and raised the issue of their sexual abuse at the 1995 Beijing conference. International women's organizations and NGOs should also recognize the crucial role women as victims in wartime play as peacemakers, organizers and survivors.

PRINCIPLE 22 After war or crisis, assessment should be made of female empowerment and capacity to mobilize and cope with post-conflict issues for themselves and their children.

Lessons for activism: Beyond food, shelter and medicine, women may need support (tools, money and other resources) in organizing activist groups to help achieve political, economic and educational stability in the post-conflict context.

PRINCIPLE 23 In cases of state feminism (e.g. Croatia, Sudan), token grants of female equity may create a false illusion of social and political change. These gestures can be revoked as easily as they are bestowed.

- Bestowing rights on women or any other humans (e.g. by a 'benign despot') is no substitute for the rights that are won by popular feminine agitation.
- Conversely, when a group has historically been victimized, it resists and reshapes imposed social change, even if it means going 'underground' to do so.

Lessons for activism: State feminism is a widespread post-colonial phenomenon offered by many political leaders and nations as a 'quick fix' to long-standing gender inequities. States may proclaim gender equity or neutrality in words but fail to deliver in practice.

Feminism and female well-being The oppression of Muslim women is a given in the political confrontation between the West and the Islamic world. The uncritical assertion that Muslim women are veiled, passive and utterly dominated by Muslim men has been used as a rationale for military interventions in Afghanistan and Iraq. The argument is that a significant benefit includes 'liberating the women'. This smacks of a new imperialism reminiscent of the old colonial model of the civilizing benefits of intervention and occupation.

For the Westerner, the veil is emblematic of the assumed inferior status of the Muslim woman. Its presence or absence is often viewed as the single most important litmus test for whether a Muslim country is repressive or free and democratic. The new imperialism is like the old in that it is not only about military, economic and political control of 'the East'; it is also about cultural domination. The symbol of the veil has become an effective dividing line between Western 'freedom' and Islamic repression. In truth, an overwhelming number of women choose voluntarily to veil or not to veil, and some Islamist regimes have violated Islamic norms by mandating veiling as part of their campaign to gain social and political control. The assertion that Muslim women need liberation is made without reflection on the state of women's freedom in the West.

This case raises also the so-called political correctness that characterized the women's movement in twentieth-century USA, Canada and Europe: women who did not switch to pants and low heels, wash off their make-up or stop dyeing their hair were considered suspect and probably not capable of being true feminists.

PRINCIPLE 24 The well-being of a Muslim woman is determined not by whether she covers herself with the hijab, but by her family's standard of living, her sense of security and freedom from harm or abuse, her level of education, her sense of agency, and her own personal preferences.

- External symbols of womanhood and femininity – certain types of clothing, make-up, high heels, or veiling for Muslim women – do not necessarily reflect the existence of women's oppression.
- Superficial choices do not always reveal the underlying realities of female well-being (or ill-being).
- External symbols of womanhood and femininity are not necessarily examples of false consciousness.
- External symbols of womanhood and femininity do not necessarily indicate women's lack of power in fighting oppression.

Lessons for activism: What we learn in trying to understand veiling can apply to women in general. When feminists in the 1970s and 1980s defined female trappings (low-cut tops or the use of make-up) as indicative of false consciousness and serving male pleasure (treating female bodies as sex objects), many women were turned away from the women's movement. We have since learned that 'true consciousness' in the Marxist sense comes in many guises, and that women are just as likely to dress for their own comfort, aesthetic sense and personal power as they are to achieve some elusive male standard. Female activism depends on tolerance and inclusiveness, not being judgemental.

PRINCIPLE 25 Real issues relating to the well-being of women are often co-opted and politically manipulated by men in control – in both imperialist and Islamic countries – and are used as a tool of state policy.

- The abortion issue and a woman's right to choose overwhelmed and co-opted the feminist movement in the USA, which had been much broader in its earlier days. Abortion rights became an arena in which men debated and determined women's reproductive freedom. In Islamist countries, notably Sudan in our sample, authorities clamped down on some of the poorest women, who are sellers of traditional beer, for example, because they are without 'honour or protection'. Their public humiliation through arrest and imprisonment, or flogging for the sake of 'public morality', is sheer political manipulation on the part of the Islamist political leaders of the state.

Towards an integrated theory of change

In very broad terms, we derived the following principles from the case studies which address the nature, sources, persistence and measurement of social change. These principles can under-gird future theory and future activism in the interests of female well-being.

PRINCIPLE 26 Social change for women as an oppressed group means moving through three essential stages: (1) penetrating the historical barriers that have kept women out of power through changing minds; (2) normalizing women's participation in the public sphere to reach the tipping point of acceptance; and (3) consolidating gains through legislation, court cases to test the legislation, ensuring implementation of existing favourable legislation, and writing further law or policy. These processes prepare the way for the next stage of change. This overriding principle is extended in the principles elaborated upon throughout the rest of this chapter.

- Symbolic gains must be institutionalized through pressure from change agents.
- In order for fundamental, positive change supporting female well-being to sustain itself, changes must penetrate and transform education, politics, the economy, the family, religion, and so forth – all social institutions.
- Political and policy gains can be lost or fail to create sustainable positive social change if commensurate structural changes are not forthcoming.
- To secure positive social change for female well-being, significant women's organizations must exist that are well organized, expertly led, powerful and firmly entrenched. These organizations must be strong and cohesive if they are to become major players after they have won significant policy shifts, legislation or revolution.

PRINCIPLE 27 Social change affecting females is rooted in power relations.
- The typical 'rules' governing gender relations may be suspended out of necessity during a time of crisis, wartime or in a concerted political movement (such as a national liberation, civil rights or freedom movement).
- The suspension of rules makes it difficult to reinstate them when the crisis is over. This produces a shift in the distribution of male and female powers.
- When men attempt to regain their dominance after a successful effort towards which women contributed substantially, the resulting bitterness may stimulate change as women resist going back to the old regime. Stefanos documents this source of change in Eritrea (2000: 56–61); the same occurred after the Vietnam anti-war movement and after the mobilization of American women during the Second World War.

PRINCIPLE 28 Social change is not as linear or progressive as Western theory has suggested.

- Social change involves advances and reversals; improved and declined status; gains and setbacks; incremental gains and subtle slippages.
- Social change is sometimes cyclical but turning back the hands of time may be impossible once freedoms and rights are entrenched.
- Positive change may deteriorate as gains are met with backlash.

PRINCIPLE 29 Social change is a product of many forces that may appear to be unrelated.

- The forces creating social change are often unpredictable and difficult to pinpoint.
- A society's dominant group can be a force for positive social change for oppressed, minority or disadvantaged groups – or a blocker of change.
- State feminism can arise out of the ashes of colonial oppression in post-colonial governments, thereby initiating sweeping change.

PRINCIPLE 30 Social change is synergistic; it takes place at multiple levels and has multiple consequences that influence each other.

- The ramifications (results and 'spin-offs') of social change may not be immediately obvious, identifiable or intended (Merton 1957).

PRINCIPLE 31 Social change is sometimes dialectical and based on structural tensions, in the Marxist vein, but can also emerge spontaneously and seren-dipitously from new technologies, ideas and inventions.

- Debate and conflict over ideas can stimulate positive social change (as Lewis Coser theorized in 1956).
- Debate generated in one society can affect the debate in other societies, especially with the advent of global communications and travel.

PRINCIPLE 32 Social change is by definition always dynamic but is often very slow and unidimensional (that is, affecting one institution at a time).

- Political, legal and policy changes at the highest levels in society may not immediately be reflected at the level of culture, values and everyday life.
- Measurement of well-being must assess the infiltration of change for females (and males) across all institutions and cultures within a society (for example, China's policy of one child per family lowered the birth rate dramatically, which may seem to be a positive step, but practice favours protecting the life of male fetuses over female fetuses, which is a negative for females).

PRINCIPLE 33 Token involvement of women in the political process or in the economy, however, does not constitute fundamental social change.

- Analysis must distinguish between full empowerment of women politically and economically and restricted or conditional political and economic participation.
- Token participation may be emblematic or indicative of future significant change, but it cannot be counted as fundamental social change.

PRINCIPLE 34 Social change cannot be measured without examining the data on the percentage of females affected by that change (for example, democracy without women's suffrage, 'body counts' in wartime that do not include civilian casualties).

Female well-being in the twenty-first century requires theory that views females as humans and not as a special category of human. It also requires theory that can be applied to decision-making that has relevance to feminism and social movements in the developed as well as the developing world. This means a feminist theory of social justice that is applicable to urgent situations – whether for women on welfare in the developed societies or women and children as refugees in failing states. As counter-intuitive as it may seem, an exclusive focus on gender is inadequate to an effective feminist theory. The next stage is to build better theory regarding human rights, inclusiveness and well-being for all world citizens.

References

Acquaro, K. and P. Landesman (2003) 'Out of madness, a matriarchy', *Mother Jones*, January/February, pp. 59–63

Coser, L. A. (1956) *The Functions of Social Conflict*, Glencoe, IL: Free Press

Helliwell, J. F. (2002) *Globalization and Well-being*, Vancouver: University of British Columbia Press

Merton, R. K. (1957) *Social Theory and Social Structure*, New York: Free Press of Glencoe

Nordstrom, C. (2004) *Shadows of War: Violence, Power and International Profiteering in the 21st Century*, Berkeley: University of California Press

OECD (Organization for Economic Cooperation and Development) (2001) *The Well-being of Nations: The Role of Human and Social Capital*, Paris: OECD Centre for Educational Research and Innovation

Stefanos, A. (2000) 'The social and economic status of Eritrean women: advances and reversals', *Trotter Review*

17 | Towards global female well-being

JANET MANCINI BILLSON AND
CAROLYN FLUEHR-LOBBAN

> The principle which regulates the existing social relations between the two
> sexes – the legal subordination of one sex to the other – is wrong in itself,
> and now one of the chief hindrances to human improvement ... it ought to
> be replaced by a principle of perfect equality, admitting no power or privi-
> lege on the one side, no disability on the other. (Mill 1989)

John Stuart Mill's observation in the eighteenth century (1989) that a full democracy must be characterized by egalitarian gender relations was not fully realized in the twentieth century. The Western first and second waves of feminism,
the 'Third World' anti-colonialist and feminist-nationalist movements, and
several decades of 'female empowerment' development activism have still not
achieved the much-desired goal of gender equity. Although Bayes et al. (2001:
5) say that democratization is progressing slowly, they also point out that
democracy often does not mean the same for women as it does for men. If so-
called democratic states do not involve full parity, equality and equity between
the sexes, these gains are experienced by the few rather than the majority.
Furthermore, long-term and extensive male domination of local, regional, national and international decision-making bodies means that issues of concern
to men are defined by default as 'general human concerns' – while 'women's
concerns' are seen as somehow limited and less important (Charlesworth
1997: 386). Democracy must be consultative, inclusive and transparent in order
to promote full participation of women and, ultimately, female well-being.

Even today, human rights are still accorded to 'peoples', but the people
often do not include females. Gendered law at all levels, nationally and internationally, has rendered females invisible and subject to male authority. Multiple levels of subordination of women (and minorities) persist in all the case
study countries. Breaking down gender as a major dividing line has not been
easy or quick. The persistence of inequities and inequality appears as oppression of women through law, social policy and practice.

Gender stratification, as reflected in differences in basic human rights, education, health, incomes, occupational types and participation in political life,
characterized all the countries in this book. Women throughout the century

and across the countries are disproportionately caught up in the interlocking identities complicated by socio-economic, religious, ethnic or racial diversity. Each of these forms of social differentiation generates social symptoms (some might call them social problems) that compromise female well-being and threaten the struggle for liberation and equality.

We conceptualize *Female Well-being*, our book's title and our common global goal, not merely as the absence of ill-being or as the substantial goal of good health with a long and full life. Rather, a substantial part of female well-being is social well-being in which women and girls enjoy not just access to but *fulfilment* of economic, political, educational and social equality. That women live longer does not necessarily mean that they are living better or more socially productive lives.

Three major implications emerge from our case studies. One is that the status of women remains lower than the status of men in all countries. This finding, though not surprising, none the less underscores the fact that there is still much work to be done. Second, the external and internal factors that impede female equality, the women's movement and female well-being still remain firmly entrenched. Third, the key to a vibrant and successful women's movement lies in understanding, accepting and leveraging our diversity. As we move in this chapter towards a vision of female well-being in the twenty-first century, we revisit the concept and recall some of the landmarks of advance in the twentieth century, especially in the areas of equal rights and human rights.

As we have seen, recent studies of globalization have not been particularly gender sensitive. This is remarkable given the fact that a major part of the success of multinationals has been the super-exploitation of female labour in the transitional agrarian countries, or the manipulation of female workers in the industrial nations through periodic mobilization and demobilization. Globalization theory must take into account female well-being in the fuller sense we are developing in this volume – a goal of optimum physical wellness and full social participation.

Redefining female well-being

We have seen in the case studies that individual well-being is essential for general human development. Governments have the capacity to support or diminish the well-being of their citizens; some are more in tune than others with the concept that female well-being may require special measures. Kaufmann et al. (1999a) developed a multi-variable index that measures the quality of government institutions via levels of corruption, agency efficiency, honesty of elections and transparency of regulations. The index is positively correlated with well-being *regardless of a country's GDP*. Government policies have a strong impact on both subjective and objective well-being, which means that change at this level could be extremely productive across the board. It also means that women do not necessarily have to spend their energies fighting for a particular piece of legislation (although that is important work) but should also be fighting for greater government transparency and honest elections and against corruption. By making government better, the chances are that more inclusive practices and gender-fair policies can more easily be enacted and enforced.

Governments should take painstaking care to *nurture* institutions rather than damage them – and to ensure that government agents and agencies are trustworthy. This requires them to be inclusive and open to all segments of society. Social movements that insist that governments reflect the profile of a country's population can go a long way towards opening up the system to greater accountability and transparency. This is a role that women in every country can play effectively. For government policies and institutions to become more responsive to female well-being, though, requires a paradigm shift.

The 'Humpty Dumpty' effect: the role of public policy and trust As we saw in the discussion of well-being in Chapter 2, individual and national well-being are integrally linked to each other. National policies impact on individual social capital and income as well as national income (GDP). Globalization has varying effects from country to country, but countries remain relatively free to craft whatever policy measures they feel will help preserve their autonomy, competitiveness and legitimacy in the community of nations. In the light of the growing realization that female well-being reflects and contributes to national well-being, regardless of time or place, policies supporting women's well-being should support societal well-being: 'Further increases in *average* income levels have little influence on self-assessed well-being, while both individual and community-level measures of education, health, employment, and social capital have continuing payoffs' (Helliwell 2002: 85).

In the 'Humpty Dumpty' effect, if a policy has the net impact of damaging a basic institution such as the educational system or families (for example, not having a coherent day care or family leave policy when there is economic pressure for both parents to work), the results may be harder to rectify than simply raising incomes for individuals. Once the eggs have been broken, it proves extremely difficult to put them back in the shell. Societies have found it easier to recover from economic depression than from institutional breakdown. The role of social policy is not to break eggs but to promote individual well-being that feeds into institutional well-being: 'Balanced evaluation of policies requires a much wider and richer canvas – one that takes full account of the sources of well-being' (ibid.: 53).

The World Values Survey shows that *trust* in national institutions (e.g. government) is positively correlated with interpersonal trust, as in Scandinavian countries. For countries to rectify inequities and build public and interpersonal trust, the quality of government must be raised (Kaufmann et al. 1999a, 1999b) because it directly affects economic growth and per capita incomes, and is a direct product of national policies. If women are to partake of and contribute to the engines of economic growth – and if they are to develop higher levels of public and interpersonal trust – then governments must make an intentional, committed effort to open doors to education and foster economic, social and political mobility for women. Theoretically, the networks and norms that feed individual health, stability and well-being must be fully open to and influenced by females in order to nourish robust institutions, a high level of national trust and a resilient social fabric. In the opposite case, when governments are fraught with cronyism, corruption and policies that serve only the elite, trust fails, institutions shatter, and the social fabric weakens.

This implies that good policy and goodwill can have good outcomes for females and males alike. Strategies should build trust and support good policy. Nations can learn from each other in figuring out how to craft gender-neutral (or gender-rebalancing) policies. We will address strategies for change in the last section of this chapter.

Social capital can be defined as 'networks together with shared norms, values and understandings that facilitate co-operation within or among groups' (OECD 2001: 41). The strength of these networks tends to decline with physical distance (and across national boundaries) – and across *social distances* as well. This is precisely why the impacts of barriers to female participation established and maintained by the 'old boys' network', in whatever country and setting, are so far reaching and devastating for females. It is as though women have been relegated to 'another country' and blocked from participating in the critical networks that produce and build social capital in their own community. For example, many constitutions written in past centuries eliminated women (and people of colour) from true citizenship as expressed in voting or the right to own land. This was true in the eighteenth-century United States, for example, but the practice persisted throughout the nineteenth and twentieth centuries and into the twenty-first. Every time females are defined as 'less than', the society as a whole is diminished. If individual well-being contributes to general social well-being, and vice versa, then both females and their communities are likely to experience a lower level of both objective and subjective well-being.

To quote Helliwell, 'protection of high standards of health care and education is worth whatever it takes to do well' (2002: 55). Governments that fail to do so miss a critical opportunity to build public trust and foster the equality of all citizens. Research has shown that all other outcome variables relating to well-being flow through education: in other words, the linkages between education and social capital have been clearly established, and 'both trust and participation depend positively both on one's own education level and on the average education in one's community' (ibid.: 44). OECD (2001) research shows that educational level is one of the best predictors of well-being if income, social capital and other outcome variables are removed. The implications of this finding are momentous for the future of female well-being and women's activism: trust and participation should rise as *all* members of a community enjoy a rise in education level – and as trust and participation rise, so should the quality of institutions and both general and individual, subjective and objective well-being.

The probability that the education of females will ultimately improve well-being for an entire community has not been lost on international development agencies which, throughout the 1990s and into the early twenty-first century, have stressed girls' education as a priority. Many have documented the far-reaching effects in improved well-being, especially in health and welfare, for communities that have finally (perhaps under pressure from international bodies) allowed and supported the education of girls (such as Thailand and Iceland in our study). Education, then, is both a route to better community functioning and to higher individual, subjective ratings of well-being. The 'public good' benefits from the individual's personal development. This Helliwell refers to as a 'community-level variable' (2002: 43–5) even though it flows through the individual girl or young woman for whom the school doors have opened. The integrative link joining these higher-level variables to individual, specific measures (such as income or health), he believes, is provided by subjective measures of well-being, such as rising educational levels, later marriage and lower fertility rates, and increasing life expectancy.

At the international level, this means that the United Nations and other bodies with a global mandate must work diligently to recognize the need for equality of representation of women in their workforces, leadership and policy-setting ranks; must train their staff in how to make practices, policies and programmes work towards equal opportunity for females (rather than assuming that interventions will automatically be open to females); write in gender-neutral and inclusive language; and challenge the gender-biased practices and policies in countries in which they operate.

The challenge of globalization for female well-being

Globalism has a human face and a female face, and the inter-cultural *mélange* is just as important as the economic and geographical aspects. We are particularly interested in the impact of globalization on the lives of women and female well-being in the world. Increasingly, it is women who provide the labour and the products that make the global marketplace possible. Women are on the move as never before in history. 'Third World' migrant women achieve their success only by assuming the cast-off domestic roles of middle- and high-income women in the 'First World' (Ehrenreich and Hochschild 2002: 3). As women from developing countries in Asia, Africa, South America and eastern Europe move into the industrialized West – as nannies, housekeepers, mail-order brides and sex workers – they bring with them more than their labour.

The darker side of globalization lies in the widening gap between rich and poor nations. Each year, tens of thousands of women leave South and South-East Asia to work in low-skill, low-paying service sector jobs. Other women leave the Philippines, Sri Lanka and India to work in the Middle East, while women from developing Asian countries, such as Thailand or urban Philippines, migrate to more prosperous places of work in Hong Kong, Singapore or Australia (Seager 1997: 64). Some women choose to migrate for higher wages; others have no choice as they are trapped in sexual slavery, as in our Thailand case, or in forced domestic servitude. Those who migrate often do so at great personal cost, leaving their families to other, even poorer care-givers as they leave to serve the wealthy in other countries. As 'Third World' women nurture the children of wealthy Western career women, their own children are left in the care of grandparents, aunts or even orphanages. As Western women abdicate the role of homemaker in increasing numbers, women from developing nations fill in the gap by doing 'women's work' for them, but by doing so they create a 'care drain' in their own countries.

The global rise in sexual slavery finds women and children sold as commodities on the world market. Young girls in brothels are often beaten, drugged and forced into sexual slavery in 'tourist' destinations (such as in Thailand and Bangladesh in our study). The largest consumers of the international sex trade are men from the USA, Canada, China, Australia, New Zealand, Japan, Saudi Arabia, France, Germany, Norway and England. Thailand, one of the most popular destinations, has one of the highest HIV infection rates in the

397

world. Girls are literally a disposable commodity, easily replaced after two to five years of sexual servitude (Ehrenreich and Hochschild 2002: 220).

As global capitalism permeates world economics, so does the need for cheap labour that makes goods accessible to the consumer masses. In the Export Processing Zones (offshore free-market manufacturing zones), the proportion of female to male workers ranges from 71 per cent in South Korea to 88 per cent in Sri Lanka. Simply put, the high standard of living that 'privileged' women and men in the industrialized West enjoy is intimately linked with and dependent on the super-exploited labour of 'commoners' in the poorest nations.

Neo-liberalism and gender agendas The economic policies of such institutions as the World Bank and the International Monetary Fund have attempted to shape developing nations by insisting on open markets and capital, stable monetary practices, structural adjustment and political stability, but only in the last two decades have they had anything to say about gender issues. Nevertheless, globalization does result in enormous and sometimes unpredictable upheavals in gender relations. As Richard Sandbrook (2001) points out, social democratic policies that might benefit large segments of the population in countries that are struggling for survival do not seem to be consonant with neo-liberal globalization policies. A 'false dilemma' has developed, according to Ugarteche (2000), which suggests that developing countries must embrace neo-liberal corporate capitalism or die economically. Alternatives to corporate globalization that employ some of the traditional subsistence techniques used for centuries by women (and men) might solve some development problems (Bennholdt-Thomsen et al. 2001; Cheru 2002).

Human rights, women's rights and female well-being

Gender apartheid has marked the twentieth century, even more pervasively than racial apartheid, according to Hilary Charlesworth (1997: 384); international and national efforts to remove or ameliorate gender apartheid have focused on 'women's rights'. This was a positive movement, but also assumed that human rights were 'men's rights'. Until the historic masculine bias in international human rights has been adequately addressed, well-being for females will not be achieved.

Although some women in developing nations have charged Western feminists with cultural bias or a qualifying of women's rights by cultural relativism, we agree with Charlesworth that 'patriarchy and the devaluing of women ... are almost universal', although they may be expressed differently from culture to culture. While we respect each other's differences, movement towards global female well-being requires us to find our common pains, values, challenges and goals.

Recognition of women's rights as universal rights As we saw in Chapter 15, the Second World Conference on Human Rights (Vienna, 1993) declared that 'the full and equal enjoyment by women of all human rights' should be a priority for national governments and for the United Nations (ibid.: 391). Issues focused on the protection of women from violence gained the world's attention in the second half of the twentieth century and finally resulted in women's rights being placed on a par with human rights (Merry 2001: 83; Benedek et al. 2002; Kerr et al. 2004). Feminists might point out that it was not until the end of the twentieth century that philosophically women achieved full humanity. Nevertheless, this accomplishment permitted a fundamentally new outlook – one that could see the systematic rape of women during wartime not only as a crime against women, but as a crime against humanity. Fluehr-Lobban (1995, 1998) has written about the limitations of cultural relativism in global human rights discourse and praxis with a focus on several culturally specific practices, such as female circumcision or 'honour' killings, as well as more general practices negatively affecting women, such as domestic violence.

Although there is much disagreement about issues such as female circumcision, there is one concept that might be used as an underpinning for human rights ethics in this new century: the need to avoid harm to females. Harm takes place when there is death, pain, disability or loss of freedom or pleasure that results from an act by one human upon another (Gert 1988: 47–9). There is nothing particularly African, Asian or American about violence or injustice. This is true of violations of human rights, whether they are in the form of arbitrary arrest, detention and torture inflicted by the state, or female circumcision imposed by custom. We believe that one could evaluate the contemporary legitimacy of cultural practices in terms of retaining useful traditions (which enhance female well-being) and abandoning practices that inflict harm or injury (which detract from female well-being). When reasonable persons from different cultural backgrounds agree that certain institutions or cultural practices cause harm, then the moral neutrality of cultural relativism must be suspended.

Avoidance of harm has been a key concept in the development of ethical guidelines in medical research and other scientific activities (Fluehr-Lobban 1994: 3). Philosophers have also refined concepts of harm and benefit; the discussion more frequently occurs, however, in terms of the prevention of harm

Box 17.1 Mary Robinson and the search for global human rights

Mary Robinson, former president of Ireland, peacemaker, coordinator of the Decade of Indigenous Peoples, and former UN High Commissioner for Human Rights (1997–2002), offers valuable insights from her practical work throughout the globe (2002). As a strong advocate of universal human rights irrespective of cultural difference, she describes how progress was made in difficult dialogues, for example with conservative Muslim scholars: 'They listened to us because for the first time we listened to them.'

Whether in Afghanistan or northern Nigeria, she found that the best way to effect change is through empowering women to raise their voices from inside their cultural framework (as in the struggle to eradicate or ameliorate FGM). If power is placed in local hands, then the superpowers have no right to preach, judge, frame or lead the dialogue. Robinson argues that the legal framework of the human rights movement must be merged with debates about globalization. This needs to be defined as a duty for all humans – citizens without borders – who are energized by a global vision in which human rights matters are the first order of business, not the last.

rather than the promotion of benefit. Listening to and incorporating the perspectives and voices of women can move the twenty-first-century agenda from prevention of harm to promotion of benefit favouring female well-being.

Beyond the standard of harm, it is increasingly evident that attempts to justify the control of female sexuality – whether using aesthetics, cleanliness, respectability or religious ideology – are being questioned and rebuked in different cultures and cannot be sustained as a justification for the continuation of a harmful practice (Box 17.1). This perspective inspires a methodology for challenging cultural and political practice in the twenty-first century which enhances female well-being.

Rethinking democracy for women in the twenty-first century

Human rights issues underlie another concern for this century – the nature of democracy. Bayes et al. (2001) argue that a 'thick democracy' recognizes women as citizens who are equal to men, as opposed to the 'thin democracy' that characterizes many emerging nation-states that are still subject to militaristic and right-wing religious leadership. As we have seen in these case studies, thin democracies are no more than a veneer under which are hidden differential opportunities – not to mention differential power and well-being.

400

All countries in this study, to a greater or lesser degree, disadvantage females in the areas of education, physical security, economic security, access to social and political institutions, and reproductive choice. The distinctive gender roles that characterize societies tend to be institutionalized and are slow to change, and gender roles and the power relations between males and females differ significantly from culture to culture (Billson 2005).

Carol Gould points out that any critique of male domination assumes a 'norm of equal freedom and a requirement of reciprocal recognition of equal agency' (1997: 326). 'Reciprocal' is the operative word, we believe, for if *only* women advocate equal agency and the end of male domination, the establishment of thick democracy cannot occur. Equal agency means that each person, regardless of gender, has the right to develop capacities and pursue goals that are in keeping with the community's values. That is, a woman has the right to pursue goals that are appropriate for any citizen. Democracy based on the norm of equal freedom also means that civil liberties must be protected and that 'the principle of equal positive freedom, which is implied in the critique of domination, constitutes a principle of distributive justice ... [for] differentiated self-development' (ibid.: 327).

Female well-being within truly democratic states, then, would entail unquestioned rights, equal power, and reciprocally supported freedom for females and males. Caring and rights would eventually be merged into individual and community values and freedoms to create a society of mutually validated agency and well-being. Within this just democracy, however, Nancy Fraser concludes that there cannot be one public sphere in which each person can equally participate. Rather, in an egalitarian but multi-cultural society there must exist the opportunity for a 'plurality of public arenas in which groups with diverse values and rhetorics participate' in a multiplicity of publics (Fraser 1997: 373; Fraser 2001). This seems obvious but dangerous. We agree that multi-culturalism is of inherent value, but we also recognize that sub-group values have been used to exclude women or as a basis for tokenism. To the extent that sub-groups create public spheres that remain open to entrenched rights, equal agency and normatively and reciprocally supported freedom for females, we can agree with Fraser's perspective.

A 'women's democracy', that is one that is responsive to women's issues and accommodates her historical inequality, is an urgent requirement for the twenty-first century. The past century was so dominated by warfare and militarism, resulting in the deaths of probably 100 million people, that alternative models must be sought and implemented. The political slogan for the twenty-first century, 'Give Women a Chance – they can't do any worse than the men', has become far more than a clever remark – it is a historical imperative. For the most part, although not exclusively, women's organizations are less hierarchical, more decentralized and empowering, and have a history of opposing wars and excessive military budgets that drain national economic resources from human ones. In our sample Iceland has experience with a 'Women's Party' and a women's list of candidates which can be studied as a potential model in enhancing democracy.

The United Nations' recommendation of 30 per cent minimum participation of women at all levels is a reform that is unlikely to be achieved soon through the electoral process. Few Western democracies have reached this goal in parliament (only the Netherlands, Sweden, and New Zealand). The developing nations that have achieved a modicum of success (such as Mozambique, Uganda, Argentina, Costa Rica, Rwanda and Romania) have done so with affirmative action measures and set-asides, as called for in the MDGs. The goal of women's democracy – taking pains to integrate women into the local development process, thus empowering women at the grassroots level – has been established as a key feature of international development agency policies (Eade 2000; Kakowski et al. 1995). This goal has not been achieved as yet, except in limited situations, but it remains a target for development work.

Women's democracy is not simply about equalizing education for girls and women – as several countries in our study have done – but ensuring that educational achievement is transformational, leading women irrevocably towards increased and informed participation at all levels of society. This longer-range outcome of educational reform has failed in nearly every country in the twentieth century. Clearly, a new praxis is required. A revitalized women's movement will be necessary to guide the discourse, craft strategies and evaluate outcomes.

Diversity and the future of the women's movement

An inclusive women's movement The second wave of the women's movement began as a massive critique of patriarchy, and has also been marked by a global strategic validation of female contributions and significant historical roles. The movement has also alienated many women around the world who are looking for more inclusive leadership. The dilemmas described in the case studies in this volume must be addressed if the international women's movement is to expand its base. Continuing improvement in female well-being depends upon the ability of other social movements and reform efforts to involve the active participation of women who have been marginalized by the interlocking oppressions of gender, ethnicity and social class. Leveraging diversity presents a daunting challenge, yet in recent years the movement has slowed, perhaps even stalled (Billson 1995).

We can see from these case studies that women are selectively incorporating the impact of the women's movement into their everyday lives, but while most applaud the new options for women, many also view with suspicion an ideology that appears to pit women against men, to deny the logic of traditional gender roles, or to devalue the concept of homemaker or mother. Culture profoundly affects attitudes towards feminism and the women's movement. Women may resist identifying themselves as feminists or participating in the movement because they view the crush of their own cultural traditions – which in part oppress them – as necessary to survival of self and community.

This dilemma becomes even more immediate as we develop a new sensitivity towards the intertwined fates of women across the globe. Many women feel hostile, suspicious or left out of the movement. Their attitudes are closely intertwined with cultural definitions of being female and with women's role as 'keepers of the culture' (Billson 2005). A new dialogue that includes women from a wide range of realities requires understanding the impact of culture on women's attitudes towards their own liberation.

A women's movement that incorporates definitions of womanhood rooted in middle-class or Western values will not attract women whose identity is complicated by the struggle against multiple barriers. On the other hand, privileged women face daily expressions of abuse, sexual harassment and discrimination simply because they are women. A viable women's movement focuses on the common experience of gender oppression, which forms a springboard for action, and on the unique experiences of gender oppression created by other differences. Understanding, accepting and leveraging female diversity is the key to advancing female well-being. Beyond the sheer force of cultural differences, the chasms between North and South, middle- and lower-income women, well-educated and poorly educated women, women of advantage and women of little advantage become clear in the light of the eleven case studies. For some women, adopting a feminist attitude feels like adopting an adversarial position against men. This may be particularly true for minority, Native and immigrant women, in their simultaneous struggle against racial or ethnic discrimination. And for a woman who feels trapped in a bad relationship for economic reasons, feminism threatens the security that she believes serves her better, at least for the time being. Feminism, with its alien ideas and strange expectations, asks her to give up too much before she in fact has the financial independence and cultural freedom to break away. For all these reasons, leveraging our diversity presents a forbidding challenge.

For far too long women's contributions have been devalued by men. We as women must not shut each other out or in any way contribute to making each other smaller or less worthy. Mutual respect, inclusiveness and shared power are the keys to making the women's movement stronger. Understanding the cultural, class, racial and other differences among us is a first step in that direction. Rather than fall into the trap of devaluing women who live different lives, we can be 'keepers of the keepers', supporting each other in our common pain, harnessing our uncommon strengths, and acknowledging and celebrating our diversity.

The movement must build coalitions on the issues that bind us within nations as well as across borders – social injustice, classism, racism, heterosexism, economic inequality and political isolation – but we must also find ways to breathe new life into a stagnating women's movement that fails to celebrate differences.

Women's organizations Women's organizations are a vital part of all social, economic and political institutions and institution-building, but inclusive means giving up 'some old notions of operating and adopting, in the name of women and for the sake of the women's movement, some new ways of operating' (Greaves 1992: 154). These new ways may be more burdensome and less efficient, but they are ultimately more authentic and more effective:

- The women's movement, through its various organizations, should 'concentrate on improving the position of women less in relation to men than in relation to society as a whole' (Vickers 1992: 58). In other words, women's place in society should be approached in terms of basic human rights, equity, access and parity. Women's organizations should consider styles of inclusion that use rotational, alphabetic or other randomized means of filling at least half of their leadership positions. Women who are inferior in society because of race, culture, sexual orientation or age may feel insecure about running for chair of a committee or even volunteering to fill a minor position. If it is assumed that all members of an organization are expected to contribute in the ways they are able, and that they do not have to play games of 'palace intrigue' or in-group politics, they will feel more at ease about participating.
- Women's organizations should make every effort to establish ties with other groups locally, regionally, nationally and globally. Being connected to women's groups all over the country, continent and world strengthens the local base.

- Women's organizations should choose accessible activities and venues in terms of timing, physical challenge and cost. Holding a monthly meeting at an expensive restaurant excludes the majority of women, especially those with children and/or a low income.
- Women's organizations should make conscious efforts to hold 'summits' for their leadership to share ideas, goals and plans. Even if this means the leadership of local shelters, rape crisis centres, programmes for women with disabilities and political caucuses meeting once a year in a park for an afternoon of talk, the movement will become more interwoven. Perspectives on reality will be expanded. Ideas for collaborative future action will be generated. Summits that include users of services, service providers and activist leaders will be particularly powerful.
- Women's organizations should make every effort to offer childcare and transportation to those who need it so women can join and participate in them.
- Larger organizations should 'adopt' smaller ones. For example, women's organizations with newsletters can reach out to smaller groups and offer to publish articles and notices of mutual interest. Similarly, the conference programmes of larger, financially stable organizations can advertise upcoming events for less well-endowed groups.
- Every women's organization should self-consciously examine its structure, modes of interaction, meeting formats and times, agendas, and tendency towards hierarchy.

Women's conferences When women meet across international boundaries, we learn more about the differential experience of common issues and chart ways to address them in mutually beneficial ways. This means that conferences must be inclusive of women from all walks of life, with or without education or jobs. Staying in touch means changing the ways in which conferences are typically planned.

- Women's conferences should be designed to include women of colour, women outside academia, and women in all kinds of disciplines, fields and groups.
- Conferences should be carefully designed not only to present and draw women from a variety of worlds, but to desegregate them during conference activities.
- Conference organizers should make every effort to avoid using the malestream model of panels of multiple presenters who have fifteen minutes

to hit the high points, which reinforces superficiality. The 'talking heads' model works against deeper understandings between women and should be replaced by more interactive models that invite participation and stimulate dialogue.

- The classroom model should be discarded; it creates an intimidating atmosphere in which only the most daring will confront or challenge a presenter's assumptions.

Changing institutions Although women's organizations exist in all the countries we examined, very few specifically address issues of women's liberation and equal access to the political, economic and social institutions that would ensure female well-being. As Datta and Kornberg conclude after looking at several countries, economic policies of global institutions and of national governments tend to disempower rather than empower women: 'Women's economic situations usually worsen as a result of structural adjustment programs', for example (2004: 164).

It will be difficult for women to exert enough pressure to overturn the prevailing asymmetries of power that flow from centuries of male domination, but we must keep in mind that humans create social institutions and that humans can change them as well. Improvements in female well-being will most likely be achieved through changing institutions, not individuals, which is precisely why it is so crucial for women's organizations to become inclusive, productive and politically powerful. 'Gender-aware planning' in India is a good example of this type of strategy (Kabeer and Subrahmanian 2000).

Unfortunately, women often resist changing institutions such as the family or the Church, which have dominated their lives since birth. Women need to understand that institutions that have been historically shaped by males must be amenable to shaping by females if they are to support female well-being. As Elena Garcés de Eder comments, women in power may not fully make this difficult but necessary paradigm shift and may use their own increasing power to disempower other women or to create new, oppressive institutions: in Colombia, women ask, 'Who is the worst enemy a woman has?' The ironic answer is 'Another woman'!

Because throughout the twentieth century (and earlier) women's contributions were devalued, mutual respect, inclusiveness and shared power are the keys to making the women's movement stronger in the twenty-first century. Barriers to female participation were established and maintained by the 'old boys' network', with far-reaching and devastating consequences for females. It is as though women have been relegated to 'another country' and blocked from parti-

> *Box 17.2 Emergent political leaders: 'Rwanda's future is on our backs'*
>
> The survivors of the genocide in Rwanda are predominantly women (about two-thirds of the population) and women have become the post-conflict leaders. 'Men think this is a revolution,' says Angelique Kanyange, a student leader at Rwanda's national university. 'It's not a revolution, it's a development strategy.'
>
> The genocide in 1994, one of the worst mass slaughters in recorded history, was triggered by the assassination of the Hutu president after a lengthy civil war between the Tutsi and the Hutu. As elsewhere, one of the tools of the genocide was a planned mass sexual assault on Tutsi women, with Hutu officials encouraging HIV-positive soldiers to take part in gang rapes. The UN estimates that at least 250,000 women were raped – 70 per cent of those who survived now have AIDS. The genocide lasted three months and left Rwanda in ruins. After the genocide ended, 800,000 Tutsi refugees who returned to Rwanda were described as the 'living dead'.
>
> In a culture that was historically pastoralist and kept women from such public roles as milking cows or climbing on roofs, women now make up 49 per cent of parliament and the country has the highest percentage of female leadership in the world, except for Scandinavia. The female literacy rate in Rwanda is also one of highest in Africa at 61 per cent; for the first time, women have the right to own property. 'Rwanda is like no other situation in the world,' says Barbara Ferris, founder and president of the International Women's Democracy Centre.
>
> (Adapted from Kimberlee Acquaro and Peter Landesman, 'Out of madness, a matriarchy', *Mother Jones*, January/February 2003, pp. 59–63)

cipating in the critical networks that produce and build social capital in their own community. For that reason, we must be especially careful that an 'old girls' network' does not similarly squeeze women out of power and participation.

On the other hand, in times of crisis, women often emerge as key leaders and decision-makers whose actions show the way to more equal societies (Box 17.2).

Towards global female well-being

A woman's movement that incorporates definitions of womanhood rooted in a vital women's movement will focus both on the commonality of gender oppression – which affects all women to some degree and forms a springboard for action – and on the unique forms of oppression created by differences in social class, nationality, religion, culture, race, age, and so forth. Attending to both the common and the unique will elevate women's political effectiveness.

Lingering questions Many questions remain for research, theory and practice in the next decade. Why is gender equity still a distant dream, when the trend towards increasing gender equality in legal and human rights was reinvigorated in 1985 with the signing of CEDAW by so many countries? Because signatories must bring their country's laws into line with CEDAW principles, CEDAW has been an important leverage point for female well-being. Yet because of reservations and manipulation of legal language, for some countries it is no more than a promissory note; similarly, other legislative measures have been less than successful. What are the implications of enacting 'equality' laws and conventions favourable to women? What are the concrete outcomes of female constitutional equality, with a concomitant prohibition of sex discrimination (Canada, Bangladesh, Japan, the UK, Iceland and Croatia)? Is token change better than no change?

If women are vital to economic systems of production and consumption and the true workers of the world, why is their work so often invisible, undervalued or ignored? While women represent 50 per cent of the world's population and one third of the official labour force, why do they work nearly two-thirds of all working hours, receive only one tenth of the world income, and own less than 1 per cent of world property? (Bella Center 1980). The question and the answer remained basically unchanged despite decades of 'women in development' praxis, second wave feminist scholarship, four international women's conferences, and scores of governments signing CEDAW.

How can the issue of cultural sovereignty versus universal human rights be responsibly resolved? How can such harmful cultural practices as FGM, dowry abuse and female infanticide be ended without violating cultural integrity? How can violence between intimates, which so often harms women and girls, be ameliorated?

Are matrifocal family forms beginning to replace more traditional extended and nuclear family forms? Is the pronounced twentieth-century trend towards female-headed families the result of a breakdown of old social orders, or the beginning of a new social formation that will mature in this century? Are the trends fundamentally different in the predominantly industrial as opposed to the predominantly agrarian countries?

How can differences between male and female life expectancies be explained in developed countries as opposed to less developed countries? What factors produce higher life expectancy for women? What factors diminish life expectancy for men? How can biology be removed as a determinant of opportunity and power?

Global strategies for change

- Develop more international women's organizations without borders as practical outgrowths of the global initiatives that have laid the foundation for future action.
- Enforce measures that guarantee equal opportunity in education and create new measures that ensure equal treatment, effective agency and equal participation in institutions directing social change.
- At the primary and secondary school levels, include re-education to teach boys and girls mutual respect.
- Extend women's studies programmes and feminist/equalist threads across the curriculum to increase understanding of equity and human rights issues; include questioning of entrenched patriarchal cultural values, demonstrate the negative social effects of patriarchy, and offer more cooperative models of social justice and social change.
- Reverse the negative sex ratio by restricting female feticide and infanticide.
- Expand access to pre-natal, maternal and post-natal healthcare for all women to continue reducing maternal and infant mortality rates HIV/AIDS, and other health threats.
- Build social support and intentional, affirmatively acting programmes that increase women's economic involvement to meet and expand female aspirations, abilities and opportunities.
- Create a new theory/praxis, a 'global standard of female well-being', for future law and policy construction: it must do no harm to females; it should be at the very least gender neutral; and most desirably, it should promote female well-being and equal rights.
- Extend 'campaign schools', set-asides and 'women's lists' to support women's political participation, candidacy, involvement and leadership in local, state and national politics to maximize political participation in the fullest sense.
- Appoint more women players in government at all levels to shape the direction of future social change.
- Review key laws, policies and practices at every level in terms of whether they meet the 'global standard of female well-being'; revise as necessary.

- Make female agency a central priority for the coming decade(s), so that women become full actors on the world stage, not beings to be acted upon or isolated from power systems.

While some of these recommendations have already been implemented in some countries, implementation still tends to be piecemeal and to be met with resistance. Renewing efforts to establish the global standard of female well-being – and taking a consistent stand on the side of equity – will undoubtedly improve the situation for women and girls wherever they happen to live. While we have used the term 'access', social change depends on more than mere access or opportunity, especially for groups that have been kept out of core systems for generations. Transformative models of change will rely on setting standards for equal school completion, equal political participation and equal economic participation and benefits, as called for in the Millennium Development Goals and other collaborative documents.

Returning to Mill's assertion that legal subordination of one sex over the other is 'wrong in itself' and a hindrance to human improvement, we conclude that his ideal of perfect equality is worth striving for in order to create female well-being throughout the world. Although the task is monumental, it is also monumentally important for the well-being of all humans. It will take

Figure 17.1 The global standard of female well-being

political will on the part of governments at every level and in every country to accomplish this task. It will take continued opportunities for women to meet locally, nationally and internationally to reflect on who we are and where we are going in this new millennium. And it will take an inclusive women's and human rights movement to make it a century of humans, neither male nor female, informed by feminist thought and action. Redefining feminism in more positive terms is an imperative element in this transformative process (Kerr 2004).

Ultimately, all who contributed to this book were motivated by a clear desire to influence practitioners, domestically and globally, and to inform policy analysis and programme development among international development experts, members of the media, the general public, and others who care about female well-being. We assume that positive social change for women will have positive implications for the well-being of children and of men, as well.

References

Bayes, J. H. et al. (2001) 'Globalization, democratization, and gender regimes', in R. M. Kelly et al. (eds), *Gender, Globalization, and Democratization*, Lanham, MD, and Oxford: Rowman & Littlefield

Bella Center (1980) 'Conclusions of the World Conference of the United Nations Decade for Women: Equality, development and peace', Copenhagen: Bella Center, 14–30 July

Benedek, W., E. M. Kiyaakye and G. Oberleitner (eds) (2002) *Human Rights of Women: International Instruments and African Experience*, London: Zed Books

Bennholdt-Thomsen, V., N. Faraclas and C. von Werlhof (eds) (2001) *There is an Alternative: Subsistence and Worldwide Resistance to Corporate Globalization*, London: Zed Books

Billson, J. M. (1995) 'A stalled movement? Women, liberation, and diversity in the United States and Canada', University of Victoria lecture sponsored by the United States Information Agency Speakers' Grant Programme

— (2005) *Keepers of the Culture: Women and Power in the Canadian Mosaic*, Boulder, CO: Rowman & Littlefield

Charlesworth, H. (1997) 'Human rights as men's rights', in C. C. Gould (ed.), *Key Concepts in Critical Theory: Gender*, Amherst, NY: Humanity Books

Cheru, F. (2002) *African Renaissance: Roadmaps to the Challenge of Globalization*, London: Zed Books

Datta, R. and J. Kornberg (2002) *Women in Developing Countries: Assessing Strategies for Empowerment*, Boulder, CO: Lynne Rienner

Eade, D. (2000) *Development with Women*, London: Oxfam

Ehrenreich, B. and A. R. Hochschild (2002) 'Introduction' (ch. 1), in Ehrenreich and Hochschild (eds), *Global Woman: Nannies, Maids, and Sex Workers in the New Economy*, New York: Metropolitan/Owl

Fluehr-Lobban, C. (1994) 'Human rights: Egypt and the Arab World', *Cairo Papers in Social Science*, 17 (3)

Global female well-being

— (1995) 'Cultural relativism and universal rights', *Chronicle of Higher Education*, 9 June, pp. B1–2

— (1998) 'Cultural relativism and universal rights', *AnthroNotes. Museum of Natural History Publication for Educators*, 20(2)

Fraser, A. S. (2001) 'Becoming human: the origins and development of women's human rights', in M. Agosín (ed.), *Women, Gender and Human Rights: A Global Perspective,* New Brunswick, NJ: Rutgers University Press

Fraser, N. (1997) 'Rethinking the public sphere: a contribution to the critique of actually existing democracy', in C. C. Gould (ed.), *Key Concepts in Critical Theory: Gender,* Amherst, NY: Humanity Books

Gert, B. (1988) *Morality: A New Justification for the Moral Rules,* New York: Oxford University Press

Gould, C. C. (1997) 'Feminism and democratic community revisited', in C. C. Gould (ed.), *Key Concepts in Critical Theory: Gender,* Amherst, NY: Humanity Books

Greaves, L. (1992) 'What is the relationship between academic and activist feminism?', in C. Backhouse and D. Flaherty (eds), *Challenging Times: The Women's Movement in Canada and the United States,* Montreal: McGill-Queen's University Press

Helliwell, J. F. (2002) *Globalization and Well-being,* Vancouver: University of British Columbia Press

Kabeer, N. and R. Subrahmanian (2000) *Institutions, Relations and Outcomes: Framework and Case Studies for Gender-aware Planning,* London: Zed Books

Kakowski, C. OECD Tinker and R. L. Blumberg (eds) (1995) *Engendering Wealth and Well-being: Empowerment for Global Change* (Latin America in Global Perspective), Boulder, CO: Westview Press

Kaufmann, D. et al. (1999a) 'Aggregating governance indicators', World Bank Policy Research Department Working Paper, Washington, DC: World Bank

— (1999b) 'Governance matters', World Bank Policy Research Department Working Paper, Washington, DC: World Bank

Kerr, J. (2004) 'From "opposing" to "proposing": finding proactive global strategies for feminist futures', in J. Kerr, E. Sprenger and A. Symington (eds), *The Future of Women's Rights: Global Visions and Strategies,* London: Zed Books

Kerr, J., E. Sprenger and A. Symington (eds) (2004) *The Future of Women's Rights: Global Visions and Strategies,* London: Zed Books

Merry, S. E. (2001) 'Women, violence, and the human rights system', in M. Agosín (ed.), *Women, Gender, and Human Rights: A Global Perspective,* New Brunswick, NJ: Rutgers University Press

Mill, J. S. (1989) *Selections* (ed.) Stefan Collini, Cambridge, UK: Cambridge University Press

OECD (Organization for Economic Co-operation and Development) (2001) *The Well-Being of Nations: The Role of Human and Social Capital,* Paris: OECD Centre for Educational Research and Innovation

Robinson, M. (2002) Presentation at the American Anthropological Association, 22 November, New Orleans, LA

Sandbrook, R. (2001) *Closing the Circle: Democratization and Development in Africa,* London: Zed Books

Seager, J. (1997) *The State of Women in the World Atlas,* 2nd edn, London: Penguin

Ugarteche, O. (2000) *The False Dilemma – Globalization: Opportunity or Threat?*, London: Zed Books

United Nations Convention on the Elimination of All Forms of Discrimination Against Women (1981), UN Document A/34/180 (1980, entered into force 3 September 1981)

Vickers, J. (1992) 'The intellectual origins of the women's movement in Canada', in C. Backhouse and D. Flaherty (eds), *Challenging Times: The Women's Movement in Canada and the United States*, Montreal: McGill-Queen's University Press

Editors and contributors

Editors

Janet Mancini Billson, director of group dimensions international, Barrington, RI, USA, and adjunct professor of sociology at the George Washington University, Washington, DC, is a consultant and social policy analyst. She served as professor of sociology and women's studies at Rhode Island College, Providence, RI, from 1973 to 1990. Dr Billson has been recognized for her theoretical work on marginality, and her 'progressive verification method', developed as a feminist approach to cross-cultural research, has been cited for its innovative and ethical stance.

Carolyn Fluehr-Lobban is professor of anthropology and women's studies at Rhode Island College. Dr Fluehr-Lobban is a leading expert on theories of the matriarchate in ancient and contemporary society. She has conducted field research in Sudan (1970–2004), Tunisia, and Egypt. She is author of *Islamic Law and Society in the Sudan* (1987; 2004 in Arabic), *Historical Dictionary of the Sudan* (with R. Lobban and J. Voll, 1992), *Islamic Societies in Practice* (1994; 2004), and *Against Islamic Extremism* (ed., 1998). Dr Fluehr-Lobban is a founder and twice past-president of the Sudan Studies Association.

Contributors

Masako Aiuchi serves as professor of political science and gender studies, School of Human Services, Hokkaido Asaigakuen University, Hokkaido, Japan. He is the author of 'Politics and Family Life' (2003) and 'Gender and the American Politics' (2003).

Vesna Barilar is a feminist activist, researcher, and editor of *Activists: 'Spelling Out' Theory,* and lecturer at the Centre for Women's Studies in Zagreb. She cooperates with numerous women's groups in Croatia and works for the Office of the Ombudsperson for Gender Equality.

Roderic Beaujot earned his doctorate at the University of Alberta, and then worked at Statistics Canada from 1974 to 1976 before becoming professor of sociology at UWO. His book *Earning and Caring in Canadian Families* (2000), received the 2001 Porter Prize of the Canadian Sociology and Anthropology Association; he is also co-author of *Population Change in Canada* with Don Kerr (2004).

Heather Eggins is visiting professor at the University of Strathclyde and the University of Staffordshire, and senior member of Lucy Cavendish College, University of Cambridge. She is also a member of the governing body of University College, Northampton. Her research interests lie in higher education, particularly issues of gender, access, strategy, and policy. Dr Eggins has edited a number of volumes, including *Women as Leaders and Managers in Higher Education*, *The Scholarship of Academic Development* and *Globalization* and *Reform in Higher Education*. She serves as editor of *Higher Education Quarterly*.

Thorgerður ('Gerda') Einarsdóttir is assistant professor and director of gender studies at the University of Iceland. She received her PhD in Sociology from the University of Göteborg, Sweden. Dr Einarsdóttir serves as principal investigator for *Work Cultures, Gender Relations and Family Responsibility*, part of a trans-national network project that includes Iceland, Norway, and Spain, and as co-investigator for *Culture, Custom and Caring: Men's and Women's Possibilities to Parental Leave*, a project funded by the European Community.

Elena Garcés de Eder is a feminist, activist, researcher, and consultant in Colombia and the United States. She earned her PhD in human sciences from George Washington University, Washington, DC (*The Construction of Radical Feminist Knowledge: Women in Colombia as an Example*). She is co-founder of *Mujeres Pazíficas*, a feminist group in Colombia that works for peace. She is also co-founder and editor of a feminist magazine, *Cábala*, published in Cali, Colombia.

Erica Halvorsen is a gender and sexual orientation policy adviser for the Equality Challenge Unit, which was set up by the higher education funding bodies of England, Scotland, Wales, and Northern Ireland to promote equality of opportunity for staff working in higher education institutions. Previously, she worked for the Association of University Teachers. She has written book, journal, and magazine pieces about women working in higher education, as well as research reports on equal opportunity.

Adriana Marulanda Herrán is a historian and political scientist at Universidad de los Andes, Bogotá, Colombia. Her main interests have been the birth and origin of the FARC guerrilla movement; the violence in Colombia since the 1930s; and the 60 years of Colombian peasants' struggle for land ownership.

Tess Hooks is a lecturer in the Sociology Department of the University of Western Ontario (UWO) in London, Ontario, where she teaches courses on social change, inequality, and minority relations, and in women's studies (courses on women and work, and gender and development). She has been an activist on behalf of academic labour with the UWO faculty association and the Canadian Association of University Teachers.

Makoto Ichimori is associate professor of history of educational thought, Faculty of Regional Sciences, Tottori University, Japan. His publications include *Education and Discrimination in Modern Japan* (1998).

Masako Inoue is associate professor of legal philosophy, history of legal ideas and theory of feminism, Faculty of Community Policy, Aichi Gakusen University, Japan. His publications include 'Significances and Tasks of Feminism as Social Theory' (1998) and 'Domestic Violence as Violence within Intimate Spheres: Roles of Law' (2004).

Ranee Itarat is with the Ministry of Finance in Bangkok.

Željka Jelavić, MA in gender studies, is an ethnologist, feminist researcher and activist. She is cofounder of the Centre for Women's Studies in Zagreb, where she lectures in Women's Studies. Former editor-in-chief of the feminist journal *Treća*, she works as a curator at the Ethnographic Museum in Zagreb, where she has been the author of several exhibitions.

Alema Karim, associate professor of economics and chair of the Department of Economics and Finance at Rhode Island College, previously worked for the Ministry of Planning, Bangladesh. She earned her PhD in economics from Boston University; her areas of research and publication include privatization in less developed countries, foreign aid, women's health, and other economic development issues.

Laura Khoury, assistant professor at Rhode Island College, received her PhD in sociology from Kansas State University in crime and criminal justice and social change. Her current research lies in race, gender, and crime. She is the author of 'History and Race Consciousness,' in *Race and Identity in the Nile Valley* (edited by Carolyn Fluehr-Lobban, Red Sea Press, 2004); 'The Rise and Demise of Oslo: Globalization and the Middle East' (*Middle East Affairs*, 2001); and 'Development, Dependency, Population Pressure, and Human Rights Performance: The Cross-National Evidence' (*Human Ecology Journal* 1999).

Keiko Kondo is acting director and cooperating representative of Non-Profit Organization Space 'ON', Japan Women's ShelterNet; she received the 1997 Kato Shizue Award for her work on domestic violence.

417

Patrice LeClerc is associate professor of sociology at St. Lawrence University, Canton, New York. Her research centers on comparative social change in the United States, Canada, and Quebec, particularly on women's movements and nationalism; she is working on a book on the development of nationalism and identity in nineteenth-century New York and Ontario. She received her PhD from Duke University and served as coordinator of the Duke Canadian Studies Center.

Farung Mee-Udon is assistant professor at the Department of Social Development, Khon Kaen University (KKU) in Thailand and a PhD student at the University of Bath, England. Her current research, connected with the ESRC Research Group on Wellbeing in Developing Countries, has been on the impact of health care policy on the well-being of women and men in rural Thailand. A graduate of Khon Kaen University and Mahidal University in Thailand, Farung obtained her masters degree in Gender and Development from the Institute of Development Studies (IDS), University of Sussex, England. She is author of 'Gender Role in Local Politics in the Northeast of Thailand' (2003); 'Equality and Inequality' (2003); 'The Constitution and New Election System' (1998); and 'The Queen of Hearts – Princess Diana and the Angel of US-Mother Teresa' (1997). Farung has been involved in various activities on gender issues, including as trainer for the election campaign of female candidates with the (Women in Politics Institute, Bangkok).

Sandra Prlenda is a historian and PhD candidate at Ecole pratique des hautes études in Paris. Her interests include nationalism studies and gender history. She is the author of several articles in Croatian, international publications, and translations. She lectures in women's history at the Centre for Women's Studies in Zagreb and participates in several historical research projects.

Fusako Seki is associate professor of social welfare law and elder law, International Graduate School of Social Sciences, Yokohama National University, Yokohama, Japan. Her publications include 'The Role of the Government and the Family in Taking Care of the Frail Elderly: A Comparison of the United States and Japan' (2001).

Nasrin Sultana earned an MA in social development from the University of East Anglia, UK, and an MPhil from the University of Dhaka, Bangladesh. She works with the Research Department of PROSHIKA, a non-governmental organisation in Bangladesh. Her focus has been on the influence of dowry, early marriage, and divorce on the lives of chronically poor women. She is pursuing her interest in the cultural construction of poverty and inequality, and is involved in the ESRC Research Group on Wellbeing in Developing Countries (WeD) research in Bangladesh.

Aletta Maria (Ria) van Niekerk (DLitt et Phil, Industrial Psychology) has been involved in human resource development since 1994. Her special interests include employee literacy training courses and self-development courses for managers from previously disadvantaged groups. She is a director of Childtypes Evaluation and Training.

Johanna (Jopie) van Rooyen (DLitt et Phil, University of South Africa) has academic and research experience relating to women in work, social, and leadership contexts. She was a director of the Women's Bureau of South Africa, an advisor to the National Family and Marriage Council of South Africa, and has contributed to a national report on labour legislation (women's issues). Jopie has lectured on Women and Organisational Leadership at the Pretoria University School of Business Leadership and on women's issues at international conferences. She is the chief executive officer of a consultancy (Jopie van Rooyen & Partners SA).

Index